ACTS

God's Word *for the* Biblically-Inept™ SERIES

Robert C. Girard

CARTOONS BY
Reverend Fun
(Dennis "Max" Hengeveld)
Dennis is a graphic de-
signer for Gospel Films and
the author of *Has
Anybody Seen My Locust?*
His cartoons can
be seen worldwide at
www.reverendfun.com.

 STARBURST PUBLISHERS®

P. O. Box 4123, Lancaster, Pennsylvania 17604

To schedule author appearances, write:
Author Appearances
Starburst Publishers
P.O. Box 4123
Lancaster, Pennsylvania 17604
(717) 293-0939

www.starburstpublishers.com

CREDITS:
Copyedited by Deb Strubel
Cover design by David Marty Design
Text design and composition by John Reinhardt Book Design
Illustrations by Mark Ammerman and Melissa A. Burkhart
Cartoons by Dennis "Max" Hengeveld

Unless otherwise noted, or paraphrased by the author, all Scripture quotations are from the New International Version of The Holy Bible.

To the best of its ability, Starburst Publishers® has strived to find the source of all material. If there has been an oversight, please contact us, and we will make any correction deemed necessary in future printings. We also declare that to the best of our knowledge all material (quoted or not) contained herein is accurate, and we shall not be held liable for the same.

READ THIS PAGE BEFORE YOU READ THIS BOOK . . .

Welcome to the *God's Word for the Biblically-Inept™* series. If you find reading the Bible overwhelming, baffling, and frustrating, then this Revolutionary Commentary™ is for you!

Each page of the series is organized for easy reading with icons, sidebars, and bullets to make the Bible's message easy to understand. *God's Word for the Biblically-Inept™* series includes opinions and insights from Bible experts of all kinds, so you get various opinions on Bible teachings—not just one!

There are more *God's Word for the Biblically-Inept™* titles on the way. The following is a list of available books. (See page 348 for ordering information.) We have assigned each title an abbreviated **title code**. This code along with page numbers is incorporated in the text **throughout the series**, allowing easy reference from one title to another.

God's Word for the Biblically-Inept™ Series

JUST FOR TEENS!

• **Learn more at www.learntheword.com** •

The Bible for Teens—Learn the Word™ Series

Who says Bible study has to be boring? Finally, there is a Bible commentary that meets the needs of today's teens by explaining biblical principles and Scripture in a fun, informative, and entertaining format. Adapted from *The Bible—God's Word for the Biblically-Inept™*.

(trade paper)   ISBN 1892016516 $14.99

Bible Bytes for Teens: A Study-Devotional for Logging In to God's Word

Teens can focus on byte-sized Scripture passages and related teaching to get clear spiritual direction for their day. Also included are reflective study questions and a power-packed design that teens will love.

(trade paper)   ISBN 1892016494 $13.99

What's in the Bible for . . .™ Teens

By Mark Littleton and Jeanette Gardner Littleton

Written to teens, this book explores biblical themes that speak to the challenges and pressures of today's adolescents, such as relationships and peer pressure. Helpful and eye-catching "WWJD?" icons, illustrations, and sidebars are included.

(trade paper)   ISBN 1892016052 $16.95

AND FOR WOMEN . . .

Bible Seeds: A Simple Study-Devotional for Growing in God's Word

Especially for women, this book combines Bible study, devotional readings, word studies, practical application, and room to write. Make this book your very own portable garden for growing in God's Word.

(trade paper)   ISBN 1892016443 $13.99

CHAPTERS AT A GLANCE

PART THREE: God's Firebrands

PART FOUR: Chained Witness

ILLUSTRATIONS

INTRODUCTION

CHAPTER HIGHLIGHTS

(Chapter Highlights)

Welcome to *Acts—God's Word for the Biblically-Inept*™. This is another in the series of books that makes the Bible fun and easy to understand. This is not a traditional Bible study or commentary. It is a REVOLUTIONARY COMMENTARY™ that I hope will change your outlook on the Bible forever. I promise to help you Learn the Word™!

To Gain Your Confidence

The New Testament Book of Acts is the history of what the first Christians did with the experiences and teachings of Jesus Christ after their face-to-face experience with him ended. I hope *Acts— God's Word for the Biblically-Inept*™ will create in you a thirst to learn even more from the book known as the "Word of God."

My most valuable researcher, first draft editor, and partner in this project was my wife, Audrey. She read everything carefully, added her insights, and served as first-responder to keep me from complicating or dumbing up this astonishing history of early Christianity.

Acts: A Sequel To The Life Of Christ

The Book of Acts was written to complete the story the author, Doctor Luke, began in the Gospel of Luke. Originally Acts was the second volume of a two-volume history of the beginnings of Christianity, which was circulated together in the **early churches**. Not long after A.D. 100 the two volumes were separated and the Gospel of Luke was circulated as part of a "fourfold **Gospel**" along with books by Matthew, Mark, and John—books that record the basic facts about Jesus Christ. The first volume of the history came to be known as the Gospel According to Luke. The second volume came to be called The Acts of the Apostles. The two books are two parts of the same story—the story of Jesus. The first tells *"about all that Jesus* began *to do and to teach"* until his ascension (Acts 1:1). The second picks up the Jesus story after his resurrec-

Let's Get Started
(Let's Get Started)

> **Acts 1:8** But you will receive power . . .

(Verse of Scripture)

THE BIG PICTURE

> **Acts 22:1–22** Paul told the story of his conversation . . .

(The Big Picture)

early churches: *local groups of believers in the early centuries of Christian history*

Gospel: *good news*

(What?)

tion and carries it forward about thirty years, tracing the spread of the Gospel from Jerusalem to Rome through the small contingent of true believers he left behind.

Author! Author!

The author of the Gospel of Luke and the Book of Acts writes anonymously. In fact, none of the writers of the **four Gospels** identify themselves by name. But church **tradition** as far back as the early part of the second century has always agreed that Luke was writer of both the Gospel of Luke and Acts.

Luke is mentioned by name only three times in the New Testament (Colossians 4:14; 2 Timothy 4:11; Philemon 24). From these passages and Luke's books we discover several things. Luke was a well-educated Greek living in Asia Minor, a **Gentile** (Colossians 4:12–14)—the only Gentile writer of the New Testament. Luke's use of the **Greek** language was superior. His lively, entertaining style resembles the writing style of Greek novelists of his time. He was also a careful historian, often tying his story to specific dates and historical <u>incidents and figures</u>. Luke was a physician (Colossians 4:14). His medical training shows in his use of technical medical terms. After he met **Paul**, Luke was the **apostle's** constant companion, even in jail. In ninety-seven verses in Acts (the so-called "we passages"), beginning with Acts 16:10, Luke uses the first person ("I," "we," and "us" rather than "they" and "them") indicating he was there and part of the action.

Okay, Doc, Where'd You Get Your Information?

Luke was not an eyewitness to anything he describes in his Gospel nor most of what he wrote in the first fifteen chapters of Acts. He never saw Jesus. The opening paragraph in his Gospel of Luke tells where and how he got his information (Luke 1:1–5). He heard about Jesus from the apostles and others who told him what they had seen and heard. Luke's two books were probably written about thirty years after Jesus rose from the dead—between A.D. 58 and 63.

The Cure For "Writers' Block"

Luke tells us that by the time he authored his books, *many* early Christian writers had begun to feel the urgency to get the facts about Jesus down on **papyrus** (Luke 1:1). Among them may have been John Mark (Mark's Gospel was written about A.D. 55) and

---

four Gospels: *Matthew, Mark, Luke, and John*

tradition: *writings and sayings of early Christians outside the New Testament*

Gentile: *non-Jew*

Greek: *"universal" language of the Roman Empire*

Paul: *Christianity's most famous convert, author of several New Testament letters*

apostle: *special ambassador of Christ*

☞ **GO TO:**

Luke 1:5, 26; 2:1–3; 3:1–2, 23 (incidents and figures)

(Go To)

KEY POINT

Jesus became a man to communicate to us what God is like.

(Key Point)

papyrus: *paper made of river reeds*

Matthew (who wrote between A.D. 50–70). Several incidents and trends may have triggered this epidemic of writer's itch:

- In many places Christians were under attack (Acts 8:1, 3; 12:1; Hebrews 10:32–34).
- Stephen and James had been **martyred** (Acts 7:57–60; 12:2).
- Paul was in a Roman prison awaiting trial (Acts 21:33; 24:27).
- The apostles faced intensifying **persecution** and death threats.
- Many of the original eyewitnesses—people who had known Jesus in the flesh—were getting older and would soon be gone; some had already died (1 Corinthians 15:6).

If the next generation was to have the facts on which the Christian faith was founded, these things had to be written down. Luke was one who felt the urgency to write what he had discovered.

Pass It On!

How did the early Christians keep alive the facts concerning Jesus and the beginnings of the church before the New Testament was written? Luke says, "*They [the facts] were handed down*" (Luke 1:2). First-century Christians told and retold the stories. People who had seen Jesus told what they had seen, heard, and felt. Jesus had given his **disciples** <u>specific responsibility</u> to pass the story on to others accurately and with authority. Luke calls them "<u>*eyewitnesses*</u> *and* <u>***servants*** *of the* ***word***</u>."

God himself oversaw the process from beginning to end (John 16:13–15), so when the writers finally began to write, there was a reliable collection of facts from which to assemble the story. Two men who were involved in this process commented on it:

- Peter: "*We did not follow cleverly invented stories when we told you about the power and coming of our Lord Jesus Christ, but we were eyewitnesses of his majesty*" (2 Peter 1:16).
- John: "*That which was from the beginning, which we have heard, which we have seen with our eyes, which we have looked at and our hands have touched—this we proclaim concerning the* **Word of Life**" (1 John 1:1).

Investigative Reporter

To ensure accuracy, Luke "*carefully investigated everything*" before reporting it (Luke 1:3). Much of Luke's investigative work may

(What Others Are Saying)

martyred: killed for their faith

persecution: harassment for religious reasons

CHURCH GROWTH

(Church Growth)

disciples: students, trainees

servants: ministers, attendants, servers

☞ **GO TO:**

Luke 24:48; John 20:21; Acts 1:8 (specific responsibility)

Acts 2:32; 3:15; 4:20 (eyewitnesses)

Matthew 20:26–28; Acts 4:33; 2 Timothy 2:15; 4:2 (servants of the word)

word: Jesus and the good news about him

Word of Life: a descriptive title for Jesus Christ

☞ GO TO:

Acts 24:27 (two years)

Acts 8:1, 3; 9:1
(persecution)

translations: literature taken from one language and expressed in another language

Dig Deeper

(Dig Deeper)

EARLY

CHURCH

WOMEN—

(Early Church Women)

Something to Ponder

(Something to Ponder)

have been done during the <u>two years</u> while Paul was in jail in Caesarea. Luke was there too, serving as Paul's physician. Luke had time to interview eyewitnesses and assemble facts from Christians who had fled to Caesarea to escape <u>persecution</u> in Jerusalem.

Which Translation Of The Bible Should I Read?

Today, English speaking people have a wide range of Bible **translations** from which to choose. I used several different translations in preparation of this book. In addition I often looked at verses in the original language of the New Testament (Greek). For this series of books we chose to use the New International Version (NIV) of the Bible. It faithfully expresses the words of original Bible writers in clear and contemporary English.

How To Use *Acts—God's Word For The Biblically-Inept*™

Sit down with this book and your Bible.

- Start the book at chapter 1.
- As you work through each chapter, read the Scripture passages from your Bible.
- Use the sidebars loaded with icons and helpful information to give you a knowledge boost.
- Answer the Study Questions and review with the Chapter Wrap-Up.
- Then go on to the next chapter.

It's simple and fun!

This book contains a variety of special features that will help you learn. They're illustrated in the outside column of this introduction. Here they are again, with a brief explanation of each.

Sections and Icons	What's It For?
CHAPTER HIGHLIGHTS	*the most prominent points of the chapter*
Let's Get Started	*a chapter warm-up*
BIBLE QUOTE	*what you came for—the Bible*
THE BIG PICTURE	*summarizes longer passages*
Commentary	*my thoughts on what the verses mean*
GO TO:	*other Bible verses to help you better understand (underlined in text)*
What?	*the meaning of a word (bold in text)*

KEY POINT	major point of the chapter or section
What Others Are Saying:	if you don't believe me, listen to the experts
Early Church Women	highlights the role of women in the early church
Church Growth	principles and conditions that made the early church grow
Persecution & Martyrdom	describes persecution of Christians in Acts and more modern times
Jesus Christ, CEO	tells how Christ supervised the early church through his Spirit
Illustrations	a picture is worth a thousand words
Remember This . . .	don't forget this
Something to Ponder	interesting points to get you thinking
Dig Deeper	find out more from other Bible passages
Study Questions	questions to get you discussing and studying
CHAPTER WRAP-UP	the most prominent points revisited

(Persecution of Martydom)

A Word About Series Cross-References

To aid you in studying various topics, biblical characters, and Bible passages, we have included cross-references to other books in the *God's Word for the Biblically-Inept*™ and *What's in the Bible for . . .*™ series. These references are scattered throughout the text of this book. The references will look similar to this: (Read more about Abraham in GWMB, pages 13–28). The four-letter code "GWMB" refers to the title of the book, in this case *Men of the Bible*. The page numbers that follow the title code tell you exactly where to look in *Men of the Bible* to find more about Abraham. Use the chart below to understand the four-letter title codes.

(Jesus Christ, CEO)

Title Code	Book Title
GWAC	*Acts*
GWBI	*The Bible*
GWDN	*Daniel*
GWGN	*Genesis*
GWHN	*Health & Nutrition*
GWJN	*John*
GWLC	*Life of Christ, Volume 1*
GWLC2	*Life of Christ, Volume 2*
GWMK	*Mark*
GWMB	*Men of the Bible*
GWPB	*Prophecies of the Bible*

Study Questions

(Study Questions)

Title Code	Book Title
GWRV	*Revelation*
GWRM	*Romans*
GWWB	*Women of the Bible*
WBFC	*What's in the Bible for . . .*™ *Couples*
WBFM	*What's in the Bible for . . .*™ *Mothers*
WBFT	*What's in the Bible for . . .*™ *Teens*
WBFW	*What's in the Bible for . . .*™ *Women*

A Word About Words

There are several interchangeable terms: Scripture, Scriptures, the Word, Word of God, God's Word, etc. All these mean the same thing and come under the broad heading called the Bible. I may use each of these terms at various times.

Yahweh: Hebrew name for God

The word "Lord" in the Old Testament refers to **Yahweh**, God. In the New Testament "Lord" is a term of respect, like "sir," a reference to God, or a title of Jesus.

Why Study Acts?

KEY POINT

Baptism with the Spirit includes everything Christ does in and for people.

After the four Gospels, where the personal story of Jesus' life, teachings, death, and resurrection are told, Acts may be the most important book in the New Testament. Here are some things you can learn from Acts that you can't get anywhere else:

- Acts is the story of how Jesus continues his work since his death and resurrection.
- Acts shows Jesus in action as head of the church.
- Acts shows how people can know Jesus through the Holy Spirit.
- Acts demonstrates practical application of Jesus' message that God loves the whole world and wants everyone to be rescued from **sin**.
- Acts records the origins of the church.
- Acts describes what true Christian fellowship is like and how important it is.

sin: choosing to disobey God; independence from God

Jesus said his Holy Spirit will guide us in discovery of *"all truth"* (John 16:13). It helps to read and study the Bible with an open heart, expecting God to light up your life in some surprising and enriching ways.

Remember
This . . .

(Remember This)

Bible Quote: This is where you'll read a quote from the Bible.

> **James 1:5** If any of you lacks wisdom, he should ask God, who gives generously to all without finding fault, and it will be given to him.

Commentary: This is where you'll read commentary about the biblical quote.

Decisions, Decisions: In Or Out?

James, the brother of Jesus, is writing to the new believers who were scattered about the Roman world (see GWBI, pages 213–214) when they fled from persecution. James knows that godly wisdom is a great gift. He gives a simple plan to get it: if you need wisdom, ask for it. God will give it to us.

Up 'til now we've concentrated on finding the wind in sails of your drifting marriage and overcoming marital problems. But you may be the reader who is shaking her head, thinking that I just don't understand what you're going through. You can't take the abuse any longer; you've forgiven the **infidelity** time after time; and in order for you and your children to survive, you see no alternative but divorce.

"What?": When you see a word in bold, go to the sidebar for a definition.

infidelity: sexual unfaithfulness of a spouse

So let m[...]
husband [...] your
get out a[...] nues.
abuse sec[...]
ing to you; they are also harmful to your children's physical and emotional state.

Go To: When you see a word or phrase that's underlined, go to the sidebar for a biblical cross-reference.

☞ **GO TO:**

Psalm 111:10 (source)

When you feel you've depleted all of your options, continue to ask God for wisdom in order to have the knowledge to make the right decisions. Wise women seek God. God is the source of wisdom and wisdom is found in Christ and the Word.

Remember This . . .

Gary Chapman, Ph.D.: Is there hope for women who suffer physical abuse from their husbands? Does reality living offer any genuine hope? I believe the answer to those questions is yes.[6]

What Others are Saying:

Give It Away

You don't have to be a farmer to understand what the Apostle Paul wrote to the Corinthian church (see illustration, page 143). A picture is worth a thousand words, and Paul is painting a masterpiece. He reminds us of what any smart farmer knows: in order to produce a bountiful harvest, he has to plan for it,

What Others Are Saying: This is where you'll read what an expert has to say about the subject at hand.

MEN OF POWER: LESSONS IN MIGHT AND MISSTEPS 9

127

Feature with icon in the sidebar: Throughout the book you will see sections of text with corresponding icons in the sidebar. See the chart on pages xvi–xvii for a description of all the features in this book.

Part One

FIRE IN THE HOLY CITY

REVEREND FUN

"Due to local fire codes, we are no longer allowed to consider ourselves 'on fire for Christ.'"

ACTS 1: LIGHTING THE FUSE

Let's Get Started

The world in which Christianity got its start was ruled by the iron fist of the Roman Empire, which had invaded Europe, North Africa, Egypt, and the Middle East, including Israel, homeland of the Jews. The imperial capital was Rome. In A.D. 30 the emperor was **Caesar** Tiberius. Nowhere was hatred of the Roman conquerors hotter nor revolutionary skirmishes more likely than Israel. Jewish historian Josephus reports that during the first century there were ten thousand incidents of insurrection in Israel alone![1]

The most radical revolution—the one the official scorekeepers forgot to count—was a nonviolent uprising that began with a handful of mostly fishermen and women in Jerusalem. In less than three hundred years, this uprising brought the mighty Roman Empire officially to its knees before the **crucified Galilean**, Jesus of **Nazareth**. This revolution was not driven by hate or political ambition but by love and belief that its hero and commanding officer had given his life for their freedom, risen from the dead, and now directed the revolution from the heavenly throne room of God!

Acts shows the **church** in its finest hour—under fierce attack but unstoppable, spiritually aflame, morally pure, impelled by love, and bound together by the living presence of Christ. It details a movement of pioneers and risk-takers breaking new ground, taking on new challenges, highly energized for assault on spiritual ignorance and wickedness.

Caesar: official title of Roman emperors; family name of Julius Caesar

crucified: executed on a cross

Galilean: resident of the province (state) of Galilee

Nazareth: Galilean town where Jesus grew up

church: community of Christian believers, not a building

Maude De Joseph West: [Acts] is a book about people who thrust their feet into sweat-stained sandals and marched out to conquer the world. They had no visible swords, they had no visible shields, they had no visible commander; nonetheless, they marched with matchless unconcern into the gates of prison, through the valley of persecution, and even into the jaws of death.[2]

> **Acts 1:1–2** In my former book, Theophilus, I wrote about all that Jesus began to do and to teach, until the day he was taken up to heaven, after giving instructions through the Holy Spirit to the apostles he had chosen.

This Could Be The Start Of Something Big!

☞ **GO TO:**

Colossians 4:14 (doctor)

Luke 1:3; Acts 1:1 (Theophilus)

Theophilus: Greek name meaning "God-Lover"

The author of Acts is a Greek <u>doctor</u> named Luke. Acts is a sequel. The author's former book is the third New Testament version of the Jesus story, the Gospel of Luke.

Both of Luke's books are addressed to an official in the Roman government that Luke calls "Your Excellency **Theophilus**." Theophilus was either a committed follower of Jesus Christ or a serious seeker on his way to becoming one. Luke's Gospel and Acts are written in the purest **Greek** in the New Testament—the language that would best communicate to an educated member of the aristocracy.

Something to Ponder

Some people think Luke may have been a slave, the personal physician of Theophilus, who was seriously ill. Through Luke's medical skills and care Theophilus was restored to health. In gratitude Theophilus gave Luke his freedom. Luke, in turn, to show his gratitude gave Theophilus the most precious gift he could think of—the message concerning Jesus.[3]

Greek: universal language of Roman Empire in which the New Testament was written

What Jesus Started

If Luke had given his second book a title, it might have been something like, "The Continuing Work of Jesus" or "More Proof Jesus Is Alive" or "You Read My First Book But Fasten Your Seat Belt, Pilgrim, You Ain't Seen Nothin' Yet!" The Gospel of Luke "began" Jesus' story (Acts 1:1). Acts tells the rest of the story. That story is still being written in the lives of Christ's followers today.

The superstar is Jesus Christ. He is the main actor in every scene. In the Gospels he moved about in a single human body and spoke with a Jewish accent. In Acts he speaks in many different voices and languages. His message and goals remain the same.

> **Acts 1:3** After his suffering, he showed himself to these men and gave many convincing proofs that he was alive. He appeared to them over a period of forty days and spoke about the kingdom of God.

Forty Incredible Days

On April 9, 30 A.D.[4] demoralized followers of the dead Nazarene, Jesus, huddled in a second-story room in Jerusalem. It was their third day of secret mourning (it was against the law to grieve openly for a condemned criminal). Their teacher, whom they had believed was the long-expected **Messiah** sent to rescue Israel from bondage, was dead. They'd watched him die (see GWLC2, pages 237–252). The depression in the room was so thick you could slice it with a knife!

Suddenly the door flew open. Breathless women who had gone to embalm the body burst in babbling confusing things about a rolling stone (Matthew 28:2), a missing corpse (John 20:2–13), angels (Luke 24:4–5) and a risen Christ (Matthew 38:8–10)!

It was the start of the most amazing forty days of their lives.

> **Acts 1:3** He . . . spoke about the kingdom of God.

The King And The Kingdom

Alive and kicking, Jesus appeared to his people in all sorts of places and situations. He spoke their names, touched them, invited them to touch him, ate with them, hiked and fished with them. The scars of the crucifixion were visible in his hands, feet, and side (Luke 24:39–40; John 20:27).

Eager partisans clustered around their **Master** in those post-resurrection meetings. They sat on the edge of their seats, unable to take their eyes off the back-from-the-dead Jesus. "The kingdom of God" had always been on his mind (see GWLC, pages 156–159). He spoke of it more than eighty times in the **four Gospels**. Alive from the dead, he talked about it more than ever.

The Kingdom In A Capsule

The kingdom centers in one major issue. In the Lord's Prayer Jesus taught us to pray: "*Our Father who art in heaven, hallowed be thy name,* thy kingdom come; thy will be done *in earth as it is in heaven*" (Matthew 6:9–10 **KJV**, emphasis added). The kingdom is the reign or rule of God. Everything in the kingdom focuses on doing God's will.

☞ **GO TO:**

Matthew 27; Mark 15; Luke 23; John 18 (watched him die)

Matthew 28; Mark 16; Luke 24; John 20–21; 1 Corinthians 15:3–8 (appeared)

2 Chronicles 10:6; Psalm 10:16; 24:1–10; 47:7–9; 93:1; 99:1–3 (kingdom of God)

Matthew 6:9–13 (Lord's Prayer)

Matthew 7:21; Luke 1:38; 22:42; Romans 12:1–2 (God's will)

Messiah: Christ, the king from God

Master: teacher, rabbi, Lord

four Gospels: New Testament books by Matthew, Mark, Luke, and John

KJV: King James Version of the Bible

---

sovereign: *absolute, excellent, supreme*

☞ **GO TO:**

Revelation 11:15
(future world)

What Others are Saying:

☞ **GO TO:**

Matthew 5–7
(character and values)

agent: *means by which God accomplishes his desired results*

☞ **GO TO:**

Matthew 4:17 (is here)

1 Peter 2:24–25; Isaiah 53:4–6 (taken the punishment)

Matthew 28:18; Romans 1:4 (Jesus rules)

Something to Ponder

Kingdom citizens are people who acknowledge God's **sovereign** authority over their lives, their world, and the universe. Their rallying cry is "God is in control!" They are linked with each other in the kingdom community, the church, the kingdom's advance contingent. Together they give the present world a taste of the <u>future world</u> where everything and everybody will bow to God's will (see GWRV, pages 307–320). They work to carry out God's grand scheme to bring every person everywhere under his benevolent reign.

Howard Snyder: The church is seen as the community of God's people—a people called to serve him and called to live together in true Christian community as a witness to the <u>character and values</u> of the kingdom. The church is the **agent** of God's mission on earth. But what is that mission? It is nothing other than bringing all things and, supremely, all people of the earth under the dominion and headship of Jesus Christ.[5]

> **Acts 1:4–5** On one occasion, while he was eating with them, he gave them this command: "Do not leave Jerusalem, but wait for the gift my Father promised, which you have heard me speak about. For John baptized with water, but in a few days you will be baptized with the Holy Spirit."

The Reign Of God—An Inside Job

As he meets with his followers after his resurrection, Jesus whistles his favorite tune: "The kingdom of God <u>is here</u>!" At last they can see what they could not see before. Having <u>taken the punishment</u> for human sin and beaten death's rap, <u>Jesus rules</u>! Even if they tried they couldn't doubt it. He's won the right to reign. He can expect his instructions to be obeyed. And he has big plans—he intends to conquer the world!

How was this fishy-smelling collection of back-country synagogue dropouts gonna conquer the world? Yielding to the reign of God in the practical stuff of life goes against lifelong habits. Sin is like fallin' off a log! Surrender to the will of God is like climbing Mount Everest every day! Conquer the world? Out of the question!

There is only one way: The King's regime must become an *inside job*! So King Jesus commands his troops: "Wait for the Spirit!" (Acts 1:5).

If You Ain't Been Dipped, You've Been Gypped!

Jesus' strategy for giving people the opportunity to live under the reign of God began with connecting his followers to the source and secret of his own power. *"John baptized with water,"* Jesus said, *"but in a few days you will be baptized with the Holy Spirit"* (Acts 1:5). In the original language of the New Testament "baptize" means the following:

- To place or dip something in water to wash it clean (like dirty laundry)
- To change the color of fabric by dipping it repeatedly in dye
- To steep, saturate, overwhelm or fill something or someone

When early Christians spoke of being "baptized with the Spirit," they had these meanings in mind:

- The Holy Spirit cleanses believers' sins away (Acts 15:8–9).
- The Holy Spirit gradually changes believers to be like Jesus (2 Corinthians 3:18).
- The Holy Spirit fills believers with his presence, giving them power to do God's will, immersing them in the thinking, values, and character of Jesus (Acts 2:4).

Splashing Down Memory Lane

"John baptized with water," Jesus said. Three years earlier on the banks of the Jordan River, the desert prophet <u>John the Baptist</u> declared: *"I baptize you with water. But one more powerful than I will come, the thongs of whose sandals I am not worthy to untie. He will baptize you with the Holy Spirit and with fire!"* (Luke 3:16). With these words of Luke 3:16, John summed up *everything Jesus Christ would do*—from teaching to dying on the cross to rising from the dead (things he was able to do in the energy of the Holy Spirit); from spiritual rebirth to forgiveness of sins to coming to live in his people's hearts (things he does in believers by giving them the Holy Spirit). *Everything* Jesus does is the Holy Spirit's work and part of his "baptism."

Don't Leave Home Without It!

Jesus gives three clues to shape his friends' expectations about the coming of the Holy Spirit into their lives (Acts 1:4–5):

1. "Don't leave Jerusalem without it!" (Acts 1:4). Don't attempt anything for God until you have the Holy Spirit.

KEY POINT

The rallying cry of the kingdom of God is "God is in control!"

Something to Ponder

☞ **GO TO:**

Matthew 3:1–12; Mark 1:2–9; Luke 3:1–20; John 1:6–8 (John the Baptist)

KEY POINT

Baptism with the Spirit includes everything Christ does in and for people.

---

gift: *grace, favor from God's goodness, not because the receiver deserves it*

2. "Wait for the Father's gift!" (Acts 1:4; 2:38; 10:45). The Spirit is a free **gift** from God.

3. "Remember what I said!" (Acts 1:4). To understand spiritual baptism, check Jesus' teachings (see chart below).

It is clear from the beginning of Acts that oversight of the expansion of God's kingdom is directed by Jesus Christ himself, living in his followers in the person of the Holy Spirit.

Dig Deeper

What Jesus Said about the Holy Spirit:

Luke 11:13 .... The Holy Spirit is given by God to people who ask.

John 3:5 .... The Holy Spirit is able to give a person "new birth" (a new start with God).

John 7:37–38 .... The Holy Spirit satisfies spiritual thirst.
The Holy Spirit is given to everyone who believes in Jesus.

John 14:16 .... The Holy Spirit is the Christian's counselor, comforter, and guide.

John 14:18–23 .... The Holy Spirit *is Jesus*—living in believers, giving life, revealing himself.

John 14:26 .... The Holy Spirit reminds us of Jesus' teachings.

John 15:26–27 .... The Holy Spirit is sent by Jesus and tells people about him.

John 16:8–11 .... The Holy Spirit enlightens the world about sin, righteousness and judgment.

John 16:12–13 .... The Holy Spirit guides people to the truth.
The Holy Spirit always agrees with Jesus.
The Holy Spirit sometimes reveals things before they happen.

John 16:14–17 .... The Holy Spirit's primary job is to glorify Jesus and make him known.

What the Bible Says about the Holy Spirit:

Hebrews 9:14 .... The Holy Spirit is eternal (no beginning, no end, not limited to time).

Luke 1:35 .... The Holy Spirit's works are acts of God.

Psalm 139:7 .... The Holy Spirit is present everywhere.

1 Corinthians 2:10–11 .... The Holy Spirit knows God's thoughts.

2 Corinthians 3:18 .... The Holy Spirit is Lord.

Acts 5:3–4 .... To lie to the Holy Spirit is to lie to God.

(See also GWJN, pages 199–203.)

What Others are Saying:

Billy Graham: There is nothing God is that the Holy Spirit is not. All the essential aspects of deity belong to the Holy Spirit. We can say of him exactly what was said of Jesus Christ in the ancient

Nicene Creed: He is very God of very God! so we bow before him, we worship him, we accord him every response Scripture requires of our relationship to Almighty God. Who is the Holy Spirit? He is God![6]

Nicene Creed: official statement of Christian beliefs adopted in A.D. 325

> **Acts 1:6–7** So when they met together, they asked him, "Lord, are you at this time going to restore the kingdom to Israel?"
>
> He said to them: "It is not for you to know the times or dates the Father has set by his own authority."

Strategy For World Conquest

Jesus' teaching about the kingdom of God was often misunderstood. Oppressed Jews looked for a military governor to throw off the yoke of **pagan conquerors** and restore national independence. These nationalistic ideas were still a sticking point in his disciples' thinking. Patriotic Jews to the core, they dreamed of reviving the old Jewish monarchy. "Lord, are you going to restore the kingdom to Israel?" (Acts 1:6).

Jesus didn't exactly say "No." Believing Jews would soon put their faith in him, surrender to God's rule, and experience the kingdom. Someday, as the prophets predicted, the kingdom of Israel would be restored (see GWPB, pages 82–86). But not yet. Jesus' response was a gentle rebuke, like saying, "The timing of national and international events is none of your business. The Father alone has authority over **times** and **dates**. Give up your dreams of worldly power. More important issues are at stake!" (Acts 1:7).

pagan conquerors: Assyrians, Babylonians, Persians, Greeks, Romans

times: interval till Christ returns to establish political as well as spiritual rule

dates: "seasons," events in establishing the kingdom

☞ **GO TO:**

Ezekiel 36–37 (restored)

Mark 13:32 (Father alone)

Luke 9:46–50; 22:2–27; Mark 10:35–45 (worldly power)

> **Acts 1:8** "But you will receive power when the Holy Spirit comes on you; and you will be my witnesses in Jerusalem, and in all Judea and Samaria, and to the ends of the earth."

The TNT Of Christ's Presence

A more important war must be fought before the war for Israel's independence. The original word translated "but" (Acts 1:8) is the strongest word in Greek to indicate contrast. It's like saying, "Hold your horses! Instead of indulging in wishful thinking or **apocalyptic** speculation, hang on to your hats, brothers. You are

apocalyptic: forecasting the ultimate destiny of the world about to grab a hot wire of power, the likes of which you have not dreamed!"

The original word for "power" in verse 8 sounds like "dynamite." It means authority and energy. To follow their Commander into battle for the kingdom, followers of Jesus need the spiritual TNT of his presence. In a few days, Jesus would supernaturally enter them in the form of the Holy Spirit. This would empower them to be what Christians must be—**witnesses**.

War Map For Revolution

Three major offensives form Jesus' plan for world conquest. The location of pins on his war map forms a table of contents for Acts[7] (see illustration, page 11).

1. Jerusalem (Acts 1–7)
2. Judea and Samaria (Acts 8–12)
3. The ends of the earth (Acts 13–28)

Acts traces the **Gospel**'s outreach as far as Rome. Before they died the **apostles** actually took the message of Jesus to Spain, Britain, Africa, and India. Before the revolution is over every people group on earth will hear it (Matthew 28:19). Strategies are in place to take the good news to the last unreached people early this century.

But don't get ahead of the Leader. Wait for the Spirit! (Acts 1:4).

Billy Graham: If you believe in Jesus Christ, a power is available to you that can change your life, even in such intimate areas as your marriage, your family relationships, and every other relationship. Also God offers power that can change a tired church into a vital, growing body, power that can revitalize **Christendom**.[8]

William Barclay: The apostles were enjoined to *wait* on the coming of the Spirit. We would gain more power and courage and peace if we learned to wait. In the business of life we need to learn to be still. . . . Amidst life's surging activity there must be time to receive.[9]

> **Acts 1:9–11** After he said this, he was taken up before their very eyes, and a cloud hid him from their sight.
> They were looking intently up into the sky as he was going, when suddenly two men dressed in white

☞ **GO TO:**

Luke 24:48; Acts 10:41; 22:20; Revelation 2:13 (witnesses)

witnesses: *literally, "martyrs"—people willing to give their lives*

Gospel: *good news about Jesus*

apostles: *Christ's specially chosen ambassadors*

What Others are Saying:

Christendom: *Christianity*

Map of the Gospel's Spread

The circles on this map show where the Gospel began in Jerusalem and spread to nearby areas of Judea and Samaria. The arrows show how the message spread to the rest of the known world at the time Acts was written. The dashed lines indicate the boundaries of the Roman Empire about A.D. 57.

> stood beside them. "Men of Galilee," they said, "why do you stand here looking into the sky? This same Jesus, who has been taken from you into heaven, will come back in the same way you have seen him go into heaven."

5-4-3-2-1 Lift Off!

The strategy sessions with the risen Jesus ended abruptly forty days after his resurrection. He led his friends into the country (Luke 24:50), raised his hands to bless them and, as they watched, lifted off, and disappeared in a strange cloud.

As the group on the hilltop strained for a last glimpse of the ascending Lord, two white-clad figures (**angels**) suddenly "beamed down" beside them. "Why are you gawking into the empty sky?" they asked. "Jesus will come back just as you have seen him go— in a cloud."

angels: *spirit beings created to serve God and help people*

☞ **GO TO:**

Mark 13:26 (in a cloud)

John 1:10–18;
 Philippians 2:5–11
 (descended)

**What Others
are Saying:**

Luke 1:31–38
 (human baby)

Mark 16:19;
 Romans 8:34
 (right hand of God)

*Dig
Deeper*

Head: *leader, director,
CEO*

intercedes: *prays for*

The ascension is the game-winning final play of an amazing life. Where did Jesus go? Thirty-three years earlier he <u>descended</u> from the heavenly dimension as a <u>human baby</u> so that he could die as a man for human sins. Mission accomplished, he returned to the heavenly dimension and reassumed his place at the <u>right hand of God</u>.

Howard Snyder: The Kingdom is both present and future, both earthly and heavenly, both hidden and becoming manifest. It is as concrete and this-worldly as the dust on Jesus' feet or the Galilean wind in his hair; it is as costly as the crucifixion; it is as heavenly as the risen Christ sitting at the right hand of the Father. . . . Its truths and values are those taught and lived by Jesus Christ and delivered to the body of his followers. But this Kingdom can become fully manifest only when Jesus Christ returns to earth.[10]

Seven Wonderful Things about the Ascension of Jesus Christ

1. The ascension fulfilled Old Testament prophecy (see Psalm 24:7–10; 68:18–19; Ephesians 4:7–11).
2. The ascension fulfilled Jesus' prophecy (see John 6:62; 7:33–34; 10:17; 14:28–29; 16:5–7).
3. With the crucifixion and resurrection, the ascension certifies Jesus is Lord, Christ, King, and **Head** (see Acts 2:32–36; Ephesians 1:18–23; 1 Timothy 3:16; Revelation 19:16).
4. The ascension puts Christ permanently in God's presence where he **intercedes** for us (see Romans 8:34; Hebrews 7:25; 9:24).
5. The ascension opens the way for Jesus to send the Holy Spirit to us (see John 16:7; Acts 2:33).
6. The ascension makes it possible for Jesus to be with us at all times (see Matthew 18:20; 28:20; Ephesians 4:10).
7. The ascension enables Jesus to prepare a place for us to be with him in heaven (see John 14:2–3).

JESUS CHRIST CEO

Jesus directs the affairs and movements of his followers and his church from the place of highest authority in the universe—the right hand of God.

> **Acts 1:12–13a** Then they returned to Jerusalem from the hill called the Mount of Olives, a **Sabbath <u>day's walk</u>** from the city. When they arrived they went upstairs to the room where they were staying.

☞ **GO TO:**

Exodus 16:29;
Numbers 35:5
(day's walk)

Anticipation In The Attic

The setting for the spiritual explosion that would rock the world was simple. Witnesses of the ascension returned to Jerusalem and climbed to the upper chamber, an upstairs room large enough to hold 120 people. Ahead lay a heart-pounding adventure. *"In a few days you will be baptized with the Holy Spirit"* (Acts 1:5). Precisely what that was going to mean they did not know. They only knew he'd told them they were about to connect with power to be his witnesses *"to the ends of the earth."*

All they had to do was . . . *wait.*

Sabbath day's walk:
three-fourth mile,
maximum distance
allowed on Sabbath

> **Acts 1:13b** Those present were Peter, John, James and Andrew; Philip and Thomas, Bartholomew and Matthew; James son of Alphaeus and Simon the Zealot, and Judas son of James.

Upper Room Roll Call: The Eleven

The upper room aggregation included "the Eleven" (the Twelve minus Judas). The Eleven were men <u>chosen by Jesus</u> as his special ambassadors and church leaders. Before being called to join Jesus' party, most had been blue-collar tradesmen (fishermen, farmers, government workers). Most were synagogue dropouts, "<u>sinners</u>" by reputation. They'd spent three years following Jesus around as his disciples (trainees). They were the original apostles whose acts are being told in Acts (see GWLC2, pages 293–294). Those present were as follows:

- Peter—Called "Rock." Quick-tongued (Matthew 16:15–16). Denied Jesus three times (Matthew 26:75). Reinstated after Jesus rose from the dead (John 21:15–17).
- John—Brother James and he were nicknamed "Sons of Thunder" for volatile personalities (Luke 9:51–55). He is the *"disciple <u>Jesus loved</u>"* of the Gospel of John.
- James—The other "Son of Thunder." First apostle **martyred** (Acts 12:1–2).

☞ **GO TO:**

Luke 6:14–16; Mark
3:16–19; Matthew
10:2–4
(chosen by Jesus)

Luke 5:8, 30; 15:1–2
(sinners)

John 13:23; 19:26;
20:2; 21:7, 20–24
(Jesus loved)

martyred: killed for
following Christ

- Andrew—Peter's brother. Brought strangers to Jesus (John 1:35–42; 12:22).
- Philip—Among first five to connect with Jesus (John 1:43–45).
- Thomas—Called Doubting Thomas for refusing to believe the resurrection until he saw Jesus alive (John 20:25–29).
- Bartholomew—Also called Nathanael. Skeptical at first, then recognized Jesus as *"King of Israel"* (John 1:46, 49).
- Matthew—Called Levi. Customs officer. Held banquet to introduce Jesus to friends (Luke 5:29). Student of Bible prophecy.
- James—"Younger" or "Junior." Matthew's brother (compare Matthew 10:3 with Mark 2:14). Christian legend says he'd been a right-wing revolutionary.
- Simon—Nicknamed "Zealot" (Acts 1:13; Mark 3:18). From militant wing of Jewish independence movement.
- Judas—Alias: Jude, Judah, or Thaddeus, to distinguish him from the betrayer Judas Iscariot. May have been the apostle James's son.

> **Acts 1:14** They all joined together constantly in prayer, along with the women and Mary the mother of Jesus, and with his brothers.

Upper Room Roll Call: The Women

Some of these women had been part of Jesus' Galilean traveling team along with male disciples (Luke 23:55). Some were wealthy and provided financial support (Luke 8:1–3). <u>Named</u> in other places are Joanna, Suzanna, Salome, and a quartet of Marys—Mary Magdalene, Mary the mother of James, Jesus' aunt Mary, and Mary his mother.

☞ **GO TO:**

Mark 16:1; Luke 8:2–3; John 19:25 (named)

EARLY CHURCH WOMEN—Luke, more than any other New Testament writer, notes the role of women in the ministry of Jesus and the church.

Specially noted is the presence of *"Mary the mother of Jesus"* (Acts 1:14). She once called herself *"The maidservant of the Lord"* (Luke 1:38). Miraculously, she was a virgin until after the birth of Jesus. (Read all about it in Luke 1:27, 34 and GWWB, pages 87–96.) The early church held Mary in high esteem. She was a major source of information about Jesus' early years. Mary not only gave Jesus birth, but also she was there to help give birth to his church!

What Others are Saying:

Craig S. Keener: Given the culture's usual downplaying of women's public roles, the equal participation of women is noteworthy, especially their apparent mixing with the men.[11]

Upper Room Roll Call: Jesus' Relatives

The roster of upper room participants contains a happy surprise: *"Jesus brothers"* were there (Acts 1:14): James, Joseph, Simon, and Judas (Matthew 13:55). Throughout most of his ministry they'd been quite unwilling to believe in Jesus (John 7:5). In fact, they thought he was mentally ill (Mark 3:21). But they've changed! Here they are among Jesus' closest disciples, waiting for the Holy Spirit. Jesus' brother James became a church <u>leader</u> and authored the **Epistle** of James.

☞ **GO TO:**

Acts 12:17; 15:13–19; 21:18 (leader)

Epistle: letter

"Together" (Acts 1:14) means more than occupying the same room. It means with <u>one mind</u> and passion. This was hardly the kind of group that could be expected to launch a worldwide revolution. Most were nobodies in polite society. However, they shared one thing in common—close relationship with Jesus. He was the superglue that held them together.

Something to Ponder

How Do You Start A Fire?

Strike a match. Spark flint on steel. Rub two sticks together. Or . . . jam 120 spiritually passionate people who've met the risen Jesus in a room like sardines, and get 'em praying . . . "**constantly**" (Acts 1:14). The early church is big on prayer—it's mentioned thirty-one times in Acts. Jesus told the early believers that their Father in heaven would give them the Holy Spirit if they prayed (Luke 24:49).

☞ **GO TO:**

Matthew 18:19–20 (one mind)

constantly: resolutely, obstinately persistent

What Others are Saying:

Sue Monk Kidd: When Jesus asked the disciples to wait, he knew that times of prayerful waiting allow something profound and necessary to take place. They create a receptiveness to God's power that enables it to sink down and revitalize our lives. . . . In every transformation there is a time to wait . . . and pray.[12]

Acts 1:15–20 In those days Peter stood up among the believers (a group numbering about a hundred and twenty) and said, "Brothers, the Scripture had to be

☞ **GO TO:**

Psalms 69:25; 109:8
(Psalms)

fulfilled which the Holy Spirit spoke long ago through the mouth of David concerning Judas, who served as guide for those who arrested Jesus—he was one of our number and shared in this ministry." (With the reward he got for his wickedness, Judas bought a field; there he fell headlong, his body burst open and all his intestines spilled out. Everyone in Jerusalem heard about this, so they called that field in their language Akeldama, that is, Field of Blood.) "For," said Peter, "it is written in the book of Psalms, 'May his place be deserted; let there be no one to dwell in it,' and, 'May another take his place of leadership.'"

Tragedy At Murder Meadow

One familiar face was missing at this upper room caucus: Judas Iscariot, Jesus' friend (see Matthew 26:50). Judas was one of Jesus' original twelve ambassadors (Luke 6:16). He turned traitor and *"served as guide to those who arrested Jesus"* (Acts 1:16). The price of his treachery was a miserable *"thirty silver coins"* (Matthew 26:15).

How Judas "Bought The Farm"

☞ **GO TO:**

Luke 22:3–6; John 12:4–6; 13:27
(turned traitor)

John 18:1–3 (guide)

The Bible gives two accounts of Judas's tragic end—here in Acts 1:18–19 and in Matthew 27:3–10. Overcome with guilt, Judas went to the Temple to return the bribe. The priests refused the money. He threw the silver into the Temple, went out, and hanged himself. His body fell, bursting open. Peter's description is graphic enough to make the strongest stomach turn.

The bribe money was used to buy the piece of land where Judas died, now considered **cursed** by his blood, as a place to bury paupers and **aliens**. Six weeks later, the locals were already calling it *"Field of Blood"* or *"Murder Meadow."*[13]

☞ **GO TO:**

Genesis 4:10–12
(cursed)

cursed: haunted

aliens: foreigners, not native to Israel.

Acts 1:21–26 "Therefore it is necessary to choose one of the men who have been with us the whole time the Lord Jesus went in and out among us, beginning from John's baptism to the time when Jesus was taken up from us. For one of these must become a witness with us of his resurrection." So they proposed two men: Joseph called Barsabbas (also known as Justus) and Matthias. Then they prayed, "Lord, you know everyone's heart. Show us which of these two you have chosen to

> take over this apostolic ministry, which Judas left to go where he belongs." Then they cast lots, and the lot fell to Matthias; so he was added to the eleven apostles.

The Election of A.D. 30

The yawn factor of 240 hours of waiting becomes apparent when we realize the most exciting thing that happened during those ten days was a church election! Actually it was quite important. The first congregational election involved four steps:

- Step 1—Instruction (Acts 1:20–21). Qualifications for office: Judas's pinch-hitter must (1) believe in the resurrection, (2) know Jesus as a result of living with him, (3) know and work well with the rest of the team.

- Step 2—Nomination (Acts 1:21–23). By **consensus** two candidates were nominated: Joseph, nicknamed Barsabbas ("son of the Sabbath") or Justus (Latin for "righteous"), and Matthias. **Eusebius** reports that Matthias was one of the seventy Jesus sent out to prepare the cities of Judea and Perea for his arrival (Luke 10:1).

- Step 3—Prayer (Acts 1:24). Ask God to <u>reveal his choice</u>.

- Step 4—<u>Casting lots</u> (Acts 1:26). Today we'd draw straws or flip a coin. In Acts 1 they wrote candidates' names on small stones, put them in a bowl, and shook the bowl till one of the stones rolled out (see illustration below). The rolling stone announced the winner—Matthias (Acts 1:26).

The story of the first church election shows how Jesus leads his movement through (1) his people's concerns, (2) their willingness to listen to each other, (3) their attitude of dependence on his leadership expressed in prayer, and (4) their consensus—agreement, harmony—about a course of action.

JESUS CHRIST CEO

consensus: agreement of the entire group

Eusebius: early church historian

☞ **GO TO:**

Proverbs 16:33 (reveal his choice)

Leviticus 16:8–10; Numbers 26:55; 1 Chronicles 26:12–16 (casting lots)

Casting Lots

Small stones or pottery pieces such as these with names or symbols written on them were used to make decisions. Biblical use of lots was not superstitious but based on a belief that God controls everything.

Lawrence O. Richards: This is the last time we read [in the Bible] any decision being made by casting lots or any similar way . . . . From that moment on the Spirit became our guide. Now we look to him, and in faith commit ourselves to obey when he shows us the way.[14]

Study Questions

1. Where did Jesus get his power to teach and do miracles?
2. Identify two things baptism with the Holy Spirit may be expected to accomplish in a person's life?
3. Jesus' strategy for world conquest involves three phases or major offensives. List them.
4. How did the people waiting in the upper room for the Holy Spirit spend their time?
5. What qualifications did Peter say should be looked for in Judas's replacement? Who were the two men who fulfilled the qualifications to be candidates for apostleship?
6. How did the group go about deciding which one should replace Judas?

CHAPTER WRAP-UP

- Acts is a sequel to the Gospel of Luke, telling how Jesus continued his work through his followers. (Acts 1:1–2)

- For forty days following Easter, Jesus appeared to people, proving he was alive. He talked about God's reign and the baptism of the Holy Spirit. He outlined his strategy for taking his message to the world. The Holy Spirit would come to his people. Then they would take his message in widening circles to the ends of the earth. (Acts 1:3–8)

- Jesus ascended to heaven, assuring vital benefits for believers. Angels promised he would return. (Acts 1:9–11)

- The disciples spent the next ten days waiting for the Spirit. They prayed and experienced oneness based on love for Jesus. (Acts 1:11–14)

- The gathering agreed Judas's vacancy on the apostolic team should be filled. Matthias was chosen by lot. (Acts 1:15–26)

ACTS 2: FIREWORKS AT THE FIESTA

Let's Get Started

Jesus told his friends they would become world travelers taking the news about him to faraway places (Matthew 28:19–20; Acts 1:8). He promised they would be *"clothed with power from on high"* (Luke 24:49). Wherever the adventure took them, he would go with them (Matthew 28:20).

Depending on your perspective, what happened next may seem strange, sensational, or spooky. In all its colorful religious history, Jerusalem had never seen anything like it. The **promise** came to the first trembling collection of 120 Jewish believers on their tenth day of waiting. Jesus suddenly stormed back into their lives like gangbusters! They found themselves with unusual opportunities to tell his story and unusual abilities for getting people to listen. They found courage to confront the people responsible for Jesus' death and to publicly appeal to their listeners to link up with the dynamic personal presence of God.

promise: God's unchangeable commitment

Michael Card: Our God is the great maker of promises. His word, the Bible, is quite simply a collection of the promises he has made to us.[1]

What Others are Saying:

> **Acts 2:1** When the day of Pentecost came, they were all together in one place.

☞ **GO TO:**

Exodus 23:16; 34:22;
   Deuteronomy 16:10;
   Numbers 28:26
   (harvest festival)

Exodus 12; Leviticus
   23:5 (Passover)

Pentecost: *called Feast of "Weeks" (seven weeks after Passover), "Firstfruits," or "Harvest"*

Passover: *celebration of Israel's freedom from Egyptian slavery*

Hebrew: *Israelite, belonging to the nation of Israel, Jewish*

Mt. Sinai: *mountain on Sinai Peninsula, between Gulfs of Suez and Aqaba*

Covenants: *binding agreements or contracts between parties*

poured out: *given freely and abundantly*

☞ **GO TO:**

2 Corinthians 1:22; 5:5;
   Ephesians 1:13–14
   (guarantees)

What Others are Saying:

Y'All Come To The Harvest Hop

Pentecost Day was the annual Jewish barley <u>harvest festival</u> held in late May or early June, fifty days after **Passover** (see GWBI, pages 25–28 and GWHN, pages 109–110). It was Israel's Thanksgiving Day. In A.D. 30 Pentecost was the day the Holy Spirit came upon the followers of Jesus (Acts 1:4). What the Jews celebrated on that day helps us understand the Spirit's coming.

God Puts His "John Hancock" On The Dotted Line

Hebrew scholars calculate that on the fiftieth day after ol' Pharaoh let God's people go (Exodus 12, 19) God gave Israel the Ten Commandments (Exodus 20:1–17) and the Law, at **Mt. Sinai**. The Law is also called "the Mosaic Covenant" because God communicated it through Israel's great liberator, Moses.

Covenants play a big part in the history of God's relationship with people. God's covenants are formal statements describing his commitments. God made covenants with Noah (see Genesis 9:8–17 and GWGN, pages 93–94); Abraham (see Genesis 12:1–3; 15:18–20 and GWGN page 112); David (1 Chronicles 17:7–15); and Moses (introduced in Exodus 19:3–6 and spelled out in Exodus, Leviticus, Numbers and Deuteronomy). The Mosaic Covenant is also called the "First" or "Old" Covenant (Hebrews 8:6–7, 13).

At Pentecost, the anniversary of the Old Covenant, the Holy Spirit introduced a New Covenant (new terms for relating to God). The Old Testament arrangement based on religious rule keeping and animal sacrifices was cancelled (Hebrews 8:13). Since Jesus came and the Spirit was **poured out**, knowing God is a whole new ball game! Today we relate to God through his Spirit who lives in everyone who trusts Jesus. God's Spirit living in us writes God's law on our minds and hearts (Hebrews 8:10; 10:16–17) and <u>guarantees</u> God's commitments will be carried out.

You see, Pentecost was not just a jazzy, goose bump–raising high. It was the start of a new way to know and live with God.

Billy Graham: The Day of Pentecost in the New Testament on which the Holy Spirit came was "a day of first fruits"—the beginning of God's harvest in this world, to be completed when Christ comes again. Pentecost in the New Testament marked the commencement of the present age of the Holy Spirit.[2]

What Pentecost Celebrates	How Celebrated	What It Pictures about the Spirit
Harvest God's goodness in providing food	The first sheaf of barley is presented to the Lord in thanksgiving and anticipation of a full harvest ahead.	The 120 are the first "sheaves" of a spiritual harvest, which will gather people all over the world to Christ through their witness.
Community Equality of God's people	Most inclusive festival. Everyone invited (Deuteronomy 16:11). All social classes participate as equals.	The Spirit is for the *whole* church; *all* who believe in Jesus are equipped by the Spirit to do God's work *together* (John 7:37–39).
Acceptance God's acceptance of imperfect people	Festival bread is common bread of Israelite homes (see GWHN, pages 8–9), made with yeast—symbol of sin (Leviticus 23:17).	God accepts and empowers ordinary people still struggling with spiritual imperfections and uses them as workers in his harvest.
Commitment God's commitments to his people	Remembering God's gift of the Mosaic Covenant, the Law, at Mt. Sinai, fifty days after first Passover (Exodus 20:1–17).	Spirit's coming inaugurated the New Covenant in Christ; the Spirit writes God's laws on believers' hearts (Hebrews 8:10).

Acts 2:2–3 Suddenly a sound like the blowing of a violent wind came from heaven and filled the whole house where they were sitting. They saw what seemed to be tongues of fire that separated and came to rest on each of them.

The Big Bang

Morning, the tenth day after Jesus was lifted to heaven, **thousands** of pilgrims moved through the streets of Old Jerusalem to the temple area for worship, unaware that in a nearby loft something was about to happen that would change the course of history. In Bible history new beginnings—especially God's covenants—are often introduced with nerve-racking <u>disturbances</u>.

The prayers of the 120 were interrupted by a deafening roar—as if a tornado had been unleashed inside the house. Today you might have described it as the roar of a superjet taking off! Wind is a symbol of the Spirit (<u>breath</u>) of God, the source of life, and cleansing judgment. The roar of this glorious gale announced that what they had been waiting for—their moment of spiritual rebirth, the beginning of a new life in the Spirit—had arrived.

Hang on to your hat! There's more to come!

thousands: 100,000 to 150,000 or more[3]

☞ **GO TO:**

Genesis 9:8–17; 15:6–20; 32:24–31; Exodus 19 (disturbances)

Genesis 2:7; Job 37:10; Ezekiel 13:13; John 3:8 (breath)

Dallas Willard: The **engulfment** came upon them—with quite a racket, right out of the sky into which only ten days earlier they had seen Jesus disappear (Acts 2:2).[4]

engulfment: baptism with the Holy Spirit

The Exploding Fireball

As if the hurricane-sound tearing through the house was not enough to scare the daylights out of them, a ball of fire suddenly appeared, exploded, separated into individual flames, and danced around the room igniting 120 secondary fires. Each person in the room seemed to be on fire.

☞ **GO TO:**

Exodus 3:2–5; 13:21–22; 19:18; Leviticus 6:13 (fire)

Psalm 1:4 (chaff)

chaff: seed coverings, straw, and other debris

- In the Bible, <u>fire</u> represents the presence of God. The Holy Spirit *is* God present.
- John the Baptist predicted Jesus would *"baptize you with the Holy Spirit and with fire."* Jesus as harvester, threshes out the good grain and incinerates the **chaff** (Luke 3:16-17). His incoming Spirit purifies a person's conscience from past guilt (Acts 15:8–9) and starts a process of cleansing away everything destructive and useless.
- The Holy Spirit's work meets both group and individual needs. He invades each person, but the impact of his cleansing, empowering work is most fully realized when believers are *together*, interacting, bumping up against each other, adjusting, dealing with irritation and frustration with each other, reconciling.

Paul Tournier: Human effort is like an endless labor in which, generation by generation, bit by bit, a monument is built, always precarious and never finished. The solution of each problem raises a thousand new problems. But when the spark of the Spirit lights up the darkness that has gathered around a person's life, it is as if there has come down from heaven, perfect and complete, a quite simple truth that sets at rest all the disquiet of the soul.[5]

Cyril of Jerusalem: Whatever the Spirit touches becomes holy and transformed.[6]

> **Acts 2:4a** All of them were filled with the Holy Spirit . . .

Engulfed In The Spirit

"Filled with the Holy Spirit"—what does it mean?

1. The Spirit of Christ fills the void created by separation from God because of sin.

2. *The Amplified Bible* says Jesus' friends were **"diffused** *throughout their souls"*[7] with the Holy Spirit. God's Spirit and the human spirit intermix. (Welcome to chemistry 101!)

3. Paul compares Spirit-filling to getting "smashed"! *"Do not get drunk on wine, which leads to* **debauchery***. Instead, be filled with the Spirit"* (Ephesians 5:18). To be filled with the Holy Spirit is to be under the Spirit's <u>influence</u> (see GWRM, pages 107–109). Getting tanked on wine leads to loss of control and destructive behavior. Spirit-filling produces joy, spiritual singing, and worship.

diffused: *molecules of one substance dispersed among those of another*

debauchery: *reckless indecency*

☞ **GO TO:**

Romans 8:5–9 (influence)

JESUS CHRIST
CEO

In order to assure that direction of his movement is dynamic and personal, Jesus comes to live in believers, in the person of the Holy Spirit. He manages the kingdom from the throne of his people's yielded desires and wills.

Kilian McDonnell: The Spirit is the turning-around point by which the way back to God is opened. . . . The Spirit is the sole source of our relationship with God.[8]

Billy Graham: All Christians are committed to be filled with the Spirit. Anything short of a Spirit-filled life is less than God's plan for each believer. . . . To be Spirit-filled is to be controlled or dominated by the Spirit's presence and power. . . . We are under the "influence" of the Spirit. Instead of doing things only with our own strength or ability, He empowers us. Instead of doing only what we want to do, we now are guided by Him.[9]

What Others are Saying:

tongues: *languages*

Acts 2:4b–11 . . . and began to speak in other **tongues** as the Spirit enabled them. Now there were staying in Jerusalem God-fearing Jews from every nation under heaven. When they heard this sound, a crowd came together in bewilderment, because each one heard them speaking in his own language. Utterly amazed, they asked: "Are not all these men who are speaking Galileans? Then how is it that each of us hears them in his own native language? Parthians, Medes and Elamites; residents of Mesopotamia, Judea and Cappadocia, Pontus and Asia, Phrygia and Pamphylia, Egypt and the parts of Libya near Cyrene; visitors from Rome (both Jews and converts to Judaism); Cretans and Arabs—we hear them declaring the wonders of God in our own tongues!"

Languages Of Wonder and Witness

Jews converged on Jerusalem for Pentecost. Thousands of travelers speaking foreign languages filled the streets. A little before nine in the morning, passersby were startled by what sounded like a violent windstorm bearing down on one particular house. They rushed toward the sound.

In the loft above, with a hurricane howl inundating their ears and a vision of flame dazzling their eyes, the roomful of Galileans began to speak with <u>languages</u> other than the Galilean-accented Aramaic they'd spoken all their lives. Men and women poured out of the upper room doors and down to the street below, loudly praising God in the new languages. It was <u>Babel</u> (see GWBI, pages 11–12) unraveled! What sounded to some like mindless babble, to others was clear declaration of the *"**wonders** of God"*! At least fifteen different languages were spoken in this **cacophony** of praise— *"Even Cretans and Arabs!"* cried one incredulous listener.

Acts 2 gives these facts concerning the "languages" phenomenon:

- Ability to speak was given by the Holy Spirit (verse 4).
- Everyone in the original group was able to speak a new language (verse 4).
- Speakers used their new languages to declare the wonderworks of God (verse 11).
- Some listeners concluded it was the babbling of a bunch of drunks (verse 13).

On two other occasions in Acts, people spoke in strange languages when first introduced to Jesus and the Holy Spirit (Acts 10:44–46; 19:5–6). Other times when people received the Spirit, the language gift is not mentioned (Acts 8:17; 9:17–18). The gift of languages (tongues) also appeared in the church at <u>Corinth</u>. There the languages were not understood and required interpretation.

☞ **GO TO:**

Isaiah 28:11–12;
   1 Corinthians 12–14
   (languages)

Genesis 11:1–9 (Babel)

wonders: *acts and characteristics of God that reveal his splendor and inspire worship*

cacophony: *discordant sound*

☞ **GO TO:**

1 Corinthians 12–14
   (Corinth)

> **Acts 2:12** Amazed and perplexed, they asked one another, "What does this mean?"

Why Would God Give Such A Goofy Gift?

The serious-minded folks were scratching their heads, wanting to know more. At Pentecost, with all those foreign visitors, the Holy Spirit's language gift shifted the worldwide witness to Jesus Christ into gear (Acts 1:8; Matthew 28:19). The pilgrims of Pentecost returned home (see illustration, page 11), taking with them news of the new thing God was doing.

Krister Stendahl: Now the Spirit is the energy and the guide engineering the life and expansion of the church in the world of the **Jewish diaspora** and through it to the **Gentile** world. The ecstatic speech, the speaking in tongues . . . is seen by Luke as a symbol of the global outreach across all barriers of language and culture.[10]

Ajith Fernando: Pentecost, then, gives us a hint of how the revolutionary breaking of social and other barriers by the gospel will work out in practical life. The implications are immense. As we take the gospel to the peoples of the world, we should not expect people to subject themselves to a language like English (which is today what Greek was in the first century). We need to learn the heart language of people and to share the gospel with them in that language.[11]

Jesus does not merely tell *the church what it should be doing; he gives the spiritual equipment and abilities needed to do it—in this case, the ability to speak the language of the people.*

JESUS CHRIST CEO

> **Acts 2:13** Some, however, made fun of them and said, "They have had too much wine."

"You're Drunk Out Of Your Skulls!"

Some people in every crowd try to hide their perplexity with cynical jokes. Or perhaps deciding the disciples were all crocked was the best explanation bewildered detractors could come up with

What Others are Saying:

Jewish diaspora: *Jews scattered in foreign countries*

Gentile: *anyone who's not Jewish*

☞ **GO TO:**

2 Kings 17:5; 25:21 (diaspora)

KEY POINT

If you want people to understand what you say about Jesus, talk their language.

☞ **GO TO:**

1 Corinthians 14:23 (explanation)

for the puzzling occurrence of a roomful of Galilean yokels making strange noises with their mouths. Ironically, in the spiritual sense, the detractors were right. This *was* the "new wine" of the new order Jesus said couldn't be contained in old bottles (Mark 2:22). In any case, the snide remark gave the full-of-Jesus believers their first real chance to be witnesses.

 Persecution & Martyrdom—It is not uncommon for Christians and their values to be ridiculed in movies, on TV, and elsewhere. People may poke fun because they don't understand or they feel uncomfortable, envious, or ashamed.

> **Acts 2:14–15** Then Peter stood up with the Eleven, raised his voice and addressed the crowd: "Fellow Jews and all of you who live in Jerusalem, let me explain this to you; listen carefully to what I say."

Hear Those Scaredy Cats Roar!

Before their very eyes they saw proof Jesus Christ rose from the dead and lives in his followers! Here's Peter the coward, who, three times, before some of these same people, denied knowing Jesus. Flanking him are eleven other guys, who, when the chips were down seven weeks earlier, ran like rabbits to save their own miserable skins leaving Jesus to face death alone. But what a difference!

The "Rock" (Peter), finally living up to his name, shouts for the crowd's attention. With good humor he pitches the cynics' joke back at them: "Drunk? It's only nine o'clock in the morning, for heaven's sake! Nobody gets drunk before breakfast." (Laughter.)

☞ **GO TO:**

Luke 22:54–62 (denied)

Mark 14:50–52 (ran)

Matthew 16:18 (Rock)

> **Acts 2:16–21** "No, this is what was spoken by the prophet Joel:
> 'In the last days, God says,
> I will pour out my Spirit on all people.
> Your sons and daughters will prophesy,
> your young men will see visions,
> your old men will dream dreams.
> Even on my servants, both men and women,

> I will pour out my Spirit in those days,
>   and they will prophesy.
> I will show wonders in the heaven above
>   and signs on the earth below,
>   blood and fire and billows of smoke.
> The sun will be turned to darkness
>   and the moon to blood
>   before the coming of the great and glorious day of
>   the Lord.
> And everyone who calls on the name of the Lord will
>   be saved.'"

A Libation At Joe's Pub

"What does this mean?" (Acts 2:12). Peter remembered the ancient prophecy of Joel (Joel 2:28–32) and quoted it to explain. The ruckus in the upper room, the happy hubbub in the streets, announced a new age. The "<u>Last Days</u> are here," Peter said. "This is the Age of the Holy Spirit." Expect miracles!

1. Expect the outpouring of the Spirit to impact everyone.
2. Expect ordinary people—men and women—to **prophesy**, see **visions**, dream **dreams**.
3. Expect awesome occurrences in the sky and on the earth. Cosmic signs were already happening! The <u>day Jesus died</u> the sky had blackened and a rock-splitting, grave-opening earthquake occurred. And now the wind roared, fire appeared, and strange languages were spoken. There would be more (see GWRV, pages 120–124).
4. Expect **salvation** to be offered to <u>everyone</u>.

EARLY CHURCH WOMEN—The Spirit gives ability, authority, and freedom to Christian women to preach and minister alongside men (Acts 2:17–18). (Read about the prophetess Deborah and how God used her even in battle in GWWB, pages 126–127.)

Watchman Nee: Because the Holy Spirit has been poured out upon all mankind, the merest cry from the sinner to God is enough.[12]

2 Timothy 3:1; Hebrews 1:2; 2 Peter 3:3; 1 John 2:18 (last days)

Matthew 1:20; 2:13, 19, 22 (dreams)

Luke 22:44–45; Mark 15:33, 38; Matthew 27:45, 51–52 (day Jesus died)

John 3:16; Romans 1:14–16 (everyone)

prophesy: *speak God's messages, preach*

visions: *insights, dream-like revelations from God*

dreams: *images with spiritual significance while asleep*

salvation: *rescue from sin's slavery; restoration of spiritual health*

What Others are Saying:

Acts 2:22–24 "Men of Israel, listen to this: Jesus of Nazareth was a man accredited by God to you by miracles, wonders and signs, which God did among you through him, as you yourselves know. This man was handed over to you by God's set purpose and **foreknowledge**; and you, with the help of wicked men, put him to death by nailing him to the cross. But God raised him from the dead, freeing him from the agony of death, because it was impossible for death to keep its hold on him . . ."

☞ **GO TO:**

Matthew 1:21; Mark
8:31; Luke 2:34–35;
John 10:14–18
(destiny)

Acts 1:9; Philippians
2:11 (exalted)

The Big Idea

Peter states the central theme of the Christian message. Some form of this message is preached over and over in Acts:

1. Jesus was approved by God (Acts 2:22).
2. His <u>destiny</u> was to die on the cross (Acts 2:23).
3. God raised him from the dead (Acts 2:24–32).
4. Jesus now occupies the <u>exalted</u> position at "*the **right hand** of God*" (Acts 2:33–35).

What Others
are Saying:

right hand: highest place
of honor and power in
the universe

William Barclay: The thought of Acts safeguards us from two serious errors in our thinking about the death of Jesus. (a) The cross is not a kind of emergency measure flung out by God when everything else failed. It is part of God's very life. (b) We must never think that anything Jesus did changed the attitude of God to men. It was *by God* Jesus was sent. We may put it this way—the cross was a window in time allowing us to see the suffering love which is eternally in the heart of God.[13]

THE BIG PICTURE 🔍

Acts 2:25–35 Peter explained that God showed King David what Messiah would <u>be like</u>. Messiah would be one of David's <u>descendants</u>. The king <u>predicted</u> Christ's resurrection and <u>return</u> to God's right hand.

☞ **GO TO:**

Psalm 16:8–11 (be like)

1 Chronicles 17:11–14
(descendants)

Psalm 16:10 (predicted)

Psalm 110:1 (return)

King David Sings The Wondrous Story

Speaking to this audience of zealous Jews, Peter used the prophetic poetry of Israel's most popular king to explain Jesus' significance. God showed King David what Messiah would be like (Acts 2:25–28; Psalm 16:8–11). Messiah would be one of David's descendants (Acts 2:29–30; 1 Chronicles 17:11–14). The singing king predicted Christ's resurrection (Acts 2:31; Psalm 16:10) and return to God's right hand (Acts 2:24; Psalm 110:1).

Peter's message is clear: The Christian Gospel offers a reality no other system of morality, religion, or philosophy offers. Genuine Christianity is packaged in the *person* of its founder and present leader—who died on the cross, rose from the dead, holds the most highly exalted position in the universe, and by his Spirit literally *lives in* his followers!

George MacDonald: Jesus departed from our sight that he might return to our hearts; he departed and, behold, he is here![14]

> **Acts 2:36** "Therefore let all Israel be assured of this: God has made this Jesus, whom you crucified, both Lord and Christ."

The Zinger: The True Identity Of The Man You Killed

Peter wraps up his speech with a whack across the head with a spiritual two-by-four. All of this—the prophecies, Jesus' crucifixion, resurrection, and ascension, the Holy Spirit's coming to the disciples, the disturbances of Pentecost—proves one great fact: Jesus (the man you crucified) is **Lord** (*Yahweh*-God) and Christ (**Messiah**-King).

Lord: Master; also a title for God

Messiah: God's Chosen One, Savior, King

Audrey I. Girard:
My sweet Messiah came to me as Savior, Lord and friend,
Anointed One by Father God, salvation in the end.
Proclaimed by David long ago, who died but did not rise.
But said his seed would be in one who would not compromise.
He'd rise again, this certain Christ, and send his Spirit back
With pow'r and comfort not yet known, providing what we lack.[15]

KEY POINT

The foremost fact of Christian faith is this: Jesus, who died for our sins, rose from the dead, is alive today, and may be known personally as Lord and Savior.

> **Acts 2:37** When the people heard this, they were cut to the heart and said to Peter and the other apostles, "Brothers, what shall we do?"

No Time To Sing "Just As I Am"

Call 911! This is an emergency! The sense of urgency that gripped people as Peter nailed home point after point was a result of the Spirit quietly doing <u>his job</u>. Peter's logic was flawless. The Spirit's power energized him as he spoke. They knew about the crucifixion. They knew who was responsible (and it wasn't Bart Simpson!) They knew Jesus' tomb was empty. They saw what they hadn't seen before: Jesus' death and resurrection fulfilled prophecies they'd read Sabbath after Sabbath in their synagogues (see GWPB, pages 46–49). The light dawned. Jesus of Nazareth *was* the Messiah!

"What shall we do?" they cried.

Something to Ponder

Were you ever *"cut to the heart"* by something you heard about Christ? What did you do? Have you made an initial commitment to follow Christ? What convinced you that you needed him?

What Others are Saying:

J. Gresham Machen: There must be the mysterious work of the Spirit of God in the new birth. Without that, all our arguments are quite useless. . . . What the Holy Spirit does in the new birth is not to make a man a Christian regardless of the evidence, but on the contrary to clear away the mists from his eyes and enable him to attend to the evidence.[16]

> **Acts 2:38–39** Peter replied, "Repent and be baptized, every one of you, in the name of Jesus Christ for the forgiveness of your sins. And you will receive the gift of the Holy Spirit. The promise is for you and your children and for all who are far off—for all whom the Lord our God will call."

Quick! Walk This Way!

Peter was ready with a road map:

1. *"Repent"*—Admit you're going the wrong way. Turn to God.
2. *"Be **baptized**" in the name of Jesus Christ for forgiveness of your sins*—Let God wash away your sins, forgiving you because of what Christ did on the cross.
3. *"Receive the gift of the Holy Spirit"*—To welcome Christ is to welcome the Spirit.

☞ **GO TO:**

Matthew 16:17; Luke 10:21–22; John 6:44–45; 16:7–15 (his job)

baptized: (in water) to publicly declare faith in Jesus

in the name of: on the basis of the character and accomplishments of

This is a promise for (1) you, (2) your children, and (3) **far off** people who don't know anything about God.

far off: Gentiles (non-Jews): future generations

F. F. Bruce: Peter's preaching proved effective, not only persuading his hearers' minds but convicting their consciences. . . . Incredible as it must appear, Peter told them that there was hope even now. Let them repent of their sin and turn to God; let them submit to baptism in the name of Jesus, confessed as Messiah. Then not only would they receive forgiveness of sins, but they would receive also the gift of the Holy Spirit—the gift which had been bestowed on the apostles themselves only a few hours before.[17]

What Others are Saying:

> **Acts 2:40** With many other words he warned them; and he pleaded with them, "Save yourselves from this corrupt generation."

"Get Out While You Can!"

The *"corrupt generation"* Peter urged his listeners to get out of was the spiritually dead, morally rotten culture of the world, including a dead religious system riddled with hypocrisy and resistance to God's will thinly masked by a facade of lifeless ritual and crotchety rule keeping. With the arrival of Jesus Christ that old system was out the window! Down for the last time! Kaput! Obsolete! A new generation is born—the generation of the Spirit. A new community, a culture responsive to Jesus as Lord, has hung up its shingle and gone into business.

☞ **GO TO:**

John 12:31–33;
Romans 7:4–6; 8:1–4; 1 John 2:15–17
(system was out)

Hebrews 8:13
(obsolete)

Dig Deeper

Spiritual Dynamite: Terms for the Holy Spirit's Work in Acts 1–2

Term	Reference	Meaning
Filled	Acts 2:4	Under the Spirit's influence
Baptized	Acts 1:5	Initiated into the Spirit's life, washed clean from sin
Gift	Acts 1:4; 2:38	The Spirit is a free gift based on God's promise
Come upon	Acts 1:8	Occupied, taken over, energized by the Holy Spirit
Poured out	Acts 2:17	God's generosity in giving the Spirit, fullness
Receive	Acts 2:38	Open the door to the Holy Spirit by welcoming Jesus

> **Acts 2:41** Those who accepted his [Peter's] message were baptized, and about three thousand were added to their number that day.

The Miracle Of The Church

Three thousand people responded to Peter's message and were baptized that very day to seal their deal to follow Christ and to welcome his Spirit into their lives. It was a day of <u>surprises</u>. The most delightful surprise was the emergence of the intense, spiritually lively community that immediately came together around the risen Jesus.

Like a magnet the Spirit drew the people who trusted Jesus to each other. They became part of a new association of people in the process of "being saved" (Acts 2:47). Elsewhere this believing community is called the <u>church</u>. The original word for "church" means "called out ones"—identifying people "called out" by the Holy Spirit to live a radically new and different lifestyle.

When a person declared his or her faith in Jesus, he or she was immediately "*added to their number*" (Acts 2:41). In New Testament jargon "added" means "fitted and adjoined"[18] (Acts 2:5–11). Fitting believers together as indispensable pieces in God's puzzle is one of the most wonderful wonders the Holy Spirit does!

☞ **GO TO:**

Acts 2:2–12, 17–20 (surprises)

Matthew 16:18; 18:17; Acts 5:11; 8:1, 3; 14:23 (church)

Acts 2:47; 5:14; 1 Corinthians 12:13 (added)

What Others are Saying:

Tertullian: How much more justly are those called and considered brothers, who acknowledge the one God as their Father; who have received the one Spirit of holiness; who have awakened from the same darkness of uncertainty to the light of the same truth? . . . We, who are united in spirit and in soul, do not hesitate to have all things in common, except wives.[19]

> **Acts 2:42** They devoted themselves to the apostle's teaching and to the fellowship, to the breaking of bread and to prayer.

On Your Mark. Get Set. Grow!

As three thousand living pieces were fitted into the early church puzzle, a unique new society developed, driven by four priorities and activities:

1 *The apostles' teaching.* Jesus had commissioned them to tell his story and teach people to obey his principles (Matthew

28:20; Luke 24:46–48). This involved three kinds of communication:

- Preaching—plain statement of the facts: Who Jesus is, and what Jesus did, including an invitation to make a decision to follow him (Acts 2:16–40)

- Teaching—explanation of the meaning of the facts aimed at helping Christians grow up in their faith (Ephesians 4:13)

- Exhortation—motivational communication urging believers to align their lives with Christ's teaching; counseling, correcting, advising one another (Acts 2:40; Romans 12:1)

What Others are Saying:

Larry Richards: Much of education is concerned with helping people know what their teachers know. Christian education is concerned with helping people become what their teachers are.[20]

2 *Fellowship.* The original word for "fellowship" (*koinonia*) means more than a handshake at the church door! New Testament-style fellowship means partnership, interaction, helping one another, sharing, sympathy, mutual communication. The first faith-based community got the crazy-loving notion that fellowship meant giving their own stuff away to meet the needs of others! (Acts 2:44–45).

3 *Breaking bread.* Jesus gave eating together <u>special significance</u>. Sharing meals was a regular part of early Christian meetings (Acts 2:42) and day-to-day fellowship (2:46). **Potluck** meals called "love feasts" (Jude 12) served three purposes:

- The hungry got a square meal.
- Sharing with each other strengthened fellowship.
- The **Lord's Supper** was celebrated, remembering Jesus and his death (1 Corinthians 11:23–26).

There is something about eating together that makes people more open to each other. A shared meal is a context where conversation happens naturally, needs become known, and friends discover how they can serve each other.

☞ **GO TO:**

Luke 9:16; 22:19; 24:30, 35, 41–43; John 21:12–13 (special significance)

Matthew 26:26–29; Mark 14:22–25; Luke 22:17–20 (Lord's Supper)

potluck: *people bring food and share it together*

Lord's Supper: *Holy Communion, Eucharist*

Remember This . . .

What Others are Saying:

Sherwood Wirt: I have learned there is no point in talking about strong churches and weak churches, big churches and little churches, warm churches and cold churches. Such categories are unrealistic and beside the point. There is only a loving church or an unloving church.[21]

4 *Prayers.* Fourteen of the first fifteen chapters of Acts and many later chapters tell how they prayed . . . "together" (Acts 4:24–31) . . . "alone" (Acts 10:9) . . . "continuously" (1 Thessalonians 5:17; Romans 8:26–27).

What Others are Saying:

Tertullian: We come together for a meeting in order to besiege God with prayers, like an army in battle formation. Such violence is pleasing to God.[22]

> **Acts 2:43–46** Everyone was filled with awe, and many wonders and miraculous signs were done by the apostles. All the believers were together and had everything in common. Selling their possessions and goods, they gave to anyone as he had need. Everyday they continued to meet together at the temple courts. They broke bread in their homes and ate together with glad and sincere hearts, . . .

The Jerusalem Philharmonic

It was hard to sleep in that church! Disturbing things kept happening. Apostles touched sick people, and they got well. Miraculous changes took place in people's attitudes toward others and material things. Love developed between people who shouldn't have been able to be in the same room without fighting. Sometimes the only response that made sense was worship.

They were "together"—really *together* (that word is used three times in this paragraph: Acts 2:44, 46). Jerusalem had many beggars and poor people. Jobs were scarce. Foreign travelers heard Peter's message, believed on Jesus, and stayed to learn more. Travel funds became depleted. <u>Destitute widows</u> joined the church. People spent enough time together to discover where the needs were. What's a Christian to do when a brother or sister in Christ is hungry or homeless? The original Jesus people responded by <u>voluntarily</u> sharing everything (2:44; 4:32). No law demanded it but the <u>law of love</u>. Private ownership was not discouraged nor ended. But surplus property was sold to get money to help the needy.

GO TO:

Acts 6:1
  (destitute widows)

Acts 5:4 (voluntarily)

Luke 9:27; John 13:34–35; Romans 13:8–10; 1 John 3:16–18
  (law of love)

What Others are Saying:

Jim Wallis: One of the very first tests of discipleship to Jesus Christ is a radical change in one's relationship to money and the possession of wealth.[23]

JESUS CHRIST CEO

The original Christians did not invent this way of living together. They simply followed Jesus' instructions, recorded in the four "Life of Christ" books—Matthew, Mark, Luke, and John. When his energy came to them through the Holy Spirit, they had no other strategy in mind but the one Jesus had given them.

Jesus' Strategy for the Church

Compare Acts 2:42–47 with Jesus' instructions to discover the source of the original Christians' ideas about how to do church.

 Dig Deeper

The Early Church in Action	The Strategy Laid out by Jesus
Acts 2:42—The priority of teaching	Matthew 28:20; Luke 6:40
Acts 2:42—The importance of prayer	Matthew 6:5–15; Luke 11:9–13; 18:1
Acts 2:43—Evidence/signs of spiritual reality	Matthew 10:8; John 13:34–35; 15:5
Acts 2:43, 46–47—Awe at God's work	Luke 4:36–37; 8:25; John 7:31, 45–46
Acts 2:44–45—Together, things in common	Luke 12:15, 22-34
Acts 2:42, 46—Shared meals, communion	Luke 10:7; 22:19; John 6:5–14
Acts 2:47—Adding to the fellowship	Luke 9:47–50; John 10:16; Matthew 28:19

> **Acts 2:47** . . . praising God and enjoying the favor of all the people. And the Lord added to their number daily those who were being saved.

Divine Arithmetic

Everyday they were together somewhere, meeting, sharing, eating, celebrating, praising. Nothing was "put on" or just for show (Acts 2:46 says they did what they did with "*sincere hearts*"). Nonbelievers watched and saw what was happening as real and good. And God <u>made it grow</u>!

☞ **GO TO:**

1 Corinthians 3:6–8 (made it grow)

Howard Snyder: Where Christian fellowship demonstrates the gospel, believers come alive and sinners get curious and want to know what the secret is.[24]

 What Others are Saying:

When the church is marked by eagerness for Christ's teaching, supportive relationships, wonder at God's working, sharing, prayer, liberality, genuineness, and joy, God adds people to their number.

 CHURCH GROWTH

Study Questions

1. What did the disciples hear, see, and experience when the Holy Spirit was first given?
2. According to Acts 2:4–13 what is the gift of tongues? What purpose did it fulfill? What was communicated? Identify three reactions of the crowd? Where in the New Testament can more information be found on the gift of tongues?
3. According to Peter, what does the resurrection prove about Jesus?
4. What did Peter say a person must do to receive the gift of the Holy Spirit?
5. To what four activities did the early believers devote themselves?
6. How far did the early Christians go in expressing their oneness and love for each other (Acts 2:44–45)? If they lacked something to give, what did some of them do?
7. Who did Luke say was responsible for the growth in numbers?

CHAPTER WRAP-UP

- The Jewish Feast of Pentecost was the setting for the initial outpouring of the Holy Spirit. The coming of the Spirit signaled the end of the Old Covenant and beginning of the New Covenant. (Hebrews 8:13)

- The Holy Spirit came with wind and fire. The disciples praised God in new languages. A crowd gathered, amazed at hearing Galileans speak their homeland (foreign) languages. The apostles told the people about the Holy Spirit. (Acts 2:2–16)

- Peter explained that these happenings fulfilled prophecy. He showed from the facts, Scripture, and eyewitness accounts that God had raised Jesus from the dead and that his resurrection proved he was Lord and Messiah. (Acts 2:16–36)

- Some were convinced. Peter explained that if they would turn to God and declare faith in Jesus, the gift of the Holy Spirit would be given to them. (Acts 2:37–40)

- Three thousand people responded and were added to their band. The new body concentrated on four activities to bring converts to spiritual maturity—teaching, fellowship, shared meals, and prayer. (Acts 2:41–42)

Wonderful things happened. All they owned was available to meet each other's needs. They welcomed one another into their homes. Their sincerity impressed everyone who watched. Their numbers grew. (Acts 2:43–47)

ACTS 3–4: SETTIN' THE WOODS ON FIRE

CHAPTER HIGHLIGHTS

- The Paralyzed Panhandler
- Jesus Is Back in Town!
- Rockin' the Boat
- Taking Trouble Home
- Normal Christianity

Let's Get Started

Jews did not stop being Jewish when they believed in Jesus and joined his band. They pursued the ancient faith with fresh enthusiasm because they understood its significance more clearly. They saw Jesus as the fulfillment of the Law of Moses.

For the committed Jew there were three special times of prayer each day—the **third hour** (about 9 A.M.), the sixth hour (noon) and the ninth hour (about 3 P.M.). Most important were the times of the <u>morning and evening</u> sacrifices. Something happened at the evening sacrifice that caused the fire of the new Jesus movement to leap the fireline and spread into the camp of its enemies. Luke, the author of Acts, does not say God created this breakout of Spirit fire, but it is not hard for believing eyes to see a divine hand arranging its escape from the comfortable parameters of the believers' community.

third hour: days were divided into twelve hours based on the position of the sun

☞ **GO TO:**

Exodus 29:29–42 (morning and evening)

THE BIG PICTURE 🔍

Acts 3:1–10 One day Peter and John went to the Temple. A man who was born with a handicap was begging there. He asked for money from Peter and John. They said they didn't have money to give him, but would give him something better. In the name of Jesus they healed him. The healed man walked and jumped and praised God so much that he attracted lots of attention.

The Case Of The Paralyzed Panhandler

Giving to the poor while entering the Temple was considered especially pleasing to God. So beggars clustered at the temple gates. This beggar chose to lie beside the *"gate called Beautiful,"* an exquisitely crafted bronze gate between the Court of the Gentiles and the Court of Women (see illustration below).

"Silver or gold I do not have," Peter said (Acts 3:6). He and John looked the lame man in the eye. "I'll give you what I have. *In the name of Jesus Christ of Nazareth, walk."* Peter grabbed the man's hand and pulled him up. The man had never stood on his own two feet before. But now he found his legs and feet supporting his weight. He jumped to his feet. Took his first step at age forty! (Acts 4:22). He was walking! He took a couple of practice leaps and then followed Peter and John through the Beautiful Gate into the Temple, walking and <u>leaping</u> and yelling praise to God! (Wouldn't you?)

☞ **GO TO:**

Isaiah 35:6; Luke 7:18–23 (leaping)

What Others are Saying:

☞ **GO TO:**

Mark 10:46–52; Luke 16:19–21 (disease or disability)

The Revell Bible Dictionary: In Middle Eastern lands begging has long been recognized as a profession. Yet the Bible has surprisingly few references to beggars. Typical beggars were crippled by some obvious <u>disease or disability</u>. . . . the beggar healed by Peter was lame from birth (Acts 3:1–10). In view of the Old Testament's often-expressed concern for the poor and oppressed, giving money to beggars was considered an important act of piety by the Jews of Jesus' time. But Christ and his disciples went to the root of the

Temple Diagram

This diagram shows the Court of the Gentiles where non-Jews could pray. The Court of the Women was in a more interior place where both men and women could worship. Women were not allowed farther into the Temple, except to sacrifice.

To Jerusalem

SLAUGHTERING PLACES

COURT OF ISRAEL To Mount of Olives

Most Holy Place

ALTAR COURT OF THE WOMEN
HOLY PLACE

COURT OF THE PRIESTS

COURT OF THE GENTILES

problem. They healed the beggars who appealed to them, combating diseases which kept them from earning their own living.[1]

What Others are Saying:

Richard C. Halverson: "What I have I give you," Peter said. You cannot give what you do not have, but you must have to give. The impotence of many Christians in this exciting, thrilling hour of history is due to the fact that they simply have nothing to offer but a few coins, and alms will not save a sick society. Healing, reconciliation, salvation can be shared only when we have it. We can give only what we have, and some of us are not giving because we do not have.[2]

JESUS CHRIST CEO

Jesus does his work through his people as they go about their ordinary daily routines if they simply share what they have with people they are with.

"In Jesus' Name"—What Does This Mean?

"*In the name of Jesus Christ of Nazareth, walk,*" Peter said (Acts 3:6). <u>Nine times</u> in eight verses in Acts 3–4 the word "name" or the phrase "in the name of" is used to refer to the authority by which a thing is done. To act in Jesus' name is to act with a kind of **power of attorney** granted by him. He gave his followers <u>authority</u> to act in his name—to represent him, speak and pray consistent with his person, character, purposes, and instructions.

☞ **GO TO:**

Acts 3:6, 16; 4:7, 10, 12, 17, 18, 30 (nine times)

John 14:12–14, 26; 15:16; 16:23–24 (authority)

power of attorney: *legal authority to act in behalf of another*

> **Acts 3:11–13a** While the beggar held on to Peter and John, all the people were astonished and came running to them in the place called Solomon's Colonnade. When Peter saw this, he said to them: "Men of Israel, why does this surprise you? Why do you stare at us as if by our own power or godliness we had made this man walk? The God of Abraham, Isaac and Jacob, the God of our fathers, has glorified his servant Jesus."

Jesus Is Back In Town!

It was as though Jesus had returned and was at his old game again! Even his enemies were forced to admit that what Peter and John did and said had a hauntingly familiar ring—"These men have been with Jesus!" they bellyached (see Acts 4:13).

"Don't look at us!" Peter began, as the crowd rushed to see the healed cripple strutting his stuff at the corner of the Temple where Solomon's Colonnade and the Royal Colonnade met. The crowd authenticated the miracle, recognizing the former lame man (Acts 3:10). "It isn't our power or godliness that makes this man able to walk," Peter said. "The <u>God of Abraham</u>, Isaac and Jacob has glorified his servant Jesus" (Acts 3:12–13).

☞ **GO TO:**

Exodus 3:24
(God of Abraham)

☞ **GO TO:**

John 18:38 (not guilty)

John 5:26; 11:25; 14:9
(author of life)

John 10:10; 11:25
(giving people life)

Luke 23:25; John 18:40
(hit man)

Ephesians 1:22; 4:15;
Colossians 1:18; 2:19
(heads)

Romans 12:4–5;
1 Corinthians 12:12–
27; Ephesians 4:4–16
(corporate body)

modus operandi:
method of operation

efficacy: power

> **Acts 3:13b–16** "You handed him over to be killed, and you disowned him before Pilate, though he had decided to let him go. You disowned the Holy and Righteous One and asked that a murderer be released to you. You killed the author of life, but God raised him from the dead. We are witnesses of this. By faith in the name of Jesus, this man whom you see and know was made strong. It is Jesus' name and the faith that comes through him that has given this complete healing to him, as you can all see."

The Master Key To Power

Peter continued, "You remember Jesus." (I'm paraphrasing.) "He's the one you insisted Pilate execute even though he found him <u>not guilty</u> and wanted to let him go. Jesus is the good guy—"*the <u>author of life</u>*"—who went around <u>giving people life</u> . . . the one you rejected and killed, voting instead for Barabbas, the <u>hit man</u> (see GWJN, pages 255–256).

"I've got news for you. God overturned your verdict! He raised Jesus from the dead. We've seen him! This healing was by faith in Jesus' name."

JESUS CHRIST
CEO

Surprise! Surprise! Surprise! The secret is out: Acts is the story of what Jesus *continues* to do since his resurrection (Acts 1:1). Jesus in Acts has the same purposes, mission, and **modus operandi** as Jesus in the Gospels. The difference? He's no longer limited to a single human body, one location at a time, one voice, one set of actions. Since ascending and sending his Spirit, Jesus <u>heads</u> a <u>corporate body</u> composed of all who receive him.

What Others are Saying:

F. F. Bruce: There is no merely magical **efficacy** in the words which Peter pronounced when, in Jesus' name, he commanded the cripple to walk; the cripple would have known no benefit had he not responded in faith to what Peter said. But once this response of faith was made, the power of the risen Christ filled his body with health and strength.[3]

THE BIG PICTURE

> **Acts 3:17–26** After acknowledging that Israel and its leaders had acted in ignorance in their rejection of Jesus, Peter showed how Jesus fulfilled what the prophets wrote about Messiah. He called for people to turn toward God, stop sinning, and listen to Jesus. If they'd do this, certain spiritual benefits are promised.

"Play It Again, Sam"

As the crowd rushed to check out the panhandler's miracle, Peter got on his soapbox. He preached the indispensable fundamentals of the Christian faith: Who Jesus is. What Jesus did (Acts 3:13–16). It's the same format as his Pentecost day sermon (Acts 2:14–40). Because the audience was Jewish, Peter quoted from the Old Testament to show how Jesus fulfilled what the prophets wrote about Messiah (Acts 3:18–25). He called for people to turn toward God, change their lives, quit their wicked ways, and listen to Jesus. If they'd do this, Peter promised these things:

KEY POINT

The early church had no message but Jesus crucified, risen from the dead, and offering a fresh start to people who trust him.

- Their sins would be wiped away (Acts 3:19; see Isaiah 44:22; Colossians 2:13–14).
- Spiritual renewal would come to them (Acts 3:19; see John 7:37–39; Matthew 11:28–30).
- Christ himself would come to them (Acts 3:20; see Acts 2:38; John 14:18–21).
- Everything broken in them would be restored (Acts 3:21; see Joel 2:12–27).
- They'd get the blessings promised to Abraham's offspring (Acts 3:25–26; see Genesis 22:18; 26:4).

But . . . if they refused, there literally would be hell to pay! (Acts 3:23).

> **Acts 4:1–3** The priests and the captain of the temple guard and the Sadducees came up to Peter and John while they were speaking to the people. They were greatly disturbed because the apostles were teaching the people and proclaiming in Jesus the resurrection of the dead. They seized Peter and John, and because it was evening, they put them in jail until the next day.

Sit Down! You're Rockin' The Boat!

The official attack against the church started here in Acts 4. Religious leaders who'd tried to terminate Jesus now arrested the first of his followers. Peter and John were hauled off to jail in mid-sermon by the captain of the **temple guard**, acting on orders from the **priests** and **Sadducees**, who controlled temple affairs. The Sadducees did not believe in life after death, the possibility of resurrection, or in the existence of angels or spirits.

Why Did Peter's Preaching Give The Chiefs The Jitters?

Acts 4:2 gives two "official" reasons Peter and John were booked:

1. They were teaching the people. And Peter and John lacked the proper credentials. (Shock! Gasp!)
2. They were proclaiming the resurrection of Jesus from the dead. This was a specific no-no to the Saducean temple leadership who didn't believe in resurrection.

Peter and John were plunked in the pokey under the pretext of protecting **orthodoxy**. Unofficially, temple leaders took a dim view of the apostles' repeated allegations that they were guilty of the Messiah's crucifixion and hoped to shut them up (Acts 2:23; 3:13).

 Persecution & Martyrdom—Arrest of Christians by religious authorities for unapproved teaching is a practice that is still alive and well! In a raid on a church in Turkey in 1999, police arrested twenty-five adults and charged them with "terrorism" for "criticizing Islam" and "forcing" people to take Bibles. According to the personal account of one of those involved, after thirty-six hours in jail, repeated interrogations, and negative newspaper publicity, a Muslim judge threw their case out of court. The incident has sparked renewal among Turkish Christians.

> **Acts 4:4** But many who heard the message believed, and the number of men grew to about five thousand.

While The Old Guard Fussed, The Church Grew

As dungeon doors clanged shut, many believed the apostles' message. The Jerusalem fellowship hit a new statistical high—five thousand men (Acts 4:4). Add women and children and the total number was probably ten thousand or more!

---

*Sidebar definitions:*

temple guard: temple police led by har habbayit—"man of the temple mount"

priests: clergymen who conducted worship at the Temple

Sadducees: religious party with political power, supporters of the high-priestly dynasty

orthodoxy: conforming to established religious doctrine or practice

The church grows by ministering to people's real needs and daring in the face of opposition to tell the truth about sin, Jesus, faith, and salvation. (Read about how the truth-telling and resulting persecution of Shadrach, Meshach, and Abednego resulted in a national decree of protection and peace in GWDN, chapter 3.)

CHURCH GROWTH

What Others are Saying:

Walter Wangerin: The council and the leaders in Jerusalem . . . were as threatened by the disciples as they had been by Jesus because the assembly growing around them was large and well-knit and committed to this Jesus as to one alive and mighty. It was an assembly distinct from the Synagogue—an *Ecclesia*, a Church.[4]

> **Acts 4:5–7** The next day the rulers, elders and teachers of the law met in Jerusalem. Annas the high priest was there, and so were Caiaphas, John, Alexander and the other men of the high priest's family. They had Peter and John brought before them and began to question them: "By what power or what name did you do this?"

Official Inquest At The Hall Of Hewn Stone

According to Jewish law no trial could be held at night, so the next day in the **Hall of Hewn Stone**, the **Sanhedrin** met to consider the case of the *unparalyzed unpanhandler*. Everybody who was anybody was there:[5]

Hall of Hewn Stone: official meeting place of the Sanhedrin

Sanhedrin: Jewish supreme court and high council

- Rulers—Temple priests and officials whose goal was preservation of the *status quo*.
- Elders—Community leaders; heads of aristocratic families.
- Teachers of the Law—Experts in Jewish law, fanatical adherents of religious rules.
- Annas, high priest—**Deposed** by Romans, Jews considered him the rightful high priest.

deposed: removed from office

- Caiaphas—Annas's son-in-law, official high priest from A.D. 18–36.
- John—Also called Jonathan. Annas's son, replaced Caiaphas as high priest in A.D. 36.
- Alexander—Just another pretty face, nothing is known about him.

> **Acts 4:8–12** Then Peter, filled with the Holy Spirit, said to them: "Rulers and elders of the people! If we are being called to account today for an act of kindness shown to a cripple and are asked how he was healed, then know this, you and all the people of Israel: It is by the name of Jesus Christ of Nazareth, whom you crucified but whom God raised from the dead, that this man stands before you healed. He is
>   'the stone you builders rejected,
>   which has become the capstone.'
> Salvation is found in no one else, for there is no other name under heaven given to men by which we must be saved."

Disorder In The Court

full: energized, under the influence

Peter was **full** of the Spirit (Acts 4:8) and chompin' at the bit. This was precisely the kind of situation Jesus told his disciples they would face. He'd said not to worry because the Holy <u>Spirit</u> <u>would teach</u> them what to say.

☞ **GO TO:**

Luke 12:11–12; 21:14–15
(Spirit would teach)

Luke 22:54–62
(done that)

Matthew 9:22; John 3:16; Romans 5:9; Ephesians 2:5; Hebrews 5:7; 7:25
(salvation)

"By what power or what name did you do this?" (Acts 4:7) the inquisitors asked.

Peter and John stood before the very court that condemned Jesus. They knew the potential consequences of confronting these hostile men with the claims of Christ. But to tell them anything but the truth would be an act of cowardice and denial. (Peter had been there, <u>done that</u>! But no more!)

The members of the high court found themselves being accused by the men they'd met to accuse (Acts 4:10–11). But Peter didn't just accuse. His charges were part of an ardent appeal in which he became a compassionate first-century Billy Graham offering **salvation** to Israel's powerful if they would put their **faith** in the name (person, character, and work) of Jesus. No "decisions for Christ" are recorded. Acts 6:7 indicates there may have been some.

salvation: rescue and forgiveness from sin's eternal consequences

What Others are Saying:

Watchman Nee: The name of Jesus . . . represents the power and dominion before which every knee in heaven and earth must bow. . . . Today the name tells us that God has committed all authority to his Son, so that in the very name itself there is power. But further, not only is it his, but it is "given to men." He has placed that authority in our hands for us to use.[6]

faith: to respond with love, trust, and obedience

JESUS CHRIST CEO

Christ is *"the capstone"* (Acts 4:11), cornerstone, or keystone. He holds God's salvation plan together.

Peter said, *"Salvation is found in no one else, for there is no other name under heaven given to men by which we must be saved."* On a scale of 1 to 10, how sure are you that Peter's statement is true? (1 = not at all sure; 10 = absolutely sure)

Something to Ponder

Who Killed Christ Jesus?

The Jews? Romans? Satan? Check these passages to see where the Bible puts the responsibility.

Dig Deeper

Responsible Party	Scripture Passages
Sanhedrin/Priests and elders (Jews)	Acts 4:5–11; 5:27–30; 7:52; Matthew 27:1, 20–23; John 19:6–7
Roman Governor Pilate (a Gentile)	Acts 4:27–28; Matthew 27:24–26; John 19:16–18
Herod (a Gentile)	Acts 4:27–28; Luke 23:6–11
Men of Israel (Jews)	Acts 2:22–23, 36; 4:27
Godless men/Romans (Gentiles)	Acts 2:23; 4:27–28; Matthew 27:27–36
People of Jerusalem (Jews)	Acts 3:13–15; 4:27–28
Judas, the betrayer (a Jew)	Acts 1:16; Matthew 27:3–4
God, to rescue us	Acts 2:23; Romans 3:25–26; 2 Corinthians 5:18–21; Isaiah 53:10
People who reject Christ (Jew/Gentile)	Hebrews 6:6; Isaiah 53:3
Human sin (Jew and Gentile)	1 Peter 2:24–25; Isaiah 53:4–6
Jesus, to be the sacrifice for our sin	John 10:14–18; Philippians 2:5–8; Hebrews 9:14; 10:5–14

John R. W. Stott: We ourselves are also guilty. If we were in their place, we would have done what they did. Indeed, we *have* done it. . . . We too sacrifice Jesus to our greed like Judas, to our envy like the priests, to our ambition like Pilate. . . . We may try to wash our hands of responsibility like Pilate. But our attempt will be as futile as his. For there is blood on our hands. Before we can begin to see the cross as something done *for* us (leading us to faith and worship), we have to see it as something done *by* us (leading us to repentance).[7]

What Others are Saying:

JESUS CHRIST CEO

Jesus never allows his people to get into a situation for which he has not made adequate provision through his indwelling Spirit for power to meet the challenge and words to say.

> **Acts 4:13–14** When they saw the courage of Peter and John and realized that they were unschooled, ordinary men, they were astonished and they took note that these men had been with Jesus. But since they could see the man who had been healed standing there with them, there was nothing they could say.

Poor, Dumb Fishermen

In spite of their animosity toward the apostles, the council members found themselves admiring their courage. Jerusalem's intellectual elite had not expected such grit and eloquence from dumb fishermen (Acts 4:13). What was it about Peter and John that showed they'd been *"with* (schooled by) *Jesus"*? Perhaps it was the Jesus-like way they rocked the establishment's boat, healed the lame, told the truth, confronted sin, and took command. Whatever it was, it was like Rabbi Jesus was back in town!

> **Acts 4:15–22** So they ordered them to withdraw from the Sanhedrin and then conferred together. "What are we going to do with these men?" they asked. "Everybody living in Jerusalem knows they have done an outstanding miracle, and we cannot deny it. But to stop this thing from spreading any further among the people, we must warn these men to speak no longer to anyone in this name." Then they called them in again and commanded them not to speak or teach at all in the name of Jesus.
>
> But Peter and John replied, "Judge for yourselves whether it is right in God's sight to obey you rather than God. For we cannot help speaking about what we have seen and heard."
>
> After further threats they let them go. They could not decide how to punish them, because all the people were praising God for what had happened. For the man who was miraculously healed was over forty years old.

The Smart Guys Paint Themselves Into A Corner

The hands of the power brokers were tied. They couldn't discredit the evidence standing in front of them in the person of the healed beggar (Acts 4:14, 22). Their law said "**unschooled**" people could not be punished without at least one warning. They were in the precarious position of opposing what the majority of people were applauding (Acts 4:16).

All they could do was order Peter and John never to speak Jesus' name in public again, threaten them with bodily harm if they did, and let 'em go (Acts 4:18, 21). But telling gung ho Christians to stop talking about Jesus is like telling the Mississippi River to go back to Minnesota! Peter and John had an irresistible urge to talk to everyone about Jesus. It turned out to be a bad day for Annas and his cronies.

 Persecution & Martyrdom—Witnessing and seeking to win converts for Christ is forbidden by law in many parts of our world today, including China and many Arab countries. Arrest can mean imprisonment, fines, torture, loss of a job, even slavery.

C. J. Klausner: This was the first mistake which the Jewish leaders made with regard to the new sect. And this mistake was fatal. There was probably no need to arrest the Nazarenes, thus calling attention to them and making them "martyrs." But once arrested, they should not have been freed so quickly. The arrest and release increased the number of believers; for these events showed on the one hand that the new sect was a power which the authorities feared enough to persecute, and on the other hand they proved that there was no danger in being a disciple of Jesus.[8]

> **Acts 4:23** On their release, Peter and John went back to their own people and reported all that the chief priests and elders had said to them.

Taking Trouble Home

Where do you go when you've spent the night in jail and seventy of the nation's powerful have shaken their fists in your face, warning of dire consequences if you dare mention Jesus' name again? Peter and John knew. They returned to the refuge of *"their own people"*—the caring community of Jesus' friends, the church.

unschooled: not trained by a recognized rabbi

 What Others are Saying:

KEY POINT

The church is not just a place to hear sermons; it's a place to share life's tough realities with supporting friends.

Chances are the brothers and sisters were together nearby, awaiting the outcome of "round one" with the city fathers.

> **Acts 4:24–30** When they heard this, they raised their voices together in prayer to God. "Sovereign Lord," they said, "you made the heaven and the earth and the sea, and everything in them. You spoke by the Holy Spirit through the mouth of your servant, our father David:
> 'Why do the nations rage
> and the peoples plot in vain?
> The kings of the earth take their stand
> and the rulers gather together
> against the Lord
> and against his Anointed One.'
> Indeed Herod and Pontius Pilate met together with the Gentiles and the people of Israel in this city to conspire against your holy servant Jesus, whom you anointed. They did what your power and will had decided beforehand should happen. Now, Lord, consider their threats and enable your servants to speak your word with great boldness. Stretch out your hand to heal and perform miraculous signs and wonders through the name of your holy servant Jesus."

Take It To The Lord In Prayer

After debriefing Peter and John, the Jesus people of Jerusalem prayed, <u>laying out</u> their situation before the Lord. First, they found Bible verses in Psalm 2:1–2 telling them opposition is normal for people identified with Christ ("God's Anointed") in a hostile world. In *The Message*, Eugene Peterson puts the Psalms passage this way: "Why the big noise, nations? Why the mean plots, peoples? Earth's leaders push for position, Potentates meet for summit talks, The God-deniers, the Messiah-defiers!"[9]

Second, they confessed confidence God was in control, <u>working out</u> his plan.

Third, they didn't ask for an easier way or destruction of their enemies. They prayed for *boldness* to speak God's message. They asked for miracles to back up their testimony.

☞ **GO TO:**

Isaiah 37:16–20
(laying out)

Romans 8:28
(working out)

What Others are Saying:

William Barclay: They had the conviction of the futility of man's rebellion. The word translated *rage* is used of the neighing of spirited horses. They may trample and toss their heads; in the end they will have to accept the discipline of the reins. Men may make their defiant gestures against God; in the end God must prevail.[10]

Maude De Joseph West: Herod . . . Pontius Pilate . . . the wily high priest and the people turned by his manipulation into a maniacal mob. . . . All these, living their own lives, scheming their own schemes, cruel, wicked, cunning, or weak, completely unaware of God Almighty, were nonetheless working out his perfect and inexorable will![11]

What Others are Saying:

> **Acts 4:31** After they had prayed, the place where they were meeting was shaken. And they were all filled with the Holy Spirit and spoke the word of God boldly.

Spiritual Booster Shot

Their prayer for miraculous signs (Acts 4:30) was answered in the surprising quality of spiritual and community life they experienced together.

First, the place was shaken and the Holy Spirit renewed his influence (filling). The first believers had been *"filled with the Holy Spirit"* at Pentecost (Acts 2:4). Since then, whenever anyone puts his or her faith in Jesus, they *"receive the gift of the Holy Spirit"* (Acts 2:38). This renewed "filling" was a "booster shot"—a fresh infusion of spiritual vitality to answer their prayer for courage.

☞ **GO TO:**

Exodus 19:18; Isaiah 6:4 (visible form)

Ajith Fernando: In the Old Testament the shaking of a place was a sign for a theophany, that is, a manifestation of God in a visible form. . . . It was God's way of indicating that he was present there and would answer the prayer.[12]

What Others are Saying:

> **Acts 4:32–37** All of the believers were one in heart and mind. No one claimed that any of his possessions was his own, but they shared everything they had. With great power the apostles continued to testify to the resurrection of the Lord Jesus, and much grace was upon them all. There were no needy persons among them. For from time to time those who owned lands and houses sold them, brought the money from the sales and put it at the apostles' feet, and it was distributed to anyone as he had need.

> Joseph, a Levite from Cyprus, whom the apostles called Barnabas (which means Son of Encouragement), sold a field he owned and brought the money and put it at the apostles' feet.

Normal Christianity

Spiritually energized, need and love combined for a unique adventure in fellowship: *"They shared everything they had."* When somebody was needy, the group didn't shrug and say, "Tsk. Tsk. Too bad. We'll pray for you." They sacrificed to meet the needs. If you had money, the normal response was to <u>cheerfully</u> dig in and shell out. Surplus possessions were sold at the local swap meet to raise funds. When need could not be filled so simply, a "For Sale" sign was slapped on the forty acres near Bethany or the summer cabin on Lake Galilee.

Sharing was voluntary. Private ownership was not ended. People had possessions and owned homes (Acts 2:46; 4:32). The difference was, possessions were treated as community property. No one was without "family"—poor, hungry, lonely, crippled, blind, retarded, homeless—all found a home in the believers' fellowship. The first Christians took material as well as spiritual responsibility for each other.

The miracle is summed up in a single amazing line: *"There were no needy persons among them"* (Acts 4:34).

Wherever you went you found "grace"—mercy, kindness, acceptance, honesty, forgiveness, generosity (Acts 4:33). The way Jesus' followers lived together was powerful proof he was alive. This visible evidence added impact to the Christians' claim that Jesus had risen and was living in them.

☞ GO TO:

2 Corinthians 9:6–15
(cheerfully)

What Others are Saying:

Ronald J. Sider: The costly sharing of the first church stands as a constant challenge to Christians of all ages. They dared to give concrete, visible expression to the oneness of believers.[13]

Jim Wallis: The Spirit had shattered the normal assumptions of the economic order, and the early believers realized that the way of Christ militated against the private use and disposition of resources and led to the sharing of all resources as needs arose in the community. Material resources, no less than spiritual gifts, were to be shared and freely given for the good of the body and not for the personal gain and advantage of the one who possessed them. A whole new system of distribution had been created in

God's new community with each person in a process of giving and receiving according to ability and need.[14]

Billy Graham: It can be so easy at times to say we love people, and be completely honest and sincere in our expression. But so often we don't see the lonely person in the crowd, or the sick or destitute man or woman whose only hope of escape may be the love we can give through Christ.[15]

Was this amazing community of generosity and grace a fluke, a once-in-history happening never to be repeated? Or is it part of the promise of the Gospel? The answer lies in the fact that the Jerusalem church lifestyle emerged in direct response to the teachings of Jesus—and those teachings are still to guide the lives and values of Christians today!

Jim Wallis: The holding of "all things in common" was not merely a futile experiment, nor did this practice end at Jerusalem. Rather the common life and sharing are shown throughout the New Testament and became the distinguishing mark of the early church.[16]

Study Questions

1. What did the man at the Beautiful Gate ask for? What did Peter and John give him? Where did Peter say the power to do this miracle came from?
2. What does it mean to do something "in Jesus' name"?
3. What two reasons were given for the arrest of Peter and John? Why were the Sadducees upset about the apostles' telling that Jesus had risen from the dead?
4. How did Peter and John respond when they were ordered never again to speak or teach in the name of Jesus?
5. In what tangible ways did the Jerusalem Christians demonstrate their love for and solidarity with one another?

CHAPTER WRAP-UP

- As Peter and John went to the Temple for prayer, they met a lame beggar asking for a handout. Peter grabbed the man's hand and pulled him to his feet. He was instantly healed and went into the Temple leaping and praising God. (Acts 3:1–10)

- A crowd gathered. Peter told them the man had been healed by faith in the name of Jesus. He urged them to listen to Jesus and quit their wickedness. (Acts 3:11–26)

- Upset because unlicensed apostles were teaching, temple officials arrested Peter and John. They were brought before the rulers to defend themselves. Peter told the rulers Jesus was their only hope of salvation. (Acts 4:1–22)
- The apostles were warned never to speak in Jesus' name and were released. They told the church. The church prayed for boldness to continue speaking and for God to provide miraculous proofs that Jesus was alive. (Acts 4:23–30)

The Lord answered by shaking the church and renewing the Spirit's influence in their lives. Jesus' followers clung more closely to each other and shared so generously to meet each other's needs that there were no needy people among them! (Acts 4:31–37)

ACTS 5: THE PERFECT CHURCH— NOT!

Let's Get Started

Once he has his readers drooling over the delicious quality of together-life experienced by the first fellowship of Jesus' disciples, the author of Acts brings us back to reality with a dull thud. Nasty termites were chawing away at what on the surface looked like the ideal support group, the beginnings of a veritable "heaven on earth." Through the shockeroo reported in Acts 5 we discover there is a vital connection between honesty, discipline, account-ability, pure motives, and spiritual power.

Charles Colson: Fellowship is more than unconditional love that wraps its arms around someone who is hurting. . . . Too often we confuse love with permissiveness. . . . True fellowship out of love for one another demands accountability.[1]

> *What Others are Saying:*

> **Acts 5:1–2** Now a man named Ananias, together with his wife Sapphira, also sold a piece of property. With his wife's full knowledge he kept back part of the money for himself, but brought the rest and put it at the apostles' feet.

The Ananias And Sapphira Affair

Ironically, the loving act of a guy named Joe set the stage for one of the most shocking moments in early church life. Joe was a transplant from Cyprus. The Christians had nicknamed him "Barnabas"

☞ **GO TO:**

Acts 9:26–27; 11:22–24; 15:36–39 (Son of Encouragement)

Numbers 18:20; Deuteronomy 10:8–9; 18:1–2 (not to own property)

John 16:13 (sensed)

Son of: *Hebrew prefix "Bar," indicates person's character*

Levite: *Israelite clan responsible to guide religious life*

Sapphira: *means "Beautiful"*

Something to Ponder

What Others are Saying:

---

or "**Son of** Encouragement." The last sentence in Acts 4 tells the innocent part he played in the sordid Ananias and Sapphira affair: *"Joseph . . . sold a field he owned and brought the money and put it at the apostles feet"* (Acts 4:36–37).

True to his reputation as encourager, Joe Barney sold land and contributed the proceeds for the needy. Others sold land and gave the proceeds too (see Acts 2:45; 4:34–35), but for some reason Joe Barney's gift was recorded. The gift was unusual not only because it was generous but also because he was a **Levite** and according to Mosaic law Levites were not to own property in the Promised Land. The land sale may not have been an act of loving generosity so much as an act of repentance for owning land contrary to the law. Joe Barney may simply have been relieving his conscience. Whatever the motive, it played a role in the tragic story that follows.

A Christian man, Ananias, and his beautiful wife, **Sapphira**, also sold some land. From the proceeds they made a generous, voluntary contribution. But there was a problem: They gave *part* of the money but gave the impression they were giving *all*. When Ananias came bearing his gift, Peter immediately sensed something was wrong, and instead of the oohs and ahs of approval that Ananias expected, Peter blew the lid off the deception.

> Wrong motivation can spoil giving. Sometimes leaders, eager to fund "the Lord's work," appeal to exactly the kind of motives that got Ananias and Sapphira in trouble! Jesus had nothing good to say about such giving (see Matthew 6:1–4).

William Barclay: This is one of the stories which demonstrate the almost stubborn honesty of the Bible. It might well have been left out because it shows that even in the early church there were very imperfect Christians.[2]

Ajith Fernando: Ananias' goal was to win the esteem of the church. The danger of doing that is real today. It is serious because it causes us to be dishonest with ourselves. A key to receiving God's grace is acknowledging our need of him; an attitude of pride can close the door that permits God's grace to enter our lives.[3]

> **Acts 5:3–4** Then Peter said, "Ananias, how is it that Satan has so filled your heart that you have lied to the Holy Spirit and have kept for yourself some of the money you received for the land? Didn't it belong to you before it was sold? And after it was sold, wasn't the money at your disposal? What made you think of doing such a thing? You have not lied to men but to God."

The Label On The Pretender's Package

Ugly dishonesty stood exposed for all to see. The exposé reveals five startling facts.

1. A <u>basic satanic strategy</u> for robbing the church of its power is to infect it with dishonesty, hypocrisy.
2. It is possible for a Christian in the best of churches, surrounded by people who are full of God's Spirit (Acts 4:31), to be "filled" (<u>influenced</u>) by Satan (Acts 5:3).
3. Satan's influence does not take away a person's responsibility for his or her choices (compare Acts 5:3 and 4).
4. <u>New Testament giving</u> is not an obligation but a free choice (Acts 5:4).
5. To lie to one's fellow believers is to lie to God (Acts 5:4).

☞ **GO TO:**

John 8:44
(basic satanic strategy)

Luke 22:3; John 13:27
(influenced)

2 Corinthians 8:1–15;
9:1–15
(New Testament giving)

What Others are Saying:

Billy Graham: We should be careful that any goodness the world may see in us is the genuine fruit of the Spirit and not a counterfeit substitute, lest we unwittingly lead someone astray. We must be constantly aware that Satan can take any human effort and twist it to serve his own purpose.[4]

> **Acts 5:5–11** When Ananias heard this, he fell down and died. And great fear seized all who heard what had happened. Then the young men came forward, wrapped up his body, and carried him out and buried him.
>
> About three hours later his wife came in, not knowing what had happened. Peter asked her, "Tell me, is this the price you and Ananias got for the land?"
>
> "Yes," she said, "that is the price."
>
> Peter said to her, "How could you agree to test the Spirit of the Lord? Look! The feet of the men who buried your husband are at the door, and they will carry you out also."

☞ **GO TO:**

Proverbs 3:11–12;
Hebrews 12:5–12
(dear children)

1 Peter 4:17;
1 Corinthians 11:30;
1 John 5:16–17
(discipline)

1 Corinthians 12:26
(whole church)

discipline: *painful experiences God allows to cleanse believers from sinful patterns*

Something to Ponder

☞ **GO TO:**

Philippians 1:21–23
(not the worst)

1 Corinthians 11:27–32
(serious consequences)

What Others are Saying:

> At that moment she fell down at his feet and died. Then the young men came in and, finding her dead, carried her out and buried her beside her husband. Great fear seized the whole church and all who heard about these events.

Dropping Dead In Church

Before the curtain came down on the sad scenario, the bodies of both Ananias and his wife were stretched out side by side in their family tomb near Jerusalem. Thank God, not everyone who lies in church drops dead. There might not be enough members left to keep cobwebs from collecting on the pews and pulpit!

The appalling passing of "Mr. and Mrs. A" were acts of a loving God correcting his <u>dear children</u>. And the **discipline** was not just for the cheerless givers—but the <u>whole church</u>. The whole Christian community quickly developed "a healthy respect for God."[5] (Read more about the godly disciplining of children in WBFM, pages 174–181 and WBFC, pages 165–179.)

Was God Too Hard on Ananias and Sapphira?

Many of us reading this story tend to think what this hapless couple did was not that big a deal—a petty sin. I mean, who hasn't pretended to be more "Christian" or "honest" than they really are? Doesn't this incident make God look like an impatient, unreasonable tyrant? Where's the love? Where's the grace?

In the first place, death is <u>not the worst</u> thing that can happen to a Christian. Second, the world sees when Christians mishandle money. The Jesus movement cries for believers who live morally pure, consistent with Christ's teachings, refusing to play the sickening game of spiritual "let's pretend." Though the consequences of hypocrisy are not always as instantaneous, visible, and shocking as what happened to Mr. and Mrs. A., phony baloney spirituality *always* carries <u>serious consequences</u>. Discipline is part of God's love and grace.

Charles Colson: *We need to know the fear of the Lord*—the overwhelming, compelling awe and reverence of a holy God. The fear of the Lord is the beginning of wisdom: It provides the right perspective on God's sovereign rule over all creation. . . . For the church in the West to come alive, it needs to resolve its identity crisis, to stand on truth, to renew its vision . . . and, more than anything else, it needs to recover the fear of the Lord. Only that will give us the holy abandon that will cause us to be the church no matter what the culture around us says or does.[6]

JESUS CHRIST CEO Jesus, in his life and ministry, modeled the truth-telling style practiced in the early church. He never sugarcoated the Gospel. He said things that pressed people's <u>hot buttons</u>. People were forced to face the truth and decide for or against him (John 3:19–21).

> **Acts 5:12** The apostles performed many miraculous signs and wonders among the people. And all the believers used to meet together in <u>Solomon's Colonnade</u>.

The Purity-Power Connection

What happened next demonstrates the spiritual impact of honesty and the death of hypocrisy. As the Jerusalem **church** shuddered with healthy fear after the Ananias and Sapphira catastrophe, new **signs** of power emerged. Until persecution made it impossible, Christians held large gatherings on the raised platform, called Solomon's Colonnade or Portico, at the east end of the Temple's outer court (see illustration below).

☞ **GO TO:**

Luke 9:57–62; John 6:53–69 (hot buttons)

John 10:23; Acts 3:11; 5:12 (Solomon's Colonnade)

church: Greek: ekklesia— "assembly of called out people"

signs: evidences of spiritual power

Solomon's Colonnade

Early Christians in Jerusalem met on the temple porch known as Solomon's Colonnade. A double row of marble columns held up its roof and provided space to gather.

Purity-Power Product One: "Miraculous Signs and Wonders"

The early Christians were "supernaturalists"—they believed in miracles. Based on their experiences with Jesus, they believed that when it serves God's purpose he is willing and capable of setting aside natural laws or controlling them to accomplish his aims.

Two kinds of miracles demonstrate the presence of God in his church:

1. Obvious miracles—when God suspends natural laws.

    Bible example—Opening the eyes of the blind (see John 9:32).

    Modern example—Five-year-old Bobby has an oral tumor; surgery is scheduled. The little boy prays for healing. The tumor disappears.

2. Hidden miracles—when God shapes and uses natural events and processes to accomplish his purposes (see Romans 8:28).[7]

    Bible examples—Fulfilled prophecies; enemy invasions God used to turn Israel back to him.

    Modern example—Our car's air conditioning breaks down in the heat of Arizona summer; childlike, Audrey prays, "Lord, please put that cloud over that sun until we get home." He does.

☞ **GO TO:**

Matthew 1:22–23; 2:5–6, 17–18; 3:3 (fulfilled prophecies)

Judges 3:7–8, 12–14; 4:1–3; 6:1–6 (invasions)

What Others are Saying:

Larry Richards: The naturalist insists that the material universe is all there is. Whatever happens *must* then be the result of natural laws, and miracles simply cannot happen. Reports of God's mighty acts in Old Testament times and of Jesus' miracles are either rejected out of hand, or some energy is expended trying to figure out reasonable natural causes to explain them away.

The supernaturalist believes that there is a reality beyond our material universe. The Christian, basing his or her faith on God's self-revelation in Scripture, has confidence in the God who is Creator and Sustainer of the physical universe. . . . There is no uncrossable gulf fixed between the natural and the supernatural. God has bridged the gap often, and has shown that he is completely capable of acting in the material world.[8]

Purity-Power Product Two: Meeting "Together"

The Greek word for "together" means "of one mind, flowing along together in harmony."

There is perhaps no greater miracle that serves as a sign—visible evidence of spiritual power and the presence of God—among Christians than the miracle of "togetherness" or unity—*flowing along together in harmony.* No other miracle gives such pure joy! (see Psalm 133).

Miracles in the Book of Acts

- Performed mainly by apostles—Acts 2:43; 3:1–10; 5:12; 9:33–34, 40–41; 13:9–11; 14:8–10; 16:16–18; 19:11–12; 20:9–10; 28:2–9
- Performed by Stephen the "**deacon**"-**apologist**—Acts 6:8
- Performed by Philip the "**deacon**"-**evangelist**—Acts 8:6
- Performed by Ananias, an ordinary disciple—Acts 9:10, 17
- Miraculous answers to prayer by groups of Christians—Acts 12:5, 12–17; 14:19–20
- Miraculous signs help Jews and others believe in the Messiah—compare Acts 2:4–12 with Isaiah 28:11–12; see also 1 Corinthians 1:22
- Highest concentration of miracles took place among Jews and Samaritans—Acts 2–12
- Reports of miracles among Gentiles not so frequent as among Jews—Acts 13–28

Dig Deeper

deacon: *one of seven assigned to care for poor*

apologist: *defender of the faith*

evangelist: *Gospel preacher*

> **Acts 5:13–14** No one else dared to join them, even though they were highly regarded by the people. Nevertheless, more and more men and women believed in the Lord and were added to their number.

A Strange Formula For Church Growth

After Ananias and Sapphira were carried out of church feet first, who, in their right mind, would want to be caught there harboring secret sin? Even with more people than ever skipping church, the believers' witness, the gracious lifestyle, the fresh purity were irresistibly attractive to people sick and tired of their culture of hypocrisy, materialism, and hatred. So their numbers grew. Most must have taken their spiritual temperature, making sure their sins were all confessed before heading for church.

CHURCH GROWTH

Healthy church growth requires discipline and account-ability. Free from hypocrisy, the church attracts people hungry for reality.

> **Acts 5:15–16** As a result, people brought the sick into the streets and laid them on beds and mats so that at least Peter's shadow might fall on some of them as he passed by. Crowds gathered also from the towns around Jerusalem, bringing their sick and those tormented by evil spirits, and all of them were healed.

The Shadow Of The Fisherman

When the church acts with integrity its leaders are respected. The people's belief that Peter's shadow could heal people may or may not have been accurate. But the fact that many believed it shows their great respect for the apostles.

Facts about early Christian healing ministry are observed in this passage (Acts 5:12–16):

- Like Jesus, the early church gave high priority to healing the sick.
- Ministry to the sick was evidence (a "sign") God's power was at work.
- Healings were done through apostles.
- Healing ministry attracted needy people.

KEY POINT

When the church is clean, its leaders are respected.

☞ **GO TO:**

Matthew 4:23–24; 8:14–17 (like Jesus)

Acts 2:43; 3:1–10; 4:30 (healing)

CHURCH GROWTH

Caring for physically, spiritually, and mentally ill people—and helping them to heal—brings healthy church growth.

> **Acts 5:17–21a** Then the high priest and all his associates, who were members of the party of the Sadducees, were filled with jealousy. They arrested the apostles and put them in the public jail. But during the night an angel of the Lord opened the doors of the jail and brought them out. "Go, stand in the temple courts," he said, "and tell the people the full message of this new life."
>
> At daybreak they entered the temple courts, as they had been told, and began to teach the people.

God's "Get Out Of Jail Free" Card

☞ **GO TO:**

Exodus 3:2; 14:19;
Isaiah 63:9
(angel of the Lord)

The twelve apostle-ambassadors were becoming highly visible and commanding great respect both in and outside the group of disciples. The jealousy of the established religious authorities boiled over. The Twelve suddenly became "Jailbirds for Jesus!"

That night "*an **angel of the Lord***" freed the jailbirds. The mysterious jailbreaker led them past the guards without being seen or opening doors! He instructed them to return to the Temple and keep telling people "*the full message of this new life.*" At sunrise, that's where they were.

angel of the Lord:
supernatural messenger; sometimes indicates the Lord's personal presence

Persecution & Martyrdom—Often in history, civil and religious authorities have thought they could stop the Jesus movement by removing its visible leaders. During the first three centuries, the Christians most likely to be martyred were bishops and other church leaders. It's a common error among enemies of the church to mistake apostles, pastors, and other leaders for the church's Head. Their removal has never stopped the movement, because the Head is Christ (see Ephesians 1:20–23). Leaders and rank-and-file disciples are his associates.

> **Acts 5:21b–26** When the high priest and his associates arrived, they called together the Sanhedrin—the full assembly of the elders of Israel—and sent to the jail for the apostles. But on arriving at the jail, the officers did not find them there. So they went back and reported, "We found the jail securely locked, with the guards standing at the doors; but when we opened them, we found no one inside." On hearing this report, the captain of the temple guard and the chief priests were puzzled, wondering what would come of this.
>
> Then someone came and said, "Look! The men you put in jail are standing in the temple courts teaching the people." At that, the captain went with his officers and brought the apostles. They did not use force, because they feared that the people would stone them.

Meanwhile, Back At The High Council

At the Hall of Hewn Stone, the high priest convened the Sanhedrin and sent guards to bring the jailbirds for questioning. Finding the cell as bare as Mother Hubbard's cupboard, the guards returned empty-handed and chagrined. Just then, someone brought news the Twelve were at the Temple, preaching. The guardsmen re-arrested them, ver-r-ry carefully, for fear of being stoned by temple-goers sympathetic to the apostles.

> **Acts 5:27–28** Having brought the apostles, they made them appear before the Sanhedrin to be questioned by the high priest. "We gave you strict orders not to teach in this name," he said. "Yet you have filled Jerusalem with your teaching and are determined to make us guilty of this man's blood."

Same Song, Second Verse

The High Priest and his cronies had tried to stop this grassroots movement by threatening Peter and John with bodily harm if they mentioned Jesus' name in public again (see Acts 4:18, 21). That was after *one* lame beggar was healed. Now, not just one, but *many* people were being healed in the forbidden name! And belief in the resurrection was spreading with "great power" (see Acts 4:33).

It was an angrier Sanhedrin this time. The high council's orders had been blatantly disobeyed. *"You have filled Jerusalem with your teaching!"* (Go, apostles!)

> **Acts 5:29–32** Peter and the other apostles replied: "We must obey God rather than men! The God of our fathers raised Jesus from the dead—whom you had killed by hanging him on a tree. God exalted him to his own right hand as Prince and Savior that he might give repentance and forgiveness of sins to Israel. We are witnesses of these things, and so is the Holy Spirit, whom God has given to those who obey him."

The Bad News And The Good News

The Twelve who had <u>run for their lives</u> when Jesus was arrested (see GWLC2, pages 223–224) were changed men. Courage replaced cowardice. *"We must obey God rather than men!"* Then, seizing the opportunity, even in this extremely hostile environment, they boldly stated the bad news and the good news.

- The bad news—You people are guilty of killing Jesus by <u>crucifying</u> him.

☞ **GO TO:**

Mark 14:50
(run for their lives)

Galatians 3:13
(crucifying)

- The good news—The God of Israel raised Jesus from the dead and exalted him to his own **right hand**. Jesus, "**Prince** and <u>Savior</u>," offers Israel "the gift of a changed life and sins forgiven."[9] We know these things because we've been changed and forgiven. The Holy Spirit verifies everything we are saying.

☞ **GO TO:**

Isaiah 9:6 (Prince)

Matthew 1:21; John 1:29 (Savior)

right hand: corulership with God

Prince: Son of God, Messiah

> **Acts 5:33–35** When they heard this, they were furious and wanted to put them to death. But a Pharisee named Gamaliel, a teacher of the law, who was honored by all the people, stood up in the Sanhedrin and ordered that the men be put outside for a little while. Then he addressed them: "Men of Israel, consider carefully what you intend to do to these men."

A Voice Of Reason In The Madness

If you've read the <u>mob scenes</u> that led to the condemnation of Jesus, you're not surprised at the explosion of rage that erupted against the Twelve witnesses. Old men in priestly robes leaped to their feet and brandished angry fists. A **cacophony** of bitter voices demanded death to the Twelve. If not restrained, some would have gladly spilled their blood right there on the pavement in the Hall of Hewn Stone.

But just in the nick of time, the stirring strains of the *William Tell Overture* are heard. There's a hearty "Hi-ho, Silver!" A masked man in a white hat riding a white stallion gallops in firing silver bullets and saving the day!

Who, I say, who was that masked man?

Into the midst of the near insanity, God sent a solitary voice of authority and reason. The man in the white hat, unexpected ally and all around cool dude was a **Pharisee**, known as "**Rabban** Gamaliel" or "Gamaliel the Elder," one of Israel's most respected teachers. Fellow teachers called him "the Beauty of the Law." His most famous student was Saul of Tarsus—the apostle Paul—(see Acts 22:3). He was, as far as we know, not a Christian, but God used him to rescue his people from a massacre.

☞ **GO TO:**

Matthew 26:67; Mark 14:65; Luke 22:63–65 (mob scenes)

cacophony: harsh sound

Pharisee: member of a group that strictly kept Jewish religious traditions

Rabban: highly respected rabbi

> **Acts 5:36–39** "Some time ago Theudas appeared, claiming to be somebody, and about four hundred men rallied to him. He was killed, all his followers were dispersed, and it all came to nothing. After him, Judas the Galilean

> appeared in the days of the census and led a band of people in revolt. He too was killed, and all his followers were scattered. Therefore, in the present case I advise you: Leave these men alone! Let them go! For if their purpose or activity is of human origin, it will fail. But if it is from God, you will not be able to stop these men; you will only find yourselves fighting against God."

"Give A Man Enough Rope And He'll Hang Himself!"

Gamaliel counseled the Sanhedrin to stop buggin' the Christians. (Go, Dude!) If their movement wasn't from God, it would fail. If it was from God, fighting Christians would be fighting God—a really stupid thing to do! It was just common, clod kickin' horse sense. And God used it to keep his ambassadors from becoming guests of honor at a first-century **necktie party**!

necktie party: stoning, hanging—first-century Jewish death penalties

What Others are Saying:

J. A. Findlay: [Gamaliel's advice was based on] sound Pharisaic teaching: God is over all, and needs no help from men for the fulfilment of his purposes; all men must do is to obey, and leave the issue to him.[10]

Remember This . . .

Sometimes Christians are protected and even rescued from persecution and martyrdom by non-Christians who are sympathetic to their cause. Examples in Acts include Gamaliel (Acts 5:34–40); Gallio (Acts 18:12–15); the Roman commander (Acts 23:23–33); and the centurion (Acts 27:42–43).

> **Acts 5:40–41** His [Gamaliel's] speech persuaded them. They called the apostles in and had them flogged. Then they ordered them not to speak in the name of Jesus, and let them go.
> The apostles left the Sanhedrin, rejoicing because they had been counted worthy of suffering disgrace for **the Name**.

the Name: Jesus

☞ **GO TO:**

2 Corinthians 11:23–25 (lashes)

Matthew 10:17–22; Mark 13:9–13; Luke 12:11–12; 21:12–19 (Christ's disgrace)

The Honor Of Dishonor

Even though Gamaliel's intervention averted a lynching, the punishment inflicted on the Twelve was harsh—thirty-nine lashes with a leather whip. As they emerged from the Hall of Hewn Stone, their backs were bloody but their hearts were full. They'd stared death in the face and demonstrated their loyalty to Jesus. They'd shared Christ's disgrace. That was reason enough for celebration!

Persecution & Martyrdom—In 1999 the Islamic fundamentalist Sudanese government was described as "the worst practitioner of religious persecution" in the world for its relentless attempts to force Islamization of Christian citizens through a systematic program of arrest, enslavement, torture, rape, starvation, and murder.[11] On a December 29, 2000, telecast, PBS commentator John McLaughlin called this "the most underreported news story of the year."[12]

F. F. Bruce: The apostles . . . found cause for joy in the thought that God had counted them worthy to endure this humiliation for the sake of Jesus' name. It was insignificant indeed when compared with the disgrace and anguish that Jesus had endured; but, as far as it went, it was a participation in his suffering, such as he had warned them to expect.[13]

What Others are Saying:

> **Acts 5:42** Day after day, in the temple courts and from house to house, they never stopped teaching and proclaiming the good news that Jesus is the Christ.

The Beat Goes On

The disciples responded to this warning not to speak in Jesus' name as they had responded to the first one—with quiet defiance. Before the bruises healed they were back teaching in the temple court and from house to house. Jerusalem was being saturated with the good news about Jesus the Messiah.

Maude de Joseph West: Sublime stubbornness, magnificent disobedience, matter-of-fact defiance! That comes close to making us "feel" for the high priest. In fact, we almost hope that he had access to the ancient world's equivalent for tranquilizer pills! Along about that time, he must have been Jerusalem's most frustrated citizen.[14]

What Others are Saying:

The link between discipline and spiritual power is obvious. The Lord dealt with dishonesty in the early church in a way that created an aversion among Christians toward hypocrisy. Cleansed motives led to renewed commitment, and the Jerusalem Christian community became a conduit for God's power. Opposition opened the door for the good news to spread into the hallowed haunts of political power! When

Something to Ponder

Christians walk together and before the world in obedience and purity without pretense, there's no telling what God's power can accomplish through them!

Study Questions

1. Who was behind the hypocrisy of Ananias and Sapphira? To whom did Peter say they had lied? Were they required to donate the proceeds of their land sale?
2. Explain the difference between "obvious" miracles and "hidden" miracles.
3. Identify three facts about the church's healing ministry observed in Acts 5:12–16.
4. Why did the priests and Sadducees put the apostles in jail? Who let them out? What did they do after being freed?
5. When members of the Sanhedrin wanted to kill the apostles, who spoke up in their behalf? What special title did his fellow teachers give him?
6. Why were the apostles so happy when they left the Sanhedrin?

CHAPTER WRAP-UP

- Ananias and Sapphira pretended to give all the proceeds of a land sale to the church. The Holy Spirit revealed their deception. Peter told them they'd lied to God. Both died. New respect for God swept the church. Hypocrisy vanished. (Acts 5:1–11)
- Christians met at Solomon's Colonnade. Miracles happened. Because of the Ananias and Sapphira affair, new people feared to join them, but still the church grew. They healed the sick and demon possessed. (Acts 5:12–16)
- Success of the Christians filled religious leaders with jealousy. They arrested the apostles. An angel freed them, and they went on preaching. Some council members wanted to kill them, but Gamaliel talked them out of it. (Acts 5:17–40)
- The apostles were flogged and released. They rejoiced for the privilege of sharing Christ's disgrace, ignored the ban, and returned to preaching. (Acts 5:40–42)

ACTS 6–7: A TEMPLE TO DIE FOR

☞ **GO TO:**

James 1:2 (trouble)

Acts 2:41; 4:4; 5:14 (huge crowds)

Let's Get Started

Write down in your little book of "Stuff that Happens" that when you decide to take Jesus' instructions seriously, you are going to find yourself in some kind of <u>trouble</u>. As chapter 5 ends, the disciples, beat up and warned *again* not to speak the name of Jesus, returned to Solomon's Colonnade where they shared the good news with <u>huge crowds</u>. (Estimates of church size at this time range from fifteen thousand to twenty thousand people.[1]) In addition to these illegal temple gatherings, they took the good news to small groups meeting in homes throughout the city (Acts 5:42). Opposition seemed to add fuel to faith's fire. The Jesus community kept growing and growing and growing.

And they kept doing the things Jesus had told them to do: Preach the good news. Heal the sick. Care for the poor. Obedience led to success. It also led right smack dab into new trouble! The dynamite believers' fellowship of Jerusalem faced up to the problem, dealt with it in Jesus' spirit, kept on obeying his instructions, and discovered God is able to use even scary problems to strengthen his people.

> **Acts 6:1–2** In those days when the number of disciples was increasing, the Grecian Jews among them complained against the Hebraic Jews because their widows were being overlooked in the daily distribution of food. So the Twelve gathered all the disciples together and said, "It would not be right for us to neglect the ministry of the word of God in order to wait on tables."

Too Big For The Mighty Twelve

In the midst of the most exciting time in its history a problem surfaced that could have torn the church apart—poor widows were overlooked in the distribution of food! *Overlooked!* It says, "You aren't important. You aren't loved." Given the church's public commitment to care for the poor, this was embarrassing—not the signal the church wanted to give.

Discrimination In The "Perfect" Church?

To complicate matters, the overlooked widows were all part of the same ethnic group. Were they being neglected because they spoke with foreign accents? The original word translated "complained" (Acts 6:1) means the Grecian Jews *muttered* indignant discontent, not openly but in behind-your-back whispers. To the widows waiting in vain for the first-century "meals on wheels" to arrive, it looked like a problem of prejudice and discrimination.

In Jerusalem two major cultural groups existed side by side:

- Hebraic Jews, born and raised in the Jewish homeland and speaking **Aramaic**
- **Grecian** Jews, born and raised in foreign countries and speaking **Greek**

Homeland Jews often looked down on foreign Jews. Some felt that Grecian Jews were contaminated by pagan culture. Actually Grecian Jews were as **orthodox** as homeland Jews.

There is no evidence of intentional discrimination in the early church (Acts 4:32). Tearing down cultural barriers was part of the church's mission (see Acts 2:5–12, 39). Still, there is no reason to suppose every blind spot was instantly whisked away, turning early believers into perfect "saints" immediately. Such changes require the processes of growing up spiritually. That takes time.

EARLY CHURCH WOMEN—In those days a woman whose husband died was often left destitute. She did not own property unless it was part of an inheritance from her father and he had no sons. Even then, she could only keep the inheritance if she married within the clan. The Bible gives special attention to the care of widows.

Caring for single women was a special concern among the original Christians. Many widows came to Jerusalem to live out their final years near the Temple, ran out of resources, and found them-

☞ **GO TO:**

Acts 9:29 (Grecian)

Ephesians 4:11–16 (growing up)

Aramaic: *a derivative of ancient Hebrew*

Grecian: *influenced by Greek culture (Hellenistic)*

Greek: *"universal" language used throughout the Roman Empire*

orthodox: *conforming to established religious doctrine and practice*

☞ **GO TO:**

Deuteronomy 24:19–21; 26:12–13; Job 31:16–23; Isaiah 1:17 (care of widows)

James 1:27; 1 Timothy 5:3–16 (special concern)

selves destitute. The church included them in its distribution of food to the poor. Some of these women had significant spiritual <u>influence</u> in the church.

☞ **GO TO:**

1 Timothy 5:9–10; Titus 2:3–5 (influence)

Development Of Helping Ministry In The Early Church

The word early Christians used for helping others is *diakonia* (service, ministry, servanthood). Some form of it occurs 101 times in the New Testament. All Jesus' followers are called to be servants. The early church's serving ministry developed in at least five stages:

1. Jesus taught his disciples to serve. Christian servanthood reflects Jesus' willingness to give his life for others (Matthew 28:25–28).

2. Spontaneous sharing occurred (Acts 2:45; 4:34). With the Holy Spirit reminding them of Jesus' teachings, a kind of unorganized, ad-lib response to needs developed.

3. Distribution was daily (Acts 6:1). Believers gathered daily for teaching, fellowship, bread breaking, and prayer (Acts 2:42–46). They ate together, and food was sent with the poor to keep them going till the next meeting. Care for the poor was patterned after Jewish practices.

4. The twelve apostles handled distribution (Acts 4:34–5:2; 6:2). They received money and goods and, in addition to preaching, directed daily food distribution.

5. Church growth demanded more organized care (Acts 6:1). As believers grew to fifteen or twenty thousand with numbers increasing daily, programless sharing developed more holes than swiss cheese. A cry went up for a better game plan.

What Others are Saying:

Larry Richards: The Jewish system of poor relief involved *tamhuy*, the "poor bowl," and *quppah*, the "poor basket." The first was a daily distribution of food provided for the homeless. The second was a weekly distribution of food and clothing provided for poor families. In both cases help was provided in goods, not in cash.[2]

Godly growth always involves growth in *love* (Ephesians 4:16; Colossians 2:19). Church growth that reflects only statistical increases is not sufficient. If people who should be cared for are "overlooked" in the scramble for size, then, however exciting it seems, it isn't godly growth.

Remember This . . .

> **Acts 6:3–5a** "Brothers, choose seven men from among you who are known to be full of the Spirit and wisdom. We will turn this responsibility over to them and will give our attention to prayer and the ministry of the word." This proposal pleased the whole group.

A Jazzed-Up Strategy For Servanthood

The church did not for a minute consider copping out on care of the poor. It never entered their heads to choose between feeding hungry mouths and feeding hungry souls. Jesus said to do both! But it was clear that twelve mere men could not handle both (Acts 6:2). If church unity and outreach were to continue unhindered the work must be *shared*.

Four things about the way they solved their problem are worth notice.

1 *No defensiveness.* Problems do not require finding someone to blame. <u>God uses</u> problems to help his church grow up.

☞ **GO TO:**

Romans 8:28
(God uses)

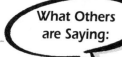
What Others are Saying:

Romans 12:6–8;
1 Corinthians 12;
Ephesians 4:11–12;
1 Peter 4:10
(wide diversity)

gifts: *abilities given by God to help people fulfill his purposes*

Keith Miller: God calls us to *problems*, not programs, in which we will find our ministries—problems which captivate our minds and imaginations and motivate us to give our lives to try to bring Christ's vision of wholeness to situations and people, as we begin to see them from his perspective.[3]

2 *Admission of human limitation.* Widow care was not just a *leader* problem—it was a problem for the whole church. *Nobody* can be everything the church needs. God's purpose is fulfilled by a <u>wide diversity</u> of people serving with their **gifts**.

Sherwood Wirt: In my own life I have learned that a lot of [spiritual] growth consists simply of my getting out of God's way. It is actually shrinkage rather than growth. I am certain that God does not want me to develop into a spiritual giant in my own eyes, even if I could. He wants me to become a spiritual pygmy so he can handle me. He wants me <u>poor in spirit</u> so he can do something with me without his having to contend with my ever-present, darling ego.[4]

☞ **GO TO:**

Matthew 5:3
(poor in spirit)

3 *Those chosen to serve met high spiritual qualifications.* The seven were not chosen because they were rich, popular, too dumb to say "No," or because they looked good in dark suits! Three qualifications for "table servers" were laid down: (1) They must

be *known* ("men . . . whom everyone trusts"[5]); (2) *full of* (directed and controlled by) *the Spirit* and (3) *full of . . . wisdom* ("good sense"[6]).

What Others are Saying:

Ajith Fernando: It is better to wait until we can find the right people rather than do good work employing the wrong people. We may achieve a lot in terms of the volume of service, but in the long run it can take the church in a wrong direction.[7]

4 *They bent over backwards to restore trust and peace.* All seven chosen represented the group that charged discrimination— all had Grecian names! The care of *all* the widows—Hebraic and Grecian—was entrusted to members of the neglected minority.

What Others are Saying:

Billy Graham: You have made your peace with God. . . . You now begin to see others through the eyes of Jesus. . . . Prejudices that you once held are beginning to slip away. Selfishness that was once characteristic of you in many areas of your life has now gone.[8]

JESUS CHRIST CEO

As Leader of the church, Jesus does more than *talk* about how problems should be handled. He *shows* how by the way he himself handled problems in his life on earth. Part of knowing what Christ wants done is looking at his model and doing it his way.

> **Acts 6:5b** They chose Stephen, a man full of faith and of the Holy Spirit; also Philip, Procorus, Nicanor, Timon, Parmenas, and Nicolas from Antioch, a convert to Judaism.

The Magnificent Seven

"The Seven," they came to be called. They were emerging leaders in the Grecian Christian community. Beyond their qualifications to serve as "table waiters" (Acts 6:2–3), Luke gives no details about Procorus, Nicanor, Timon, and Parmenas. About Stephen he says he was *"a man full of the Holy Spirit"* and *"a man full of God's grace and power"* (Acts 6:8). Philip (not the apostle) became known as "Philip the evangelist" (Acts 21:8). Nicolas was a Gentile convert to Judaism.

They were never officially given the title "**deacons**," though Christians often refer to them that way. They were prepared for service by

☞ **GO TO:**

Acts 21:8 (the Seven)

deacons: *men and women involved in practical "helping" ministries of the church* six years of living in the growing Christian community. It takes time to grow honest, spiritual leaders with good ol' horse sense.

William Barclay: It is extremely interesting to note that the first office-bearers to be appointed [in the church] were chosen not to talk but for practical service.[9]

According to New Testament teaching every Christian is gifted (see Romans 12:6–8; 1 Corinthians 12:4–11, 27–31; Ephesians 4:11; 1 Peter 4:8–11). Read a list of the spiritual gifts in WBFT, page 126. What abilities do you have that can be used in service to others? What do you enjoy doing that might help the church?

> **Acts 6:6–7** They presented these men to the apostles, who prayed and laid their hands on them. So the word of God spread. The number of disciples in Jerusalem increased rapidly, and a large number of priests became obedient to the faith.

The Laying On Of Hands

The early church used these steps in the selection process for the Seven:

- The apostles clarified their spiritual and practical qualifications (Acts 6:3).
- The congregation selected the seven by consensus or mutual agreement (Acts 6:5–6).
- The apostles **confirmed** the congregation's choices by praying for them with the traditional laying on of hands (Acts 6:6). Laying on of hands was a Jewish tradition. It signified (1) *blessing* (see Genesis 48:13–30); (2) *identification* (see Leviticus 1:4; 4:4; 16:21); and (3) *authority* (see Numbers 27:22–23) for an assigned task.

The problem the Seven were appointed to solve is never mentioned again. Evidently, these guys did a bang-up job.

Early Christians expected the Holy Spirit to guide them to solution of problems through the agreement (consensus) of leaders and people about a course of action (see Matthew 18:15–20; Acts 1:21–26).

JESUS CHRIST CEO

KEY POINT

The church grows in numbers and influence when there is harmony among Christians, the work is shared, and the needs of people are met.

confirmed: ratified, demonstrated approval

blessing: spiritual support, prayer for success

identification: oneness and equality

Seven Habits of Highly Effective Churches

1. Listen to people.
2. End discrimination based on language, culture, or social distinctions.
3. Serve with your gift—don't do somebody else's work—and let others help.
4. Care for people and their needs, especially the poor.
5. Spread the Word of God.
6. Pray often and about everything.
7. Appoint spiritual leaders or servants—approve their ministry.

Results: People are pleased, hungry are fed, Word is spread, numbers increase, and priests believe. (See timeline below.)

CHURCH GROWTH

☞ **GO TO:**

Romans 12:6–8;
1 Corinthians 12:4–11; Ephesians 4:11;
1 Peter 4:8–10 (gift)

Charles Colson: Harmony and oneness in spirit can be achieved only when Christians put aside their personal agendas and submit themselves to the authority of the Holy Spirit. . . . when the people of God, united in his name, proclaim the Word of God, they can turn their world upside down.[10]

What Others are Saying:

> **Acts 6:8** Now Stephen, a man full of God's grace and power, did great wonders and miraculous signs among the people.

This Deacon Could Really "Deac"!

Few Bible characters are described in as glowing terms as Stephen. A Grecian transplant, he was part of Jerusalem's foreign-born community. In the course of his food distribution work, Stephen had an unusual impact. He performed miracles and convinced many people in the Grecian Jewish community that Jesus is Messiah.

Timeline of How the Church Grew

A.D. 30 Pentecost/3,000 added Acts 2	➡	A.D. 32 Lame man healed/ 5,000 men Acts 3–4	➡	A.D. 36 (some say A.D. 42) The Seven chosen/20,000 in the church Acts 6

> **Acts 6:9–14** Opposition arose, however, from members of the Synagogue of the Freedmen (as it was called)—Jews of Cyrene and Alexandria as well as the provinces of Cilicia and Asia. These men began to argue with Stephen, but they could not stand up against his wisdom or the Spirit by whom he spoke.
>
> Then they secretly persuaded some men to say, "We have heard Stephen speak words of blasphemy against Moses and against God."
>
> So they stirred up the people and the elders and the teachers of the law. They seized Stephen and brought him before the Sanhedrin. They produced false witnesses, who testified, "This fellow never stops speaking against this holy place and against the law. For we have heard him say that this Jesus of Nazareth will destroy this place and change the customs Moses handed down to us."

The Frame-Up

synagogues: 480 Jewish gathering places for study and prayer in Jerusalem

Stephen distributed food to the poor in the **synagogues** of Greek-speaking Jews like himself, including the Freedmen synagogue. Freedmen were liberated slaves. They were usually very poor. So it was natural that his relief work would bring Stephen into their community.

In the Freedmen's synagogue Stephen found himself in red-hot debate with unbelieving Jews. The debate revolved around what Stephen believed about the Temple and Jewish religious traditions. These small-minded men were no match for Stephen's *"wisdom or the Spirit by whom he spoke."* (In other words, they lost the debate!) So they attacked Stephen on two other fronts.

blasphemy: slander; misuse of God's name

Judaism: Jewish religious system

- Slander—In a first-century version of "being tried in the press," they stirred up the people. Stephen was guilty of *"**blasphemy** against Moses and God,"* they said.

☞ **GO TO:**

Leviticus 24:10–23 (death penalty)

John 2:19; Matthew 26:59–61; Mark 15:29–30; Luke 21:5–6 (tear down)

- Formal charges—They officially accused Stephen before the Jewish High Court on two counts: Count 1: Blasphemy against the Temple and the Law (Acts 6:13). Conviction carried the <u>death penalty</u>. Count 2: Plotting destruction of **Judaism** by claiming Jesus would <u>tear down</u> the Temple (Acts 6:14).

Did The Christians Plan To Tear Down The Temple?

It was a lie. Christians were not plotting to destroy the Temple. Jesus and his disciples had great <u>respect for the Temple</u> and the <u>Law</u>. But some Christian beliefs were twisted by their enemies to form a condemning accusation of Stephen. Christians believe the following:

- The Temple is not the only place to meet God. People can meet God anywhere (see Matthew 18:20; John 4:21–24; Acts 17:24).
- The Law and temple services are **fulfilled** in Christ (see Matthew 5:17).
- God writes his Law on people's hearts and minds by the Holy Spirit (see Jeremiah 31:33; Hebrews 8:10).
- God's grace is not exclusively for Jews; it's for Gentiles too (see Matthew 28:19; Acts 2:39).

These beliefs were misinterpreted as a threat to traditional Jewish religion.

> **Acts 6:15–7:2** All who were sitting in the Sanhedrin looked intently at Stephen, and they saw that his face was like the face of an angel.
> Then the high priest asked him, "Are these charges true?"
> To this he replied: "Brothers and fathers, listen to me!"

Angel Face For The Defense

Jews associated a <u>glowing face</u> with a person close to God. Stephen, on trial for his life, experienced the intimate presence of Jesus (Matthew 28:20). He addressed his judges with respect (Acts 7:2). But before his defense rested, he would charge them with the very crimes for which they accused him.

THE BIG PICTURE 🔍

> **Acts 7:3–43** Stephen used the examples of Israel's forefathers Abraham, Joseph, and Moses in his defense. He gave his listeners a star-studded history lesson.

The Defense Calls Its Only Witness—History!

Stephen marshaled case histories from the Old Testament to prove four points:

☞ **GO TO:**

John 2:14–17; Matthew 21:12–16 (respect for the Temple)

Matthew 5:17–20; Romans 13:8; Galatians 3:24 (Law)

fulfilled: *spiritual transactions pictured in Law and temple worship have become reality*

☞ **GO TO:**

Exodus 34:29–35 (glowing face)

Promised Land:
Palestine, land promised
to Abraham and his
descendants

circumcision: removal of
the foreskin of the penis
as a symbol of faith and
belonging to God's Old
Testament people (not
required of Christians)

Pharaoh: title of Egyptian
kings

Hebrews: Israelites, Jews

1. God's presence and work are not confined to the geographical boundaries of Israel.

2. Meeting God is not limited to a manmade house of worship or any "holy place."

3. True faith does not need "holy places" or visible structures to thrive; it only needs the presence and Word of God.

4. Israel had a history of rejecting God by rejecting his representatives and idolizing manmade structures.

God revealed himself to <u>Abraham</u>, revered father of the Hebrew nation, when he was a pagan in Mesopotamia, far from the **Promised Land**. Acting on "the bare word of God,"[11] Abraham followed the Lord not knowing where he would be led. He never owned a square foot of the Promised Land, but believed God's promise to give it to his offspring. He received **circumcision** as a symbol of confidence in God's promise. (Read more about Abraham in GWMB, pages 13–28.)

Three generations later jealous brothers (Israel's founding "fathers") sold <u>Joseph</u> into slavery. But exile from the Promised Land did not separate him from God. He had nothing to hang on to but promises God made in his <u>dreams</u>. From slavery he rose to rule Egypt under a grateful Pharaoh. When famine struck, his brothers found themselves at the mercy of the brother they'd rejected. As God's representative, Joseph forgave and rescued them. (Read more about Joseph in GWMB, pages 55–70.) He brought his whole family to live in Egypt where they flourished.

A later Egyptian **Pharaoh** forgot Joseph's role in Egypt's survival and turned the **Hebrews** into slaves. He decreed that Hebrew newborn babies should be thrown out like garbage and allowed to die of exposure. Moses' parents <u>defied the decree</u> and protected their infant son for three months. When they could hide him no longer, they set him afloat in a special basket on the Nile River. An Egyptian princess found the infant in the basket, fell in love with the unusual baby, and raised <u>Moses</u> as her son. He was educated in Pharaoh's palace (right under ol' Pharaoh's nose!).

As an adult, Moses threw in his lot with the Hebrew slaves and offered himself as their deliverer (Acts 7:23–25). They would have nothing to do with him. He escaped to Arabia (Midian) where he spent the next forty years herding sheep. There, in Gentile territory, 250 miles across the desert from the temple site, God met Moses in a burning bush and called it *"holy ground"* (Acts 7:33). (All it takes to make a holy place is God's holy presence!)

To make a long story short (the <u>unabridged version</u> is four volumes in the Old Testament!): God heard the cries of the slaves down in Egypt land—far from any holy place (Acts 7:34). He sent Moses back to Egypt to lead them to freedom amid Fourth of July fireworks courtesy of God! (Acts 7:36).

Fifty days later, God met Moses on **Mt. Sinai**. The mountain shook with God's presence. God gave Moses *"living words to pass on"* to the Hebrews (Acts 7:38)—the <u>Ten Commandments</u> and the Law. Moses' faith did not depend for a millisecond on a holy place. He knew he had the presence and living Word of God.

While Moses was on Sinai's summit getting God's words, the Hebrews were in the foothills slapping together a hasty, nasty golden **calf** (Exodus 32:4)—something tangible to believe in. No matter that their mooless moo-cow was nothing but a chunk of cold metal. For a lifeless little bull they turned their backs on the living words of God! Tragically, this was only the beginning of their idolatry (Acts 7:42–43).

Points to ponder from the comical caper of the bullion bullock:

- "Holy" places do not make people holy. This dastardly deed with its rampant <u>rowdyism</u> was done at the "mountain of God," Mt. Sinai.

- **Idolatry** is worshiping what our grubby little hands have made (Acts 7:41).

> **Acts 7:44–45a** "Our forefathers had the tabernacle of the Testimony with them in the desert. It had been made as God directed Moses, according to the pattern he had seen. Having received the tabernacle, our fathers under Joshua brought it with them when they took the land from the nations God drove out before them."

A Pop-Up, Fold-Up Holy Place

On Sinai God gave Moses the blueprint for the **tabernacle**, a temporary place for Israel to meet God (see illustration, page 78). It was designed with these features:

- Its furnishings were <u>shadowy pictures</u> of **spiritual transactions** that would later be part of a relationship with God through Jesus Christ (Hebrews 8:5; 10:1).

☞ **GO TO:**

Exodus, Leviticus, Numbers, Deuteronomy (unabridged version)

Exodus 20:1–17 (Ten Commandments)

Mt. Sinai: *volcanic mountain in southern Arabia*

calf: *bull; Egyptian fertility god some Hebrews worshiped while in slavery*

Something to Ponder

☞ **GO TO:**

Exodus 32:6, 19 (rowdyism)

idolatry: *worship of objects*

☞ **GO TO:**

Exodus 25–31 (tabernacle)

Hebrews 9, 10 (shadowy pictures)

Tabernacle: *tent, temporary dwelling*

spiritual transactions: *prayer, intercession, new birth, forgiveness, salvation*

Wilderness Tabernacle

God designed each feature of this portable tent or church that the Israelites carried with them. It was called a tabernacle.

- It could be folded up and moved at a moment's notice, so Israel could choose to believe God was among them wherever they went (Acts 7:45).

> **Acts 7:45b–47** "It remained in the land until the time of David, who enjoyed God's favor and asked that he might provide a dwelling place for the God of Jacob. But it was Solomon who built the house for him."

No Dream House For God

Stephen continued his history lesson: Years later King David <u>dreamed</u> of replacing the collapsible chapel with a permanent house for God. The Lord slammed on the brakes, telling David he didn't need a house and never asked anyone to build him one! One day, God promised, <u>a **descendant**</u> of David would build the *spiritual* house God really wanted (1 Chronicles 17:3–14).

David's son <u>Solomon built</u> the first, most magnificent Jewish temple. And God met with his people there (1 Kings 8:10–11). But even as he prepared to build it, Solomon acknowledged that no manmade building could ever contain God: "*Who is able to build a temple for him [God], since the heavens, even the highest heavens, cannot contain him?*" (2 Chronicles 2:5–6).

☞ **GO TO:**

Psalm 132:2–5
(dreamed)

Luke 1:26–33
(a descendant)

2 Chronicles 2–7
(Solomon built)

descendant: *Messiah, Christ*

> **Acts 7:48–50** "The Most High does not live in houses made by men. As the prophet says:
>
> 'Heaven is my throne, and the earth is my footstool. What kind of house will you build for me? says the Lord.
>
> Or where will my resting place be?
>
> Has not my hand made all these things?'"

God Doesn't Live In A Manmade House

Stephen stood accused of blasphemy for suggesting the Temple is not essential. This was not true. His defense strategy was to explain what he and the other Christians did believe and he quoted from Isaiah 66:1–2. The Temple had served a purpose. But even temple worshipers must understand—the house is *not God* and God *"does not live in houses"*—not even the Temple.

Pagans think temples <u>contain gods</u> and to threaten a temple is to <u>threaten a god</u>. But it's not a biblical idea. It makes God out to be small and distorts people's perception of him, confusing him with religious institutions, "sacred" places, and manmade traditions. God is none of these "religious" things. He is *the Most High*—too great to be stuck in a manmade structure. Not even the *universe* can contain him, for heaven's sake!

Remember This . . .

Ajith Fernando: There is no place in the New Testament for holy places where people go on pilgrimage, expecting merit to accrue to them by being there. The popularity of these places . . . may be traced to a lack of intimate knowledge of God.[12]

What Others are Saying:

God's New "Temple"

As caregiver working among the *people* of the early church, Stephen saw God building a new kind of temple. This unique, new "holy place" was rising amid the rubble of ruined religion. The old Temple would be destroyed (not by Christians, but pagan Romans, in A.D. 70). But the new living temple would be <u>forever</u>! New Testament writers describe it this way:

- 1 Corinthians 3:16—*"Don't you know that you yourselves are God's temple and that God's Spirit lives in you?"*

- Ephesians 2:22—*"In him [Christ] you too are being built together to become a dwelling place in which God lives by his Spirit."*

☞ **GO TO:**

1 Kings 8:27 (contain gods)

Acts 19:27 (threaten a god)

Revelation 21:2–4 (forever)

- 1 Peter 2:5—*"You also, like living stones, are being built into a spiritual house to be a holy priesthood, offering spiritual sacrifices acceptable to God through Jesus Christ."*

With Jesus as their foundation, his followers *are* the lively, flesh-and-blood house of God. Their love, loyalty, and care are focused less and less on religious structures, like the gold and marble building that dominated Jewish life, and are becoming refocused on the living, breathing family bonded together by their common connection to Christ.

Something to Ponder

> **Acts 7:51–54** "You stiff-necked people, with uncircumcised hearts and ears! You are just like your fathers: You always resist the Holy Spirit! Was there ever a prophet your fathers did not persecute? They even killed those who predicted the coming of the Righteous One. And now you have betrayed and murdered him—you who have received the law that was put into effect <u>through angels</u> but have not obeyed it."
> When they heard this they were furious and gnashed their teeth at him.

☞ **GO TO:**

Deuteronomy 33:2–3;
  Galatians 3:19;
  Hebrews 1:4; 2:2
  (through angels)

☞ **GO TO:**

Isaiah 63:10 (resistance)

Righteous One: *Messiah, Christ*

The Maddening Truth!

Stephen ended his defense with an in-your-face indictment of not only Israel past but the arrogant Sanhedrin itself. They accused Stephen of slander against God, Moses, the Law, and the Temple. But it is they who slandered Moses and God and destroyed the Temple. Stephen pronounced them guilty on four counts:

- Count 1—Persistent <u>resistance</u> against the Holy Spirit (Acts 7:51).
- Count 2—Persecution and martyrdom of the prophets (Acts 7:52).
- Count 3—Betrayal and murder of the **Righteous One** (Acts 7:52).
- Count 4—Disobedience of the Law they claim to defend (Acts 7:53).

Needless to say, this was not a page from Dale Carnegie's *How to Win Friends and Influence People.* The room erupted with rage verging on insanity. Powerful politicos reacted with bestial **grinding of teeth**.

> **Acts 7:55–56** But Stephen, full of the Holy Spirit, looked up to heaven and saw the glory of God, and Jesus standing at the right hand of God. "Look," he said, "I see heaven open and the Son of Man standing at the right hand of God."

☞ **GO TO:**

Psalm 35:16; Luke 13:28
(grinding of teeth)

grinding of teeth: *sign of rage*

Hero's Welcome For The Faithful Witness

Freshly **infused** with the Holy Spirit, Stephen was given a rare glimpse into the heavenly world. He saw Jesus *standing* at God's right hand. Usually, Jesus is pictured as seated. Here he stands to welcome a faithful witness laying his life on the line for his Lord's sake. Jesus' place at **God's right hand** guarantees Stephen's salvation.

☞ **GO TO:**

Acts 4:8, 31
(freshly infused)

Mark 8:35
(laying his life)

1 John 2:1–2
(guarantees)

infused: permeated, controlled

JESUS CHRIST CEO

Jesus stands by his people as they do what he has sent them to do. They never face suffering or death alone. He stands with them, strengthening, seeing them through it, welcoming them with his affirming, "Well done!" (See Matthew 25:21, 23; Luke 19:17.)

God's right hand: coruler with God the Father

> **Acts 7:57–60** At this they covered their ears and, yelling at the top of their voices, they all rushed at him, dragged him out of the city and began to stone him. Meanwhile, the witnesses laid their clothes at the feet of a young man named Saul.

The Rock Of Execution

The judges heard Stephen's description of Jesus at God's right hand as the ultimate blasphemy. Law-trained, robed jurists stuffed their fingers in their ears and yelled to drown out the voice of the witness. The tribunal entrusted with justice and order, became a pack of junkyard dogs. The Law's provisions for justice were trampled under furious feet in a rush to snuff out Stephen's life.

Stoning was the capital punishment prescribed by the Law of Moses for blasphemy. According to legal rules, after a fair trial with witnesses and careful deliberation (a death sentence required

☞ **GO TO:**

Leviticus 20:27; Deuteronomy 17:5–7; Joshua 7:25
(stoning)

witnesses: accusers, those who testified against him at the trial

executioners: witnesses against the accused led the stoning

overnight consideration), the convicted person was taken out of the city to an eleven-foot-deep pit known as "The Rock of Execution." On the way he was urged to confess his guilt, with the promise of "a share in the age to come" if he did. He was stripped, bound hand and foot, and pushed headfirst into the pit. If he died from the fall, the execution was ended. If not, the **witnesses** against him led others in throwing heavy stones down on him until he died.

There is no indication that any of the "proper" procedures were followed in Stephen's case. In fact, the Sanhedrin had no legal right to execute anyone without permission from Roman authorities. Their rage blinded them to the risks.

A young man named Saul witnessed the execution. He guarded the **executioners'** clothes and applauded (Acts 7:58; 8:1). Just what every lynch mob needs—a cheerleader!

 Persecution & Martyrdom—Stephen was the first Christian martyr. Thousands in every generation have died for their loyalty to Jesus. In Kenya, East Africa, in 1950 hundreds of African Christians who agreed with the goal of national freedom but refused to join Mau Mau fighters in their campaign of murder were strangled or hacked to death with machetes in their homes. When government authorities offered them guns to protect themselves, their answer was, "No. We love you and we love our Kikuyu brothers as well. How can we tell them about the love of God if we are holding guns?" They continued to testify . . . as they died.[13]

> **Acts 7:59–60** While they were stoning him, Stephen prayed, "Lord Jesus, receive my spirit." Then he fell on his knees and cried out, "Lord, do not hold this sin against them." When he had said this, he fell asleep.

A Spirit Stones Could Never Crush

As the stones of death fell, Stephen mirrored Jesus on the cross.

- Jesus prayed: *"Father, into your hands I commit my spirit"* (Luke 23:46).
  Stephen prayed: *"Lord Jesus, receive my spirit"* (Acts 7:59).

- Jesus prayed: *"Father, forgive them"* (Luke 23:34).
  Stephen prayed: *"Lord, do not hold this sin against them"* (Acts 7:60).

Why Did Stephen Die?

Reasons for Stephen's Death Sentence	Reference in Acts 7
He suggested the Temple was no more holy than any place God meets people.	Verses 2, 9, 30–34, 38, 44
He insisted God does not live in manmade institutions or traditions.	Verses 48–50
He accused religious officials of resisting and rejecting God.	Verses 51–52
He accused the Law's "champions" of failure to obey the Law.	Verse 53
He placed Jesus on the same level as God.	Verses 55–56

Religious people will kill for "sacred" buildings and institutions. Jesus' people will die for him, with shining faces and forgiving hearts.

Something
to Ponder

Study Questions

1. What specific qualifications did the apostles tell the church to look for in the people chosen to care for the poor?
2. What Christian beliefs may have been twisted by Stephen's enemies to charge that he spoke against the Temple and conspired to destroy the Temple and Judaism?
3. Of what four things did Stephen say his accusers were guilty?
4. What two prayers did Stephen pray while being stoned to death? What two prayers did Jesus pray at his death?

CHAPTER WRAP-UP

- As the young church grew, its care of the poor developed gaps. Greek-speaking widows were overlooked in the food distribution. Complaints of neglect and discrimination surfaced. The solution was to share the work. (Acts 4:34–5:2; 6:1–4)

- Seven spiritually mature, practical-minded men were chosen from the Grecian community to care for the distribution to the church's poor. The apostles prayed and laid hands on the men selected and turned the work over to them. (Acts 6:5–7)

- Stephen, one of the seven, was a whiz at proving Jesus was the Messiah. When enemies of Christ couldn't win an argument with him, they hatched a plot to bring him before the Sanhedrin on trumped-up charges. (Acts 6:8–14)

- As he defended himself, Stephen's face glowed. He showed from history how God is not confined to any "holy place" but meets people when and where he chooses. He traced Israel's history of rejection. (Acts 6:15–7:45)

- David wanted to build a house for God, but God said "No." Solomon built the Temple. But building a house to contain God is impossible, Stephen said. (Acts 7:44–50)

Stephen ended his defense with an indictment of the Sanhedrin. When he described his vision of Jesus at God's right hand, infuriated council members dragged him out and stoned him. As he died, he asked the Lord to forgive them. (Acts 7:51–60)

Part Two

FIRE IN THE COUNTRY

REVEREND FUN

"And all of the apostles were no longer in one 'Accord.'"

ACTS 8: SCATTERGUN!

Let's Get Started

Stephen was the first to die for Jesus. He met Christ's enemies' mindless rage with a shining face. Even as the boulders of death crushed his body, somewhere inside Stephen found superhuman strength to forgive his killers (Acts 7:54–60).

A young man named Saul was there. He threw no stones. He held the killers' coats (Acts 7:58). He could not have known that from that moment on his destiny would be bound together with the Christians.

> **Acts 8:1a** And Saul was there, giving approval to his death.

Stompin' Out The Fire

Who was this *Saul* guarding the killers' cloaks? His participation in Stephen's execution suggests three "may haves":

- He may have been a member of the Sanhedrin.
- He may have acted as *praeco*, the official herald who announced the crime for which the condemned man was executed.[1]
- He may have been one of the rabbinical students who attended Sanhedrin meetings to learn. (If so, he wouldn't have missed the execution for a trip to Disneyland!)

> **Acts 8:1b–3** On that day, a great persecution broke out against the church of Jerusalem, and all except the apostles were scattered throughout Judea and Samaria. Godly men buried Stephen and mourned deeply for him. But Saul began to destroy the church. Going from house to house, he dragged off men and women and put them in prison.

A Whole Lotta Shakin' Goin' On!

Saul was convinced traditional Judaism and the faith of Jesus could never coexist. To preserve the ancient religion, the new sect must be smashed—and he was just the guy to do it! The Sanhedrin's approach of ordering Jesus' partisans <u>not to speak</u> in their founder's name had failed.

☞ **GO TO:**

Acts 4:18; 5:40
(not to speak)

Acts 2:47; 4:21; 5:13
(high esteem)

The day Stephen died, Saul, with approval of the Sanhedrin (Acts 9:2), launched an all-out campaign to wipe the name of Jesus from his followers' lips and to drive faith in him from their hearts (Acts 8:1, 3; 22:4). Saul was an equal opportunity persecutor—targeting both men and women. Some paid with their lives (Acts 22:4).

His goal was to destroy the church! (The Greek word for "destroy" means ferocious, animal-like devastation.)

Until Saul's onslaught, the young church had been held in <u>high esteem</u> by the citizens of Jerusalem. Now believers ran for their lives! The Twelve stayed in town (wearing dark glasses, hats pulled down, and collars pulled up—as we say in the spy business: "incognito"). Facing danger with their brothers and sisters was an act of courage.[2]

 Persecution & Martyrdom—Saul's was the first general persecution of the church. Over the next 250 years, ten imperial Roman persecutions, plus hundreds of local incidents of arrest, beating, and lynching, would try to force Christians to renounce their faith. But it is estimated that more Christians have been killed for their faith in the last fifty years than in the first three centuries of the church![3]

What Others are Saying:

Henry Halley: Saul . . . laid waste the church, dragging men and women to prison, beating them that believed, putting many to death, making havoc of the church beyond measure.[4]

EARLY CHURCH WOMEN—Among the first to lay their lives on the line for Jesus were women (Acts 8:3). Just as Christian women witnessed, so they suffered and died.

> **Acts 8:4** Those who had been scattered preached the word wherever they went.

Backfire!

Had it not been for Saul, the first disciples might have hung around enjoying the lively Jerusalem fellowship indefinitely. But the world was waiting. The first disciples had been *"witnesses . . . in Jerusalem"* for seven or eight years. Phase two of the Jesus revolution—*"in all Judea and Samaria"* (Acts 1:8)—was like a racehorse in the gate, stomping, snorting, chomping at the bit for a gallop on the open track.

In a sweet irony, the searing pain of Saul's hot breath on their necks sent reluctant disciples scurrying to fulfill their <u>commission</u>. With the help of this little Pharisee crazy with <u>misdirected zeal</u>, the faith of Jesus broke out all over Judea and leaped the walls of prejudice to ignite Samaria.

☞ **GO TO:**

Matthew 28:19–20 (commission)

Philippians 3:6; 1 Timothy 1:12–15 (misdirected zeal)

JESUS CHRIST CEO

Behind the scenes, the Lord of the church is at the controls of his movement. He uses the "disaster" of persecution to spread his message. An early Christian, Tertullian, wrote, "The blood of the martyrs is the church's seed." Early believers had spent several years in the faith-building environment of the Jerusalem Christian community. Now the faith that had been built must be taken out to a world waiting for the good news, and as director of world events, Jesus saw to it that it was (see illustration, page 90).

Dragged Kicking And Screaming Into God's Work

Did the early Christians—those paragons of spiritual love and power—really have to be *kicked* out of the nest to get them to get on with God's work?

Oh, yeah. Early Christians apparently had the same problems modern Christians do. They clung to the status quo too long. Now, as then, willingness to risk sharing one's faith outside the security of the believers' circle sometimes requires a hefty shove!

When Paul's persecution of the church began, Christians ran for their lives in all directions. They took the Gospel with them from Jerusalem to Joppa in Samaria, where Peter had his vision (Acts 9:32–10:48); to Caesarea, the home of Cornelius (Acts 9:32–10:48); and to Judea and Gaza when Philip met the Ethiopian (Acts 8:26–39).

What Others are Saying:

Robert E. Coleman: Jesus . . . [foresaw] the day when the Gospel of salvation in his Name would be proclaimed convincingly to every creature. Through that testimony his church militant would someday be the church universal even as it would become the church triumphant. It was not going to be an easy conquest. Many would suffer persecution and martyrdom in the battle. Yet no matter how great the trials through which his people would pass, and how many temporal skirmishes were lost in the struggle, the ultimate victory was certain. His church would win in the end. . . . (Matthew 16:18).[5]

Billy Graham: Again we face a dark time in the history of God's people. In spite of some encouraging signs, the forces of evil seem to be gathering for a colossal assault on the work of God in the world. . . . Our world needs to be touched by Christians who are Spirit-filled, Spirit-led, and Spirit-empowered. Are you that kind of Christian?[6]

> **Acts 8:5–8** Philip went **down** to a city in Samaria and proclaimed the Christ there. When the crowds heard Philip and saw the miraculous signs he did, they all paid close attention to what he said. With shrieks, evil spirits came out of many, and many paralytics and cripples were healed. So there was great joy in that city.

down: Jews leaving Jerusalem always go "down"; it's in the mountains and high in their hearts

The Greater Samaria Miracle Crusade

Philip, highly visible in Jerusalem as one of the seven who cared for the poor (Acts 6:5), hightailed it north across the Samaritan border. He stopped in an unnamed town—perhaps a Greek-speaking city, where a language barrier wouldn't hinder sharing the Gospel—perhaps <u>Sychar</u> where Jesus met the woman at the well (see WBFW, page 18).

Samaritans were a people of mixed ancestry—a combination of poor northern Israelites and <u>transplants</u> from other conquered nations. Their religion was a corrupted form of Judaism. They accepted as Scripture only the first five books of the Old Testament. They shared the Jews' <u>anticipation</u> of the Messiah. "Pure" Jews never accepted Samaritans as real Jews. In turn, Samaritans despised Jews for their rejection.

Philip introduced Jesus to the Samaritans as their Messiah (Acts 8:5). The Holy Spirit authenticated his preaching with miracles (Acts 8:6). Hundreds believed, and there was joy all over town (Acts 8:8)!

☞ **GO TO:**

John 4:4–42 (Sychar)

2 Kings 17:24–28 (transplants)

Deuteronomy 18:15–19; John 4:25 (anticipation)

> **Acts 8:9–13** Now for some time a man named Simon had practiced sorcery in the city and amazed all the people of Samaria. He boasted that he was someone great, and all the people, both high and low, gave him their attention and exclaimed, "This man is the divine power known as the Great Power." They followed him because he had amazed them for a long time with his magic. But when they believed Philip as he preached the good news of the kingdom of God and the name of Jesus Christ, they were baptized, both men and women. Simon himself believed and was baptized. And he followed Philip everywhere, astonished by the great signs and miracles he saw.

The Great Wizard

The town's most notorious celebrity was a slight-of-hand artist named Simon—early Christian literature calls him "Simon **Magus**." He wowed the local citizens with illusions ("magic" tricks) and sorceries. Sorcery involved **occult practices** and, often, drug-induced "magical" effects. ("Just snort a little of this white powder and *voila!* you're off to la-la land!" One "trip" and you're convinced the drug dealer is "God's man of faith and power"!) When this first-century magician saw Philip's miracles— paralytics walking, demon-harassed people restored to sanity (Acts 8:7)—he was impressed. These were not illusions! No tricks, no drugs, no hallucinations.

Simon's skills as an illusionist and <u>**sorcerer**</u> convinced the Samaritans he had a pipeline to God (Acts 8:10). Simon "believed," and Philip baptized him (Acts 8:13). His faith appeared to be sincere. After his baptism Simon followed Philip everywhere, like a wizard's apprentice, trying to figure out the evangelist's "magic."

Magus: practitioner of illusions, sorcery, and quackery

occult practices: incantations calling for action or influence by supernatural (demonic) powers

sorcerer: person who uses drugs to produce "magical" effects

☞ **GO TO:**

Exodus 7:11–12; Acts 13:4–12 (sorcerer)

What Others are Saying:

William Barclay: Simon was by no means an unusual type in the ancient world. There were many astrologers and soothsayers and magicians, and in a credulous age they had great influence. . . . Even the twentieth century has not risen above fortune-telling and astrology, as almost any popular newspaper or magazine can witness. It is not to be thought that Simon and his fellow-practitioners were all conscious frauds. Many of them had deluded themselves before they deluded others and believed in their own powers.[7]

> **Acts 8:14–17** When the apostles in Jerusalem heard that Samaria had accepted the word of God, they sent Peter and John to them. When they arrived, they prayed for them that they might receive the Holy Spirit, because the Holy Spirit had not yet come upon any of them; they had simply been baptized into the name of the Lord Jesus. Then Peter and John placed their hands on them, and they received the Holy Spirit.

Spirit Link

Big guns from Jerusalem, Peter and John, were dispatched to check out what was happening in Samaria. Philip was a "new kid on the block." He needed help. Many Samaritans believed and were baptized in Jesus' name, but something was missing: *"the Holy Spirit had not yet come upon any of them"* (Acts 8:16). Usually, the gift of the Spirit came with believing in Jesus (Acts 2:38; 10:44). What tipped the evangelist and apostles off that the Holy Spirit had not yet been given to the Samaritans?

- It may have been the absence of visible <u>spiritual gifts</u>— speaking in new languages, sharing spiritual insights, caring for one another, etc.
- It may have been the absence of <u>spiritual life</u>—liveliness of spirit—eagerness for spiritual things, thirst for fellowship, worship, knowledge of Christ.
- It may have been confusion left over from the Samaritans' involvement in the occult, drugs, and other deceptions of Simon's magic—things Peter exposed in Acts 8:20–23.
- It may have been special knowledge or insight given by the Holy Spirit—the "gift of **discernment**"—that tipped the leaders off to what was missing.

☞ **GO TO:**

Romans 12:6–8; 1 Corinthians 12:7–11, 28–30; Ephesians 4:11 (spiritual gifts)

1 John 5:12 (spiritual life)

1 Corinthians 12:10; Hebrews 5:14 (discernment)

discernment: *ability to distinguish between good and evil*

Audrey I. Girard: When God's Spirit resides within us, he communicates to us an antsy feeling when other people's spirits are not in tune with his. That's the time to pray. Being insightful (discerning) is a gift from God to make us knowing and caring.[8]

What Others are Saying:

The Holy Spirit Dances To His Own Tune

Peter and John's dual task was to bring believing Samaritans under the full influence of the Spirit and to establish a solid connection between the new Samaritan church and the "mother" church in Jerusalem. Three things were unique about the Holy Spirit's coming at Samaria:

1. The Spirit came when the apostles prayed for them (Acts 8:15).
2. There was a waiting period between believing and receiving the Spirit (Acts 8:16).
3. The Spirit's coming coincided with the apostles' touch (Acts 8:17).

F. F. Bruce: It was one thing for them to be baptized by a freelance evangelist like Philip, but not until they had been acknowledged and welcomed by the leaders of the Jerusalem church did they experience the signs which confirmed and attested their membership in the Spirit-possessed society.[9]

What Others are Saying:

"I'll Buy That Trick!"

Philip had not hesitated to accept the magician's confession of faith as real. But Simon's faith was shallow. Instead of adopting the thinking and lifestyle of Jesus, he continued to be dazzled by Philip's miracles and the apostle's ability to influence people (Acts 8:13, 18). <u>Faith based on miracles</u> and signs isn't trustworthy. Simon's faith had more holes than a fishnet:

☞ **GO TO:**

John 2:23–24; 4:48; 7:3–5 (faith based on miracles)

grace: *unearned, unmerited favor*

1. He was confused about **grace**. He thought he could buy God's favor (Acts 8:18–20).

2. He was confused about power. He couldn't see the difference between the power of the occult, magic, and superstition and the power of the Holy Spirit.

3. He was confused about ministry. He saw the work of the apostles as another kind of showmanship (Acts 8:21). If he had the formula, he could do it too!

4. He was confused about the Holy Spirit's work. His entrepreneurial mind saw it as a way to get rich, influence people, and satisfy his ego.

Acts 8:20–25 Peter answered: "May your money perish with you, because you thought you could buy the gift of God with money! You have no part or share in this ministry, because your heart is not right before God. Repent of this wickedness and pray to the Lord. Perhaps he will forgive you for having such a thought in your heart. For I see that you are full of bitterness and captive to sin."

Then Simon answered, "Pray to the Lord for me so that nothing you have said may happen to me."

When they had testified and proclaimed the word of the Lord, Peter and John returned to Jerusalem, preaching the gospel in many Samaritan villages.

Rotten Money

Peter blows the lid off Simon's mixed-up priorities. The idea that God's gifts go to the highest bidder is so corrupt it could only come straight from **hell**! J. B. Phillips translates Peter's response in Acts 8:20, *"To hell with you and your money!"*[10] Although he confessed faith in Christ, Simon's heart was not **right**. He was up to his pointy wizard's hat in spiritual trouble: He needed inner change—repentance.

Simon's "prayer request" was a magician's illusion. Sources outside the Bible report[11] he continued to chase his badly motivated dream of spiritual authority. After this, he moved to Rome where he became a hero of heretics whose ideas created disunity in the church for centuries. Non-Christian Romans honored him with a statue inscribed, *Semoni Sancto Deo,* "To Simon the holy god."

Christians rightly rejoice whenever a public figure or celebrity confesses faith in Christ and becomes identified with the Jesus movement. But fame and notoriety should not be confused with spiritual maturity. New Christians need time to grow in their faith and understanding of God's grace and Christ's way of life before they are pushed forward as spokesmen for the Gospel or leaders in the church.

> **Acts 8:26–29** Now an angel of the Lord said to Philip, "Go south to the road—the desert road—that goes down from Jerusalem to Gaza." So he started out, and on his way he met an Ethiopian **eunuch**, an important official in charge of all the treasury of Candace, queen of the Ethiopians. This man had gone to Jerusalem to worship, and on his way home was sitting in his chariot reading the book of Isaiah the prophet. The <u>Spirit told</u> Philip, "Go to that chariot and stay with it."

Holy Hitchhiker

As Peter and John returned to Jerusalem, the Lord gave Philip new orders: "Take a hike!"

Obedient, Philip headed back into dangerous Judean territory where Saul was still harassing Christians. He hadn't gone far when the entourage of an important **Ethiopian** government official came down the road, headed home after a pilgrimage to the Holy City. He was the treasurer and personal attendant of Queen Candace (pronounced "kan-da-kee"), and a worshiper of Israel's God.

hell: *place of the dead; eternal punishment; Satan's domain*

right: *straight, true, honest*

Remember This . . .

eunuch: *castrated male servant*

☞ **GO TO:**

1 Kings 19:12–13; Isaiah 30:21 (Spirit told)

Ethiopian: *person from African kingdom on the Nile River near modern Sudan*

JESUS CHRIST CEO

Jesus is the church's strategist. He puts people where he needs them if they listen to his voice.

What Others are Saying:

☞ **GO TO:**

Ephesians 4:15–16 (Head)

Head: *title for Christ emphasizing his role as CEO of the church*

Watchman Nee: Divine work must be divinely initiated. A worker may be called directly by the Spirit, or indirectly through reading the Word, through preaching, or through circumstances; but whatever the means God uses to make known his will to a man, *his* must be the Voice heard through every other voice. *He* must be the One who speaks, no matter through what instrument the call may come. . . . It is from the **Head** that all our direction comes.[12]

> **Acts 8:30–35** Then Philip ran up to the chariot and heard the man reading Isaiah the prophet. "Do you understand what you are reading?" Philip asked. "How can I," he said, "unless someone explains it to me?" So he invited Philip to come up and sit with him.
>
> The eunuch was reading this passage of Scripture:
>
> "He was led like a sheep to the slaughter,
> and as a lamb before the shearer is silent,
> so he did not open his mouth.
> In his humiliation he was deprived of justice.
> Who can speak of his descendants?
> For his life was taken from the earth."
>
> The eunuch asked Philip, "Tell me, please, who is the prophet talking about, himself or someone else?" Then Philip began with that very passage of Scripture and told him the good news about Jesus.

Seeker's Question: Who's The Lamb?

As he traveled, the African read aloud from the scroll of Isaiah 53:7–8. Philip ran to the chariot and asked if the Ethiopian understood what he was reading. "Come and ride with me," the man said. "Explain it to me."

Philip simply told the man what he knew: Isaiah was talking about Jesus bearing the injustice of the cross to save people from their sins. No sales pitch. No pulpit pounding. He just told the man what he knew.

> **Acts 8:36, 38–40** As they traveled along the road, they came to some water and the eunuch said, "Look, here is water. Why shouldn't I be baptized?" And he gave orders to stop the chariot. Then both Philip and the eunuch went down into the water and Philip baptized him. When they came up out of the water, the Spirit of the Lord suddenly took Philip away, and the eunuch did not see him again, but went on his way rejoicing. Philip, however, appeared at Azotus and traveled about, preaching the gospel in all the towns until he reached Caesarea.

Soul-Dipper

From what happened next, we can guess Philip, in his conversation with the African, included something like what Peter said at Pentecost: "You need to *repent and be baptized in the name of Jesus Christ for the forgiveness of your sins*" (Acts 2:38).

The entourage approached a desert stream, and the man got the idea to be baptized.

Note: Acts 8:37 is not in some older **manuscripts** of Acts. For that reason, translators of the New International Version (NIV) did not include it. But it is the kind of thing a Christian witness like Philip would say: *"If you believe with all your heart, you may be baptized."* To which the Ethiopian responded: *"I believe that Jesus Christ is the Son of God."* [13]

It was a statement of faith. So together, Philip, founding president of Hitchhikers for Jesus, and the eager-beaver black believer splashed into the water. Philip baptized the man while his royal troupe watched. As they came out of the water, the Spirit whisked the wet hitchhiker away to his next assignment, and a dripping Ethiopian went home to tell the story and lay the foundation for the Ethiopian Christian church.

manuscripts: handwritten copies in Greek on which Bible translations are based

☞ **GO TO:**

Romans 6:1–4 (rose with Christ)

What Others are Saying:

William Barclay: To the early Christians baptism was, whenever possible, by immersion and in running water. It symbolized . . . cleansing. . . . It marked a clean break. . . . [It] was a real union with Christ. As waters closed over a man's head he seemed to die with Christ and as he emerged he <u>rose with Christ</u>. [14]

When things got hot in Jerusalem, Philip and other Christians didn't stand around waiting to get clobbered! They "got outta Dodge" as quickly as possible. As they fled they talked about Jesus. Whatever happens, wherever Jesus' follower

Something to Ponder

goes, he or she is there as Christ's witness—a storyteller of the good news. Contrary to what my sixth grade teacher Ms. Anderson told me, *neatness* does not always count. The storyteller doesn't have to look good or be eloquent. He or she simply tells what he or she knows. And the news spreads!

JESUS CHRIST CEO

Driving witnesses out of Jerusalem through Saul's persecution seems drastic. But as head of the church, Jesus Christ knew best what it would take to get his message out.

Study Questions

1. What did God use to get Christians to leave Jerusalem and take the message of Christ to Judea and Samaria?
2. What happened in Samaria when Philip proclaimed Christ? Who was his most notable "convert"?
3. Identify three things that were different about the Holy Spirit's coming to the Samaritans. Why was it important for the apostles to be there?
4. Simon's attempt to buy the power to give people the Holy Spirit showed his confusion. Identify at least three areas of his confusion.

CHAPTER WRAP-UP

- The day Stephen died, Saul launched a crusade to destroy the church. Men and women were jailed for the crime of following Jesus. Many escaped to the outlying villages, telling the Jesus story wherever they went. (Acts 8:1–4)

- Philip went to Samaria, where he preached and performed miracles. Many Samaritans believed in Jesus. One who believed and was baptized was a magician named Simon, whom some people thought was some sort of god. (Acts 8:5–13)

- Peter and John were sent from Jerusalem to help establish the Samaritan church. They touched people, and the people received the Holy Spirit. (Acts 8:14–17)

- Simon the magician was impressed when he saw what happened when the apostles touched people. He offered to buy the ability to do what they were doing. Peter was outraged. (Acts 8:18–24)

An angel told Philip to take a hike down the Gaza Road where he thumbed a ride with an African official on his way home after a visit to Jerusalem. The African believed on Jesus and was baptized. (Acts 8:25–40)

ACTS 9: U-TURN ON STRAIGHT STREET

Let's Get Started

Saul of Tarsus could not erase the memory of Stephen's shining face. Stephen's last words, *"Lord Jesus, receive my spirit"* (Acts 7:59), played over and over in Saul's mind like a broken record. *"Lord . . . do not hold this sin against them"* (Acts 7:60). *Lord Jesus . . . Lord Jesus . . . Lord Jesus.*

He tried to drown the images by persecuting more people. Again and again, the zealous persecutor was secretly astonished at the serenity—even joy—with which these men and women met danger and death.

Bishop Festo Kivengere: I remember [a former Mau Mau fighter who had turned to Christ] . . . he said, "I was one who led a group of fighters to attack a Christian family at night. We were ordered to do it because they were 'hard-core resisters.' But to my surprise, that man loved us. He said he was not at all afraid to die, for he would immediately be with Jesus. Then he pleaded with us, not for his life, but for ours, that we awake and repent while there was still time. We killed him, but he died praying, 'Father, forgive them and give them time to turn about.' We went back to the forest, but the face of that man and his love never left me. At last his Jesus has found me, and now I want to tell everyone about him."

How do you destroy Christians like that? You beat them; they love you. You put them to shame; they think you have given them an opportunity to be creative. You kill them and they win you![1]

> **What Others are Saying:**

> **Acts 9:1–2** Meanwhile, Saul was still breathing out murderous threats against the Lord's disciples. He went to the high priest and asked him for letters to the synagogues in Damascus, so that if he found any there who belonged to the Way, whether men or women, he might take them as prisoners to Jerusalem.

Blind Fury

Self-appointed champion of traditional religion, Saul boasted publicly of his intent to <u>kill</u> Christians if they did not renounce Jesus. The religious establishment gave his campaign of terror its approval. When harassed disciples fled, spreading the message of the Messiah as they went, Saul and the high priest agreed the campaign against **the Way** (Acts 9:2) should be taken beyond the walls of the Holy City.

In the Roman Empire the various peoples were governed by the laws of their own nations. According to Jewish law, the Sanhedrin in Jerusalem had authority over the six million Jews scattered throughout the Roman world. **Extradition** of escapees back to Jerusalem for punishment required authorization from the high priest. The "letters" Saul carried would be honored both by the secular government and synagogue officials in Damascus.

☞ **GO TO:**

Acts 22:4; 26:10 (kill)

John 14:6; Acts 18:25–26; 19:9, 23; 22:4; 24:14, 22 (the Way)

the Way: *nickname emphasizing Christianity as a distinct style of living*

extradition: *surrender of an accused person in one state to be tried by another state*

Persecution & Martyrdom—Martyrdom is a regular, ongoing feature of church life in 25 percent of (present-day) global Christianity that we call the "underground church." According to David Barret of World Evangelization Research Center, in one part of the globe, over ten thousand Christians have been killed every year since 1950, due to clashes with anti-Christian mobs, infuriated relatives, state-organized death squads, and so on.[2]

Profile Of A Persecutor

From references in Acts—mostly what the man says about himself—we develop the following profile of this obsessed man Saul—later called Paul. He was

- a "young man" (see Acts 7:58)—meaning he was between twenty-four and forty years of age;
- a Jew, born a Roman citizen in **Tarsus** (see Acts 21:39; 22:3, 25–29);

Tarsus: *important Roman city three hundred miles north of Jerusalem*

- fluent in Greek, Aramaic, and Hebrew (see Acts 21:37, 40; 22:2);
- raised in Jerusalem (see Acts 22:3);
- a disciple of the respected Pharisee, <u>Gamaliel</u>, under whom he received a superior rabbinical education that probably began at age thirteen (see Acts 22:3);
- an <u>expert</u> in Jewish law (see Acts 22:3); and
- motivated in his persecution of Christians by <u>zeal</u> for God (see Acts 22:3).

"The rest of the story" of Saul of Tarsus is the subject of most of the rest of the Book of Acts.

☞ **GO TO:**

Acts 5:34–39 (Gamaliel)

Philippians 3:5–6 (expert)

Philippians 3:6 (zeal)

What Others are Saying:

A Second-Century Church Leader: [Paul was] a man of middling size, and his hair was scanty, and his legs were a little crooked, and his knees were far apart; he had large eyes, and his eyebrows met, and his nose was somewhat long.[3]

Eugenia Price: Saul . . . believed himself to be serving the Lord God of Israel when he persecuted the disciples of Jesus. His service had become an obsession.[4]

The Road To Truth

As Saul and his entourage of temple police reached a high point on the trail over Mt. Hermon, suddenly spread out below them lay a white city on a green plain—like "a handful of pearls in a goblet of green."[5] **Damascus**, one of the oldest cities in the world, is 150 miles north of Jerusalem. Ten thousand Jews lived there. Consequently, there were many synagogues from which to flush out Christians to drag back to Jerusalem in chains. The trip took a week—time for the Holy Spirit to penetrate Saul's dark fury with questions.

Within sight of Damascus, the questions raised by his encounters with Christians were answered. Acts records three accounts of this moment—this one in Acts 9 and two first-person accounts in Acts 22 and 26 (see also 1 Corinthians 15:8–10; Galatians 1:13–17; and 1 Timothy 1:12–14).

Damascus: *capital of modern Syria*

> **Acts 9:3–4** As he neared Damascus on his journey, suddenly a light from heaven flashed around him. He fell to the ground and heard a voice say to him, "Saul, Saul, why do you persecute me?"

Smack Down!

It was high noon (see Acts 22:6; 26:13). A flash of light brighter than the sun knocked Saul flat! Some people think a mountain thunderstorm broke over the travelers, striking Saul with a lightning bolt and the Lord spoke to him out of the storm. Others suggest Saul was dazzled by what the Old Testament calls the **shekinah**, the radiance of God's personal **glory**, shining from Jesus' face.

☞ **GO TO:**

Exodus 14:19–20;
24:15–18;
2 Chronicles 7:1
(shekinah)

Luke 9:28–32;
2 Corinthians 4:6
(from Jesus' face)

shekinah: Hebrew for the special, visible presence of God

glory: splendor, radiance

☞ **GO TO:**

Acts 9:17, 27; 26:15–
16; 1 Corinthians 9:1;
15:8 (saw Jesus)

> **Acts 9:5** "Who are you, Lord?" Saul asked.
> "I am Jesus, whom you are persecuting," he replied.

The Last Appearance Of Christ

In that blazing light Saul saw something that changed him forever. Prostrate in dirt and camel dung on the Damascus Road, Saul saw Jesus—not a dream or vision of Jesus, but Jesus *in person*—the crucified, risen-again Christ (Acts 9:17, 27). Jesus spoke the persecutor's name, *"Saul, Saul, why do you persecute me?"*

Saul did not recognize his confronter. But he had sense enough to realize that whoever knocked him down and was talking to him was *the Boss!*

"I am Jesus, whom you are persecuting."

Talk about a whack upside the head! A swift kick in the convictions! A bop on the belief system! Judaism's "hero" fighting the influence of a dead Nazarene whose claims he thought could be dismissed, suddenly, in a flash of insight, realized that while he'd been chasing Christians, the Nazarene was alive and well and taking it all very personally!

What Others are Saying:

John R. W. Stott: To begin with, we must hear his voice. . . . Sometimes we hear his voice through the prickings of the conscience, sometimes through the gropings of the mind. Or it may be a moral defeat, or the seeming emptiness and meaninglessness of our existence, or an inexplicable spiritual hunger, or a sickness, bereavement, pain or fear, by which we become aware that Christ is . . . speaking to us. Or his call may come through a friend, a preacher or a book. Whenever we hear, we must listen.[6]

KEY POINT

To attack a Christian is to attack the Lord.

> **Acts 9:6–9** "Now get up and go into the city, and you will be told what you must do."
> The men traveling with Saul stood there speechless; they heard the sound but did not see anyone. Saul got

> up from the ground, but when he opened his eyes he could see nothing. They led him by the hand into Damascus. For three days he was blind, and did not eat or drink anything.

Three Blind Nights

"Go into town and wait for instructions." The light disappeared. The avenger of Judaism blinked his eyes. He was blind as a bat! His traveling companions saw the light and Saul's tumble, heard a strange sound (unintelligible to them), listened to Saul's side of the conversation, but had not the foggiest idea of what had just happened.

At Judas's Bed-and-Breakfast, Saul skipped breakfast. He spent three days and nights in the dark, fasting—no food, no drink—the radical sort of fasting reserved for urgent repentance and seeking God. He prayed. While he waited Saul had a **vision** of someone named Ananias coming to touch and heal him.

☞ **GO TO:**

Genesis 46:2; Daniel 10:7; Luke 1:22; Acts 10:3, 9–23; 18:9 (vision)

vision: *a revelation from God, often received when the person is in a dream-like state*

William Barclay: There is all of Christianity in what the Risen Christ said to Paul, "Go into the city, and you will be told what to do." Up to this moment Paul had been doing what *he* liked, what *he* thought best, what *his* will dictated. From this time forward he would be told what to do. The Christian is a man who has ceased to do what he wants to do and who has begun to do what Christ wants him to do.[7]

What Others are Saying:

THE BIG PICTURE

Acts 9:10–16 Meanwhile, in Damascus a disciple named Ananias had a vision in which God told him to go to the house of Judas on Straight Street and ask for a man from Tarsus named Saul. God told Ananias that Saul had a vision that Ananias would come, place his hands on him, and restore his sight. Ananias was willing to go, but he'd heard all about Saul's murderous mission. Ananias wondered if God knew what he was doing. God said, "Go, I have chosen this man as my instrument."

Reluctant Gofer

Ananias was a well-respected, law-abiding member of the Jewish community in Damascus (see Acts 22:12) and a Christian *disciple*—follower of Christ—(Acts 9:10). He was listening for the Lord's voice.

His first response (before he knew the assignment) was *"Yes, Lord."* When the Lord told him what he wanted him to do on Straight Street (see illustration below), Ananias began to make like a motorboat—"But-but-but-but . . . " (Acts 9:13). Saul was at the bottom of Ananias's list of people he was dying to meet. In his imagination, he could hear dungeon doors clanging shut behind him!

"Hold the phone, Lord! Me 'reach out and touch' the Christian-hater of all time? That's like sending Chicken Little to lay hands on the Big Bad Wolf!" (Acts 9:13–14).

But the Lord insisted. *"Go! This man is my chosen instrument to carry my name before the Gentiles and their kings and before the people of Israel"* (Acts 9:15).

After making his funeral arrangements and notarizing his will (just joking!), Ananias did as he was told. By the time he reached the Straight Street Hotel, confidence and acceptance replaced suspicion. His first word to Saul, the sightless spiritual upstart, was "Brother" (Acts 9:17).

What Others are Saying:

William Barclay: In Christ, Paul and Ananias, the men who had been the bitterest of enemies, came together as brothers.[8]

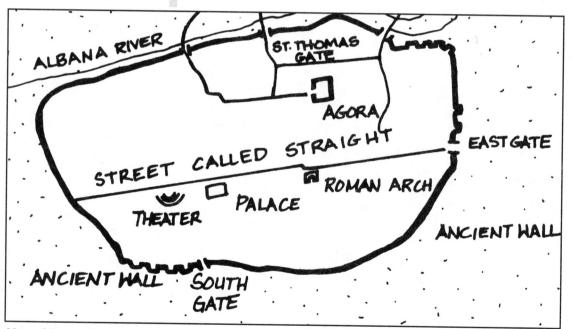

Map of Damascus

This map of Damascus shows Straight Street, the main east to west thoroughfare, which is called Darb al-Mustaqim today. Ananias was sent to see Paul at the house of Judas on this street.

> **Acts 9:17–19** Then Ananias went to the house and entered it. Placing his hands on Saul, he said, "Brother Saul, the Lord—Jesus, who appeared to you on the road as you were coming here—has sent me so that you may see again and be filled with the Holy Spirit." Immediately, something like scales fell from Saul's eyes, and he could see again. He got up and was baptized, and after taking some food, he regained his strength. Saul spent several days with the disciples in Damascus.

Transformation Of The Troublemaker

Saul's spiritual **metamorphosis** wasn't complete until Ananias came. He emerged from his three-day encounter with the risen Jesus with four fundamental certainties, which became the driving force in his life:

1. Jesus is Lord (Acts 9:5–6).
2. Gentiles and Jews alike must be told about Jesus (Acts 9:15).
3. Saul was God's chosen representative to take the message to the Gentiles (Acts 9:15).
4. This calling would be costly in terms of <u>personal suffering</u> (Acts 9:16)

Saul's Process Of Spiritual Reconstruction

The miracle of spiritual rebirth involved five important processes for Saul:

1. A personal encounter with Jesus (Acts 9:3–6). Jesus initiated it. Saul did <u>nothing to deserve</u> it. Like a hound on the scent of a 'coon Jesus pursued him and turned the <u>light on</u> in his rebellious, self-righteous brain so Saul could see him.
2. He surrendered to Jesus as Lord of his life (Acts 9:5).
3. Other Christians played an important role in Saul's conversion (Acts 9:10–19, 27–28). They forgave him for harm he'd done and accepted him as "brother" (Acts 9:17).
4. Saul was filled with the Holy Spirit (Acts 9:17–18).
5. Saul's conversion was personal but not private. He (a) was baptized—public confession of his faith in Jesus (Acts 9:18); (b) was commissioned as Christ's ambassador-witness (Acts 9:15); and (c) became part of the believers' fellowship (Acts 9:19).

metamorphosis:
scientifically—process by which larva becomes butterfly; spiritually—rebirth, awakening

☞ **GO TO:**

2 Corinthians 11:23–29
(personal suffering)

☞ **GO TO:**

Ephesians 2:8–9;
1 Timothy 1:16
(nothing to deserve)

2 Corinthians 4:6
(light on)

What Others are Saying:

Dig Deeper

Billy Graham: Conversion occurs when we repent and place our faith in Christ. But what is the process like as we approach the point of conversion? . . . The key word is *variety*. . . . The night I came to Christ there were several people around me weeping. I had no tears at all and wondered if my act of commitment was genuine. . . . Conversion is no less real to quiet people than to the more expressive or dramatic ones. . . . Jesus described the conversion experience like the movement of the wind (John 3:8). Wind can be quiet, gentle, or it can reach cyclone proportions. So it is with conversion, sometimes easy and tender, and other times a tornado which alters the entire landscape.[9]

Bible Terms for Conversion

Term	Definition	Scripture
Conversion	Turn to Christ; change beliefs, attitudes, behavior	Acts 15:3; 16:13–15; Romans 16:5; 1 Thessalonians 1:9; 1 Timothy 3:6
Renewal	Restore spiritual life and relationship with God	Titus 3:5; Jeremiah 31:23–34
Born again	Become a child of God by receiving Christ	John 1:12–13; 3:3, 5; 1 John 3:9
Resurrection	Become alive to God; end separation caused by sin	Ephesians 2:1–7; Philippians 3:10–11
New creation	Become a new person, one of God's new people	2 Corinthians 5:17; 1 Peter 2:9–10
Receive Christ	Actively welcome Christ into one's life	John 1:12; Revelation 3:20
Reconciliation	Restoration of harmony with God	Romans 5:10–11; 2 Corinthians 5:16–21
Saved	Rescued from sin's consequences	John 3:16; Romans 10:9–10
Decision	Choice, commitment to follow Christ	Matthew 16:24; Joshua 24:15

THE BIG PICTURE

Acts 9:20–24 After his encounter with the Lord, Saul told the story of his conversion in the synagogues, announcing that Jesus is God's Son, the Messiah. The change in Saul shocked his hearers, who knew he had been sent to Damascus to arrest Christians. An assassination plot developed.

Maddening Metamorphosis

At first, Saul was welcomed as a respected traveling teacher. His letters from the high priest (Acts 9:2) opened the door. But the story he told was different from the one they expected to hear. He had changed 180 degrees. And the change drove the enemies of Jesus crazy!

A group of overzealous Jews decided Saul must be terminated! So they posted assassination squads at the town gates to rub the "turncoat" out if he ventured outside the city. Saul's past now mirrored his future. The fulfillment of Ananias's prophecy had begun (Acts 9:16).

> **Acts 9:25** But his **followers** took him by night and lowered him in a basket through an opening in the wall.

followers: sympathizers, friends

A Freshman In The School Of Dependence

Meanwhile, back at the church, the very people Saul had been sent to arrest became his spiritual family. He soon discovered how absolutely essential other Christians were to his physical as well as spiritual survival. When his would-be assassins hatched their plot, it became clear Paul had to make himself scarce if he was going to see sunrise. In the middle of the night his Christian friends sneaked him out a hole in the city wall, letting him down in a basket (see illustration, page 108). He escaped into the night, headed for Jerusalem.

From the start, Saul learned the vital principle of mutual dependence by which the healthy Christian community functions. First, he found his way into the city after being blinded only with the help of his traveling companions. Then, his information about God's plan for his life came through Ananias. Then came his escape through the wall—if not for his Christian brothers, his career would have ended in Damascus, with an assassin's knife.

 The Lord's instructions often come to us through others. It is essential that we learn the principle of interdependence: *We need each other.* Direct revelation from God can sometimes lead to independence, individualism, spiritual pride, and separation from others in the community of faith. The Lord arranged for Saul to learn this principle early.

JESUS CHRIST CEO

> **Acts 9:26–27** When he came to Jerusalem, he tried to join the disciples, but they were all afraid of him, not believing that he really was a disciple. But Barnabas took him and brought him to the apostles. He told them how Saul on his journey had seen the Lord and that the Lord had spoken to him, and how in Damascus he had preached fearlessly in the name of Jesus.

Paul's Escape by Basket

Paul's friends helped him escape capture by hiding him in a large wicker basket or hamper such as this.

Never Trust A Transformed Troublemaker

Another lesson in dependence on other Christians waited for Saul in Jerusalem. When he left for Damascus, he had been *"breathing out murderous threats against the Lord's disciples"* (Acts 9:1). He'd done a pretty good job of wrecking the Jerusalem church (see Acts 8:1, 3). And his name was definitely not on the top of the Christians' "Most Desirable Dinner Guest List"! When he tried to make contact with them on his return from Damascus, they prudently slammed the door in his face. They were sure it was a scheme to infiltrate the believers' circle to destroy it. Nobody would let him get close enough to tell his story.

Until Barnabas. "Barney the Encourager" (see Acts 4:36) took the risk of listening to Saul's story and became convinced his conversion was real. He became Saul's access into the wary Jerusalem fellowship. Later Saul and Barnabas <u>teamed up</u> for ministry.

☞ **GO TO:**

Acts 11:25–26; 13:2–3 (teamed up)

> **Acts 9:28–30** So Saul stayed with them and moved about freely in Jerusalem, speaking boldly in the name of the Lord. He talked and debated with the Grecian Jews, but they tried to kill him. When the brothers learned of this, they took him down to Caesarea and sent him off to Tarsus.

Agitator, Go Home!

In Jerusalem, Saul took up where Stephen left off, ministering among the Grecian Jews, as if the former persecutor felt driven to continue the martyr's unfinished work. The reaction was a rerun. Stephen's killers added Saul to their hit list. Once again, Saul's Christian brothers saved his neck, whisking him out of town and sending him packing to Tarsus, his boyhood home.

It is impossible to imagine the spread of the Christian Gospel throughout the Roman Empire apart from Saul's conversion and ministry. As the Lord's "instrument" (Acts 9:15) Saul devoted the rest of his life, including all his material and physical resources, to the service of Christ the Lord who surprised him on the Damascus Road.

Once we see who Jesus is, we are never the same again. We too become his *"chosen instruments."* Whether the vision comes in dramatic Damascus Road fashion or through quiet interaction with the Bible and the Spirit, the only reasonable response is to give ourselves, including all our energies and material resources, to serving him.

> **Acts 9:31–32** Then the church throughout Judea, Galilee and Samaria enjoyed a time of peace. It was strengthened; and encouraged by the Holy Spirit, it grew in numbers, living in the fear of the Lord.
> As Peter traveled about the country, he went to visit the **saints** in Lydda.

Pete, The Power Ranger

After Saul the converted troublemaker—whose capacity for causing a ruckus wherever he went is legendary—left Jerusalem, there was a little window of peace for the early Christians.

Peter used the window to visit Christian communities outside Jerusalem. During his trip to the country two miracles powerfully impacted the Judean coastal area along the Mediterranean Sea.

> **Acts 9:33–35** There he found a man named Aeneas, a paralytic who had been bedridden for eight years. "Aeneas," Peter said to him, "Jesus Christ heals you. Get up and take care of your mat." Immediately Aeneas got up. All those who lived in Lydda and Sharon saw him and turned to the Lord.

☞ **GO TO:**

Acts 6:1, 8–10
(Grecian Jews)

Something to Ponder

☞ **GO TO:**

Romans 12:1–2
(give ourselves)

Acts 9:13, 32, 41;
26:10 (saints)

saints: "holy ones"; Christians, God's people

Dance, Quadraplegic, Dance!

The first miracle took place at the junction between two trade routes—the Egypt to Babylon Road and the Joppa to Jerusalem Highway—at the town of Lydda. A man named Aeneas had been disabled for eight years. Peter said, *"Jesus Christ heals you!"* Aeneas got up; his paralysis vanished. He went around showing people what had happened, and people turned to the Lord.

What Others are Saying:

Mother Basilea Schlink: Cures, which are effected in the name of Jesus, reveal to people that the stream of divine life is continually flowing from the One who is life. His strength is given not only to revive soul and spirit, but also to heal the bodies of sick people and to awaken new life.[10]

> **Acts 9:36–38** In Joppa there was a disciple named Tabitha (which, when translated, is Dorcas), who was always doing good and helping the poor. About that time she became sick and died, and her body was washed and placed in an upstairs room. Lydda was near Joppa; so when the disciples heard that Peter was in Lydda, they sent two men to him and urged him, "Please come at once!"

Sad Song Of The Selfless Seamstress

Eleven miles from Lydda in the Mediterranean coastal city of **Joppa** (now part of Tel Aviv) lived a Christian woman named **Tabitha**, noted for the lovely way she <u>used her material resources</u> and sewing skills to help the poor. In that mixed community of Aramaic- and Greek-speaking peoples, this woman was a byword in both cultures for kindness and caring.

Tabitha died. Her body was prepared for burial, which, according to Jewish custom, would take place before sundown the day of her death.

Joppa: *seaport for Jerusalem*

Tabitha: *means "gazelle," a small, graceful antelope with soft, bright eyes*

☞ **GO TO:**

Joshua 19:46;
2 Chronicles 2:16;
Ezra 3:7; Jonah 1:3
(Joppa)

Proverbs 31:20, 31;
Matthew 5:16
(used her material
resources)

EARLY CHURCH WOMEN—Christian women like Tabitha used their skills and talents to help the poor in Jesus' name. Their down-to-earth witness for Christ had a powerful impact on the people they helped.

> **Acts 9:39–43** Peter went to Joppa. He prayed and then commanded Tabitha to get up. She did. When people saw the miracle Peter had performed through God's power, many became believers.

Miracles and answers to prayer convince people to put their faith in Jesus.

Hold The Funeral Till I Get There!

News reached Joppa that Peter was a few miles away. When the selfless seamstress succumbed, two men went to Lydda to get him. To make it to Joppa (thirty-five miles away) before sundown, Peter had to leave without packing his toothbrush!

Peter had seen Jesus raise the dead. So when they took him upstairs to where Tabitha's body lay in state, he did <u>almost exactly</u> what he'd watched Jesus do—even down to the words he said. He sent the mourners out, prayed, and said to the dead woman, *"Get up!"* Then he called the teary-eyed mourners back and presented her to them . . . *alive!*

The impact was powerful—all over Joppa people *"believed in the Lord."*

☞ **GO TO:**

Mark 5:40–41 (almost exactly)

Ajith Fernando: Can this [raising of the dead] happen today too? Jesus did it, the apostles did it, and there is no prohibition to Christians in later ages praying for the dead. We must, of course, remember that death is God's gateway to ultimate triumph, and many wonderful Christians, like Stephen and James in Acts, were not spared "untimely" deaths. Therefore, we must have considerable discernment and sensitivity before praying for the raising of the dead. But submission to Scripture prohibits me from saying that we should never pray this way.[11]

What Others are Saying:

Biblical church growth is measured in (1) impact in the lives of people, (2) encouragement or hope, (3) additions to the community of faith, and (4) the extent to which believers' lives honor the Lord (Acts 9:31).

CHURCH GROWTH

Study Questions

1. With what question did Jesus confront Saul on the road to Damascus? What spiritual principle did this question reveal concerning Jesus and his followers?
2. Identify four of the five important spiritual processes involved in Saul's spiritual reconstruction or conversion.
3. What happened when Saul first came back to Jerusalem, and who helped him become accepted among the believers?

4. What resulted from the healing of Aeneas and the raising of Tabitha from the dead?

CHAPTER WRAP-UP

- When Christians escaped Saul's persecution in Jerusalem, he pursued them to Damascus. On the way, Jesus appeared to him and turned his life around. (Acts 9:1–6)

- Saul was left blind and waiting for the Lord's instructions. Ananias came. The Holy Spirit filled Saul, healed his eyes, and disclosed God's plan for him. (Acts 9:7–17)

- Saul immediately preached Christ in Damascus. Enemies plotted to kill him. Christian friends helped him escape. In Jerusalem, Christians were afraid of him. Barnabas believed in him and convinced them his conversion was real. (Acts 9:19–31)

- After Saul left for Tarsus, the church in Judea, Galilee, and Samaria experienced a time of peace and growth. Peter visited the Christians in the Judean countryside, where two notable miracles convinced many to believe in Jesus. (Acts 9:31–43)

ACTS 10–11: PETER GOES WALL CRASHING

Let's Get Started

Peter with his sidekick John were in Samaria when the Samaritans, a mixed breed of "**impure Jews**," received the Holy Spirit and became followers of Jesus (Acts 8:25). Acceptance of the Samaritans into the church was a big stretch even for fully informed *Christian* Jews like Peter and John. It went against lifelong anti-Samaritan prejudice. But Jesus <u>always accepted</u> Samaritans. What else could his followers do?

Even with inclusion of the Samaritans, however, Christianity remained mostly a Jewish thing. But the young church's CEO had bigger plans! He'd outlined his strategy in Acts 1:8—*"You will receive power when the Holy Spirit comes on you; and you will be my witnesses in Jerusalem, and in all Judea and Samaria, and to the ends of the earth."* With the Jerusalem campaign going strong and new churches popping up *"in all Judea and Samaria,"* the movement took a deep breath (Acts 9:31). The most challenging phase of the revolution was just around the next bend in the road.

The importance of what happened next is underscored by the amount of space given to it by Luke—the story is repeated <u>three times</u> in Acts! The dramatic revelation to the young church that non-Jews were to be accepted as full participants was a major turning point.

> **Acts 10:1–2** At Caesarea there was a man named Cornelius, a centurion in what was known as the Italian Regiment. He and all his family were devout and God-fearing; he gave generously to those in need and prayed to God regularly.

impure Jews: *Samaritans were a mix of Jew and Gentile parentage*

☞ **GO TO:**

John 4:4–42 (always accepted)

☞ **GO TO:**

Acts 10; 11:4–17; 15:7–9 (three times)

Herod the Great: "King" of Judea when Jesus was born

Gentiles: non-Jews

centurion: commander of one hundred soldiers

Italian Regiment: detachment of soldiers recruited in Italy

God-fearers: Jews called them "Proselytes of the Gate"—almost Jews

☞ **GO TO:**

Matthew 27:54; Acts 23:17; 27:43 (centurion)

Acts 13:26, 50; 17:4, 17 (God-fearers)

Acts 11:3 (short of circumcision)

The God-Fearer

Thirty-five miles up the coast from Joppa was Caesarea, center of Roman occupational government in Judea and a showplace of Roman culture. The city was built by **Herod the Great** and named for Emperor Caesar Augustus. Its citizens included both Jews and **Gentiles**. A military officer named Cornelius was stationed there.

Cornelius was a Roman. He was a **centurion**, like a captain today (see illustration below), assigned to the **Italian Regiment**. He and his family were "**God-fearers**," a term for Gentiles attracted to Judaism who attended the synagogue, prayed to God, and lived by Jewish moral principles, but were not fully converted to Judaism because they stopped <u>short of circumcision</u>.

Centurion

Cornelius was a Roman centurion. He would have worn a ceremonial helmet and carried a battle shield as shown here.

Roman Military Structure

1. Legion .... Six thousand men. Modern equivalent: Division.
2. Cohort .... Each Legion divided into ten Cohorts of 600 men. Modern equivalent: Battalion.
3. Centuries ...... Each Cohort divided into six Centuries of 100 men. Modern equivalent: Company.
4. Centurions .... Each Century commanded by a Centurion. Modern equivalent: Captain. Centurions were called "the backbone of the Roman army."[1]

Maude De Joseph West: Cornelius . . . was a good man, a devout man, a generous man, but he was still a Gentile and no Jew would have eaten at table with him any more than you would get down on the floor and drink milk from a dish with your cat.[2]

John Kennedy: In the heyday of Greek and Roman culture the Jewish way of life had a definite appeal to many [Gentiles]. . . . Proselytes (to Judaism) were of two orders, "Proselytes of Righteousness" and "Proselytes of the Gate." The former were obliged to undergo the rite of circumcision and baptism, undertook to obey all the observations of Jewish law, and received all the privileges of a born Jew. . . . The latter had a much looser, yet none the less vital attachment to the Jewish community. They were not circumcised, and probably not baptized, neither were they bound by the ceremonial observances of the law, but they worshipped regularly in the synagogue, and were bound by the moral precepts of the law which the Jews regarded as binding on all mankind. In the Acts of the Apostles these people are referred to as "devout men" or those that "fear God."[3]

> **Acts 10:3–8** One day at about three in the afternoon he had a vision. He distinctly saw an angel of God, who came to him and said, "Cornelius!"
>
> Cornelius stared at him in fear. "What is it, Lord?" he asked.
>
> The angel answered, "Your prayers and gifts to the poor have come up as a memorial offering before God. Now send men to Joppa to bring back a man named Simon who is called Peter. He is staying with Simon the tanner, whose house is by the sea."
>
> When the angel who spoke to him had gone, Cornelius called two of his servants and a devout soldier who was one of his attendants. He told them everything that had happened and sent them to Joppa.

Your Prayers Are Answered!

God did not wait for Jewish Christians to reach out to the Gentiles. (He might still be waiting!) Captain Cornelius was a **devout**, generous Gentile seeking God. An angel appeared to this noble Roman during observance of evening prayers. God had observed his devotion and generosity. The angel's terminology is straight out of the

devout: devoted to religious duties, sincere

☞ **GO TO:**

Joshua 4:7; Exodus 12:14; Luke 22:19; 1 Corinthians 11:24–25 (memorial)

Acts 3:1 (3 P.M.)

grace: *loving-kindness, mercy*

multiplicity: *a great number*

Jewish worship manual: Cornelius's prayers and gifts to the poor had *"come up"* to God like the aroma of a pleasing sacrifice. God accepted his devotion and generosity as a *"memorial offering"* (Leviticus 2:2), an act of gratitude for God's **grace**.

Captain Cornelius longed for God. As a pagan he was sick of the **multiplicity** of immoral and powerless pagan deities. "The answer to your spiritual hunger is nearby," the angel told him. (The angel might have added: "If the wind is blowing in from the sea, just follow your nose to the tanner's house!" Tanning hides is a smelly business.)

Cornelius wasted no time. Even though it was after 3 P.M., he dispatched three men to Joppa (about thirty-five miles away) with orders to bring back Peter (Acts 10:7–8).

> **Acts 10:9–13** About noon the following day as they were on their journey and approaching the city, Peter went up on the roof to pray. He became hungry and wanted something to eat, and while the meal was being prepared, he fell into a trance. He saw heaven opened and something like a large sheet being let down to earth by its four corners. It contained all kinds of four-footed animals, as well as reptiles of the earth and birds of the air. Then a voice told him, "Get up, Peter, kill and eat."

What's For Lunch?

☞ **GO TO:**

Psalm 55:17; Daniel 6:10 (prayer time)

Leviticus 11 (no-no list)

ekstasis: *"a displacement of the mind from its ordinary state and self-possession, an ecstacy, a trance"[4]*

unclean: *prohibited by Old Testament laws of ritual purity*

It was midday at Simon the Tanner's odoriferous cottage by the sea—prayer time, not mealtime. Jews ate two meals a day—a light meal in mid-morning and a more substantial meal in late afternoon. Peter was on the roof of the house, where he could catch the Mediterranean breezes. He was praying. He was hungry.

His rooftop experience is called ***ekstasis*** in Greek—in NIV English, "a trance" (Acts 10:10). As Peter saw the huge tablecloth being lowered from the sky and spread before him containing animals, reptiles, and birds—all on the Jewish no-no list of "**unclean**" creatures to be avoided—he was shocked!

Lunch was served! A voice told Peter to get up, kill something to eat, and dig in! (We might say, "Pig out!")

> **Acts 10:14–16** "Surely not, **Lord**!" Peter replied. "I have never eaten anything impure or unclean."
>
> The voice spoke to him a second time, "Do not call anything impure that God has made clean."
>
> This happened three times, and immediately the sheet was taken back to heaven.

Lord: *God the Father, Jesus, and the Holy Spirit are all addressed this way in Acts*

KEY POINT

The Lord speaks to people when they pray.

☞ **GO TO:**

Leviticus 11:43–44 (commitment to God)

Start The Revolution Without Me!

The sight before him and the instruction to *"kill and eat"* left Peter dumbfounded. As a moderately orthodox Jew he'd carefully observed the Jewish prohibitions against contact with anything impure—and what was "impure" was carefully spelled out in the Mosaic Law. These laws of ritual purity were so deeply ingrained in his psyche he was even willing to debate God!

Lawrence O. Richards: In the Old Testament community of faith, commitment to God was demonstrated by isolation from anything or anyone that was ritually unclean. Laws of ritual purity touched on every phase of a person's life—from conception and birth to clothing that might be worn, food that might be eaten, and treatment of the dead. The intent of these laws of separation was to constantly remind the Jewish people that they were set apart to God, and that they were to honor God in every aspect of their lives.[5]

What Others are Saying:

Dig Deeper

Clean and Unclean Animals[6] according to Leviticus 11

Category	Classification Principle	Examples
Land animals	If it has a split hoof *and* chews the cud it is clean. Animals with paws or that travel in any other way are unclean.	Camel, badger, pig, weasel, rat, lizards of all types are unclean. Cattle, goats, sheep, deer are clean.
Water creatures	If it has fins *and* scales it is clean.	Catfish, eels, shellfish are unclean.
Birds	Specific birds are restricted. Birds of prey and carrion eaters are unclean.	Eagles, vultures, hawks, ravens, owls, cormorant, osprey, storks, heron, hoopoe, bats are unclean.
Insects	Flying insects that walk, *except* those with jointed legs, are unclean.	Locusts, katydids, crickets, grasshoppers are clean.

JESUS CHRIST CEO

Christ's word is final on all matters of faith and practice. In Peter's case, the Spirit of Jesus made it clear that arbitrary Old Testament prohibitions had ended. The New Testament way of relating to God would not be by keeping rules, but by responding to the Spirit.

> **Acts 10:17–20** While Peter was wondering about the meaning of the vision, the men sent by Cornelius found out where Simon's house was and stopped at the gate. They called out, asking if Simon who was known as Peter was staying there.
>
> While Peter was still thinking about the vision, the Spirit said to him, "Simon, three men are looking for you. So get up and go downstairs. Do not hesitate to go with them, for I have sent them."

Pete And The Pagans

Peter had never "done lunch" like this before! He wrestled with the meaning of what he'd just experienced. As the disquieting smorgasbord faded from view, he heard foreign voices. They were at the tanner's front gate asking for Peter. At this point the voice in the vision became a personal, inner voice. The **voice of the Spirit** told him to go downstairs, meet the visitors, and not to hesitate to go with them. The Spirit added, *"I have sent them."*

☞ **GO TO:**

1 Kings 19:11–13; Isaiah 30:21 (voice)

What Others are Saying:

Mother Basilea Schlink: Every morning I ask [the Holy Spirit] for his leading and guidance. Then it is as if there were someone standing beside me and speaking to me, and yet I hear no voice. . . . What a gift! We can trust in the Holy Spirit and leave the guidance to him.[7]

voice of the Spirit: *inward conviction; sense of the right thing; silent, personal message from God perceived in back of one's mind*

> **Acts 10:21–22** Peter went down and said to the men, "I'm the one you're looking for. Why have you come?"
>
> The men replied, "We have come from Cornelius the centurion. He is a righteous and God-fearing man, who is respected by all the Jewish people. A holy angel told him to have you come to his house so that he could hear what you have to say."

Breakthrough!

All his life Peter had been taught to see Gentiles as impure. He would not enter a Gentile's house for fear of touching something "unclean." Contact with anything unclean required a process of ritual cleansing before one could participate in worship. Israel must be a "separated" people, **consecrated** to God.

But it was time for change. The old rules of separation must be scrapped if the Jesus movement was to take the next step toward

consecrated: *set apart for a holy purpose*

world conquest: witness *"to the ends of the earth"* (Acts 1:8). If not, the Jesus revolution would end before it had scarcely begun because it would be forever trapped behind the growth-stifling walls of Judaism. For the good news of salvation through Jesus Christ to be offered to "whoever" (John 3:16; Acts 2:21), the barriers between Jews and Gentiles had to come down.

Eating With The Enemy

Specifically the voice in the vision told Peter to *eat* what is unclean. That very day and in the days following he would find himself *eating* with "unclean" Gentiles (Acts 10:23; 11:2). But food wasn't really the issue, although scrapping the outdated food laws was necessary if Jewish and non-Jewish believers were to eat together. Acceptance and fellowship were the issues. Eating together is an act of fellowship and acceptance. It's why Christians often "break bread" (share meals and celebrate the Lord's Supper) together. But at issue in Peter's mind-altering vision was God's plan for the church to open its doors (and hearts) to believing Gentiles and accept them as part of Christ's body . . . without reservations.

☞ **GO TO:**

Acts 1:4; 2:42, 46 (eating together)

1 Corinthians 12:13 (part of Christ's body)

THE BIG PICTURE 🔍

> **Acts 10:23–33** Peter invited the men at the gate to be his overnight guests. The next day he and six Jewish Christian men from Joppa headed for Caesarea. The centurion had invited his Gentile relatives and friends to meet Peter. Peter told how God had dealt with him about his prejudice toward Gentiles and asked Cornelius why he'd sent for him. Cornelius told about the angel's visit.

The Bungie Jump Of Faith

Peter the brash was not one to let grass grow under his feet when it came to acting on orders from the Lord. Ignoring his personal discomfort and tossing aside the risk of censure by fellow Jews, he went down to meet the men from Caesarea. The light began to dawn: "Unclean" animals in the vision were metaphors for *people* he had been seeing as "unclean." Peter's actions and words show in four ways that he got the message and broke through to a new way of seeing people:

1. Peter welcomed as guests the Gentile messengers who stood at the gate not expecting to be invited into a Jewish

kosher: *suitable for Jews to eat*

home (Acts 10:23). It was an easy first step. It didn't involve eating anything that wasn't **kosher**.

2. Peter returned with Cornelius's men—no questions asked (Acts 10:23, 29). Anticipating the need for witnesses to stand with him when the inevitable storm of criticism struck, he took along six Christian brothers from Joppa (Acts 11:12).

3. When Peter arrived Captain Cornelius met him at the door, wondering if he would cross the threshold into a Gentile's house. Peter walked right in (Acts 10:25, 27).

4. The house was full of people—*Gentile* people—Cornelius's friends and relatives. Peter told them about his change of mind: *"You are well aware that it is against our law for a Jew to associate with a Gentile or to visit him. But God has shown me that I should not call any man impure or unclean. So when I was sent for, I came without raising any objection"* (Acts 10:28–29).

What Others are Saying:

Ajith Fernando: Making changes is often difficult. . . . Peter's willingness to change was fueled by his being willing to do things he was uncomfortable with, such as living in the home of a tanner. . . . Some great Christian advances are made not in the strategy sessions of our air-conditioned boardrooms but in the difficult and uncomfortable situations to which love for people takes us.[8]

THE BIG PICTURE

Acts 10:34–43 Peter talked to the Gentiles at Cornelius's house about Jesus, his anointing with the Holy Spirit, his goodness and healing, how God was with him, his death on the cross and resurrection from the dead, and how trusting him brings forgiveness.

GO TO:

Acts 10:1–8 (angel's visit)

Gentile God-Fearers Gain The Gospel

When Cornelius told about the angel's visit and his instructions to send for Peter (Acts 10:30–32), Peter responded with a declaration of the Gospel's inclusiveness: *"I now realize how true it is that God does not show favoritism but accepts men from every nation who fear him and do what is right"* (Acts 10:34–35).

Like Cornelius, the friends and relatives gathered to hear Peter were "God-fearers" (Acts 10:2, 35)—Gentiles who, though not converts to Judaism, prayed to Israel's God, and gave money to the synagogue and the poor. They were not in the dark about Jesus—they'd heard the Christian message (Acts 10:36–38). They only needed to be reminded of the facts and told the good news was for *them*.

Peter's talk clues us in to the things early Christians' shared when they witnessed to non-Jewish people:

- Jesus is Lord of *all* people, sent by God to bring the good news of peace with God (Acts 10:34–36).
- Jesus was empowered by the Holy Spirit to do good, heal, and free people from the devil's bondage (Acts 10:37).
- Jesus was crucified (Acts 10:39).
- God raised him from the dead; many saw him alive (Acts 10:40–41).
- Christians are witnesses to the reality of his resurrection life (Acts 10:41).
- God has appointed Jesus to judge *all* the world's people (Acts 10:42).
- *Everyone* who believes in Jesus receives forgiveness through **his name** (Acts 10:43).

his name: *Jesus' person, who he is and what he did*

> **Acts 10:44–48** While Peter was still speaking these words, the Holy Spirit came on all who heard the message. The circumcised believers who had come with Peter were astonished that the gift of the Holy Spirit had been poured out even on the Gentiles. For they heard them speaking in tongues and praising God.
>
> Then Peter said, "Can anyone keep these people from being baptized with water? They have received the Holy Spirit just as we have." So he ordered that they be baptized in the name of Jesus Christ. Then they asked Peter to stay with them for a few days.

Pardon The Glorious Interruption!

The crowd of God-fearers was ready to take the plunge. Before Peter could end his sermon his listeners were *all* <u>filled</u> with the Holy Spirit and spoke in <u>new languages</u>! Turning to the Jewish Christians who'd come with him, Peter asked if there were any <u>objections</u> to these Gentiles being baptized as Christians. No objection was heard, and all were baptized, declaring their faith in Jesus (Acts 10:44–48).

☞ **GO TO:**

Acts 2:4; Ephesians 5:18 (filled)

Acts 2:4; 19:6; 1 Corinthians 12–14 (new languages)

Acts 8:36; 11:17 (objections)

Peter and his Jewish compadres stayed a few more days to teach and help establish the new church at Cornelius's house in Caesarea.

The barriers of culture and race began to crumble. The door to the Gentiles was flung open. It was just the beginning of God's strategy for broadcasting the Gospel. Within a few decades, what began at Cornelius's house expanded to encompass the entire Roman world. Paul, soon to be known as "the apostle to the Gentiles," expressed the principle involved: *"There is neither Jew nor Greek, slave nor free, male nor female, for you are all one in Christ Jesus"* (Galatians 3:28).

What Others are Saying:

F. F. Bruce: The descent of the Spirit on those Gentiles was outwardly manifested in much the same way as it had been when the original disciples received the Spirit at Pentecost: they spoke with tongues and proclaimed the mighty works of God (see Acts 2:4, 11). Apart from such external manifestations, none of the Jewish believers present . . . would have been so ready to accept the reality of the spirit's coming on them. . . . As in Peter's vision the voice of God overruled food restrictions . . . so now the act of God in sending the Spirit overruled the sacred tradition which forbade association with Gentiles.[9]

> **Acts 11:1–3** The apostles and the brothers throughout Judea heard that the Gentiles also had received the word of God. So when Peter went up to Jerusalem, the circumcised believers criticized him and said, "You went into the house of uncircumcised men and ate with them."

Backlash! Pete On The Carpet

Peter's extended time with Cornelius's family and friends at Caesarea did two things. First, it gave time for news of what Peter had done to reach Jerusalem and be discussed over the back fence and down at the fish market before he returned from his trip to the country. Second, the fact that he spent several days living and (especially) *eating* with Gentiles intensified the anxiety and ire of concerned Jewish Christians in Jerusalem.

What Others are Saying:

Ajith Fernando: Not only had their leader baptized Gentiles, he was also having continuous table fellowship with them. The table fellowship, which is what Peter's critics objected to (Acts 11:3), indicated in a powerful way that Cornelius and company were indeed accepted into the Christian community.[10]

The Purists: Loaded For Bear!

The whole church heard the gossip (Acts 11:1). Most disturbed was a group called "the circumcised believers." Actually, all Jewish males were circumcised, but this phrase designated a group of Christian Jews who were especially concerned that Gentiles should submit to the rite of circumcision (in other words, become Jews) before being fully accepted into the church. Today's English Version calls them "those who were in favor of circumcising Gentiles."[11]

Of course, these folks had seen no vision nor heard the Lord's voice sweeping away the old prohibitions. They'd not been there when the Spirit came to the Gentiles. The very idea of Peter going in to ceremonially unclean homes and eating nonkosher food with ceremonially unclean people made the hair stand up on the back of their sanctified necks!

THE BIG PICTURE

> **Acts 11:4–17** Peter told about his rooftop vision, the trip to Caesarea, the conversation with Cornelius, and the coming of the Holy Spirit on the Gentiles just as the Spirit had come on the disciples at Pentecost.

"The Spirit Made Me Do It!"

Peter simply reported what had happened. The six brothers from Joppa were there to back up his story (Acts 11:12). Having had a little time since the Cornelius incident to reflect on it, Peter also shared his interpretation:

1. The episode at Caesarea was a fulfillment of Jesus' promise to baptize believers with the Holy Spirit (Acts 1:5; 11:16).

2. God's acceptance of the Gentiles was verified by the exact same gift he'd given the 120 on the day of Pentecost—the gift of his Spirit (Acts 2:38–39; 11:17).

3. Besides—"What do you want me to do? Pick a fight with God?" (Acts 11:17). Peter tried that on the roof of the tanner's scented seaside domicile. God had the last word then. Peter wasn't about to try to talk him out of it now.

> **Acts 11:18** When they heard this, they had no further objections and praised God, saying, "So then, God has granted even the Gentiles repentance unto life."

The Miracle Of Acceptance

Considering they had all grown up indoctrinated in prejudice, the ease with which the other disciples accepted Peter's conclusions was nothing short of miraculous! No sullen grumbling, muttering under their breath, or opposition. They praised God!

Something to Ponder

As believers in the twenty-first century, we are also called to a radical acceptance of others. The world sees and judges people on the basis of race, background, occupation, age, and appearance. But we are to see others as fellow believers or as people who need the Lord. It is not easy learning to accept others; the early Christians are proof of that. But it is one of the changes followers of Jesus Christ are called to make. With whom do you associate that no minister would normally contact?

What Others are Saying:

Ajith Fernando: For the moment the circumcision party is silenced. They will emerge again in chapter 15 when they see what large numbers of Gentiles have come into the church. Not everyone has undergone the permanent change of conviction that Peter has. They join in praise now, but as they see the wider implications of this step, they will rise up again in protest.[12]

JESUS CHRIST CEO

Gentiles have always been included in the Lord's plan to restore people to fellowship with God. When the time was right, he cut through the barriers of human prejudice, reluctance, and fear and drew them to himself. It was so clearly an act of God that even the mouths of the detractors were shut for a while.

> **Acts 11:19** Now those who had been scattered by the persecution in connection with Stephen traveled as far as Phoenicia, Cyprus and Antioch, telling the message only to Jews.

Fugitives On Mission

The persecution following Stephen's martyrdom had sent Jesus' followers scurrying to the hills (Acts 8:1). As they fled they shared the good news all over Judea and Samaria (Acts 8–10). Even so the faith of Christ spread no farther than a 100-mile radius of Jerusalem. But some fugitives kept going—to places like Phoenicia (150 miles), Cyprus (250 miles) and Antioch (300 miles) (Acts 11:19). Those who escaped beyond the 100-mile limit were mostly Greek-speaking Jews. Raised outside the **Holy Land** (Acts 11:20), they were at home in foreign places.

Holy Land: *Israel*

> **Acts 11:20** Some of them, however, men from Cyprus and Cyrene, went to Antioch and began to speak to Greeks also, telling them the good news about the Lord Jesus.

The Queen Of The East

A few persecution-escapees stopped when they reached the free Roman city of Antioch on the Orontes, third largest city in the Roman Empire, with a population of 500,000. Antioch was one of the most beautiful cities in the empire, often called "Antioch the Beautiful" or "Queen of the East." Its balmy air was fragrant with the scent of roses from which rare Antiochene perfumes were made.

It was a cosmopolitan town. From all over the empire people moved there to share the prosperity. Among the migrants were many Jews. Jews were well treated in Antioch. The synagogue there was considered the second most beautiful on earth. Gentile converts to Judaism and "God-fearers" were numerous.

Antioch was a pagan city filled with temples. At the foot of Mount Silpius, south of the city, was a huge rock formation that looked like a faceless human head. Pagan mythology said this was the head of Charon, the god in charge of transporting dead souls to the underworld. Nearby was the Grove of Daphne, worship center for Apollo, Artemis, Astarte, and other gods. Worship at the grove featured ritual prostitution. "The morals of Daphne" was a worldwide expression for sexual immorality.

Luke's Hometown?

Early Christian writers (**Eusebius** and **Jerome**) state that Luke, author of Acts, was a native of Antioch. He may have been one of the Greeks who came to Christ during the spiritual awakening of Acts 11. From this point, much of what is reported is based on the author's eyewitness accounts.

Eusebius: *early church historian*

Jerome: *early church theologian*

> **Acts 11:21** The Lord's hand was with them, and a great number of people believed and turned to the Lord.

Revolutionizing The Revolution

Everywhere the fugitives went they preached Christ . . . to Jews. But when they got to Antioch, a metropolis oozing with spiritual hunger and open to new ideas, a few—some from the Island of Cyprus and some from Cyrene, North Africa (Acts 11:20)—began to talk about Jesus to **Greeks** too. Luke's terminology indicates they made a noteworthy adjustment in their approach: Instead of talking about Jesus as *Messiah*, a Jewish term non-Jews would not relate to, these smart witnesses emphasized the good news about the **Lord** Jesus (Acts 11:20). "Lord" was a familiar term in the religious culture of Antioch. Many searched in various cults for a "lord" and "savior" who could guarantee salvation and life after death.

Greeks turned to the Lord in great numbers! This was revolutionary. Unnerving. Jewish witnesses soon found themselves surrounded by "pagan believers."[13]

Greeks: *Gentiles, not just people from Greece, but anyone influenced by Greek culture*

Lord: *title emphasizing Jesus' deity and authority*

☞ **GO TO:**

John 20:28; Philippians 2:6–11; Ephesians 1:21–23; 1 Peter 3:22 (Lord)

> **Acts 11:22–23** News of this reached the ears of the church at Jerusalem, and they sent Barnabas to Antioch. When he arrived and saw the evidence of the grace of God, he was glad and encouraged them all to remain true to the Lord with all their hearts.

Send In Barney

By this time the leaders of the church at Jerusalem should have been accustomed to the relentless efforts of the Holy Spirit to widen the circle of the church. With each leap of the faith <u>outside</u> the comfortable confines of Jewish orthodoxy, they had <u>carefully checked</u> to verify that what was happening was the work of God. This time they sent Barnabas—on his first apostolic assignment. Barney was the right man for the job.

☞ **GO TO:**

Acts 8 and 10 (outside)

Acts 8:14–17; 11:1–18 (carefully checked)

> **Acts 11:24–26a** He was a good man, full of the Holy Spirit and faith, and a great number of people were brought to the Lord.
>
> Then Barnabas went to Tarsus to look for Saul, and when he found him, he brought him to Antioch. So for a whole year Barnabas and Saul met with the church and taught great numbers of people.

All-Around Great Guy

Barnabas had a nickname based on his spiritual giftedness: Son of Encouragement. He lived up to his name (see Acts 4:36; 9:27; 11:23). A Cypriot Jew, he was born on an island 150 miles west of Antioch (see Acts 4:36). His native language was Greek. Barney was a Levite (see Acts 4:36), the clan from which priests were chosen, hence he was well trained in the Scriptures. If anyone was "sold out" for Jesus Christ, it was this man (see Acts 4:36–37). He had experienced the daily life of the original community of believers (see Acts 2:41–47; 4:32–35; 9:26–27). An apostle (see Acts 14:14) and a good man (see Acts 11:24), he lived by faith, under the Holy Spirit's influence (see Acts 11:24).

Barnabas accomplished four things in Antioch: (1) He affirmed God was at work (Acts 11:23); (2) he participated in successful **evangelism** (Acts 11:24); (3) he linked up with Saul (Paul) to create an effective spiritual leadership team (Acts 11:25–26); and (4) he and Saul successfully **discipled** the new converts for a year (Acts 11:26).

evangelism: *introducing new people to Christ*

discipled: *trained, helped grow in knowledge of Christ and spiritual maturity*

That Wild And Crazy Church

Jewish followers of Christ had their churches in Jerusalem, Judea, and Galilee. Believing Samaritans had theirs. Since Peter's visit, a church of Gentile God-fearers was meeting at Cornelius's house in Caesarea. But not until Antioch was there a church where believing Jews steeped in the law met regularly with Gentile believers who'd grown up entirely outside the influence of Judaism. These former pagans knew nothing of the strict moral and social discipline of the Ten Commandments.

The spiritual explosion going on among Antiochene Gentiles happened so fast the Jewish believers quickly gave up making an issue of circumcision, purification ceremonies, and other traditional observances. The Antioch church's meetings were probably roughly modeled after synagogue meetings, but the flood of untutored Gentiles made a shocking difference. Manners, clothing styles, and hair lengths, so important to Jews, had to be overlooked for the sake of fellowship around Christ.

Most shocking of all to Jewish sensibilities was the sharing of meals with the Gentile believers. Christians <u>ate together</u>. In Antioch, Jews and Gentiles shared meals in ways strict Jews considered uncouth and irreverent. By choosing to build fellowship on the simple basis of mutual faith in the Lord Jesus, the Jewish pioneers in Antioch blazed a trail for the acceptance of Gentiles by the whole church.

☞ **GO TO:**

Acts 2:42, 46; Galatians 2:11–13
(ate together)

Gene Edwards: [The Gentile believers at Antioch] were so rowdy and noisy! "Reverence" was not part of their experience. They were completely uninhibited. As they ate (no Jew could ever overlook this), they did so with dirty hands. No Jewish prayer. . . . Just eating and rejoicing in the Lord. Their clothes were not like Jewish clothing. Nor did they seem as clean. . . . The length of their hair, by Jewish standards, was an abomination. And, to top it off . . . [none of them] had ever been circumcised![14]

> **Acts 11:26b** The disciples were called Christians first at Antioch.

The First "Christians"

It may be significant that the watching world first recognized disciples of Jesus as "Christians" after the walls of separation fell, and Jews and Gentiles were observed living together in harmony in the same community of faith. "Christians" is not the name Jesus' followers usually chose for themselves. Only two other verses in the New Testament use that term (Acts 26:28; 1 Peter 4:16).

- They usually call themselves "brothers" (Acts 1:16), "believers" (Acts 4:32), "disciples" (Acts 6:7), "saints" (Acts 9:32), or "followers of the Way" (Acts 22:4).
- Their Jewish enemies derided them as "Galileans" (Acts 2:7), "Nazarenes" (Acts 24:5), or "this sect" (Acts 28:22).

"Christians" may have been a nickname of ridicule—as "Puritan," "Quaker," or "Methodist" first were. But hiding in the nickname was a spark of respect. The Greek word is *Christianous*, which can mean "members of Christ's party," "belonging to Christ," "Christ-people," or "little Christs."

The Grace-People

heterogeneous: mixed

When Barnabas arrived to check out the spiritual revolution in Antioch, he saw in this **heterogeneous** group *"evidence of the grace of God"* (Acts 11:23). "Grace" is a Bible word for "God's free and spontaneous action taken to meet human need, especially in providing salvation."[15] Attitudes and actions of the Antioch disciples were visible proof of God's grace:

- They were willing to cross racial, cultural, and social barriers to share Jesus with others (Acts 11:20). This was hugely successful (Acts 11:21, 24).

- They displayed a refreshing spirit of unity as diverse people from diverse cultures (Jews and Gentiles) **accommodated** one another in order to be together.
- They were eager to learn and willing to actively pursue spiritual growth (Acts 11:26).
- They responded generously to needs of their fellow Christians when they heard about them (Acts 11:28–30).

Something to Ponder

accommodated:
adjusted, accepted diversity

You could get a picture of "grace" by looking at the way Antioch believers were together. Acceptance, harmony, gratitude, teachableness, enthusiasm, willingness to risk, accommodation, fellowship, joy, caring, generosity—do you suppose these might be reasons their neighbors called them "*Christians*"? Do others think of you as a Christian? If so, what do you think convinces them?

What Others are Saying:

Maude De Joseph West: It was the pagans who gave the adherents of the new religion the title which set them apart from Jews. *The disciples were called Christians first at Antioch.* A title of pious respect and regard? Hardly! An epithet hurled at a group of wild-eyed fanatics? Possibly. A distinct term, matter-of-factly distinguishing the strange new sect from proselytes of the Jewish religion? Quite likely. In any event, it is the name which Christ's followers have worn from that day onward, sometimes to his glory and sometimes, alas, to his embarrassment.[16]

> **Acts 11:27–30** During this time some prophets came down from Jerusalem to Antioch. One of them, named Agabus, stood up and through the Spirit predicted that a severe famine would spread over the entire Roman world. (This happened during the reign of Claudius.) The disciples, each according to his ability, decided to provide help for the brothers living in Judea. This they did, sending their gift to the elders by Barnabas and Saul.

Three You'll Hear From Again

Keep the names of three people in mind: Barnabas, Saul, and Agabus. Barnabas and Saul (Acts 11:25–26) spent a year at Antioch. Then they were sent out as an apostolic team to plant churches in other Gentile cities (Acts 13:3). Agabus (Acts 11:27–28) was a

☞ GO TO:

Acts 15:32; 19:6;
Romans 12:6;
1 Corinthians 14:3,
29–39 (prophet)

prophet: speaker for God, preacher, exhorts believers, sometimes foretells the future

traveling **prophet** who predicted *"severe famine"* in the Roman Empire and a food shortage in Jerusalem. He appears again in Acts 21:10. A thirteen-year drought (A.D. 41–54) had already begun when Agabus prophesied in A.D. 44.

Study Questions

1. What did Peter see in his vision on the roof of the tanner's house? What did the voice tell him to do? When he protested, what did the voice say?
2. Name three of the five things Peter did to show he had gotten the message of the vision and changed his mind?
3. What revolutionary thing did Christian witnesses do in Antioch that was not usually done?
4. Identify three of the four things Barnabas accomplished in Antioch.
5. Identify three of the four visible proofs that may have caused Antiochenes to refer to disciples of Jesus as "Christians"?

CHAPTER WRAP-UP

- Cornelius, a God-fearing Gentile in Caesarea, was told by an angel to send for Peter. Peter, in Joppa, saw a vision that confronted his prejudice against Gentiles and prepared him to go to Cornelius. (Acts 10:1–20)

- When Peter arrived at Cornelius's house, he shared the Gospel with a group of Gentiles who, while listening, believed on Jesus and were filled with the Spirit. (Acts 10:21–48)

- Peter was called on the carpet by Jewish Christians to explain his interaction with Gentiles and eating nonkosher food. When they heard the facts and how the Holy Spirit had come on the Gentiles, they praised God. (Acts 11:1–18)

- Some Christians who escaped Saul's persecution ended up in Antioch, where they began sharing Jesus with Greeks. Many Antiochenes turned to the Lord. Barnabas was sent from Jerusalem to check it out. (Acts 11:18–21)

- Barnabas saw God's grace at work in the mixed fellowship of Jewish and Gentile believers. He got Saul to join him, and for a year they discipled a throng of newly converted Antiochenes. (Acts 11:22–30)

ACTS 12: KING OF HOT AIR AND MAGGOTS

Let's Get Started

Jesus didn't sugarcoat anything. He never hid the fact that people who linked up with him would suffer the same rejection and persecution he did . . . which finally got him killed. Jesus said, *"If the world hates you, keep in mind that it hated me first. . . . If they persecuted me, they will persecute you also. . . . All this I have told you so that you will not go astray (when it happens). . . . A time is coming when anyone who kills you will think he is doing a service to God. They will do such things because they have not known the Father or me. I have told you this, so that when the time comes you will remember that I warned you"* (John 15:18, 20; 16:1–4).

Secular authorities mostly ignored the Jesus movement as just another Jewish internal squabble, and of no concern to the Roman occupation government—the *real* government. Ridiculing disciples in Antioch as "Christians" (Acts 11:26) was the church's worst trouble from the secular world.

Secular government's hands-off policy ended with events reported in Acts 12. Religious and civil authorities began to combine their efforts to stop the Jesus movement. The first foray of government into the anti-Christian cause was also short-lived. It did some damage. But in the long run its greatest accomplishment was to affirm the principle that though believers suffer and die in the battle for God's kingdom, the ultimate outcome is assured. Victories are won through the prayers of God's people. The proud and powerful anti-God-players are brought down. In the process God's truth captures more territory and captivates more minds and hearts.

> **Acts 12:1** It was about this time that King Herod arrested some who belonged to the church, intending to persecute them.

Here A Herod, There A Herod, Everywhere A Herod

This is the first mention in Acts of the New Testament's notorious succession of puppet rulers bearing the title "Herod." Here's the whole Herod **dynasty** in the order of their appearance in the New Testament (see also GWLC, page 40):

- Herod the Great—King of Judea from 37–4 B.C. Rebuilt the Temple. Slaughtered the babies of **Bethlehem** in an attempt to destroy the baby Messiah, Jesus.
- Herod Antipas—**Tetrarch** of Galilee and Perea, 4 B.C.–A.D. 39. Beheaded John the Baptist. Jesus stood trial before him on his way to crucifixion.
- Herod Archelaus—**Ethnarch** of Judea, Samaria, and Idumea, 4 B.C.–A.D. 6. So cruel, ineffective, and universally hated, the Romans replaced him with a governor.
- Herod Philip—Tetrarch of Iturea and Trachonitis, 4 B.C.–A.D. 34. Founder of Caesarea-Philippi, where Jesus spent some time.
- Herod Agrippa 1—King of Judea, A.D. 37–44. *"King Herod"* of Acts 12. Grandson of Herod the Great by his Jewish queen Mariamne.
- King Herod Agrippa 2—Son of Agrippa 1 (Acts 25–26).

Get Agrippa Yourself, Man!

Herod Agrippa 1 was a "puppet" king answerable to Rome. He was a savvy politician and realized the effectiveness of his reign depended on maintaining a good relationship with the Jewish leaders. The fact that his grandmother was a Jewess helped. Many Jews liked him because he kept the Jewish law and all the Jewish holy days. His attack against the church was pure politics.

> **Acts 12:2** He [Herod Agrippa 1] had James, the brother of John, put to death with the sword.

dynasty: succession of rulers from one family line

Bethlehem: Judean town where Jesus was born

Tetrarch: ruler of a minor province

Ethnarch: ruler of a country

☞ **GO TO:**

Matthew 2:1–20; Luke 1:5 (Herod the Great)

Matthew 14:1–11; Mark 6:14–29; Luke 3:1, 19; 13:31–33; 23:7–12; Acts 4:27 (Antipas)

Matthew 2:22 (Archelaus)

Luke 3:1 (Philip)

Political Correctness Turned Deadly

Earlier Christian leaders were held in such high esteem by the people it had been unwise to attack them directly (Acts 5:26). By Acts 12 public opinion (always fickle) had turned against them. Agrippa, reading the political winds, decided his popularity in the polls would get an upward kick with an attack against the church—especially targeting its high profile leaders. So he arrested several Christians, including the apostle James.

The recorded details of James's martyrdom are scant. He was hacked to death with the sword (beheaded), the first apostle martyred for his faith in Jesus. Several New Testament characters have the name James. This one is James, son of Zebedee, the brother of John. Jesus nicknamed him and his brother "Sons of Thunder." He was one of Jesus' inner circle of confidants. Jesus once predicted that James would drink the same cup of suffering and experience the same "baptism" as he. Thanks to Herod, he did.

☞ **GO TO:**

Mark 4:17
(Sons of Thunder)

Luke 9:28; 22:8
(inner circle)

Mark 10:39 (same cup)

What Others are Saying:

Samuel Rutherford: Through many afflictions we must enter into the kingdom of God. . . . It is folly to think to steal to heaven with a whole skin.[1]

Billy Graham: It is never easy to be a Christian. The Christian life can still bring its own loneliness, unpopularity, and problems. It is human nature to dislike, resent, or regard with suspicion anyone who is "different.". . . To suffer for the faith is not a penalty; it is a privilege. In doing so, we share in the very work and ministry of Christ. If we are united with Christ and his sufferings, we shall also be united with Christ in his resurrection.[2]

Persecution & Martyrdom—James was martyred with the sword. Another prominent New Testament character, Paul, would face the same fate in Rome. In modern times, Christians are killed for their faith in the same way. China is one such place. In 1934, John and Betty Stam of China Inland Mission were put to death with the sword by Chinese communists.[3] In 1966–1976, the Chinese Cultural Revolution forced religious activity underground, destroyed most Bibles, looted Christians' homes, and imprisoned or executed many Christians.[4]

> **Acts 12:3–4** When he saw that this pleased the Jews, he proceeded to seize Peter also. This happened during the Feast of Unleavened Bread. After arresting him, he put him in prison, handing him over to be guarded by four squads of four soldiers each. Herod intended to bring him out for public trial after the Passover.

Peter In The Pokey

religious establishment: Jewish leaders and supporters, not the people in general

Fortress Antonia: Roman "barracks" adjacent to the temple area

night watches: four watches of three hours each[5]

☞ **GO TO:**

Mark 14:2 (dim view)

Acts 21:31–22:29 (Fortress Antonia)

The **religious establishment** rejoiced to see James's head roll. A good politician knows the expediency of pleasing the special interests, so when what he did to James got good press, Agrippa decided to nab another apostle, Peter.

Agrippa decided not to terminate the Big Fisherman until *after* the twin festivals of Passover and Unleavened Bread. The festival schedule that year was carefully planned to go like this:

Thursday—Search and destroy all yeast (leaven).
Friday noon—Sacrifice Passover lambs at the Temple.
Friday after sundown—Eat Passover meal with family and guests.
Next seven days—Celebrate Israel's escape from Egypt. Eat only unleavened bread.
Day after the festival—Chop off Peter's head!

The Jews took a <u>dim view</u> of executions during this high holy season. One must operate by certain priorities, you understand: First, we must take a few days off to worship God. Then we can get back to killing Christians! So, in the spirit of the holidays, Peter "celebrated" in prison (probably at the Roman **Fortress Antonia**), guarded by four relays of four soldiers each—one squad for each of the **night watches**. This was unusually heavy security, reserved for the most dangerous felons. (Sarcasm intended.)

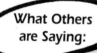

What Others are Saying:

William Barclay: The great tragedy of this particular wave of persecution was that it was not due to any man's principles, however misguided; it was due simply to Herod's bid to gain popular favor with the people.[6]

Persecution & Martyrdom—Between 1917–1953 in the Soviet Union, 88 percent of Russian Orthodox churches were closed and four hundred leaders of unregistered Baptist churches were in prison. Ten thousand Christians were sent to Siberian gulags or exiled, and a thousand Christians were prisoners in psychiatric wards. It is estimated that half the sixty million people killed during those years by the Communist government were Christians.[7]

> **Acts 12:5** So Peter was kept in prison, but the church was earnestly praying to God for him.

The Miracle Of Uncertain Praying

What were the Christians doing while Peter was "on holiday" in the slammer? They grabbed their most potent weapon—prayer—and aimed it at the powers-that-be. The original Greek word Luke uses to describe their praying indicates considerable energy was exerted; their praying was intense, fervent, and extended. They prayed all night (Acts 12:6, 12). They were <u>united</u>—"*the church was . . . praying.*" James had been killed. Unless God rescued him, Peter was next. It was time for serious prayer.

Theirs was, we shall soon discover, imperfect prayer. But it was enough to unleash the power of Almighty God.

Paul Billheimer: Heaven holds the key by which decisions governing earthly affairs are made but we hold the key by which those decisions are implemented. . . . Prayer is not overcoming the reluctance of God. It is not persuading him to do something he is unwilling to do. It is "binding on earth" that which already has been bound in heaven (Matthew 12:19). It is implementing his decision. It is enforcing his will upon earth.[8]

☞ **GO TO:**

Matthew 18:19–20 (united)

What Others are Saying:

> **Acts 12:6–11** The night before Herod was to bring him to trial, Peter was sleeping between two soldiers, bound with two chains, and sentries stood guard at the entrance. Suddenly an angel of the Lord appeared and a light shone in the cell. He struck Peter on the side and woke him up. "Quick, get up!" he said, and the chains fell off Peter's wrists.
>
> Then the angel said to him, "Put on your clothes and sandals." And Peter did so. "Wrap your cloak around you and follow me," the angel told him. Peter followed him out of the prison, but he had no idea that what the angel was doing was really happening; he thought he was seeing a vision. They passed the first and second guards and came to the iron gate leading to the city. It opened for them by itself, and they went through it. When they had walked the length of one street, suddenly the angel left him.
>
> Then Peter came to himself and said, "Now I know

without a doubt that the Lord sent his angel and rescued me from Herod's clutches and from everything the Jewish people were anticipating."

Dreamy Escape

Here's the picture. It's the night before Peter is to stand trial before King Herod; the church is up all night, praying, dreading the worst. The two guards to whom Peter is chained wrist-to-wrist are at attention. The two guards at the cell door are on high alert against any plot to "spring" the prisoner. Everybody—Christians, soldiers—is tense, vigilant, on the job.

Peter? It's the night before his almost certain death sentence. What's he doing? Ho-hum. He's taking a siesta—sawing logs! He's resting like a baby in its mother's arms! His conscience is clear. He's confident of God's sovereign control—whether it means <u>life or death</u>. He's in dreamland.

Suddenly the dream changes. Whack! Somebody slaps him on the side. He opens his eyes. His cell is full of light. Someone is there who isn't dressed like a Roman soldier. *"Quick, get up!"* the dream visitor says. Suddenly the chains fall off Peter's wrists, clattering to the cell floor. The guards are still at attention, looking straight ahead, chained to nobody, unaware their prisoner is loose. "Get dressed and put on your shoes," the bright intruder says. "Don't forget your coat (it's cold outside). Follow me."

Peter follows like an obedient puppy, past the two guards in the cell and the two at the entrance. Nobody notices. They come to the front gate of the fortress. It swings open. Out on the cobblestones they walk till the street dead ends. "Wow!" Peter thinks, "I'm having <u>another vision</u>!"

Suddenly he's alone. Reality hits him: He's awake, busted out of jail . . . and it's no dream! "God has rescued me!" he says.

☞ **GO TO:**

Philippians 1:20
(life or death)

Acts 10:9–16
(another vision)

KEY POINT

God controls circumstances and answers our prayers according to his purposes.

**What Others
are Saying:**

Charles Wesley:

Long my imprisoned spirit lay
    Fast bound in sin and nature's night;
Thine eye diffused a quick'ning ray,
    I woke; the dungeon flamed with light.
My chains fell off, my heart was free,
    I rose, went forth, and followed thee.[9]

> **Acts 12:12–17** When this had dawned on him, he went to the house of Mary the mother of John, also called **Mark**, where many people had gathered and were praying. Peter knocked at the outer entrance, and a servant girl named Rhoda came to answer the door. When she recognized Peter's voice, she was so overjoyed she ran back without opening it and exclaimed, "Peter is at the door!"
>
> "You're out of your mind," they told her. When she kept insisting that it was so, they said, "It must be his angel."
>
> But Peter kept on knocking, and when they opened the door and saw him, they were astonished. Peter motioned with his hand for them to be quiet and described how the Lord had brought him out of prison. "Tell James and the brothers about this," he said, and then he left for another place.

☞ **GO TO:**

Acts 13:5, 13; 15:37–
40; Colossians 4:10;
2 Timothy 4:11;
1 Peter 5:13 (Mark)

Mark: *author of the Gospel of Mark*

The Grinning Ghost At The Garden Gate

The first thing Peter had to do was let the Christians know of his escape. Next, he had to head for cover—Agrippa was sure to be after him. From the fortress he went directly to Mary's house where a group was praying through the night. Her home was the meeting place of one of Jerusalem's early **house churches** (see illustration, page 138).

Peter knocked on the entrance. Rhoda, a servant girl, part of the praying group, went to the gate. Peter identified himself. She recognized his voice, and in her excitement she left him standing in the street while she rushed back inside with the incredible news.

Not all the reactions show evidence of "mighty, <u>mountain-moving faith</u>."

Rhoda was overjoyed. But others said, "You're nuts!" (Too many sleepless nights of prayer, perhaps, had driven the sensitive young thing over the edge!) Another theory: *"It's his angel."* (Many believed a person's <u>guardian angel</u> could take on the appearance of the person under his care.)

When they stopped arguing about who or what was at the gate and opened it, they saw Peter and "went wild!"[10] He waved his hand to calm them down, "Shh! You'll wake the neighbors!" He stayed only long enough to ask them to report his escape to James (another James—brother of Jesus, now a leader among Jewish Christians). Then he disappeared into the night. He left Judea, possibly for Antioch or someplace in **Asia Minor** (Galatians 2:11; 1 Peter 1:1), beyond Herod's jurisdiction.

house churches: *Jerusalem church was divided into groups that met in homes*

☞ **GO TO:**

Matthew 17:20; 21:21
(mountain-moving faith)

Matthew 18:10
(guardian angel)

Asia Minor: *modern Turkey*

Typical House Church

Christians in Jerusalem gathered at homes of wealthy believers. Most homes had an inner courtyard, such as the one shown here, that could accommodate large groups. A gate, not shown, opened from the street onto the courtyard leading to the living quarters.

Remember This . . .

Even though their reactions to Peter's knock at the door reveal they weren't at all sure God was going to answer their prayers, the disciples prayed anyway. It was the right thing to do. It was the *only* thing to do! They prayed because they cared. They prayed because Jesus taught them to pray. They prayed because God uses prayer in his war against the powers of this world. And, even though their prayers were not perfect and their faith was shaky, God heard them.

What Others are Saying:

Watchman Nee: There are people today who claim to have greater faith than those gathered in Mary's house. They are certain God will send an angel, and every door in the prison will swing open before him. If a gust of wind blows: "There's Peter knocking at the door!" If the rain begins to patter: "There's Peter again!" These people are too credulous, too cock-sure. For even the most devoted Christian, while exercising a faith which must surely bring an answer from God, knows what it is to have lurking just around the corner the question whether perhaps he might be mistaken.[11]

EARLY CHURCH WOMEN—Two Christian women of different social rank play important roles in this incident: (1) Mary, Mark's mom, hosts and perhaps leads a church in her home and (2) Rhoda, a simple, believing servant girl recognizes that the answer to their prayers has arrived.

This story contains a mystery: Why should James be martyred while Peter escapes martyrdom? It's a question for which only the Lord has the answer. F. F. Bruce reminds us this scenario "has been repeated countless times in the history of the people of God."[12] By faith, says Hebrews, some *escaped the edge of the sword* (Hebrews 11:34); and by faith others *were put to death with the sword* (Hebrews 11:37). Go figure!

Something to Ponder

> **Acts 12:18–19** In the morning, there was no small commotion among the soldiers as to what had become of Peter. After Herod had a thorough search made for him and did not find him, he cross-examined the guards and ordered that they be executed.
> Then Herod went from Judea to Caesarea and stayed there a while.

King Of Hot Air And Maggots

Herod suspected Peter's jailbreak was an "inside job" and the guards had been bribed. Roman military law required punishment of guards who let a prisoner escape to match the punishment the prisoner would have received. In this case, the sentence was death (Acts 12:18–19). If all the guards watching Peter were held responsible, sixteen men were sacrificed on the altar of Herod's political ambitions that day!

Frustrated, Herod Agrippa retreated to the town founded by his grandfather. He was soon to discover there is no retreat from the justice of God. God was not finished answering his people's prayers.

> **Acts 12:20–21** He had been quarreling with the people of Tyre and Sidon; they now joined together and sought an audience with him. Having secured the support of Blastus, a trusted personal servant of the king, they asked for peace, because they depended on the king's country for their food supply. On the appointed day Herod, wearing his royal robes, sat on his throne and delivered a public address to the people.

All Dressed Up And No Place To Go!

The people of Tyre and Sidon on the Phoenician seacoast west of Galilee, depended on good relations with Herod to maintain the flow of food supplies from Galilee on which they had depended for a <u>thousand years</u>. Somehow they had offended Herod Agrippa. To keep from starving, they decided to seek peace. Perhaps with a well-placed bribe they secured the support of Blastus, one of Herod's advisers, who arranged a peace conference.

Agrippa knew how to strut his stuff!

☞ **GO TO:**

1 Kings 5:9–12
(thousand years)

What Others are Saying:

propitious: benevolent, favorably disposed

Flavius Josephus: [Agrippa] entered the theater at daybreak. There the silver, illuminated by the touch of the first rays of the sun, was wondrously radiant and by its glitter inspired fear and awe in those who gazed upon it. Straightway his flatterers raised their voices from various directions—though hardly for his good—addressing him as a god. "May you be **propitious** to us," they added, "and if we have hitherto feared you as a man, yet henceforth we agree that you are more than mortal in your being!"[13]

> **Acts 12:22–23** They shouted, "This is the voice of a god, not of a man!" Immediately, because Herod did not give praise to God, an angel of the Lord struck him down, and he was eaten by worms and died.

Dances With Worms

The citizens of Tyre and Sidon believed flattery will get you anything! In his arrogance, Agrippa accepted their cheers. His willingness to usurp God's place spelled his doom. Agrippa the "god" died from being *"eaten of worms"* (Acts 12:23). Possible medical diagnosis: intestinal round worms. Roundworms can grow to sixteen inches long, clog the intestines, and cause extreme pain, vomiting, and death (all of which makes James's beheading sound like a walk in the park!).

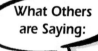

What Others are Saying:

Maude De Joseph West: [Agrippa] was seized with agonizing pains in his belly. His wondrous silver garment was nothing more than extra weight upon his outraged flesh as he was carried back to his palace. There, five days later, he died of the same loathesome disease which had claimed the life of his grandfather, Herod the Great. . . . Josephus describes in graphic and revolting detail the illness which killed Herod's grandfather. Oh, yes indeed, there were worms—lots of worms![14]

> **Acts 12:24–25** But the word of God continued to increase and spread.
>
> When Barnabas and Saul had finished their mission, they returned from Jerusalem [to Antioch], taking with them John, also called Mark.

Our God Is Marching On

With the demise of the great god-pretender, the Romans appointed a governor to rule Judea. All that was left was for Luke to contrast Agrippa's miserable end with the unstoppable progress of the Word of God.

 Persecution & Martyrdom—Herod Agrippa 1 was not the first nor would he be the last tyrant to try to stomp out Christian faith. Add to the list Nero, Diocletian, Hitler, Stalin, Mao, Idi Amin, and a thousand others who set themselves against the church. All are dead. The Gospel of Jesus lives on.

> God personally oversees the spread of his Word. When Christians are left at peace, their witness spreads and numbers grow. When they are martyred, their blood sprouts new believers anyway.

CHURCH GROWTH

Check out these lessons on prayer from the church at Mary's house.

- The *church* prayed together (Acts 12:5; also, Matthew 18:19).
- The prayer group was inclusive—rich and poor; men and women; servants, masters (Acts 12:12–13).
- They prayed *"earnestly,"* with intensity (Acts 12:5).
- They prayed over an extended time—eight days (Acts 12:2, 4–5).
- They prayed *"to God"* (Acts 12:5).
- They prayed all night (Acts 12:12).
- They prayed in spite of their doubts and were surprised when Peter escaped (Acts 12:15–16).
- With prayer, they used common sense. Not waiting to be rearrested, Peter left town (Acts 12:17).
- God did more than they prayed for. Herod's fraud was exposed and he died (Acts 12:23–24).

Dig Deeper

Something to Ponder

Worldly circumstances and forces can seem all-powerful. It is easy to forget God is at work in everything. How does this chapter help you put world leaders and events in perspective?

Study Questions

1. How was the apostle James martyred? What was different about this persecution?
2. What did the church do to get Peter out of prison? Where did they do this?
3. What happened as a result of what the believers did? What does this reveal about who holds the real power—secular authorities or the Lord of the church?
4. When Peter knocked at the door of Mary's house, who did members of the group think was really out there? What would you have said if you were there? What do these responses reveal about the prayers of the group?
5. What did Herod Agrippa do that showed him to be the fraud he was?

CHAPTER WRAP-UP

- King Herod arrested several Christians at Jerusalem and killed the apostle James. When he saw this pleased the religious leaders, he arrested Peter and placed him under heavy guard at Fortress Antonia. (Acts 12:1–4)

- While Peter was in jail awaiting certain execution, the people of the church gathered to pray for his release. The night before his trial and execution, an angel came into the prison, woke Peter up, and led him past the guards to freedom. (Acts 12:5–11)

- When he realized he hadn't dreamed the escape, Peter went to Mary's house where a group was praying. At first, they couldn't believe it was him. After welcoming him, he talked with them, and they sent him off to a safe place. (Acts 12:12–17)

- Herod met his deserved end after he allowed the Phoenicians to call him a god. After his death, the church experienced another spurt of growth. (Acts 12:18–25)

Part Three

GOD'S FIREBRANDS

REVEREND FUN

"This isn't what I had in mind when they asked if I enjoyed working on church boards."

ACTS 13–14: WORLD AMBASSADORS

CHAPTER HIGHLIGHTS

- Dream Team
- Dr. Know-It-All
- Take Your Sinuses to Antioch!
- Power and Poison
- Get Real!
- Watering Baby Plants

Let's Get Started

Meanwhile, back in Antioch, Cilicia, Jesus' followers continued to develop the faith-based community that was about to become the bridge over which the good news of Jesus could cross from the Holy Land to the rest of the world. Antioch's uniqueness was its disturbingly glorious mix of people from all sorts of religious, racial, and social roots drawn together around the risen Jesus without the hang-ups of Judaism's fellowship-inhibiting religious rules or society's class structure.

Give Antioch fellowship a blue ribbon! It was the *first place* Jews freely shared the good news with pagans (Acts 11:20). It was the *first place* large numbers of non-Jews believed and were welcomed into the church (Acts 11:23). It was the *first place* Jesus' disciples were called "Christians" (Acts 11:26). It was the *first church* to send humanitarian aid to hungry Jerusalem Christians (Acts 11:28–30). It was the *first church* to recognize the partnership of Barnabas and Saul (Acts 11:30), who had just returned from delivering the aid package (Acts 12:25).

Antioch's destiny as a launching pad for Christian ambassadors was about to become clear.

> **Acts 13:1** In the church at Antioch there were prophets and teachers: Barnabus, Simeon called Niger, Lucius of Cyrene, Manaen (who had been brought up with Herod the tetrarch) and Saul.

☞ **GO TO:**

Ephesians 4:11 (gifted)

Matthew 28:19–20 (disciple)

Ephesians 4:11–16 (equip converts)

shepherds: *pastors*

prophecy: *communication of God's message*

teaching: *explanation of the meaning and application of God's message*

disciple: *(verb) teach and train to live as followers of Christ*

Something to Ponder

Dream Team

A committed group of **shepherds** watched over development of the Antioch church. This team was spiritually <u>gifted</u> to provide two things needed to help people grow up in relationship to Jesus Christ: **prophecy** and **teaching**. The leadership team at Antioch included these men:

- Barnabas—"Son of encouragement," a good man, full of the Holy Spirit and faith (Acts 11:24).
- Simeon—Nickname: "Niger" (Latin for "dark-skinned" or "black"), probably an African.
- Lucius—A North African from Cyrene (modern Libya).
- Manaen—His name means "comforter," a man with aristocratic connections.
- Saul—A trained rabbi, former persecutor of Christians, brought to Antioch by Barnabas to help **<u>disciple</u>** and <u>equip converts</u> (Acts 11:25–26).

Antioch's spiritual leadership team was as racially and socially varied as the people they served. Many challenges that keep today's Christians apart were met and overcome in that ancient fellowship. This "wild and crazy," racially mixed church was the Holy Spirit's choice for a bridge over which to reach the world.

> **Acts 13:2–3** While they were worshiping the Lord and fasting, the Holy Spirit said, "Set apart for me Barnabas and Saul for the work to which I have called them." So after they had fasted and prayed, they placed their hands on them and sent them off.

"Your Mission, Should You Accept It . . ."

These prophets and teachers were doing two things together: (1) worshiping the Lord and (2) **fasting**. In this context they sensed the Holy Spirit was calling Barnabas and Saul to a wider mission and that the Antioch church should send them out with their support.

How did the Spirit communicate his desires? No self-destructing cassette tape outlined an "impossible" mission. No mysterious cat brought tomorrow's newspaper today. The word probably came through a gift of <u>prophetic insight</u>. The group reached a

fasting: *skipping meals to concentrate on spiritual things—mostly prayer*

☞ **GO TO:**

1 Corinthians 12:8, 10 (prophetic insight)

place of harmony when the five found themselves with a single persistent conviction. All (including Barnabas and Saul) agreed the Spirit was speaking.

What Others are Saying:

Oswald Chambers: The key to the missionary problem is not the key of common sense, nor the medical key, nor the key of civilization or education or even evangelization. The key is prayer. "Pray ye therefore the Lord of the harvest, that he will send forth workers into his harvest" (Matthew 9:38). Naturally, prayer is not practical, it is absurd . . . from the ordinary common-sense point of view.[1]

JESUS CHRIST CEO

From the Antioch experience we discover that the head of the church guides and communicates his will to his people best when they are (1) worshiping—expressing their love and respect for him; (2) setting aside their own wants and desires—fasting; (3) experiencing spiritual harmony—unity amid diversity—with each other; (4) listening for his voice; (5) responding as they understand what he wants them to do; and (6) willing to support each other in doing God's will.

> **Acts 13:4–5** The two of them, sent on their way by the Holy Spirit, went down to Seleucia and sailed from there to Cyprus. When they arrived at Salamis, they proclaimed the word of God in the Jewish synagogues. John was with them as their helper.

Boldly Go Where No One Has Gone Before

The Christians at Antioch surrounded Barnabas and Saul and John Mark, the young man who would go with them, touching them in a show of love and support, sending them on their way.

John Mark, the third member of the missionary team, was Barnabas's cousin (Colossians 4:10). John Mark was an eyewitness, unlike Barnabas and Saul, of Jesus' life and death. He was raised in a godly home. His mother's house was a gathering place for Christians in Jerusalem (Acts 12:12). Later, he authored the first "Life of Christ" ever published—the Gospel of Mark.

The church's sending act was significant for three reasons. First, Christ's ambassadors were sent out not as independents but connected to the sending church. Second, the laying on of hands symbolized the congregation's support. Third, the church's willingness to deny itself the ministry of two of its valued leaders in order to share the good news with strangers demonstrates a spirit of liberality.

Barney, Saul, and John Mark trekked the fifteen miles down the Orontes River to Seleucia, Antioch's seaport, and boarded a ship for the sixty-mile sail to the island of Cyprus, their first stop (see illustration below). For Saul, later called Paul, it was the first sixty miles of a ministry itinerary that would consume the rest of his life and take him a total of more than seventeen thousand miles—more than halfway around the world.[2]

Dig Deeper

Examine Acts 13 and 14 for the seven-point strategy this missionary group used for planting new churches.

1. Go where the Gospel has not been heard.

2. Concentrate on population, governmental, and commercial centers.

Paul's First Missionary Journey

The first missionary journey of Paul, formerly called Saul, began at Seleucia, near Antioch. Arrows show the route he took from there.

3. First, share the good news with Jews and God-fearers at the synagogue.

4. Stay a short time teaching new believers and establishing the church.

5. Move on, trusting new believers to the Holy Spirit and each other.

6. Revisit young churches to encourage believers and confirm leaders.

7. Return to home base (the sending church) and report.

> **Acts 13:5–8** When they arrived at Salamis, they proclaimed the word of God in the Jewish synagogues. John was with them as their helper.
>
> They traveled through the whole island until they came to Paphos. There they met a Jewish sorcerer and false prophet named Bar-Jesus, who was an attendant of the proconsul, Sergius Paulus. The proconsul, an intelligent man, sent for Barnabas and Saul because he wanted to hear the word of God. But Elymas the sorcerer (for that is what his name means) opposed them and tried to turn the proconsul from the faith.

Dr. Know-It-All

The island of Cyprus was a Roman province famous for copper mining and shipbuilding. The team landed at the Greek city of Salamis and preached in synagogues across the island. Acts 11:19 says that Christian fugitives escaped to Cyprus and told the story of Jesus. The team may have run into Barney's relatives—Cyprus was his home turf (Acts 4:36).

The last stop was the provincial capital, Paphos, a pagan city notorious for immorality connected with worship of the love-goddess, "the **Paphian**." When the **proconsul**, Sergius Paulus, got wind of what Barnabas and Saul were teaching, he wanted to hear more.

Their attempts to share the good news with him were opposed by Bar-Jesus Elymas, a Jewish <u>sorcerer</u>, who pulled every trick in the book to keep the proconsul from believing in Jesus. In that superstitious first-century culture it was common for government officials to employ sorcerers, fortune-tellers, and wizards as advisers. With his boss on the verge of becoming a Christian, Elymas

Paphian: Syrian version of the Greek god Aphrodite

proconsul: provincial governor, a judicial and military position

☞ **GO TO:**

Acts 8:9–13, 18–24 (sorcerer)

saw his source of income evaporating before his beady, greedy, lying, drug-glazed eyes!

> **Acts 13:9–12** Then Saul, who was also called Paul, filled with the Holy Spirit, looked straight at Elymas and said, "You are a child of the devil and an enemy of everything that is right! You are full of all kinds of deceit and trickery. Will you never stop perverting the right ways of the Lord? Now the hand of the Lord is against you. You are going to be blind, and for a time you will be unable to see the light of the sun."
>
> Immediately mist and darkness came over him, and he groped about, seeking someone to lead him by the hand. When the proconsul saw what had happened, he believed, for he was amazed at the teaching about the Lord.

Wizardry Hung Out To Dry

It was a critical moment for Sergius Paulus and Cyprus. The governor's spiritual restoration and that of many islanders hung in the balance. It was no time for tolerance. The Holy Spirit energized **Paul**. His eyes blazed with anger as he stared Elymas straight in the eye and, in the presence of the governor, confronted the anti-Christ wizard with a point-by-point exposé of his spiritual rottenness. What Paul said to the bogus "Jesus" of Paphos expresses fairly well the Bible's <u>evaluation of wizards</u>, witches, and practitioners of black and white magic, spiritualism, and the occult:

- You are no son or follower of Jesus—you're a son of the devil. (Wham!)
- You are "an enemy of everything right." (Pow!)
- "You are full of all kinds of deceit and trickery." (Socko!)
- You never stop making right seem wrong and wrong seem right. (Bam!)
- The Lord is against everything you stand for. (Splat!)

Here is your sentence from the Lord himself, Paul added, *"You are going to be blind, and . . . unable to see the light of the sun!"* Immediately Dr. Know-It-All[3] found himself groping in the dark, begging for somebody to take his hand and show him the way out. The blindness would be temporary.

As for Sergius Paulus, as the misty darkness fell on his "adviser," he believed in Jesus and stepped into God's sunlight.

Paul: Saul's Greek name

☞ **GO TO:**

Leviticus 19:26, 28, 31; 20:6; Deuteronomy 18:9–14; Isaiah 8:19–20; Malachi 3:5 (evaluation of wizards)

Venerable Bede: Remembering <u>his own case</u>, [Paul] knew that by the darkening of the eyes the mind's darkness might be restored to light.[4]

What Others are Saying:

Billy Graham: It is the Spirit-filled Christian who knows when to have "righteous indignation" and when to be patient, and who knows when long-suffering becomes an excuse for inaction or a crutch to hide a defect of character.[5]

☞ **GO TO:**

Acts 9:8–12
(his own case)

Alias, Paul

In Acts 13:9 the author sneaks the information about Saul's name change into the narrative without explanation. From then on, except when telling the story of his conversion, Saul is Paul. Saul is his Jewish name. His parents, members of the tribe of Benjamin (Philippians 3:5), named their son after Israel's first king, Saul, a Benjamite. Like many Jews, especially those living outside the Holy Land, they also gave him a Greek name. "Paul" (*Paulus*) is Greek for "little."

When working with Gentiles he used his Greek name. The first time it's noticed is when he shares the Gospel with his namesake, Governor Sergius *Paulus* of Cyprus.

☞ **GO TO:**

Acts 9:1–29
(radical change)

Walter Wangerin: To indicate the <u>radical change</u> within himself, [Saul] changed his name to Paul, and . . . began to tell the story—in Greek, to the Greeks.[6]

What Others are Saying:

> **Acts 13:13a** From Paphos, Paul and his companions sailed to Perga in **Pamphylia**, . . .

Pamphylia: Roman province on the south coast of Asia Minor (Turkey)

Paul Takes The Lead

Until the incident at Sergius Paulus's palace in Paphos, Barnabas had been the <u>leader</u> of the apostolic expedition; his name is listed first. After Cyprus, Barnabas and Paul were still the inseparable one-two Gospel punch, but Paul was named first, indicating a subtle change in team leadership. To his credit, Barnabas (Barney the encourager) was okay with this.

☞ **GO TO:**

Acts 11:25–26, 30;
12:25; 13:1–2, 7
(leader)

William Barclay: Without his name being mentioned this verse (Acts 13:13) pays the greatest of all tributes to Barnabas. . . . there is from him no word of complaint. He was a man prepared to take second place so long as God's work was done.[7]

What Others are Saying:

> **Acts 13:13b** . . . where John left them to return to Jerusalem.

Little John Goes Home To Mama

John Mark, the team's young helper (Acts 13:5), left the mission at Perga and returned to Jerusalem. We're not told why. Guesses include (1) the confrontation with Elymas shook him up; (2) he resented Paul replacing cousin Barnabas as team leader; (3) he had second thoughts about preaching to Gentiles; (4) he was homesick and needed his mommy; or (5) your guess is as good as mine!

> **Acts 13:14a** From Perga they went on to Pisidian Antioch.

Take Your Sinuses To Antioch!

☞ **GO TO:**

Galatians 4:13
(reference)

No preaching was done in Perga. A <u>reference</u> in his letter to the Galatians suggests Paul became sick in the coastal lowlands and headed to higher altitude to recuperate. After Mark sailed for Jerusalem, Paul and Barnabas climbed the rugged and dangerous trail across the Taurus Mountains to the city of Antioch, Pisidia, (see illustration, page 148) on a plateau 3,600 feet above sea level. Antioch was a common town name. Sixteen first-century towns had that name. This one was in Pisidia province. The team would return and preach in Pamphylia later (Acts 14:24–25).

> **Acts 13:14b–16** On the Sabbath they entered the synagogue and sat down. After the reading from the Law and the Prophets, the synagogue rulers sent word to them saying, "Brothers, if you have a message of encouragement for the people, please speak."
>
> Standing up, Paul motioned with his hand and said: "Men of Israel and you Gentiles who worship God, listen to me!"

☞ **GO TO:**

Matthew 13:54;
Luke 4:16
(pattern Jesus used)

1 Corinthians 9:19–23
(tailored his message)

Globe-Trotting Sermonizer Shakes Up Synagogue

In first-century synagogues, distinguished visitors were often asked to speak. For the apostle-ambassadors this represented a wide-open door to present the good news about the Messiah. It was a <u>pattern Jesus used</u>. Paul <u>tailored his message</u> to communicate to his Jewish audience.

Acts 13:17–41 Paul traced the history of God's involvement with Israel from the patriarchs to King David. David was special because he was willing to do whatever God wanted. Jesus, David's descendant, was sent by God to be Israel's Savior. John the Baptist announced him. The people and leaders at Jerusalem rejected Jesus, and Pilate executed him. Jesus rose from the dead, and many people saw him. His resurrection fulfilled Old Testament prophecies. People who believe in Jesus are forgiven and **justified** before God.

justified: declared righteous, acceptable to God

Synagogue Shocker: Judaism And Christianity Are One

In this message Paul does something very important. He shows how Judaism and Christianity are not different religions. Both are part of a single, wonderful, loving process by which God reveals himself to human beings and makes it possible for the estrangement caused by sin to be taken away so God and people can live together in peace.

Here's the gist of Paul's sermon in a few sound bites:

- Sound bite 1—Israel has always been the object of God's special care (Acts 13:17–19).

- Sound bite 2—God gave Israel Canaan as their homeland and great leaders—judges, kings—especially King David, *"a man after God's own heart"* (Acts 13:16–22).

- Sound bite 3—God promised to send David's descendant to rescue both Jewish children of Abraham and Gentile friends of God. He's here! He's *"the **Savior** Jesus"* (Acts 13:23–26).

- Sound bite 4—The people and their leaders in Jerusalem failed to recognize the Savior. He was crucified and buried, but God raised him from the dead. Everything <u>God promised</u> Israel is fulfilled in the resurrected Jesus (Acts 13:27–37).

- Sound bite 5—Here's what it comes down to: <u>Anyone</u> may be forgiven of his or her sins and justified (judged "not guilty" and "okay") before God through Jesus and what he accomplished. The Law of Moses could never do that! This leaves you with a choice: Trust Jesus, or play the cynic and refuse to believe (Acts 13:38–41).

☞ **GO TO:**

Psalm 2:7; Isaiah 55:3; Psalm 16:10; Acts 13:33–37 (God promised)

John 3:16; Acts 2:21; Romans 1:16 (anyone)

Savior: *Rescuer from sin's control and consequences; Redeemer*

☞ **GO TO:**

Acts 14:1–5; 17:1–5; 18:5–8; 19:8–10 (story hidden)

appointed: chosen by God

> **Acts 13:42–45** The people of the synagogue urged Paul and Barnabas to continue teaching the following Sabbath. Next Sabbath a large crowd gathered to hear about Jesus. Synagogue leaders were jealous and spoke abusively against Paul's teaching.

Next Sabbath's Special Guest: The Green-Eyed Monster

Many who listened to the apostles' message accepted God's offer of grace (forgiveness and justification—Acts 13:38–39). That's the often-unnoticed, success <u>story hidden</u> in the reports of negative responses in synagogue after synagogue. During the next week Paul and Barnabas spent many hours encouraging those who chose to follow Jesus as their Messiah to continue in their newfound freedom (Acts 13:42–43).

The word got around and the following Saturday *"almost the whole city gathered to hear the word of the Lord!"* (Acts 13:44).

When regular synagogue-goers arrived, they found strangers sitting in their pews! (I hate it when that happens!) Leaders and unbelieving rank-and-file Jews, consumed with jealousy, heckled Paul, making it impossible for him to speak.

> **Acts 13:46–49** Then Paul and Barnabas answered them boldly: "We had to speak the word of God to you first. Since you reject it and do not consider yourselves worthy of eternal life, we now turn to the Gentiles. For this is what the Lord has commanded us:
>
> 'I have made you a light for the Gentiles,
>   that you may bring salvation to the ends of the earth.'"
>
> When the Gentiles heard this, they were glad and honored the word of the Lord; and all who were **appointed** for eternal life believed.
>
> The word of the Lord spread through the whole region.

Casting Pearls Before Appreciative Pagans

Paul and Barnabas cited Isaiah's prophecy about how God expected the Jews to be a saving *"light to the Gentiles"* (Isaiah 49:6). They left the synagogue to focus on non-Jewish townspeople who were thrilled to hear the news of forgiveness and justification through Jesus.

The apostolic strategy was the same in every city: Take the good news of Messiah Jesus to the Jews *first*. God loves the Jewish people. He sent the Messiah to reveal his plan of salvation to them *first*. They were the ones to whom the ancient messianic promises and prophecies were given. They anticipated Christ's arrival. The invitation to receive Christ was offered to them before anyone else. Many—an estimated one-third of first-century Jews—believed and welcomed Jesus as Messiah. Tragically twice as many chose to turn him away. And often for such a tawdry substitute—jealousy! (Acts 13:45).

Something to Ponder

The early church grew rapidly when it gave up trying to convince hardhearted religious people and targeted the people who'd never heard of Jesus.

CHURCH GROWTH

What Others are Saying:

J. R. Dumelow: God desires the salvation of all men (1 Timothy 2:4; 4:10, etc.), but inasmuch as he foresees that some (in the expression of their free will) will actually repent and believe, while others will refuse to do so, he ordains the former to eternal life, and the latter to eternal death (Romans 8:28–30, etc.).[8]

> **Acts 13:50–52** But the Jews incited the God-fearing women of high standing and the leading men of the city. They stirred up persecution against Paul and Barnabas, and expelled them from their region. So they shook the dust from their feet in protest against them and went to Iconium. And the disciples were filled with joy and with the Holy Spirit.

"This Town Ain't Big Enough Fer The Two Of Us!"

As the green-eyed monster flexed its muscles and flapped its lying lips, unbelieving synagogue leaders convinced some leading women and the town fathers to join their attack against the apostles. When last seen, Paul and Barnabas were headed east-southeast, waving to a joyful bunch of new Christians who'd come to the city limits to see them off. As they passed a dour-faced collection of synagogue officials, "Tiny" (Paul) and Barney paused for a moment, pulled off their sandals, and, in a defiant gesture, **shook off the dust** of Antioch's streets in the faces of the religious high mucky-mucks.

☞ GO TO:

Luke 10:10–11 (shook off the dust)

shook off the dust: *traditional Jewish declaration of separation and warning of judgment*

Something to Ponder

messianic: belonging to the Messiah, Christ

The story of the Jewish reaction at Antioch, Pisidia is repeated again and again in Acts. Some believed in Jesus as Messiah; others refused. Believing Jews joined believing Gentiles to become part of the **messianic** movement sweeping the world. Unbelieving Jews went back to their traditions, but it was never the same. God had visited them, eternal life had been within their reach, but out of fear, jealousy, or blindness, they had said "No" to their destiny.

> **Acts 14:1–7** At Iconium Paul and Barnabas went as usual into the Jewish synagogue. There they spoke so effectively that a great number of Jews and Gentiles believed. But the Jews who refused to believe stirred up the Gentiles and poisoned their minds against the brothers. So Paul and Barnabas spent considerable time there, speaking boldly for the Lord, who confirmed the message of his grace by enabling them to do miraculous signs and wonders. The people of the city were divided; some sided with the Jews, others with the apostles. There was a plot afoot among the Gentiles and Jews, together with their leaders, to mistreat them and stone them. But they found out about it and fled to the Lycaonian cities of Lystra and Derbe and to the surrounding country, where they continued to preach the good news.

Power And Poison

Ninety miles east of Pisidian Antioch, on the east–west road from Syria to Ephesus was Iconium (modern Konya, Turkey). *"As usual"* the apostle-ambassadors began their work at the synagogue. Luke describes their preaching as *"the message of [God's] grace"*—the news that God loves people and has provided salvation as a free gift to those who put their faith in Jesus (Acts 14:3). Their witness was punctuated with healing miracles.

Real love is too much for some people to handle. They are more comfortable with hate. So *as usual* the good news led to division. Some believed. Some refused and poisoned the minds of others against the missionaries. An assassination plot developed. Paul and Barnabas managed to avoid the conspirators for a while, but the time came when getting out of town fast was the only sensible thing to do. On, to the twin cities of Lystra and Derbe!

☞ **GO TO:**

Ephesians 2:8–9
(free gift)

Persecution & Martyrdom—Verbal abuse and slander are favorite weapons of the enemies of Christ. First-century Christians were (falsely) accused of atheism, cannibalism, child-sacrifice, incest, worship of an ass's head and human sex organs, illegal assembly, arson, and hatred of the human race. During the 1950s in China, Christian leaders were routinely accused of hostility to Communist government policies, womanizing, counter-revolutionary activities, poisoning water supplies, and espionage, among other things. Many Chinese Christians were sentenced to long prison terms based on such charges.

> **Acts 14:8–13** In Lystra there sat a man crippled in his feet, who was lame from birth and had never walked. He listened to Paul as he was speaking. Paul looked directly at him, saw that he had faith to be healed and called out, "Stand up on your feet!" At that, the man jumped up and began to walk.
>
> When the crowd saw what Paul had done, they shouted in the **Lycaonian** language, "The gods have come down to us in human form!" Barnabas they called Zeus, and Paul they called Hermes because he was the chief speaker. The priest of Zeus, whose temple was just outside the city, brought bulls and wreaths to the city gates because he and the crowd wanted to offer sacrifices to them.

Lycaonian: the local language

Get Real!

Who could have anticipated such a devilish turn of events! Instead of giving glory to God for the healing of the believing lame man, the people's appreciation turned to idolatry—a complete misunderstanding of the truth—a lie!

In this case it was a lie based on fear (as most idolatry is). A local legend held that two of the gods, **Zeus** and **Hermes**, had once assumed human form and visited the town of Lystra. Only an old man and woman offered them hospitality. The two gods became angry and destroyed the town, wiping out the entire population, except for the old couple! The Lystrans were determined not to make the same mistake again. This led to the bizarre incident with Paul and Barnabas.

Religious fervor, powered by sheer terror, escalated out of control. Paul and Barnabas, not understanding the local language,

Zeus: Jupiter, father of gods and human beings

Hermes: Mercury, the messenger-god

did not realize at first what was happening. The priest of Zeus, whose job it was to keep the gods happy, brought bulls to sacrifice to the visiting "deities."

KEY POINT

A starting place for witness is to show people God's work in creation and his supply of human needs.

> **Acts 14:14–18** But when the apostles Barnabas and Paul heard of this, they tore their clothes and rushed out into the crowd, shouting: "Men, why are you doing this? We too are only men, human like you. We are bringing you good news, telling you to turn from these worthless things to the living God, who made heaven and earth and sea and everything in them. In the past, he let all nations go their own way. Yet he has not left himself without testimony: He has shown kindness by giving you rain from heaven and crops in their seasons; he provides you with plenty of food and fills your hearts with joy." Even with these words, they had difficulty keeping the crowd from sacrificing to them.

Mosh Pit Meeting

The apostles' drastic action barely managed to stop the sacrifices. They tore their clothes to rags and plunged into the crowd of would-be "worshipers" yelling, *"We too are only men, human like you!"* Half naked, they forced the people to touch and look and see that they were mere flesh.

Not only did Paul and Barnabas expose themselves as humans to a crowd determined to make them gods, but they dared call this "great honor" a *"worthless thing."* In fact, the entire pagan system of worship is a worthless thing from which people must turn to find the real God.

The real God is

☞ **GO TO:**

Acts 17:30; Romans 2:4; 2 Peter 3:9 (patient God)

Genesis 8:22; Psalm 4:7; Ecclesiastes 9:7; Isaiah 25:6; Acts 2:46 (crops and food)

Psalm 19:1–4; Acts 17:24–28; Romans 1:19–20 (testimony)

- the *living* God (Zeus and Hermes were lifeless figments of human imagination!),
- the Creator who made everything in heaven, earth, and sea,
- the patient God who *"let all nations go their own way,"* waiting for them to turn to him, and
- the kind God who provides rain and crops and food that bring joy to human hearts.

To people who pay attention, the created universe, rain, and food, are visible testimony in every generation to the existence, power, and goodness of God.

The authenticity of Christian leaders demands they <u>reject the exalted</u> positions people build for them. In Lystra there could be no mistake about the fact that, even though they were God's messengers, Paul and Barnabas were nonetheless ordinary humanity. Their vulnerability nearly cost Paul his life (Acts 14:19)!

Remember This . . .

Oswald Chambers: There is no room for . . . the crank or the fanatic in missionary work. A fanatic is one who has forgotten he is a human being. Our Lord never sent out cranks and fanatics, he sent out those who were loyal to his domination. He sent out ordinary men and women . . .[9]

What Others are Saying:

☞ **GO TO:**

Matthew 23:8–12 (reject the exalted)

> **Acts 14:19–20** Then some Jews came from Antioch and Iconium and won the crowd over. They stoned Paul and dragged him outside the city, thinking he was dead. But after the disciples had gathered around him, he got up and went back into the city. The next day he and Barnabas left for Derbe.

Down But Not Out

Embarrassed and feeling foolish, the Lystran crowd was an easy target for clever enemies of the Gospel who used the confusion to create a riot. The attack focused on Paul, since he was the main speaker. Stones flew. Paul went down. To hide what they had done from Roman authorities (who would strongly disapprove of such a riot), they dragged what they thought was Paul's dead body out of the city and dumped it. Christians—Barnabas, the healed lame man, and other believers—gathered around the <u>battered Paul</u>, who revived and went back into the city with them.

☞ **GO TO:**

2 Corinthians 11:25; Galatians 6:17 (battered Paul)

William Barclay: It was John Wesley's advice, "Always look a mob in the face." There could be no braver thing than Paul's going straight back amongst those who had tried to murder him. A deed like that would have more effect than a hundred sermons. Men were bound to ask themselves where a man got the courage to act in such a way.[10]

What Others are Saying:

> **Acts 14:21–25** They preached the good news in that city and won a large number of disciples. Then they returned to Lystra, Iconium and Antioch, strengthen-

---

ing the disciples and encouraging them to remain true to the faith. "We must go through many hardships to enter the kingdom of God," they said. Paul and Barnabas appointed elders for them in each church and, with prayer and fasting, committed them to the Lord, in whom they had put their trust. After going through Pisidia, they came into Pamphylia, and when they had preached the word in Perga, they went down to Attalia.

Watering Baby Plants

Next, the church planters headed for Derbe, sixty miles southeast on the border of Galatia. The good news had good success there. (It's amazing how much work you can get done when you're not dodging flying bricks!)

From Derbe they returned for a brief visit to each place where they had left a knot of believers, a baby church. In most places, their first visit had been cut short by the pressing necessity to "get outta Dodge" quickly to keep from being killed. On these return visits the apostles did four things:

1. They **strengthened** the disciples (Acts 14:22), instructing them further concerning the Christian way.

2. They encouraged them to remain true to the faith (Acts 14:22). The little flocks of believers in each place faced the same persecution and pressure as the apostles.

3. They appointed **elders** in each church (Acts 14:23). They helped believers in each place to recognize people the Holy Spirit had gifted for servant-leadership.

4. They committed them to the Lord (Acts 14:23). The most effective leaders and committed people cannot make church happen as it is intended. The church, like the Christian life, requires a walk of faith—a dependence on Christ to function as Savior and leader of his church, his body.

strengthened: literally, "confirmed the minds of"

elders: Greek: presbuteros—overseers, pastors, spiritually mature leaders

☞ **GO TO:**

1 Timothy 3; Titus 1; 1 Peter 5 (elders)

Ephesians 4:11 (Spirit had gifted)

Matthew 20:25–28 (servant-leadership)

Ephesians 5:23; Colossians 1:18 (leader)

What Others are Saying:

Ajith Fernando: The plural is always used in connection with the appointment of leaders. While it is true that one person must emerge as the key leader in a group, biblical leadership operates in the context of a team.[11]

> **Acts 14:26–28** From Attalia they sailed back to Antioch, where they had been committed to the grace of God for the work they had now completed. On arriving there, they gathered the church together and reported all that God had done through them and how he had opened the door of faith to the Gentiles. And they stayed there a long time with the disciples.

Full Circle

Back at "home base" in Antioch on the Orontes, the "sending church" waited and prayed for the return of their favorite sons. When Barnabas and Paul returned after two-plus years on the campaign trail, that whole wild and crazy, gung ho-for-Jesus group came together to hear the report of what God was doing among the Gentiles. Why shouldn't they? They had been there at every turn in the road in their hearts and prayers.

Paul Billheimer: The **Moravians** . . . carried on a chain of prayer day and night which continued uninterrupted for 100 years. This was the beginning of the modern missionary movement.[12]

What Others are Saying:

Moravians: *Protestant denomination arising in fifteenth-century Bohemia and Moravia*

Study Questions

1. Identify and describe two types of ministry the leaders at Antioch used to help people grow up in relationship to Jesus?
2. What two things did the prophets and teachers do when they got together as a team? What did the Spirit tell them to do?
3. Identify three of the five things Paul said to Elymas the sorcerer which express the Bible's evaluation of wizards, witches, and practitioners of magic, spiritualism, and the occult (Acts 13:9–11).
4. After the lame man's healing, who did the people of Lystra think the apostles were? What did Paul and Barnabas do to show they were human?
5. What "testimony" to his reality and kindness has God given to all people?

CHAPTER WRAP-UP

- A group of spiritually powerful prophets and teachers met, fasted, and prayed in Antioch. The Holy Spirit communicated his desire that Barnabas and Saul be sent out to take the message of Jesus into the Gentile world. (Acts 13:1–3)

- The team sailed to Cyprus, where they preached in the synagogues. At Paphos, the governor wanted to hear the Gospel, but a Jewish sorcerer kept him from it. In an outburst of power, Paul stopped the sorcerer and struck him blind. (Acts 13:4–12)

- From Cyprus the team traveled to Antioch, Pisidia. Paul showed how Christianity grew from Judaism's roots. When synagogue leaders opposed them, they shared Jesus with Gentiles. Many believed. When a persecution started, they left. (Acts 13:13–52)

- The apostolic team had an effective ministry in Iconium until a campaign of slander turned many against them and a plot developed to stone them to death. They found out about the plot and headed for Lystra and Derbe. (Acts 14:1–7)

- At Lystra, a lame man was healed. People thought Paul and Barnabas were gods. The apostles tore their clothes and dived into the crowd to show they were human, then told them to turn to the real God. Paul was stoned and left for dead. (Acts 14:8–20)

- After preaching at Derbe, the team revisited the towns where they'd preached. They confirmed the believers' faith, encouraged them, and appointed elders in each city. Then they returned to their home base in Antioch on the Orontes. (Acts 14:21–28)

ACTS 15: OUTSIDERS CRASH THE CHRISTIAN PARTY

Let's Get Started

To some early Christians it seemed the Gospel had leaped out of its corral and was galloping across the world landscape like a herd of mustangs—beyond control, free, and wild. Wonderful things were happening among non-Jewish people. Whoa, Nellie!

Strict Jews who believed in Jesus were happy when the first Gentiles found the Lord. But then they watched as changes took place that made them extremely uncomfortable. From childhood it had been drilled into them that circumcision was *the* symbol separating God's people from pagans. Naturally, they expected believing Gentiles to start acting like Jews!

This set up a showdown that led to another important turning point in early Christianity. The shoot-out at the Jerusalem Council lets us observe a fine example of creative conflict resolution.

> **Acts 15:1** Some men came down from Judea to Antioch and were teaching the brothers: "Unless you are circumcised, according to the custom taught by Moses, you cannot be saved."

Breaking Out Is Hard To Do

Gentiles would soon outnumber Jews in the church. No one in leadership seemed to be raising the all-important circumcision issue. Everyone danced around the subject of the sacred surgery. Paul and Barnabas's two-year mission brought a quadrillion more

---

non-Jews into the church without telling them they had to obey Jewish rules!

To some Hebrew Christians this was unacceptable. Two questions bugged them:

1. How can non-Jews be saved and considered the people of God if they don't observe the Law of Moses (Acts 15:1)?

2. How can Christians who keep the traditions of Judaism "break bread" with ceremonially unclean Gentiles who ignore Moses' rules about the "right" food and the "right" way to prepare it (see Acts 11:3) and who don't get circumcised?

Some concerned Jewish believers decided that if their leaders weren't going to deal with these issues they'd have to. They packed their bags and headed for Antioch to "enlighten" the Gentile believers there.

> **Acts 15:2–4** This brought Paul and Barnabas into sharp dispute with them. So Paul and Barnabas were appointed, along with some other believers, to go up to Jerusalem to see the apostles and elders about this question. The church sent them on their way, and as they traveled through Phoenicia and Samaria, they told how the Gentiles had been converted. This news made all the brothers very glad. When they came to Jerusalem, they were welcomed by the church and the apostles and elders, to whom they reported everything God had done through them.

Much Ado About Nothing?

Intense argumentation followed as Paul and Barnabas challenged the erroneous suppositions of the legalist teachers. Since these Pharisaic "evangelists" claimed to represent the Jerusalem church, it was decided the Jerusalem church and the apostles should be brought into the controversy. So Antioch dispatched Paul and Barnabas and others to powwow with the apostles and elders at Jerusalem.

The churches along the way were glad to hear of Gentiles coming to Christ. When the duo arrived, the Jerusalem church treated the two missionaries like conquering heroes.

This debate had to happen because it raised questions that were at the heart of the Christian message: First, can a person be good and law abiding enough to earn God's favor, or must he simply admit his helplessness and humbly throw himself on God's mercy and grace? Second, what must a person do to be saved—work or believe?

In his letter to the Galatians, Paul states the principle behind his and Barnabas's contention that Gentiles must be accepted into full fellowship in the church *without* being required to be circumcised and practice the Old Testament ceremonies: "We . . . know *that a man is not justified by observing the law, but by faith in Jesus Christ. . . . because by observing the law no one will be justified!"* (Galatians 1:15–16).

justified: right with God, accepted

Some issues are so essential to the good news they cannot be compromised! The truth that salvation is by <u>faith not works</u> is one of those issues. (Read more about faith and circumcision in GWRM, pages 51–57.)

Remember This . . .

> **Acts 15:5–6** Then some of the believers who belonged to the party of the Pharisees stood up and said, "The Gentiles must be circumcised and required to obey the law of Moses."
> The apostles and elders met to consider this question.

☞ **GO TO:**

John 6:28–29;
Galatians 5:6;
Ephesians 2:8–9
(faith not works)

The Council Of Jerusalem, A.D. 50

In case you haven't heard, conflict is not foreign to the church. Never has been. (Well, duh!) Here we are taken inside an early church business meeting called to consider an issue so crucial, if not dealt with correctly, it could have created a gigantic roadblock to the progress of the Gospel at a time when it was just beginning to penetrate the world at large. It gives us our best view of the early church's approach to corporate problem solving.

Who Was There?

It was an open meeting. The decision would affect the *whole church* (Acts 15:4, 22). So grassroots members were there along with the church's leaders. Two types of leaders are identified (Acts 15:2, 4, 6, 22, 23).

- Apostles—Members of the original Twelve still in Jerusalem, plus Paul and Barnabas. James had been martyred (see Acts 12:2). Peter was on the lam but, at considerable personal risk, came back for this meeting (see Acts 12:19; 15:7).

- Elders—Spiritual leaders (shepherds) appointed for pastoral care of the local congregation in Jerusalem. This local leadership team is first mentioned in Acts 11:30. James, Jesus' brother, is recognized as the leader of this pastoral team (see Acts 12:17; 15:13; 21:18).

The debate was set up by Christian **Pharisees**. Pharisees in the New Testament are <u>not usually</u> pro-Jesus. But these exceptional Pharisees were followers of Jesus and part of the church. They kept philosophical ties with the legalistic Pharisee party. Their argument: *"Gentiles must be circumcised and required to obey the law of Moses."*

Pharisees: meticulously observed the Law of Moses and ceremonial rules developed by rabbis

☞ **GO TO:**

Matthew 3:1–12; 9:1–13; 12:12–14; 23:23–24 (not usually)

Principles of Church Decision-Making

Thorough discussion of all viewpoints and willingness to listen (Acts 15:7, 12) are essential to turn division into unity. The Greek words the author of Acts uses to describe the debate tell how thorough the discussion was:

- Acts 15:2—*"sharp dispute and debate"* (Greek: "not a little discord and questioning")
- Acts 15:7—*"much discussion"* (Greek: "seeking, dispute, debate, controversy")

Howard Marshall calls it "a general free-for-all."[1] Eugene Peterson's interpretation of Acts 15:7 says, "The arguments went on and on, back and forth, getting more and more heated."[2]

The early church historian Luke doesn't give the arguments of those in favor of demanding that Gentiles live under Jewish law. Focus is on statements that carried the day and led to the harmonious conclusion.

CHURCH GROWTH

Two basic Christian beliefs guided the discussion:

1. Christians believe Jesus is personally involved with them in the affairs of the church, through his Holy Spirit (Acts 15:28; see Matthew 18:20; 28:20).
2. Christians believe agreement among themselves carries great power and authority (Acts 15:22, 25; see Matthew 18:17–19).

> **Acts 15:7–12** After much discussion, Peter got up and addressed them: Brothers, you know that some time ago God made a choice among you that the Gentiles might hear from my lips the message of the gospel and believe. God who knows the heart, showed that he accepted them by giving the Holy Spirit to them, just as he did to us. He made no distinction between us and them, for he purified their hearts by faith. Now then, why do you try to test God by putting on the necks of the disciples a yoke that neither we nor our fathers have been able to bear? No! We believe it is through the grace of our Lord Jesus that we are saved, just as they are."
>
> The whole assembly became silent as they listened to Barnabas and Paul telling about the miraculous signs and wonders God had done among the Gentiles through them.

Crashing The Party Or Invited By God?

Peter, the apostle with a price on his head, stood to remind them what God did in the Captain Cornelius affair—an incident still fresh in their minds. His arguments were simple and convincing:

1. God initiated the outreach to the Gentiles (Acts 15:7; 10:3–20; 11:17).

2. God verified his acceptance of Gentiles by giving them the Holy Spirit, just like he did us Jewish believers (Acts 15:8; 10:44; 11:15–17).

3. God makes no distinction between Jews and Gentiles. The hearts of both are purified on the basis of faith in Jesus (Acts 15:9).

4. To lay the burden of Moses' Law on people God has accepted amounts to questioning God's judgment (Acts 15:10; 11:17).

5. If lifelong Jews have found the Law an <u>impossible burden</u>, what sense does it make to expect Gentiles to bear it (Acts 15:10)?

6. The Law never saved anyone. Jews and Gentiles alike are saved through the grace (undeserved favor) of the Lord Jesus (Acts 15:11).

To buttress Peter's arguments, Paul and Barnabas related their

☞ **GO TO:**

Romans 7:7–25;
Galatians 3:10–14
(impossible burden)

experiences, reporting visible evidence of God at work among the Gentiles in Asia Minor (Acts 15:12). The assembly fell silent, listening. The facts had a calming effect.

multifarious: *diverse, great variety*

William Barclay: The attempt to obey the Law's **multifarious** commands and so to earn salvation was a losing battle which left every man in default. There is only one way—the acceptance of the free gift of the grace of God in an act of self-surrendering faith.

Peter went right to the heart of the question. . . . Can a man *earn* the favor of God? Or must he admit his own helplessness and be ready in humble faith to accept what the grace of God gives? In effect, the Jewish party said, "Religion means earning God's favor by keeping the Law." Peter said, "Religion consists in casting ourselves on the grace of God." . . . The paradox of Christianity is that the way to victory is through surrender; and the way to power is through admitting one's own helplessness.[3]

> **Acts 15:13** When they finished, James spoke up: "Brothers, listen to me."

Yes! To The Revolution

After the arguments had been heard, a respected member of the local church leadership team offered a decision he felt was consistent with the facts and on which he felt the body could agree. Who was this "James," and why should the church listen to him?

James was Jesus' biological brother (Mark 6:3). He'd seen Jesus after his resurrection (2 Corinthians 15:7). He'd become acknowledged leader of the Jerusalem church because of his mature Christian character and spiritual giftedness. He was nicknamed "Old Camel Knees" because he spent so much time on his knees in prayer. He was known and respected both in and outside the church as a faithful observer of the Law of Moses.

William Barclay: [James's] leadership was not a formal office; it was a moral leadership conceded to him because he was an outstanding man.[4]

GOD'S WORD FOR THE BIBLICALLY-INEPT

> **Acts 15:14–18** "Simon has described to us how God at first showed his concern by taking from the Gentiles a people for himself. The words of the prophets are in agreement with this, as it is written:
>
> "'After this I will return
> and rebuild David's fallen tent.
> It's ruins I will rebuild,
> and I will restore it,
> that the remnant of men may seek the Lord,
> and all the Gentiles who bear my name,
> says the Lord, who does these things'
> that have been known for ages."

The Last Argument

Though James was a committed keeper of Jewish religious law, he could see only one direction for the church to take. Two things convinced him:

1. God's actions (Acts 15:14). No believer would suggest God goofed in gathering "a people for himself" from the Gentiles (as reported by Peter, Paul, and Barnabas).

2. God's Word (Acts 15:15–18). A prophecy from the Book of Amos convinced him it had always been God's plan for Gentiles to be welcomed into the church *as Gentiles*— not forced to become Jews! (See Amos 9:11–12.)

> **Acts 15:19–21** "It is my judgment, therefore, that we should not make it difficult for the Gentiles who are turning to God. Instead we should write to them, telling them to abstain from food polluted by idols, from sexual immorality, from the meat of strangled animals and from blood. For Moses has been preached in every city from the earliest times and is read in the synagogues on every Sabbath."

Consensus For Freedom And Fellowship

The facts were obvious: (1) God accepts Gentiles on the basis of faith (Acts 15:8); and (2) Judaism's ceremonial laws hinder the Gospel's growth among non-Jews and create barriers to fellowship between true believers (Acts 15:10–11). Confronted by the facts and the group's expressed concerns, James pulled together a **consensus** and proposed it be communicated to the churches.

consensus: *what the group can agree on*

The "requirements" of the Jerusalem Council were aimed at removing the main barriers to fellowship between Jewish and Gentile Christians.

☞ **GO TO:**

Acts 1:4; 2:42, 46; 6:1–2; 11:3 (eat together)

Exodus 20:4–6 (idolatry)

Genesis 9:4; Leviticus 17:10; Deuteronomy 12:23–25 (eating blood)

What Others are Saying:

sacrificed to idols: food in Gentile markets was often offered to an idol before being sold

1. No roadblocks to faith (Acts 15:19). The church should not make it difficult for Gentiles to turn to God. Circumcision isn't mentioned, but the intent is Gentiles are off the hook. No Jewish rituals are required, including circumcision.

2. No roadblocks to fellowship (Acts 15:20). Gentiles should make accommodations to their Jewish friends so they can <u>eat together</u> freely. Two things Jews find especially repulsive are <u>idolatry</u> (anything to do with idols) and <u>eating blood</u>. Non-Jewish believers can make it easier for Jews to break bread with them if they stop serving food **sacrificed to idols** or unbled meat.

3. The moral high road (Acts 15:20). Guarding against sexual sin of all kinds must have high priority. Lust, sexual sin, and marital unfaithfulness destroy fellowship.

4. No anxiety about Moses (Acts 15:21). Pharisees wanted Gentiles to live under Moses' influence. They feared erosion of his authority if new believers didn't keep the Law. Not to worry! *"Moses has been preached in every city . . . and is read in the synagogues every Sabbath."* Christians will always be influenced by Moses. (James was right.) Christians love the Old Testament. Moses still speaks to Christians!

F. F. Bruce: Idolatry, fornication, and murder were the three cardinal sins in Jewish eyes; avoidance of these was held to be binding on the whole human race.[5]

Maude De Joseph West: It comes as a shock to most of us that the sin of gross immorality was mentioned in the same breath with dietary customs. Among Gentiles, chastity was not something to be cherished, nor impurity a sin to be avoided. They simply did not know any better. How could they have known? Their very religions were filthily immoral.

We know better. Nonetheless, we are moving swiftly toward that abyss of immorality from which those Gentiles were rescued by the grace of our Lord and Savior, Jesus Christ.[6]

JESUS CHRIST CEO

When the letter was composed reporting the decision to the Gentile churches, it read: *"It seemed good to the Holy Spirit and to us . . ."* (Acts 15:28). The Holy Spirit had this great idea, and we all agreed. In this case, the Spirit of Jesus, the church's Head, led his people through the processes involved in consensus making.

What Others are Saying:

Lawrence O. Richards: In many ways the first church council can serve as a model for resolving disputed issues today. We note especially that:

1. The issue was clearly defined.
2. The issue was brought to the entire leadership for open discussion and debate.
3. Differing positions were actively argued.
4. Evidence from what God was currently doing was considered.
5. The interpretation of what God was doing was tested for harmony with Scripture.
6. Special concern was shown for the sensibilities of those who "lost" the debate.
7. The "winners" were asked to surrender some of the rights they had won in view of some of the convictions of the "losers."

. . . We cannot expect everyone to surrender convictions which are wrong, however clear the voice of God through church and Scripture. What we can do is seek to hear the Holy Spirit's voice through our brothers and the Word of God. And, as we debate, remember always that we are one family in Christ, and that those who differ from us remain brothers and sisters whom we have a duty to love.[7]

The Lord leads his church in practical matters through consensus (agreement, harmony). Keys to consensus are dependence on the Holy Spirit to guide the process, commitment to unity rather than "winning," valuing each other personally, and willingness to listen to each other's concerns.

CHURCH GROWTH

THE BIG PICTURE

Acts 15:22–35 The apostles and elders and the Jerusalem church sent Paul and Barnabas back to Antioch accompanied by Judas and Silas. They carried a letter restating the decision to free believing Gentiles from Jewish rules. The Antioch Christians welcomed the lib-

> erating letter. Judas and Silas returned to Jerusalem. Paul and Barnabas continued to teach and preach in Antioch.

Risk-Takers Deliver The Mail

Four men were dispatched with the letter from Jerusalem to *"the Gentile believers"* in Antioch and the provinces of Syria and Cilicia. Acts 15:26 identifies Paul and Barnabas as *"men who have risked their lives for the name of our Lord Jesus Christ."* Judas Barsabbas and Silas, two members of Jerusalem's leadership team (Acts 15:22), both preachers (Acts 15:32), were sent along to authenticate and explain the letter.

The straight-talking letter repudiated the unauthorized teachers who'd caused such angst in Antioch, freed Gentiles from Judaism's religious rituals, and encouraged a "Just say No!" attitude toward sexual sin and things that strain cross-cultural Christian fellowship.

Howard Marshall: After the delegates had received their instructions from the church, they went down to Antioch where a meeting of the members of the church was held and the letter was handed over and read aloud to the assembly. . . . It was greeted with joy, for its contents showed that the decisive point had been accepted: the Gentiles were not to be required to be circumcised and keep the law of Moses.[8]

> **Acts 15:36–39a** Some time later Paul said to Barnabas, "Let us go back and visit the brothers in all the towns where we preached the word of the Lord and see how they are doing." Barnabas wanted to take John, also called Mark, with them, but Paul did not think it wise to take him, because he had deserted them in Pamphylia and had not continued with them in the work. They had such a sharp disagreement that they parted company.

Coming Apart At The Teams

At this strategic moment in the history of the church, when it began to radically change from a movement within Judaism to a predominantly Gentile movement, two of its most important visionaries could no longer see eye to eye and parted company—never to work together again.

GOD'S WORD FOR THE BIBLICALLY-INEPT

The Devil In The Details

Luke gives so few details that we can only guess why the conflict between Paul and Barnabas could not be resolved. Here's what we know:

They agreed to revisit the churches they'd planted. But Mark, Barnabas's younger cousin, became the focus of *"sharp disagreement"* (Acts 15:39). The original word means "an angry dispute." A fight.

- In this corner, wearing white trunks and weighing 200 pounds: BARNEY THE ENCOURAGER—the "people person," underlineunderline no one else wants to help. He wanted to take Mark with them even though he'd jumped ship on the first voyage (Acts 13:13). "Come on, Paul, give the kid another chance!"

- In this corner, wearing purple trunks and weighing 190 pounds: PAUL THE PERFECTIONIST—the "do or die person," the get up and keep punching guy, intense, concerned for success of the mission. Mark had blown his chance, leaving them shorthanded on the first trip. "The kid's not dry behind the ears! A quitter! Excess baggage!"

☞ **GO TO:**

Acts 9:26–27; 11:23 (champion of young believers)

Acts 14:19–20 (get up and keep punching)

> **Acts 15:39b–41** Barnabas took Mark and sailed for Cyprus, but Paul chose Silas and left, commended by the brothers to the grace of the Lord. He went through Syria and Cilicia, strengthening the churches.

Breaking Up The Old Gang

The original missionary team split in two:

- Team Cyprus: Barnabas and Mark
- Team Europe: Paul and Silas

Who was right, and who was wrong? The song says, "It takes two to tango!" As in every rancorous split-up, there was no doubt plenty of blame to go around.

Barnabas turned out to be right in his assessment of Mark. After a few more years of discipling with the "son of encouragement," early church tradition says Mark ministered with Peter and wrote a New Testament Gospel. According to 2 Timothy 4:11, even Paul changed his mind about Mark. Paul continued to es-

☞ **GO TO:**

Acts 15:37–39
(break-up)

2 Corinthians 1:19;
1 Thessalonians 1:1;
2 Thessalonians 1:1
(Sylvanus)

Matthew 20:25–28
(Jesus' teaching)

**Something
to Ponder**

**Remember
This . . .**

**What Others
are Saying:**

☞ **GO TO:**

Romans 8:28
(worked good)

☞ **GO TO:**

2 Corinthians 4:7
(weaknesses)

teem Barnabas as an equal in commitment and sacrifice for the Gospel (1 Corinthians 9:6).

After the <u>break-up</u> of the original missionary team, Paul chose Silas and headed for Asia Minor to follow up the young churches there. It was rebuilding time for Paul's team. His new partner, Silas a.k.a. <u>Sylvanus</u>, was an elder in the Jerusalem church, sent with Paul and Barnabas to explain the decision of the Jerusalem Council freeing Gentiles from Jewish religious rules. He was a preacher or speaker for God with an effective ministry with the Gentiles in Antioch (see Acts 15:32). Like Paul, he was a Roman citizen (see Acts 16:37–38).

<u>Jesus' teaching</u> and example suggest that bringing along weak, failing individuals is high on the list of Christian leadership priorities. His patience with the weak and failing is legendary. Look what he put up with from those twelve deficient disciples closest to him!

God <u>worked good</u> from the conflict. Two teams went two directions sharing the good news. New Testament readers are left with the comforting assurance that God uses people in his work who are very, very human.

Larry Richards: Was Paul a hypocrite? He urged others to reconcile their differences but became so angry with Barnabas that he broke up with his friend. Paul . . . was a fallible human being. None of us are without weakness; all of us are susceptible to sin. . . . Later Mark . . . became reconciled to Paul, who wrote to Timothy to, "get Mark and bring him with you, because he is helpful to me in my ministry" (2 Timothy 4:11). This tacit admission that he was wrong clears Paul of the charge of hypocrisy but not of acting foolishly in breaking up with Barnabas over giving Mark a second chance.[9]

Ajith Fernando: We can be grateful that Luke did not gloss over crises in the early church and hide the <u>weaknesses</u> of its leaders. It was not an ideal church, with saints whose perfect lives leave us panting with frustration over our failures and imperfections. It was a church with people just like us but who nevertheless were available to God and were used to do great things for him.[10]

JESUS CHRIST CEO

Division between Christians can have disastrous results. But the Lord is able to use (and often has used) division to get his people to move in new directions which fulfill his goals. One thing is certain: Division cannot stop the spread of the good news.

Study Questions

1. When unauthorized teachers from Jerusalem came to Antioch insisting that Gentile believers had to be circumcised in order to be saved, how did Paul and Barnabas respond? What was the real issue?
2. In his argument before the apostles and elders at Jerusalem, Peter stressed six points. Identify three of them.
3. What two things convinced James that the Gentiles should be accepted into the church as Gentiles and not expected to become Jews?
4. What two things did James feel Gentiles should do to make fellowship with their Jewish counterparts easier?
5. What was the issue that led to the break up of Paul and Barnabas?

CHAPTER WRAP-UP

- The Gentile-Jewish fellowship at Antioch was disrupted by teachers who insisted Gentiles must be circumcised. Paul and Barnabas debated them. The church sent them to discuss the issue with elders and apostles in Jerusalem. (Acts 15:1–4)

- The first world church council met to discuss the issue. Christian Pharisees insisted Gentiles come under Moses' Law. Peter, with Paul and Barnabas's support, told how God accepted Gentiles on the same basis as Jews—by faith in Jesus. (Acts 15:5–12)

- James, leader of the Jerusalem church, proposed freeing Gentile believers from the Law and called for them to adjust to their Jewish brothers and sisters by a couple of dietary changes and to avoid sexual sin. Church leaders agreed. (Acts 15:13–22)

- Two local leaders, Judas and Silas, were sent to Antioch with Paul and Barnabas and a letter outlining the council's decision. The Gentile believers were overjoyed with the decision freeing them from the obligation of circumcision. (Acts 15:22–34)

- Paul and Barnabas made plans to go on another missionary journey, but got into an argument about whether John Mark should go along again. The disagreement became so intense, the team split up. (Acts 15:35–41)

ACTS 16: JAILHOUSE ROCK

Let's Get Started

The decision by the Jerusalem Council (see Acts 15) to release Gentiles from the Law of Moses kicked into motion a time of transition for the young church. Christians were no longer merely another Jewish sect. The Jesus movement was rapidly becoming a predominantly Gentile movement. The story, as told in Acts, shifts attention to the Gospel's penetration deep into the Roman world and to the widening ministry of Paul.

> **Acts 16:1** [Paul] came to Derbe and then to Lystra, where a disciple named Timothy lived, whose mother was a Jewess and a believer, but whose father was a Greek.

Rebuilding The Dream Team

Paul regrouped with Silas, his new partner, and left on another missionary journey (see illustration, page 178). When Paul and Barnabas visited Lystra five years earlier, Paul was nearly killed by a crowd of "adoring fans" who suddenly turned violent and stoned him (Acts 14:8–21). He was left for dead outside the city. Out of that pile of bloody stones rose not only a battered-but-unbowed Paul but also a Christian church. And out of that church emerged a gifted young man named Timothy who was to become one of Paul's most trusted coworkers and dearest friends.

Tim Terrific!

Timothy was the son of a Jewish Christian mother and a Greek father. His name means "God honoring." He was a lifelong student of the Bible (see 2 Timothy 3:14–15) but was not raised a strict Jew. His mother Eunice and grandmother Lois were excellent spiritual models (see 2 Timothy 1:5). Tim possessed **spiritually valuable abilities**, but needed encouragement to use them (see 1 Timothy 4:14; 2 Timothy 1:6). Even so, he was respected by fellow Christians who commissioned him for Christian ministry (see Acts 16:2; 2 Timothy 4:14).

spiritually valuable abilities: gifts of the Holy Spirit

> **Acts 16:2–3** The brothers at Lystra and Iconium spoke well of him. Paul wanted to take him along on the journey, so he circumcised him because of the Jews who lived in that area, for they all knew that his father was a Greek.

Paul's Second Missionary Journey

Paul's second missionary journey began at Antioch, north of Jerusalem. Paul's travels with Silas are shown. The dashed line shows where Barnabas and Mark left Paul and headed for Cyprus.

The Wondrous Wisdom Of Holy Inconsistency

Whoa, Nellie! What's this? Paul, the champion of spiritual freedom who argued successfully for liberation of Gentiles from the necessity of circumcision, who was in Lystra to pass that good news to the church there, now does a 180 by circumcising Tim Terrific. What's wrong with the picture? Whatchadoin', Paul?

Some people accuse Paul of inconsistency. Perhaps. But "foolish consistency," wrote R. W. Emerson, "is the hobgoblin of little minds."[1] Paul's was no "little mind." He was never as committed to the wisdom of the Jerusalem Council as to the <u>mind of Christ</u> and the day-to-day leadership of the Holy Spirit. No set of rules can cover all the surprises and **serendipities** involved with the Holy Spirit's personal leading. In circumcising Timothy, Paul acted according to higher principles than the principles of freedom, personal preference, or doing the least the church demands. Far more important to him were the following things:

- The principle of personal obedience to Christ (see 2 Corinthians 10:5)
- The principle of living by the spirit not the letter of the law (see 2 Corinthians 3:6)
- The principle of accommodation on **nonessentials** in order to communicate the Gospel to diverse people (see 1 Corinthians 9:19–23)
- The principle of love (see 1 Corinthians 13:4–8)

Why Did *Tim Let Paul Perform "The Surgery"?*

There were two main reasons Tim Terrific chose this elective surgery. Both are *"because of the Jews"* (Acts 16:3), and both have to do with the team's priority of taking the Gospel to the Jews in every city first (Acts 13:5, 14; 14:1; 16:13; 17:2, 10, 17; 18:4; Romans 1:16). First, Tim wanted to assure Jews that following Christ did not mean they had to stop being Jewish. Second, he wanted all the credibility he could get with the Jews they would be trying to reach.

Timothy did not have to submit to circumcision to be accepted by God or the church. But because he <u>loved</u> the Jewish people, he <u>surrendered</u> his rights in order to serve them.

Something to Ponder

☞ **GO TO:**

1 Corinthians 2:9–16; 2 Corinthians 10:5 (mind of Christ)

serendipities: unexpected, delightful discoveries and experiences

nonessentials: religious practices, preferences, and opinions not required for salvation

☞ **GO TO:**

Romans 14:19; 15:1–3; 1 Corinthians 8:9 (loved)

Matthew 20:27–28 (surrendered)

Remember This . . .

> **Acts 16:4–10** Paul and his friends delivered the Jerusalem apostles' decision, and the churches grew. The Holy Spirit kept Paul from preaching in Asia and from entering Bithynia. Paul had a vision of a man asking him to come to Macedonia, so he went.

Following The Holy Spirit Around

Christian workers' movements are a blend of strategic planning and sensitivity to the Spirit. Acts 16:6–10 describes four ways the team experienced the Lord's step-by-step leadership.

1. Spiritual roadblocks. The Holy Spirit "kept" them from preaching in Asia province (Acts 16:6). *"Kept . . . from"* means "hindered, restrained, prevented, or forbidden." How the Spirit did this we're not told. <u>Prophecy</u>? <u>Uneasiness</u> about a planned action?

2. Adverse conditions and physical limitations. The Spirit of Jesus *"would not allow them to"* go north toward Bithynia (Acts 16:7). Perhaps Paul became sick and needed a doctor. So they went to Troas where their friend, Dr. Luke, was. Paul's sickness was the Lord's way of denying permission to visit a place not on the divine itinerary.

3. Vision (Acts 16:9): "A vision through the night" (literal translation). The same mental picture came to Paul repeatedly that night: A Macedonian stood pleading for Paul and the team to cross the Aegean Sea to Europe and *"help us."*

4. Team agreement. When Paul shared his vision, the team—Paul, Silas, Timothy, and Luke—started packing, "concluding" the vision was a call from God (Acts 16:10). The whole team agreed the vision was God communicating his will.

"Closed doors" and circumstances had kept them moving west-northwest to Troas. There, with their toes in the Aegean, the orders they'd been listening for came in an all-night vision and team consensus.

Dr. Luke Signs On

At Troas (Acts 16:10), so quietly the average reader may miss it, another member joined the team aboard the ship for Macedonia and would stick with Paul like flypaper until the last chapter of

---

☞ **GO TO:**

1 Timothy 4:14 (prophecy)

Colossians 3:15 (uneasiness)

KEY POINT

God leads his people through the Holy Spirit.

"closed doors": *circumstances making a course of action impossible or impractical*

Acts. He doesn't wear a nametag. The subtle insertion of the little two-letter first person plural pronouns, "we" and "us" (Acts 16:10 and ninety-six other verses in Acts), reveals that the author of Acts had signed on. Most of what he writes from this point on is eyewitness recall.

Luke was a Greek. Paul calls him, "dear friend Luke, the doctor" (Colossians 4:14). Unconfirmed early church stories about Luke suggest these intriguing possibilities:

- He was Theophilus's slave, (see Acts 1:1) freed after he restored his master's health.[2]
- He was a "charter member" of the Antioch church.[3]
- He was in Troas waiting to sign on as a ship's doctor.[4]
- He joined the team as personal physician to the frequently ailing Paul.[5]

> **Acts 16:11** From Troas we put out to sea and sailed straight for Samothrace, and the next day on to Neapolis.

Europe Calls!

At last, the Spirit said, "Go!" The team headed for the dock with "Europe or bust!" stickers on their luggage. Their first port o' call on the way to Macedonia was Samothrace, a mountain island rising five thousand feet above the sea. The next day passengers and cargo were unloaded at Neapolis (modern Kavalla, Greece), seaport for Philippi.

John Pollock: They did not think of themselves as passing from the continent of Asia to Europe. [These] terms were in use, but the Aegean was Greek on either side. They had, instead, the excitement of approaching a new province, bringing them nearer Rome. They knew that beyond Macedonia they could reach Achaia and Italy, and the vast lands of Gaul, Spain, Germania, even the mist-bound island of Britain lately added to the empire: all save Rome untouched by the Good News. They were not bringing force of arms or a political program: just four men—and Another, invisible. . . .[6]

What Others are Saying:

> **Acts 16:12–13** From there we traveled to Philippi, a Roman colony and the leading city of that district of Macedonia. And we stayed there several days.
>
> On the Sabbath we went outside the city gate to the river, where we expected to find a place of prayer. We sat down and began to teach the women who had gathered there.

River Sisters

Roman colony: citizens dressed Roman, spoke Latin, lived by Roman law

Philippi was a **Roman colony** and commercial center on the Via Ignatia, the main overland route between the Aegean and Adriatic Seas. It was named for Philip of Macedon, father of Alexander the Great. Much of the population was retired military personnel.

The Jewish population of Philippi was too small for a synagogue, which required a minimum of ten men. Jews gathered at the riverside for Sabbath prayers. At the River Gangites the apostles found a group of Jewish and God-fearing Gentile women and told them about Jesus.

EARLY CHURCH WOMEN—The Philippian church began with a group of praying women. As Christianity spread in the Roman Empire, women greatly outnumbered men among early converts.

> **Acts 16:14–15** One of those listening was a woman named Lydia, a dealer in purple cloth from the city of Thyatira, who was a worshiper of God. The Lord opened her heart to respond to Paul's message. When she and the members of her household were baptized, she invited us to her home. "If you consider me a believer in the Lord," she said, "come and stay at my house." And she persuaded us.

Lady In Purple

freed-woman: liberated female slave

Macedonian women were noted for their independence. Under Roman law a freeborn woman with three children or a **freed-woman** with four children had the right to own property and enter into legal transactions without the consent of a husband or father. Many Macedonian women became highly influential.

One such woman was Lydia, a God-fearing Gentile who heard Paul preach at the riverside prayer meeting. She conducted a successful business in purple cloth dyed with the secretions of a rare

GOD'S WORD FOR THE BIBLICALLY-INEPT

Mediterranean shellfish. So rare and costly was this dye only the wealthy could afford the cloth. Trading in this exquisite fabric had made Lydia wealthy. And she was head of her own **household**.

The <u>Lord opened</u> Lydia's heart, and she believed in Jesus, becoming the first person on the European continent to turn to Christ. After she and her entire household were baptized she persuaded the team to stay at her home.

household: family, servants, slaves, and other dependents

☞ **GO TO:**

John 6:44 (Lord opened)

EARLY CHURCH WOMEN—Women were attracted to early Christianity because within the Christian community women enjoyed higher status and security than among their pagan neighbors. By contrast to pagan women, who were married very young (often before puberty), Christian women had more freedom to decide if and when they would marry. Christian husbands could not easily divorce their wives. Marital faithfulness was expected of both Christian husbands and wives.

> **Acts 16:16** Once when we were going to the place of prayer, we were met by a slave girl who had a spirit by which she predicted the future. She earned a great deal of money for her owners by fortune-telling.

The Case Of The Unfortunate Fortune-Teller

The second European impacted by the good news came from the opposite end of the social spectrum from Lydia. She was a slave, physically and spiritually. She was mentally ill, tormented by an evil spirit Luke describes as *pneuma pythona*—the spirit of **Python**—which controlled her speech. "The ancient world had a strange respect for mad people because, they said, the gods had taken away their wits in order to put the mind of the gods into them."[7] The Philippians believed this girl was clairvoyant—that she could tell the future. Her owners charged high fees for her services as a fortune-teller.

Python: mythical snake guarding ecstatic speeches of the god Apollo

> **Acts 16:17–18** This girl followed Paul and the rest of us, shouting, "These men are servants of the Most High God, who are telling you the way to be saved." She kept this up for many days. Finally Paul became so troubled that he turned around and said to the spirit, "In the name of Jesus Christ I command you to come out of her!" At that moment the spirit left her.

Fortune-Teller Gets A Future

When this tormented girl followed Paul and the others around announcing that they were God's servants telling *"the way to be saved,"* Paul did not take it as a compliment. This continued several days. Paul became "troubled." (That's putting it mildly. The Greek word means strongly irked, provoked, and "worked up" with anger or grief.) The tortured girl told the truth, but when the <u>devil tells the truth</u>, the effect is always confusion.

Finally, Paul whirled around and, in Jesus' name, commanded the evil spirit to come out of her. Instantly, the mental anguish ended and the slave girl was free from her spiritual bondage! Luke doesn't say she became a Christian. Likely she did.

☞ **GO TO:**

Mark 1:23–26
 (devil tells the truth)

> **Acts 16:19–24** When the owners of the slave girl realized that their hope of making money was gone, they seized Paul and Silas and dragged them into the marketplace to face the authorities. They brought them before the magistrates and said, "These men are Jews, and are throwing our city into an uproar by advocating customs unlawful for Romans to accept or practice."
>
> The crowd joined in the attack against Paul and Silas, and the magistrates ordered them to be stripped and beaten. After they had been severely flogged, they were thrown into prison, and the jailer was commanded to guard them carefully. Upon receiving such orders, he put them in the inner cell and fastened their feet in the stocks.

The Gospel—A Pain In The Pocketbook!

When they realized their profits had flown the coop along with the evil spirit, the girl's owners hit the ceiling! (Luke uses the same Greek word in verse 18 for departure of the evil spirit as in verse 19 for departure of the owners' profits. Their ill-gotten gain was literally "**exorcised**" along with the tormenting spirit!) Typical of people whose bottom line is money, they had no concern for the girl's welfare and no gratitude for her healing. She was, after all, **property**. By healing her Paul violated their property rights!

The owners played on the crowd's **anti-Semitic** sentiments. Their charges never mentioned the real reason for their ire, their <u>loss of revenue</u>. They accused Paul and Silas of being anti-Roman. (If the truth won't sell, try hogwash!)

exorcised: *expelled, gotten rid of*

property: *Romans referred to slaves as "living tools"*

anti-Semitic: *against the Jews*

☞ **GO TO:**

Acts 19:23–27
 (loss of revenue)

Without investigating the charges, the magistrates ordered Paul and Silas **beaten** and jailed. The jailer was ordered to *"guard them carefully."* He locked them in the local jail's maximum-security cell and clamped their feet in stocks.

Persecution & Martyrdom—The economic effects of Christians' commitment to help people can trigger animosity.

During A.D. 257–258 in Rome, Laurence, a deacon of the church at Rome, was ordered to hand over the treasures of the church to the head of the empire's pagan religion. Laurence promised to comply. Next day he gave all the money to the city's poor. (The church cared for 1,500 Roman widows and orphans at the time.) When officials asked where the treasures were, Laurence pointed to the poor. *"These* are the treasure of the church!" he said. He was beheaded for his disobedience.[8]

In the 1990s in suburban Phoenix, Arizona, a church ministering to the homeless came under attack by neighbors who claimed the presence of the homeless people was causing their property values to drop. City government intervened and ordered the church to stop its outreach to the homeless.

> **Acts 16:25–26** About midnight Paul and Silas were praying and singing hymns to God, and the other prisoners were listening to them. Suddenly there was such a violent earthquake that the foundations of the prison were shaken. At once all the prison doors flew open, and everybody's chains came loose.

Papa Sang Bass—Me And Little Brother Joined Right In!

Philippi's maximum-security cell was no Holiday Inn. It was colder than a witch's elbow and blacker than the ace of spades and smellier than road tar. The stocks were ingeniously designed to immobilize the feet and legs for maximum discomfort (see illustration, page 186). This torture was often used on early Christians. Such were the accommodations enjoyed in the Philippian stockade.

Backs bruised and torn, punished illegally for an act of mercy, these crazy Christian fanatics had no time for self-pity. Rejoicing was the order of the evening! About midnight the stockade echoed with the sound of two Jewish-accented male voices singing hymns! As a kid in church, I remember an old fire-and-brimstone preacher saying, "Paul sang tenor, Silas sang baritone, and God joined in

☞ **GO TO:**

2 Corinthians 11:25 (beaten)

beaten: caned; Greek—"beaten with wooden rods"

☞ **GO TO:**

Matthew 5:10–12; Acts 5:41 (rejoicing)

with a thundering bass that shook the prison so violently stocks fell off, locks shattered, doors flew open, and the prisoners' chains fell away!" All might have escaped, but none did.

JESUS CHRIST CEO In the dungeon dark, the Lord Jesus touched people who could be reached no other way. *"The other prisoners were listening"* (Acts 16:25). Their chains broke too. They could have escaped but didn't. The jailer found Jesus. The other prisoners got a taste of the Gospel.

> **Acts 16:27–28** The jailer woke up, and when he saw the prison doors open, he drew his sword and was about to kill himself because he thought the prisoners had escaped. But Paul shouted, "Don't harm yourself! We are all here!"

Jailerbreak!

The jailer knew, according to Roman military law, that if prisoners had escaped he would be given the punishment the fugitives would have received. An executed criminal's property would be confiscated. To protect his family from loss of their property, he grabbed his sword to take his own life. Just in the nick of time, Paul shouted, "Don't do it! *We are all here!*"

Prison Stocks

Paul and Silas were clamped in this favorite Roman torture device in the inner cell.

> **Acts 16:29–30** The jailer called for lights, rushed in and fell trembling before Paul and Silas. He then brought them out and asked, "Sirs, what must I do to be saved?"

The Million Dollar Question

"What must I do to be saved?" As a Roman and a pagan, did the jailer understand what he was asking?

- He may have heard the fortune-teller say these men came to tell people how to be saved (Acts 16:17).
- He'd felt supernatural power in the earthquake and believed Paul and Silas were connected with it.
- He'd been on the brink of suicide—perhaps he was asking how he could escape his superior's punishment (Acts 16:27, 29).
- His response to the answer shows he understood his need for spiritual restoration and sincerely wanted to know how to get it (Acts 16:33–34).

> **Acts 16:31–32** They replied, "Believe in the Lord Jesus, and you will be saved—you and your household." Then they spoke the **word of the Lord** to him and to all the others in his house.

word of the Lord: *the good news about Jesus*

The Million Dollar Answer

The answer was that there was nothing the jailer needed to *do*. Everything necessary for his salvation had been done for him by Christ. All that was required was to believe in Jesus! Furthermore, the same offer was extended to everyone in his house. It's a familiar pattern in Acts: The head of the house trusts Jesus, and the rest of the family follows, believing and being baptized (Acts 10:2; 16:14–15, 33–34). All are included in God's promise of salvation. Each must simply make his or her personal decision to believe.

> **Acts 16:33–34** At that hour of the night the jailer took them and washed their wounds; then immediately he and all his family were baptized. The jailer brought them into his house and set a meal before them; he was filled with joy because he had come to believe in God—he and his whole family.

Was The Jailer "Saved"?

Luke reports four evidences of the authenticity of the jailer's conversion:

1. Making amends—he nursed Paul's and Silas's wounds.
2. Baptism—he and his family confessed their faith and were baptized.
3. Table fellowship—he shared a meal with Paul and Silas in his home.
4. Joy—he and his family <u>rejoiced</u> over their new faith in God.

☞ **GO TO:**

Isaiah 55:1–2, 10–13
(rejoiced)

What Others are Saying:

spurious: illegitimate, falsified origin

William Barclay: Unless a man's Christianity makes him kind it is not real. Unless a man's professed change of heart is guaranteed by his change of deeds it is a **spurious** thing.[9]

> **Acts 16:35–39** When it was daylight, the magistrates sent their officers to the jailer with the order: "Release those men." The jailer told Paul, "The magistrates have ordered that you and Silas be released. Now you can leave. Go in peace."
>
> But Paul said to the officers: "They beat us publicly without a trial, even though we are Roman citizens, and threw us into prison. And now do they want to get rid of us quietly? No! Let them come themselves and escort us out."
>
> The officers reported this to the magistrates, and when they heard that Paul and Silas were Roman citizens, they were alarmed. They came to appease them and escorted them from the prison, requesting them to leave the city.

Red Carpet For The "Bad Guys"

At daybreak officers came with orders to release the prisoners. To their chagrin the prisoners refused to leave! Paul and Silas demanded the magistrates who had plunked them in the pokey illegally and unjustly come, apologize for their gross negligence, and personally escort them out. *"We are Roman citizens,"* said Paul.

Oops! A shiver of alarm ran up and down the magistrates' collective spines! By law, Roman citizens could not be executed, beaten, tortured, or placed in stocks without a public hearing.

When the judges showed up to escort the apostles to freedom, it was with a markedly more conciliatory tone than when they ordered their incarceration. They did, however, politely suggest the apostles leave town!

Paul and Silas did not hesitate to use their rights as Roman citizens to protect themselves and others from unjust and arbitrary treatment. Philippian Christians would soon face <u>persecution</u>. The apostles' protest may have helped protect some.

Something to Ponder

Lawrence O. Richards: Christians do have a dual citizenship. We owe total allegiance to heaven. Yet even as we live by the laws of our earthly nation, so we can claim all the rights granted us here as well.[10]

What Others are Saying:

☞ **GO TO:**

Philippians 1:27–30 (persecution)

Persecution & Martyrdom—During 1999 in Turkey, Turkish Christians experienced a Paul-and-Silas-like situation. They were arrested and interrogated for thirty-six hours for being "terrorists." While in jail they cooked and shared meals with the other prisoners, who thanked them for their kindness. Upon their release, guards who had observed their attitudes and actions, apologized for the arrest.

> **Acts 16:40** After Paul and Silas came out of the prison, they went to Lydia's house, where they met with the brothers and encouraged them. Then they left.

The Church At Lydia's House

A small cadre of Christian believers gathered at Lydia's villa for final exhortations. A baby church was beginning. Its membership spanned the social spectrum: an upper-class seller of expensive fabric, a slave girl, a middle-class jailer, and others you can read about in Paul's letter to the Philippians. At this point Luke, the author, switches to third person pronouns ("they," "them"). The good doctor stays behind to help deliver the baby church. Good choice. Philippi was a medical center.[11]

Study Questions

1. Since the Jerusalem Council (Acts 15) agreed that Gentiles need not be circumcised to be Christians, what four "higher principles" may have guided Paul in circumcising Timothy?
2. What are two reasons Tim was willing to submit to "the surgery"?
3. What finally convinced Paul and the missionary team that it was God's will to go to Europe? Who joined the team at this point? How do we know this?
4. Stories of three people whose lives were touched by the Gospel are told in Acts 16. Who were they? What were their occupations? Where were they on the social scale?
5. When the Jailer asked Paul and Silas, "What must I do to be saved?" (Acts 16:30), what was the answer? What four things did the jailer do to show he had been converted to Christ?

CHAPTER WRAP-UP

- After the breakup with Barnabas, Paul chose Silas as his partner and headed for Asia Minor. At Lystra, Timothy was added to the team. (Acts 16:1–5)

- By various hindrances, circumstances, and sensitivities, the Holy Spirit led the team to Troas. There Paul had a vision revealing God's will for them to take the Gospel to Europe. Dr. Luke joined them at Troas. (Acts 16:6–11)

- At Philippi, a group of women met at the river to pray. When Paul shared the Gospel, Lydia, a Philippian businesswoman, believed and was baptized. (Acts 16:12–15)

- Paul expelled an evil spirit from a clairvoyant slave girl. The apostles were arrested, beaten, and jailed. At midnight they sang. An earthquake broke chains and opened prison doors. The jailer and his family received the Lord. (Acts 16:16–34)

- Paul and Silas refused to leave jail until the judges apologized for mistreating them. When they left Philippi, a new church was meeting at Lydia's house. (Acts 16:35–40)

ACTS 17: JUNKYARD OF THE GODS

Let's Get Started

Everyone is **religious**—even those who pretend not to be. All people **worship** something. It may be a decorated stick in the forest, statue of a pot-bellied eastern philosopher, world leader, teacher, river, mountain, science, success, sports, music, "fun," a cause—their own glands—even their own face in the mirror. They may not call it "god." But they ascribe supreme worth to it and expend their best energies for it. They expect the god to give them meaning and comfort—maybe even immortality.

Some say, or hope, God does not exist. Others don't know. Or if he exists they insist there's no way to know for sure. I have a friend who calls himself a *"devout* agnostic." He's devoted to (in other words quite *religious* about) not knowing God. Still others claim to know there's a living God, but have all but lost him in a maze of lifeless religious trappings, ceremonies, and rules.

John wrote, *"No one has ever seen God, but **God the One and Only**, who is at the Father's side, has made him known"* (John 1:18).

As early Christian witnesses fanned out across the world, they were confronted with humanity's vast ignorance about God. They met people whose struggle to know (or avoid) God had caused them to create thousands of deities to whom they looked for good fortune, protection, and something to fill the emptiness inside. The Christian challenge was how to share with such people the good news of Jesus, whom Christians believe is the *Only One* who reveals God as he really is.

religious: *devoted to an ultimate reality or deity*

worship: *regard with great respect, honor, or devotion*

God the One and Only: *God's Son Jesus Christ*

> **Acts 17:1–4** When they had passed through Amphipolis and Apollonia, they came to Thessalonica, where there was a Jewish synagogue. As his custom was, Paul went into the synagogue, and on three Sabbath days he reasoned with them from the Scriptures, explaining and proving that the Christ had to suffer and rise from the dead. "This Jesus I am proclaiming to you is the Christ," he said. Some of the Jews were persuaded and joined Paul and Silas, as did a large number of God-fearing Greeks and not a few prominent women.

World Class Troublemakers

Sixty-two miles west of Philippi was Thessalonica, the most important city in Macedonia. Paul, Silas, and Timothy followed the same strategy there as in other towns—they went first to the synagogue and shared their message with the Jews and "**Proselytes of the Gate**" who met there. Paul showed from the Old Testament the necessity for the death and resurrection of Jesus, and declared that he was the promised Messiah. Some Jews and Greeks became convinced and "*joined* Paul and Silas.*"

Proselytes of the Gate:
Gentiles worshiping with Jews, but not fully converted to Judaism

joined: *"threw in their lot with Paul and Silas"[1]*

 EARLY CHURCH WOMEN—Influential Gentile women were charter members of several New Testament churches, including Thessalonica.

> **Acts 17:5–9** But the Jews were jealous; so they rounded up some bad characters from the marketplace, formed a mob and started a riot in the city. They rushed to Jason's house in search of Paul and Silas in order to bring them out to the crowd. But when they did not find them, they dragged Jason and some other brothers before the city officials, shouting: "These men who have caused trouble all over the world have now come here, and Jason has welcomed them into his house. They are all defying Caesar's decrees, saying that there is another king, one called Jesus." When they heard this, the crowd and the city officials were thrown into turmoil. Then they made Jason and the others post bond and let them go.

Let's Start A Ruckus!

Trouble from synagogue leaders was not triggered by desire to protect the traditional faith so much as plain mud-ugly, yellow-bellied, green-eyed *jealousy*! In Thessalonica synagogue leaders found some disreputable characters hangin' around the market itchin' to make a lot of noise and beat somebody up. Unable to find Paul and Silas, they grabbed Jason and some other believers and hauled them off to the **politarchs**.

They trumped up charges against the Christians: (1) they were world class troublemakers—this riot was *their* fault; (2) they defied Caesar's decrees; and (3) they promoted a king to replace Caesar. All pure hogwash. But shrewdly calculated to turn super-patriotic Romans into a tizzy.

It worked. The crowd and officials went into orbit! But since there was no real evidence the charges were true, Jason and the others were released after being forced to *"**post bond**"* guaranteeing Paul and Silas would leave town and never come back. To protect Jason and the others, Paul and Silas slipped out of town after sundown and did not return. Paul kept in touch with <u>letters</u>.

politarchs: Macedonian city officials

post bond: put up bail money

☞ **GO TO:**

1 Thessalonians and 2 Thessalonians (letters)

What Others are Saying:

Dig Deeper

Howard Marshall: The Jews were "jealous" because here as elsewhere Paul won over the "devout Greeks," those already attracted to Judaism—the very people they themselves hoped to win as converts.[2]

Of what "crime" were the Christians accused? *"These men . . . have caused trouble all over the world!"* (Acts 17:6). Is it true? The original Greek statement from which this is translated can be interpreted several ways. Check out these translations and verses:

- *"Christians turn the world upside down"* (King James Version). It's true. Jesus changes people. Examples: Luke 19:1–10; Acts 9:1–20; Acts 19:18–20; 1 Corinthians 6:9–11.

- *"Christians upset the civilized world"* (William Barclay's translation[3]). It's true. Jesus' values conflict with society's values. See Matthew 5:3–10; Luke 6:20–36; Luke 16:15; Luke 18:14.

- *"Christians subvert the whole world"* (F. F. Bruce's translation[4]). It's true. When the Gospel gets into people they become part of a secret force seeking to undermine and overturn the unjust, immoral principles and practices on which godless culture is founded. See Matthew 13:33; Luke 17:20–21; John 19:36; Romans 12:1–21; 1 Corinthians 13:1–13.

- "*Christians cause trouble all over the world*" (New International Version). It's true. Christ's teachings do not please people who don't want their selfish lifestyles disturbed. Christ's claims and ideas are often met with discomfort and rage, which leads to trouble. See Luke 12:49–53; John 15:18–16:4.

What Others are Saying:

Billy Graham: Jesus Christ . . . was the greatest of all revolutionaries, and he seeks true revolutionaries today who have been transformed by the power of his gospel and who are prepared to row against the mainstream, to go through the straight gate and follow the narrow way (see Matthew 7:13–14). This way may be filled with suffering, hardships, ridicule, and ostracism from the group. It is difficult to follow Jesus Christ. The problem of applying his teachings to our lives is often confusing; that is why it is so important to rely upon the Scripture and upon the Holy Spirit.[5]

Persecution & Martyrdom—The accusation that Christians "*turn the world upside down*" (Acts 17:6 KJV) is still in vogue. In Peru in 1989, Justino Huaman Quicana, chief of the Quicana Indians, was tortured and murdered by Shining Path terrorists, who accused him of confusing the people [by preaching the gospel].[6]

> **Acts 17:10–11** Now the Bereans were of more noble character than the Thessalonians, for they received the message with great eagerness and examined the Scriptures every day to see if what Paul said was true. Many of the Jews believed, as did also a number of prominent Greek women and many Greek men.

KEY POINT

Wise listeners check the Bible to see if a preacher or teacher is telling the truth.

Searching The Bible For God

After the fierceness of opposition in Thessalonica, Berea was a breath of fresh air. The message of Jesus Christ sounded no less strange to Berean ears than to Thessalonian ears. But the Bereans did their homework. They compared what Paul was saying with Old Testament Scripture. The final word, for them, was the written Word of God. When they realized the missionaries were telling the truth, they embraced it.

Ajith Fernando: [The Bereans'] nobility (Acts 17:11) lay in their willingness to acknowledge their need, resulting in an eagerness to hear from God and to receive what they heard. This in turn resulted in their salvation. They came down from their pedestals . . . and, <u>like hungry children</u> in need of food, they sought God's Word.[7]

What Others are Saying:

☞ **GO TO:**

Matthew 18:3–4
  (like hungry children)

> **Acts 17:13–14** When the Jews in Thessalonica learned that Paul was preaching the word of God at Berea, they went there too, agitating the crowds and stirring them up. The brothers immediately sent Paul to the coast, but Silas and Timothy stayed at Berea.

Mail Order Riot

Back in Thessalonica synagogue leaders got wind that Paul was preaching in Berea. Zealous "Keepers of the Ancient Ways,"[8] they made the fifty-mile trip to Berea to start another riot, which led to another hasty hiatus for Paul.

It was too late to stop the Lord's work. A group of eager Bible students was already being drawn together around Jesus. Timothy and Silas stayed to get the church founded, while Paul hightailed it to the coast.

> **Acts 17:15–16** The men who escorted Paul brought him to Athens and then left with instructions for Silas and Timothy to join him as soon as possible. While he was waiting for them in Athens, he was greatly disturbed to see that the city was full of idols.

Junkyard Of The Gods

For Paul, Athens was culture shock! A common saying was that there were more **idols** in Athens than in all the rest of Greece combined! Others—artists, tourists—might have noted the skill of the sculptors, the costliness of the rare collection of statuary and fine art. Paul saw it differently. He was overwhelmed by a sense of tragedy that a city so noted for intellectual brilliance could be so abysmally ignorant and confused about God!

<u>Behind every shrine</u>, temple, and altar, the sensitive spirit of Christ's apostle saw a sinister spirit—a demon committed to stupefying brilliant minds. The great intellects of Athens soared

idol: *any object one shapes or uses as an object of worship*[9]

☞ **GO TO:**

1 Corinthians 8:4–6;
  10:18–20
  (behind every shrine)

among the stars, but their shriveled spirits crawled like oversized infants groping for God in a junkyard of "sacred" toys!

What Others are Saying:

Howard Marshall: The apostle Paul was a strategist. He campaigned in the great cities of the Roman World. He selected centers on trade routes, seaports, places where there was much coming and going. From these centers the message could run like fire far and wide. . . . So he came . . . to Athens, a city with 1000 years of history . . . founder of democracy, home of . . . the greatest university of the world, center of philosophy, literature, science and art—but hard ground for the gospel.[10]

> **Acts 17:17–18** So he reasoned in the synagogue with the Jews and the God-fearing Greeks, as well as in the marketplace day by day with those who happened to be there. A group of Epicurean and Stoic philosophers began to dispute with him. Some of them said, "What is this babbler trying to say?" Others remarked, "He seems to be advocating foreign gods." They said this because Paul was preaching the good news about Jesus and the resurrection.

A New Slant On God

The Athenian marketplace was crowded with people haggling over produce and goods. Mixed with the businesspeople were philosophers, politicians, and teachers "haggling" over the latest philosophical and political ideas. Paul dived into this mix with both feet. Among those who listened to him were Epicurean and Stoic philosophers.

- Epicureans—Disciples of Epicurus (341–271 B.C.). They believed pleasure (happiness) is "the chief end of life." The most worthy pleasure is to be pain-free. Intellectual pleasure is superior to sensual pleasure. Matter is eternal. Existence ends when the body dies—there is no resurrection. The gods have no interest in human affairs.

- Stoics—Disciples of Zeno (340–265 B.C.). They were **pantheistic**—"The Force be with you!" and all that jazz. Life's goal is harmony with nature and its laws and strict control of all human passions, emotions, and affections. Duty is more important than love. Suicide is recommended as a means of escape from a life that can no longer be sustained with dignity.

pantheistic: belief that impersonal forces and laws of nature are gods

When the philosophers called Paul a "babbler" (Acts 17:18), the word they used literally meant "seed-picker." Their first impression was that Paul was a hawker of secondhand scraps of learning. The name they called him reveals an overblown view of their own wisdom. Some thought Paul was promoting two new foreign gods—one named *Iasous* (Jesus) and the other named *Anastasis* ("Resurrection") (Acts 17:18). Why not listen? The streets of Athens were overloaded with gods from all over the world. What could it hurt to add a couple more to the gaudy crowd?

> **Acts 17:19–21** Then they took him and brought him to a meeting of the Areopagus, where they said to him, "May we know what this new teaching is that you are presenting? You are bringing some strange ideas to our ears, and we want to know what they mean." (All the Athenians and the foreigners who lived there spent their time doing nothing but talking about and listening to the latest ideas.)

The Mars Hill Society

For centuries this small hill in Athens, called the **Areopagus,** had been the location for a court that heard criminal cases. In Paul's day it had become a center for the discussion of philosophical ideas among local and foreign experts in history, philosophy, and religion. This "thinkers' club" had taken on the name of the hill, Mars Hill. Nothing got their intellectual juices flowing like a hot new idea.

Areopagus: Hill of Ares, Greek god of war (Roman: Mars)

> **Acts 17:22–23** Paul then stood up in the meeting of the Areopagus and said: "Men of Athens! I see that in every way you are very religious. For as I walked around and looked at your objects of worship, I even found an altar with this inscription: TO AN UNKNOWN GOD. Now what you worship as something unknown I am going to proclaim to you."

The God Nobody Knows

Six hundred years B.C. the city of Athens was in the grip of a terrible plague. Hundreds died. The town fathers consulted with a **Pythian** priestess to find out the source of the plague and why

☞ **GO TO:**

Acts 16:16 (Pythian)

Pythian: possessed with the serpent-spirit who guarded the oracles of Apollo

their sacrifices to the gods were having no effect. They were told the city was under a curse because of the treachery of King Megacles who had promised amnesty to a group of people if they would surrender. When they did, the king broke his word and killed them all!

Athenians had sacrificed to every god they could think of, but the plague persisted. The priestess said there was another god who held the city accountable for their king's crime. Problem: She couldn't tell them his name!

The priestess received an **oracle** instructing the town council to send a delegation to the island of Crete to bring back a prophet named Epimenides who would be able to tell them how to appease the unknown deity.

Epimenides instructed the council members to bring to the Areopagus (where the council held its meetings) a flock of hungry sheep—half of them white and half, black. Stonemasons should also be brought along with a supply of stones and mortar.

At dawn the flock was released on the grassy hill. Epimenides prayed a humble prayer, acknowledging their pitiful ignorance of his name and asking the unknown God to look with compassion and forgiveness on the city. He prayed that this God would reveal his willingness to help by causing the sheep that pleased him—black or white—to lie down on the grass instead of grazing. Each sheep that laid down was sacrificed to the unknown God on an altar constructed on the spot where the animal laid down. Some of these altars bore the inscription *agnosto theo*—"to an unknown God" (see illustration, page 199).

According to Greek storytellers,[11] the plague began to lift the very next day! Within a week, the sick had recovered and Athens was praising Epimenides' "unknown God." But after six centuries, all they knew of this God was that he had forgiven Athens and removed its plague.[12]

Something to Ponder

All creation and God's continuing forgiveness, healing, protection, and supply of daily human needs make it clear to all but the most closed minds that there exists a good and powerful Being who cares for his creatures and provides a place for them to live. Even so, to most people he continues to be the Unknown God. It's hard to find God in an information vacuum! To *know* God requires his personal self-disclosure. He does this through his written Word (the Bible), his Holy Spirit, and his messenger-witnesses.

THE BIG PICTURE

Acts 17:24–31 "The God who made the world and everything in it is the Lord of heaven and earth and does not live in temples built by hands," Paul said. He proceeded to introduce the philosophers to this Creator God.

The God Who Wants To Be Known

The nameless God of Athens had a name! Introducing him to the Athenian intellectuals, Paul called him by the Greek name *Theos.* The name rang a bell with his educated listeners because it was the name the great Greek philosophers had used when writing about the Supreme God in whose existence they believed. Drawing his information from the Bible, Paul unmasked their "unknown" Theos-God with these facts:

1. Theos-God made the world and everything in it (Acts 17:24; Genesis 1).

2. Theos is Master of heaven and earth, sky and land—too great to be confined to a manmade temple or altar (Acts 17:24; 1 Kings 8:27; Isaiah 66:1–2).

3. Theos is not dependent on people to meet his needs or run his errands. *Au contraire!* People are dependent on him for *"life and breath and everything else"* (Acts 17:25).

4. Theos created all nationalities, beginning with one man (Acts 17:26; Genesis 1:27; 2:7). (Athenians believed they "sprang from the soil of their native [Greece],"[13] and were superior to other races and nationalities. Paul punctures their balloon!)

5. Theos planned specific times and places for people to live and created an inhabitable planet before putting them on it (Acts 17:26; Genesis 1:1–26).

6. Theos provided everything needed for life and security so people could see what he's done and reach out to him (Acts 17:27). (If God remains "unknown," it is because humans suppress the truth about him visible in the created universe [Romans 1:18–23].) He wants people to know him. *"He is not far from each one of us!"* (Acts 17:27).

7. Theos doesn't play hide and seek. In fact, we "can't get away from him!"[14] To make his point, Paul quotes two poets familiar to his listeners.

   • Epimenides, 600 B.C., wrote of Theos: "In him we live and move and have our being" (Acts 17:28).

   • Aratus, 300 B.C., wrote: "We are his offspring" (Acts 17:28).

8. Theos originated humans. It makes no sense to think he could be a statue chiseled by a human sculptor from gold, silver, or stone! (Acts 17:29; Isaiah 44:9–20).

9. Theos overlooked Athenian ignorance about him in the past, but no more! Now they must turn from *un*knowing and *know* God (Acts 17:30).

10. Theos has set a time for the world to be judged (Acts 17:31; Psalm 9:8; 96:13; Hebrews 9:27). The identity of the presiding judge has been revealed: He's the man God raised from the dead! (Acts 17:31; John 5:25–27; Romans 1:4).

☞ **GO TO:**

Acts 14:15–17;
Romans 3:25
(Theos overlooked)

Romans 6:23; 14:12;
2 Corinthians 5:10;
Revelation 20:11–15
(judged)

What Others are Saying:

Epimenides, *in the poem from which Paul quotes:*
They fashioned a tomb for thee O holy and high one—
The Cretans always liars, evil beasts, idle bellies!
But thou art not dead; thou livest and abidest forever.
For in thee we live and move and have our being.[15]

Michael Green: To the cultured [pagans] . . . the Christians seek to establish the fact that there is one God, discredit idolatry and through the light of natural revelation (God the Creator and Sustainer) to prepare the way for the special revelation of God contained in Christ.[16]

> **Acts 17:32–34** When they heard about the resurrection of the dead, some of them sneered, but others said, "We want to hear you again on this subject." At that Paul left the Council. A few men became followers of Paul and believed. Among them was Dionysius, a member of the Areopagus, also a woman named Damaris, and a number of others.

Eggheads For Jesus

At <u>mention of resurrection</u> the Mars Hill Society disintegrated into cynical laughter. To Epicureans and others end-time judgment and resurrection were absurd. According to legend, when Athena, patron goddess of the city, founded the Areopagus, the god Apollo said: "Once a man dies and the earth drinks up his blood, there is no resurrection."[17] Stoics did not believe in resurrection but believed in continuing existence after this life. Perhaps they were the ones who said they'd like to hear more.

☞ **GO TO:**

Matthew 27:62–66; 28:11–12; Acts 4:2; 23:6–8 (mention of resurrection)

EARLY CHURCH WOMEN—Some listeners believed. Two are named: Dionysius, a member of the Mars Hill Society, and Damaris. The Society had no women members so Damaris may have been a bystander listening to the discussion or a street woman plying her trade in the market. She made history as a charter member in the tiny infant church at Athens.

Maude De Joseph West: Paul did not gain many converts among the Greek intellectuals. It is so even today. Men, wise in their own conceits, smug in their self-sufficiency, are not easily persuaded that their souls are wearing <u>filthy rags</u> and <u>feeding on husks</u>. God is only for the weak and the stupid, and they, the intelligentsia, have absolutely no need of him.[18]

John Pollock: Athens had rejected (Paul). He could not know that his speech would go down to posterity . . . as one of the greatest speeches of Athens. He could not know that whole books would be written about it or that in a few hundred years the **Parthenon** would become a Christian church; and that nineteen centuries on, when Greece after long suppression became once more a sovereign state, the national flag which flies beside the ruins of the Parthenon would be lowered to half-mast each Good Friday, and raised on Easter Day in honor of Christ's resurrection.[19]

What Others are Saying:

☞ **GO TO:**

Isaiah 64:6 (filthy rags)

Luke 15:16 (feeding on husks)

Parthenon: *temple to the goddess Athena, built on the Acropolis at Athens*

1. Of what three "crimes" did enemies accuse the Christians in Thessalonica?
2. How did the Berean Jews respond to the message of Christ?
3. What did Paul use as a starting place for his teaching about God at the Areopagus (Mars Hill Society) in Athens?
4. Using Paul's Mars Hill teaching (Acts 17:24–31) fill in the blanks:
   a. People are dependent on God for "_____ and _____ and everything else."
   b. God is "not far from _____."
   c. "In him we ____ and move and _____."
   d. "We are his _____."
5. What did Paul say that made some of the Areopagus members sneer?

CHAPTER WRAP-UP

- Paul's team preached in Thessalonica. Jews and God-fearing Greeks (including prominent women) became persuaded Jesus was the Messiah. Jealous synagogue leaders accused Christians of being troublemakers. (Acts 17:1–9)

- Bereans received the message about Jesus after carefully studying Old Testament Scripture to see if what they were hearing was true. Enemies from Thessalonica came to Berea and stirred up trouble. Paul went on to Athens. (Acts 17:10–15)

- Athenians' idolatry distressed Paul. Sabbaths, he taught in the synagogue; weekdays, he preached to pagan philosophers in the marketplace. (Acts 17:16–21)

- Speaking at the Areopagus, Paul revealed the identity of the "Unknown God" whose altar he found there. (Acts 17:22–31)

- When Paul told them about the resurrection of Jesus, the Epicureans made jokes about it. A few people said they wanted to hear more. A few Greeks—Dionysius and Damaris and a few other intellectuals—believed in the Lord. (Acts 17:32–34)

ACTS 18: SIN CITY SAINTS

Let's Get Started

From the frying pan of intellectual, idolatrous Athens, Paul leaped into the fire of sex-saturated, materialistic Corinth. Traveling alone, he approached Corinth through the five-hundred-year-old **Isthmian wall** that spanned the five-mile Corinthian **isthmus**. He may have wondered if this hotbed of **hedonism** could possibly be convinced to respond to the invitation of the pure and selfless Nazarene he had come to introduce.

> **Acts 18:1** After this, Paul left Athens and went to Corinth.

Isthmian wall: twenty-five feet high

isthmus: narrow strip of land connecting northern and southern Greece

hedonism: belief that pleasure is the most important good in life

The Swingin' City Of Aphrodite And Apollos

Corinth was famed as "the Bridge of Greece." Situated on the Corinthian Isthmus, the narrow neck of land that keeps southern Greece from being an island, its geographical position made it a key commercial center. The only overland trade route between northern and southern Greece passed through Corinth. It had two seaports, one on the Aegean Sea and one on the Adriatic Sea. Small ships were carried from one port to the other across the isthmus on a tramway, saving two hundred miles of treacherous sea travel.

Its strategic location gave Corinth potential as a center from which the news of Jesus could spread in all directions.

For The Love Of Sport

The first thing Paul saw as he passed through the Isthmian wall was the huge stadium where the Isthmian Games were held. This biennial sporting event was second only to the Olympics in importance. The games began with a sacrifice to Poseidon, the sea god, followed by athletic, equestrian, and musical competitions.

The Isthmian games were notoriously corrupt. Athletes broke training rules and sold themselves to the highest bidder. Magicians and fortune-tellers bilked the gullible. Every sort of huckster hawked his wares. Philosophers gathered to argue. It was just the kind of carnival atmosphere where a brash evangelist like Paul would be found declaring the news of Jesus Christ. His letters reveal he was somewhat of a "sports fan" and often used sports to illustrate spiritual truth.

To "Act The Corinthian"

Six miles south of the stadium was the city of 100,000 to 700,000 (depending on who you asked). A city of sailors, traveling salesmen, and government officials—"everybody" was from someplace else!

Fifteen hundred feet above the city atop the Acrocorinth (Corinthian **Acropolis**) was the town's most impressive feature, the Temple of Aphrodite, goddess of love and Poseidon's coruler of the sea. Every night a thousand prostitute-priestesses descended from the temple to the town to engage its male citizens and visitors in "worship" of the goddess.

In the first-century world to be called a "Corinthian" did not necessarily mean you came from Corinth—it meant you were hooked on pleasure and sexual excess. Prostitutes were called "Corinthian girls." To "act the Corinthian" meant to engage in sex outside of marriage. And when a Corinthian was portrayed in a play, he was always drunk.

John Pollock: In the city itself, the archaic Temple of Apollo . . . also glorified sex as well as music, song, and poetry, for Apollo was the ideal of male beauty. The temple's inner recesses held nude statues and friezes of Apollo in various poses of virility. . . . If the love of Christ Jesus could take root in Corinth, the most populated, wealthy, commercial-minded, and sex-obsessed city of eastern Europe, it must prove powerful anywhere.[1]

☞ **GO TO:**

1 Corinthians 9:24–27;
Colossians 4:12;
1 Timothy 4:7–9;
2 Timothy 2:5; 4:7–8
(to illustrate)

Acropolis: Greek city's fortified high ground; mountain overlooking the city

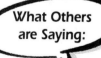

What Others are Saying:

What's A Nice Jewish Boy Doing In A Place Like This?

Though born in the pagan city of Tarsus, Paul was brought up Jewish. He cut his teeth on the Ten Commandments. He trained in Jerusalem to be a rabbi. Since his conversion (see Acts 9) he was a committed follower of the lofty moral teachings of Jesus.

As he moved about Corinth, at the games, the Forum, the market, and in the neighborhoods, he was surrounded by prostitutes and their customers, practicing homosexuals, cheating business people, drunks, and addicts. It was not unusual to be accosted by a harlot. Everyday conversation was filled with lust and moral filth, cursing and slander (see 1 Corinthians 6:9–10). The town lived for money, pleasure, wine, gambling, sports.

The Christian mind is <u>trained</u> by Scripture and the Holy Spirit to be sensitive, repulsed by sin, saddened by immorality. The realization that so many were trapped in destructive lifestyles seems to have nearly overwhelmed Paul. As his ministry in Corinth began, he experienced a deep sense of *"weakness and fear, and . . . much trembling"* (1 Corinthians 2:3).

☞ **GO TO:**

2 Timothy 3:14–17;
Hebrews 5:14
(trained)

> **Acts 18:2** There [in Corinth] he met a Jew named Aquila, a native of Pontus, who had recently come from Italy with his wife Priscilla, because Claudius had ordered all the Jews to leave Rome. Paul went to see them, . . .

Soul Mates

Paul did not like to work alone. It wasn't simply a matter of personal preference—spiritual <u>teamwork</u> was the principle on which the early church nearly always operated. Jesus set the <u>pattern</u>. Silas and Timothy had stayed in Berea to help the young church get on its feet (Acts 17:15).

Corinth had a significant Jewish colony. Following his usual pattern, Paul went to the synagogue. There he met a Christian couple, newly arrived from Rome—a man named Aquila and his wife, Priscilla. The three of them became close friends and co-workers for Christ.

Aquila and Priscilla moved easily around the Roman Empire (see illustration, page 206). Aquila was a Jew. Priscilla may also have been Jewish, but some scholars speculate she was from the aristocratic Roman family Prisca. <u>Prisca</u> is the formal name Paul uses to refer to her in his letters. Luke uses her familiar name, Priscilla. Before Corinth, they lived in Rome and were part of the church

☞ **GO TO:**

Acts 2:14; 6:3–6; 8:14;
11:25–26; 13:1, 4–5;
15:39–40 (teamwork)

Matthew 10:5; Luke
9:28; 10:1 (pattern)

Romans 16:3;
2 Timothy 4:19
(Prisca)

there. They were forced to leave Rome in A.D. 49 when Claudius Caesar issued an order banishing Jews from the capital city.

The **cardinal** principle for function in the church is interdependence (1 Corinthians 12:21–27). Church leadership as seen in Acts follows that cardinal principle. No apostle, elder, deacon, or pastor is called to "go it alone" or to be a "Lone Ranger" running everything. (Even the Lone Ranger had his Tonto!)

> **Acts 18:3** . . . and because he was a tentmaker as they were, he stayed and worked with them.

Preacher With Dirt Under His Fingernails

cilicium: *cloth made of goat hair from Paul's home province of Cilicia*

One of the things that first linked Aquila, Priscilla, and Paul was their common trade. The original word for "tentmakers" literally means "leather workers." They made leather tents from goatskin and wove goat fleece into waterproof cloth called **cilicium**, which was used to make tents and cloaks.

Aquila and Priscilla's Travels

The lines and numbers on this map indicate the mobility of Aquila and Priscilla. They came from Pontus (1), lived in Rome (2), met and worked with Paul in Corinth (3), moved to Ephesus (4), and later moved back to Rome (5).

Paul sometimes <u>accepted gifts</u> in order to spend full time in ministry (he taught that the minister has <u>the right</u> to be supported by those he or she serves). But in Corinth and as a general policy he chose to earn his living and that of his fellow team members by working as a tentmaker. In his rabbinical training he'd been taught it was improper to demand payment for teaching the Scriptures. "He who makes a profit from the crown of the **Torah** shall waste away," said Rabbi Hillel.[2] Rabbi <u>Gamaliel</u> said, "All study of the Torah which is not combined with work will ultimately be futile and lead to sin."[3]

Paul was always careful to avoid the impression that the Gospel was just another way to make a buck! His motive for preaching was not profit (2 Corinthians 2:17). Besides, working with his hands put Paul side by side with the ordinary working stiffs of Corinth—people he wanted to reach with the good news about Jesus.

☞ **GO TO:**

Philippians 4:10–19 (accepted gifts)

1 Corinthians 9 (the right)

Acts 5:34–39; 22:3 (Gamaliel)

Something to Ponder

Torah: Old Testament Scripture

Bernard of Clairvaux: Learn the lesson that, if you are to do the work of a prophet, what you need is not a scepter but a hoe.[4]

Read the following passages to discover why Paul continued to make his living doing ordinary, non-religious work while engaged in ministry, instead of being a "full-time" minister.

Acts 20:33–35
2 Corinthians 2:17
1 Thessalonians 2:9

1 Corinthians 9:13–19
2 Corinthians 11:7–12
2 Thessalonians 3:7–10

What Others are Saying:

Dig Deeper

> **Acts 18:4–6** Every Sabbath he reasoned in the synagogue, trying to persuade Jews and Greeks.
> When Silas and Timothy came from Macedonia, Paul <u>devoted</u> himself exclusively to preaching, testifying to the Jews that Jesus was the Christ. But when the Jews opposed Paul and became abusive, he shook out his clothes in protest and said to them, "Your blood be on your own heads! I am clear of my responsibility. From now on I will go to the Gentiles."

☞ **GO TO:**

1 Corinthians 2:2 (devoted)

Try *Gentile* Persuasion!

On Sabbath days Paul was given opportunity to teach at the synagogue. Silas and Timothy completed their work with the young churches of Macedonia and rejoined him. Hearing how well the Thessalonians and Bereans were doing gave the apostle a shot in the arm. The Philippians sent a gift which freed Paul to lay aside tent making to concentrate on a last ditch effort to convince his Jewish brothers to welcome Jesus as their Messiah.

History repeated itself in Corinth when Jewish resistance became so intense there was nothing to do but to leave the synagogue and take the Gospel to pagans. Paul's shaking his clothes was a dramatization the Jewish congregation would have understood as an announcement of futility and separation, and warning of judgment. A strict Jew returning to Israel from a pagan land would shake the dust of that land from his clothing so as not to bring pagan contamination into Israel.

"You've made your bed," Paul was saying, "Now lie in it!"

☞ **GO TO:**

1 Thessalonians 3:6–10 (Thessalonians)

2 Corinthians 11:9; Philippians 4:16 (Philippians)

Luke 9:5; 10:1; Acts 13:51 (announcement)

> **Acts 18:7–8** Then Paul left the synagogue and went next door to the house of Titius Justus, a worshiper of God. Crispus, the synagogue ruler, and his entire household believed in the Lord; and many of the Corinthians who heard him believed and were baptized.

"Somewhere, God Always Opens A Window!"[5]

As synagogue doors slammed shut, the house next door, the home of a Gentile named Titius Justus, opened its doors to welcome the Christian messengers. The greatest shock waves felt in the Jewish community must have been when its leading citizen, Crispus, with his entire family, joined the Christian meeting next door!

These verses read like a Who's Who in Corinth. Titius Justus, also known as "Gaius," was a wealthy Roman God-worshiper who attended the synagogue. One of the few people in Corinth whom Paul personally baptized (see 1 Corinthians 1:14), his home was spacious enough to host *"the whole church"* at Corinth.

Crispus was synagogue president, an ordained rabbi, and trained in the Law. As president he was in charge of congregational life, arranged Scripture readers and speakers, and presided at meetings. Paul's teaching would have been cleared through him. He and his entire family believed in Jesus as Messiah. Paul personally baptized him (see 1 Corinthians 1:14).

☞ **GO TO:**

Acts 10:2, 44; 16:15, 31–34 (entire family)

Romans 16:23 (host)

> **Acts 18:9–11** One night the Lord spoke to Paul in a vision: "Do not be afraid; keep on speaking, do not be silent. For I am with you, and no one is going to attack and harm you, because I have many people in this city." So Paul stayed for a year and a half, teaching them the word of God.

The Undiscovered Church

Paul had faced opposition in every city—mob violence, stoning, beating, imprisonment, sickness, threats, ridicule, rejection, hatred, and verbal and personal abuse. In Corinth he was confronted with sin so open and glamorized, morally degenerate lifestyles so foreign, that his mind went into overload. He may have been tempted to move on before the Lord's work in Corinth was solidly established.

At that crucial moment, Jesus spoke to Paul in a vision, telling him to keep talking without fear (Acts 18:9–10). The Lord gave three reasons he shouldn't cut and run.

- The Lord's presence: *"I am with you."*
- The Lord's protection: *"No one is going to attack or harm you."*
- The Lord's people: *"I have many people in this city."*

Paul stayed a year and a half, teaching God's Word to anyone who would listen. One of the greatest churches in the New Testament emerged. A burgeoning fellowship of previously lost souls came to Christ out of the depths of moral and spiritual darkness. "Here's what some of you were," wrote Paul in a letter after he left, "sexually immoral, idolaters, adulterers, male prostitutes, practicing homosexuals, thieves, greedy, drunks, spreaders of lies about others, swindlers!" "But," he added, *"you were **washed**, you were **sanctified**, you were **justified** in the name of the Lord Jesus Christ and by the Spirit of our God!"* (see 1 Corinthians 6:10–11).

washed: forgiven, cleansed from past sins, kept clean

sanctified: set apart for God's service, useful to God

The church at Corinth was a fellowship of people whose lifestyles were turned right side up through the straightforward telling of Jesus' story—especially his death on the cross and what it means (see 1 Corinthians 2:1–5; also 1:18–25).

justified: declared "not guilty," right with God

While in Corinth, Paul wrote **two letters** to the Christians in Thessalonica. These two letters became part of the New Testament.

two letters: First and Second Thessalonians

Something to Ponder

The amazing thing about this story is that before the Corinthian church existed, the Lord looked at this infamously wicked city and saw something wonderful even the visionary apostle Paul could not see. *"I have many people in this city!"* The church was there, waiting to be discovered not only among the nice, moral folks, but among the druggies, prostitutes, gays and lesbians, cheats and jailbirds. Jesus loves and wants to rescue all kinds of people!

THE BIG PICTURE

> **Acts 18:12–16** Jewish leaders in Corinth brought Paul up on charges before the Roman provincial official, Gallio. Gallio ruled in favor of Paul and the Christians.

Christians Win A Round In Court

The Lord promised Paul protection (Acts 18:10). That protection came from an unexpected source. In summer, A.D. 51, a noble Roman named Gallio was appointed **proconsul** of the province of **Achaia**. Gallio was a son of the famous Roman orator Seneca and brother of the Stoic philosopher, Seneca (Junior). He was known for kindness and fairness. His brother wrote: "No man was ever as sweet to one as Gallio is to all."[6]

proconsul: *governor*

Achaia: *southern Greece*

Paul's enemies thought they could buffalo the new proconsul into silencing Paul and the Christians. Judaism was a protected religion under Roman law. By charging that Paul *"is persuading people to worship God in ways contrary to the law"* (Acts 18:13) they hoped to convince Gallio that Christianity was not Jewish and could not be included in the protections the government granted Judaism.

Gallio, however, ruled that what Paul was doing was no crime against Roman law. He saw the whole case as nothing but a fuss among rival Jews over theology, and he had no intention of getting the government involved in it (Acts 18:14–15).

What Others are Saying:

F. F. Bruce: Gallio's ruling meant in effect that Paul and his associates, so long as they committed no breach of public order, continued to share the protection which Roman law granted to the practice of Judaism. . . . It meant that for the next ten or twelve years . . . [until Nero reversed this policy] the gospel could be proclaimed in the provinces of the empire without fear of coming into conflict with Roman law.[7]

> **Acts 18:17** Then they all turned on Sosthenes the synagogue ruler and beat him in front of the court. But Gallio showed no concern whatever.

Poor Sosthenes

Gallio ejected the accusers from his court. Then he sat there with a disinterested look on his face while an unidentified "they" beat the stuffin' out of Sosthenes, the synagogue president! Sosthenes was the successor to Crispus, who lost his job as synagogue officer when he became a Christian (see Acts 18:8). Quite possibly he is the same Sosthenes who coauthored Paul's first letter to Corinth (see 1 Corinthians 1:1), which would mean he too became a Christian.

> **Acts 18:18** Paul stayed on in Corinth for some time. Then he left the brothers and sailed for Syria, accompanied by Priscilla and Aquila. Before he sailed, he had his hair cut off at Cenchrea because of a vow he had taken.

A Haircut, A Vow, And A Trip

After Gallio's favorable decision, Paul stayed a while longer in Corinth. Then he left, headed for . . . ? Luke skimps on the why's and wherefore's and doesn't tell how much time it took to do this or that, so we are left to make "educated" guesses. Here's the itinerary I'm guessing (with the scholars' help) Paul took:

1. He packed his bags and hiked to Cenchrea, Corinth's Aegean seaport. Before embarking he went to Ye Olde Tonsorial Shoppe for a haircut, *"because of a __vow__."* When Jews were especially thankful they "took a vow" promising to demonstrate their gratitude to God publicly. Paul had entered Corinth with fear and trembling. By God's mercy he'd survived the dangers of the wicked city unscathed, leaving behind a gifted, growing church. Getting a haircut was his Jewish way of saying "Thanks!"

2. His final destination was the Roman province of Syria, which included both Antioch—his home church—and Jerusalem—everybody's "mother" church (Acts 18:18).

3. Priscilla and Aquila traveled with him as far as Ephesus (Acts 18:19). Anxious to get on his way, Paul left, promising to return *"if it is God's will."*

☞ **GO TO:**

Deuteronomy 23:21–23 (vow)

vow: *promise made to God*

4. He boarded a ship to Caesarea, Jerusalem's nearest seaport. In Jerusalem he *"greeted the church"* (Acts 18:22). For some reason only his mother knows for sure, Luke doesn't mention Jerusalem. His use of "up" and "down" tells us Paul went there. Jews always went "up" to Jerusalem no matter where they came from and "down" no matter where they were going when they left.

5. From Jerusalem Paul went *"down"* to Antioch, his home base (Acts 18:22).

6. After time in Antioch he took another "missionary journey" (see illustration, page 216). No details are given here (Acts 18:23).

THE BIG PICTURE

Acts 18:19–28 Priscilla and Aquila got involved in the life of the synagogue. Their quiet <u>infiltration</u> of the Ephesian Jewish community contributed to Paul's success when he returned. One person this dynamic duo influenced was a silver-tongued Egyptian Jew named Apollos. Apollos was of great help to believers and was a good debater for Christ.

☞ **GO TO:**

Luke 13:20 (infiltration)

Silver-Tongued Stranger

Apollos was a native of Alexandria, Egypt, where a million Jews lived. Highly educated, he knew his way around the Old Testament. He believed in Jesus through the teachings of John the Baptist. A skilled orator, he was a fiery, courageous preacher.

As a student of John the Baptist, Apollos knew the basics about Jesus, but lacked important facts needed to effectively communicate the good news.

- He knew Jews demonstrated readiness to receive Christ by repentance and baptism (see Luke 3:3–14).

Lamb: *sacrifice to take away the world's sins*

- He knew Jesus was the Savior—John called him "**Lamb** of God" (see John 1:29–34).

- He knew Christ would baptize people with the Holy Spirit (see Luke 3:16).

- He *"had been instructed in the way of the Lord"* (Acts 18:25)—the *way* of life modeled by Jesus.

He was probably in the dark about the church's decision to accept Gentiles without requiring them to live under Jewish law (see Acts 15:28–29). Also Alexandrian Jews tended to interpret the Bible **allegorically** rather than literally—perhaps Apollos needed correction at that point. Priscilla and Aquila took him under their wing and *"explained to him the way of God more adequately"* (Acts 18:26).

After that Apollos was an unstoppable **apologist** for Christ (Acts 18:27–28). He went to Europe and developed an appreciative following at <u>Corinth</u>.

allegorically: seeing questionable hidden meanings in straightforward Bible passages

apologist: defender of the faith, debater

William Barclay: One of the commonest titles in Acts is The Way (see Acts 9:2; 19:9, 23; 22:4; 24:14, 22); and that title shows us at once that Christianity means not only believing certain things but putting them into practice.[8]

What Others are Saying:

Aquila and Priscilla Served Christ Together

☞ **GO TO:**

1 Corinthians 1:12; 3:4–9 (Corinth)

Dig Deeper

- Acts 18:3—Worked together to earn a living
- Acts 18:3—Opened their home to Paul
- Acts 18:3–4—Helped start the church at Corinth
- Acts 18:18–19—Moved to Ephesus to help start another new church
- Acts 18:24–25—Spotted potential in Apollos as a Christian communicator
- Acts 18:26—Opened their home to Apollos, corrected, filled gaps in his knowledge of the Gospel
- Acts 18:2, 18–19, 26—Ministered together without concern about whose ministry got noticed. (In the beginning Aquila is named first. Later Priscilla is mentioned first, probably indicating her gifts were more prominent. Still they were inseparable in ministry.)
- Romans 16:3–4—Paul's "fellow-workers," their risking-everything, apostolic-style ministry impacted churches in Corinth, Ephesus, and Rome.
- Romans 16:5—In Rome (and probably in Ephesus) they opened their home to a house church.

EARLY CHURCH WOMEN—After Acts 18:2, Priscilla's name is nearly always listed before Aquila's. When Paul greets the two in his letters, he mentions Priscilla first (see Romans 16:3; 2 Timothy 4:19). She probably was the more prominent of the two. In a culture that tended to put women down, the Christians valued the special contribution of its women to God's work.

Vickie Baker: Step out in holy boldness—Live life on the edge. No apathy, no boredom, No comfort zone in sight! Empowered by the Spirit. Opportunities abound. Vibrant Christianity—Life lived on the edge.[9]

Study Questions

1. Who did Paul link up with in Corinth? What did he have in common with them?
2. Where did Paul go to preach when he could no longer preach in the synagogue? What important person followed him there? How did the Corinthians respond?
3. What three reasons did the Lord give for Paul to stay in Corinth and continue to courageously preach the Gospel?
4. What Egyptian Jew was influenced by Aquila and Priscilla, and what were his strengths related to Christian ministry?

CHAPTER WRAP-UP

- Corinth was a hotbed of hedonism, sports fanaticism, and sexual excess disguised as religion. Paul's need for support was filled by Aquila and Priscilla, with whom he worked as a tentmaker. (Acts 18:1–3)

- Some Jews, including the synagogue president and his family, embraced Jesus as their Messiah. But opposition forced Paul to take his teaching outside the synagogue to the home of Titius Justus, a Gentile believer. (Acts 18:4–8)

- Paul felt a great sense of inadequacy as he ministered in Corinth. The Lord assured him in a vision that he had many people in the city. If Paul kept speaking in spite of his fears he would find them. The Lord would protect him. (Acts 18:9–10)

- Enemies accused Paul before the Roman governor Gallio, who ruled in favor of the Christians. (Acts 18:12–17)

- As Paul left Corinth with Aquila and Priscilla he demonstrated thankfulness to God with a vow. He left Aquila and Priscilla in Ephesus and went on to Jerusalem and Antioch. (Acts 18:18–23)

- When Apollos, an educated Alexandrian Jew and student of John the Baptist, arrived in Ephesus and taught in the synagogue, Priscilla and Aquila took him in and filled the gaps in his theology. He went on to Europe and became a highly successful Christian apologist. (Acts 18:24–28)

ACTS 19: FREEDOM AND FURY IN THE CITY OF THE NO-GODS

Let's Get Started

Ephesus was a deceptively beautiful metropolis. The magnificent temple to the fertility goddess Artemis—one of the seven wonders of the first-century world—dominated its skyline and religious, social, and economic life. No sensual pleasure was denied. It was a world financial center. Dreams of material success and affluence captivated the minds and consumed the energies of the people. All the happiness money could buy was at their fingertips. Life for the Ephesians should have been "the good life."

But when the early Christians looked at Ephesus, they saw something very different. They saw a culture of fear scarcely veiled by the architectural, artistic, and sensual beauty on display. Christ's followers saw a half-million souls trapped in a devil-dominated world of **necromancy**, **occultism**, witchcraft, and useless worship of a lifeless, powerless goddess. Magic symbols and **incantations** failed to give them control over their world. Worship failed to connect them with the living God. Nearly the entire populace lived on a treadmill of **superstition**, confusion, and terror.

Into this environment went Paul.

> **Acts 19:1a** While Apollos was at Corinth, Paul took the road through the interior and arrived at Ephesus.

necromancy: *contact with spirits of the dead*

occultism: *belief in, influence by, involvement with supernatural powers*

incantations: *spells and verbal charms*

superstition: *trust in magic, chance, or false ideas of cause*

The Long Road To Ephesus

Ephesus was an evangelistic prize that had eluded Paul. Twice before, the city and its surrounding province had been on his planned itinerary. Twice, the Lord overruled his plans. The first detour occurred on the second apostolic foray into Asia Minor when *"Paul and his companions . . . [were] kept by the Holy Spirit from preaching the word in the **province of Asia**"* (Acts 16:6). Instead, the team was sent to <u>Macedonia</u> (Acts 16:10).

Paul's heart again drew him to Ephesus after a fruitful ministry in Corinth. This time he went there, accompanied by Aquila and Priscilla, and preached in the synagogue. The synagogue congregation was responsive. But Paul had been antsy. He couldn't stay. Indicating it was "God's will," he left for Antioch, Syria, with a stopover at Jerusalem (see Acts 18:18–22 and illustration below).

Luke, the early church historian, doesn't tell how long this detour took. Paul rejoined Aquila and Priscilla in Ephesus *"after spending some time in Antioch"* and an overland trip to churches he and Barnabas had planted in Galatia and Phrygia—in the Asia Minor interior (Acts 18:23).

province of Asia: Roman state where Ephesus was the largest city; today—western Turkey

☞ **GO TO:**

Acts 16:11–18:18 (Macedonia)

Paul's Third Missionary Journey

This map shows the route of Paul's third missionary journey, which began in Antioch, Syria, north of Jerusalem. From there he traveled overland toward Ephesus.

Why did Paul keep skirting Ephesus? Paul was <u>no super-hero</u>. Ephesus represented a new kind of challenge. Never had he encountered a city so completely given over to the occult. As a mere man, he may have needed time to get his soul and mind ready for the fierce spiritual warfare he knew he'd face inside the Ephesian city limits.

> **Acts 19:1b–2** There he found some disciples and asked them, "Did you receive the Holy Spirit when you believed?"
>
> They answered, "No, we have not even heard that there is a Holy Spirit."

The Key To The City

Finally, Paul arrived in the great city. The Lord provided a welcome mat. In a special encounter the Holy Spirit handed Paul the "key to the city."

He had not been in Ephesus long before he bumped into a small group of disciples. Luke, the early church historian, reserves that term for followers of Jesus. These men believed. They'd been baptized. They talked and looked like Christians. Their faith *appeared* to be the real McCoy. But Paul had an uneasy feeling. Something was missing.

"Did you receive the Holy Spirit when you believed?" Paul asked. (Good question. The New Testament doesn't recognize the possibility of being a real Christian unless the Spirit comes to live <u>in a person</u>. The Holy Spirit comes in the package <u>with faith</u>.)

"We have not even heard that there is a Holy Spirit," was the incredulous response.

John Kennedy: There is no detailed description given whereby we may know God's people. . . . It may be difficult to explain in terms that would satisfy the **unregenerate** man how children of God recognize one another, but the witness of the Spirit is a reliable guide.[1]

> **Acts 19:3–4** So Paul asked, "Then what baptism did you receive?"
>
> "John's baptism," they replied.
>
> Paul said, "John's baptism was a baptism of repentance. He told the people to believe in the one coming after him, that is, in Jesus."

Something to Ponder

☞ **GO TO:**

1 Corinthians 2:3; 2 Corinthians 12:7–10 (no superhero)

☞ **GO TO:**

1 Corinthians 12:3; Galatians 3:2; 1 Thessalonians 1:5–7; Hebrews 6:4 (in a person)

Acts 2:38; Romans 8:9 (with faith)

What Others are Saying:

unregenerate: *not Christian; lacking Christ's inner life*

The Unheard-Of Spirit

Paul quizzed them about baptism: "Whodiptcha?" Turns out they'd been baptized by John the Baptist or one of his followers.

Their professed ignorance about the Holy Spirit cannot mean they'd never heard of him. John's disciples knew the Old Testament, which is loaded with <u>references</u> to the Holy Spirit. What's more, they knew John the Baptist. John clearly prophesied that Christ's main work would be to baptize people with the Holy Spirit (see Matthew 3:11; Luke 3:16; John 1:33).

What these disciples most likely meant was that they didn't know the prophecy about Christ baptizing people with the Holy Spirit had been <u>fulfilled</u>. They hadn't heard about Pentecost, the day the Holy Spirit came to live in people who believe in Jesus.

☞ **GO TO:**

Genesis 1:2; Numbers 11:16–17; Isaiah 63:10–11; Joel 2:28–32 (references)

Acts 1:5; 2:4; 2:38 (fulfilled)

> **Acts 19:5** On hearing this, they were baptized into the name of the Lord Jesus.

Double Dip

The Ephesian "disciples" also didn't seem to know John had identified Jesus as Messiah and told people to put their trust in him (see John 1:29–35). When they heard this, they believed and were baptized *"into the name of the Lord Jesus."*

This is the only place in the New Testament where anyone is said to have been rebaptized. It highlights the fact that there was a huge difference between John's baptism and baptism into Jesus Christ.

- *John's baptism* was a ceremonial bath of repentance. It represented a commitment to a radical life-change[2] and an announcement of intent to live a better life in preparation to receive Christ when he arrived (see Luke 3:3–14; John 1:6–9, 14).

- *Jesus' baptism* is a dramatized declaration in which believers in Jesus are dipped in water (or have it poured or sprinkled on them) to announce they believe in Jesus, have welcomed him into their lives as Savior and Lord, and are united with him and everything he has done and stands for (see Romans 6:1–11).

In the Bible, to act "into" or "in the name of" someone means to act depending on and consistent with the character, values, and accomplishments of the person whose name is used.

Remember This . . .

Authentic Christian faith does not depend on saying the right words or doing the right religious rituals, but on the character and faithfulness of Jesus Christ.

> **Acts 19:6–7** When Paul placed his hands on them, the Holy Spirit came on them, and they spoke in <u>tongues</u> and <u>prophesied</u>. There were about twelve men in all.

☞ **GO TO:**

Acts 2:4–11, 17; 10:44–46 (tongues)

Acts 4:31, 33; 9:17–20; 10:44–46 (prophesied)

The Energizer Enters

When Paul placed his hands on the "Ephesian Twelve," it symbolized acceptance into Christian fellowship. The Holy Spirit's coming to them at their baptism points up the most important difference between John's and Jesus' ministries. John could bring people to the point of readiness to change. But only Jesus, coming to live in them in the person of his Holy Spirit—*spiritually baptizing* them—could make it possible for people to live changed lives.

What Others are Saying:

Billy Graham: The filling of the Holy Spirit should not be a once-for-all event, but a continuous reality every day of our lives. It is a process. We must surrender ourselves to him daily, and every day we must choose to remain surrendered. In every situation involving conflict between self and God's will, we must make our decisions on the basis of our constant submission to Christ.[3]

> **Acts 19:8–9** Paul entered the synagogue and spoke boldly there for three months, arguing persuasively about the kingdom of God. But some of them became obstinate; they refused to believe and publicly maligned the Way. So Paul left them. He took the disciples with him and had discussions daily in the lecture hall of Tyrannus.

Extracurricular Activities At Tyrannus U.

The aggressive and relentless preaching and teaching of Paul, combined with Jesus' "<u>yeast-in-dough</u>" principle, produced amazing results in Ephesus and the surrounding province. For three months the synagogue **pulpit** was open. Many Jews were persuaded to believe in Jesus. At the same time some hardened their hearts. Inevitably the opposition became too disruptive for Paul to continue. When the synagogue door slammed shut, Paul took the

☞ **GO TO:**

Matthew 13:33 (yeast-in-dough)

pulpit: *Hebrew: migdal ez—desk where Torah scrolls were read*

Tyrannus: *philosopher whose hall Paul rented*

daily: *11 A.M.–4 P.M.— siesta time for Professor Tyrannus's students[4]*

believers with him and moved his base of operations to the lecture hall or school of **Tyrannus** where **daily** he shared the good news of Jesus with all comers.

> **Acts 19:10** This went on for two years, so that all the Jews and Greeks who lived in the province of Asia heard the word of the Lord.

The Incredible Statistic

☞ **GO TO:**

Revelation 2–3
   (seven churches)

During Paul's two years at Tyrannus's hall, the <u>seven churches</u> mentioned in Revelation were probably founded. Paul taught, then he and his colleagues fanned out across the province sharing what they were learning of Jesus.[5] Paul spent a total of three years in Ephesus (see Acts 20:31). His coworkers included Aquila, Priscilla, Silas, Timothy, Erastus, Gaius, Aristarchus, Luke, the "Ephesian Twelve," believers from the synagogue, and others (see Acts 18–19). Little knots of believers sprang up throughout the area. And *everyone*—can you believe it?—*everyone* in the province heard the good news from someone! (Acts 19:10).

 Persecution & Martyrdom—In the mid-1700s in England, an Anglican priest named John Wesley was barred from preaching his message of spiritual renewal in Anglican churches. So he preached anywhere people would listen—the streets, mines, countryside—even cemeteries. Result? The Methodist revival in which tens of thousands came to Christ.

Faith Versus The Boogie Man

In spite of its grand emphasis on religion, philosophy, and material acquisition, the culture of Ephesus displayed glaring evidence that none of these met the spiritual needs of the people. The literature of early Ephesus contains much evidence that the study and practice of occultism and magical arts was pervasive. "Witches came out of the woodwork!"[6] Superstition substituted for faith. Famous parchments, called "Ephesian Letters," contained incantations of secret names and words guaranteed to bring safe travel, fertility, and success in business or love.

Even Jews who lived there dabbled in the forbidden stuff. A book of first-century Jewish magic, **Sefer ha-Rasim**, lists names of angelic beings used in casting good and evil spells.[7]

Sefer ha-Rasim: *Book of Mysteries*

> **Acts 19:11–12** God did extraordinary miracles through Paul, so that even handkerchiefs and aprons that had touched him were taken to the sick, and their illnesses were cured and the evil spirits left them.

Sweaty Hankies And Healing Power

In the witchy atmosphere of Ephesus, God worked in mysterious ways. Paul's <u>healing ministry</u> took a bizarre twist: Handkerchiefs (the Greek word means "sweat rags") and aprons worn by Paul in his tentmaking work were taken to sick and mentally ill people and they got well!

Now hold the phone! Don't ring up Billy Graham or the Pope and ask them to send you their used hankies! Keep the story straight:

1. *God* did the miracles, not Paul.
2. The healing power was in *God*, not sweat-soaked rags Paul wore around his head or goat-oil stained aprons he wiped his hands on.
3. Paul's dirty laundry was a visual aid to help people make the leap into faith in *God*.

Some people need visual aids. Healing people who needed to touch Paul's cast-off clothing before they could believe (even though, in reality, such things are unnecessary) was a loving God's gracious way of meeting people where they were.

☞ **GO TO:**

Acts 14:3, 6–10;
Romans 15:17–19;
2 Corinthians 12:12
(healing ministry)

Dig Deeper

Some Visual Aids to Faith in the New Testament

Reference	Visual Aid	What Happened
Mark 5:27–34; 6:56	Touched edge of Jesus' cloak	Woman, and all who touched were healed.
John 9:6–7	Mud on blind man's eyes, washing	Blindness healed. Man converted.
Acts 2:38, 41	Baptism	Spirit received. Believers added to church.
Acts 5:15–16	Passed by Peter's shadow	Sick, tormented people healed.
Acts 19:11–12	Touched Paul's hankies and aprons	Illnesses cured. Evil spirits left.
1 Corinthians 11:23–26	Lord's Supper, bread and wine	Remember Jesus. Proclaim his death.

> **Acts 19:13–16** Some Jews who went around driving out evil spirits tried to invoke the name of the Lord Jesus over those who were demon-possessed. They would say, "In the name of Jesus, whom Paul preaches, I command you to come out." Seven sons of Sceva, a

Jewish chief priest, were doing this. One day the evil spirit answered them, "Jesus I know, and I know about Paul, but who are you?" Then the man who had the evil spirit jumped on them and overpowered them all. He gave them such a beating that they ran out of the house naked and bleeding.

It Takes One To Know One

A troupe of professional exorcists billed as "The Seven Sons of Sceva" claimed to drive demons out of "possessed" people and things (I could have used their services for a car I once owned!). They heard about Paul's success casting out evil spirits in Jesus' name and decided to add the name of Jesus to their bag of tricks and incantations.

One day Sceva's boys were hired to cast out an evil spirit. To their surprise, when they intoned the name of Jesus over the harassed soul, the evil spirit yelled back, *"Jesus I know, and I know about Paul, but who are you?"* At which point the demon attacked the exorcists, and they were last seen "streaking" out of the house and down the street, leaving a trail of bloody footprints!

What Others are Saying:

Mark Galli: Jews and pagans had their own exorcism prayers and rituals . . . long before Christianity arrived. But Christian exorcism was impressive in that it used no elaborate invocations or rituals—just prayer, Scripture, and the name of Jesus.[8]

Remember This . . .

Jesus' name is not a "magic" word to use to make a profit or get fame for yourself. Jesus' name represents a mighty person whose power is for making the name and character of his Father God known and for doing his will.

Acts 19:17–20 When this became known to the Jews and Greeks living in Ephesus, they were all seized with fear, and the name of the Lord Jesus was held in high honor. Many of those who believed now came and openly confessed their evil deeds. A number who had practiced sorcery brought their scrolls together and burned them publicly. When they calculated the value of the scrolls, the total came to fifty thousand drachmas. In this way the word of the Lord spread widely and grew in power.

The Great Ephesian Ouija Roast

News of the Sceva boys' fiasco got around quickly—probably accompanied by a lot of loud laughing. Not everyone thought it was funny. The incident became the epicenter of a spiritual earthquake. Jesus' name was suddenly known and respected all over town. Misuse of it could send you to the emergency room!

Christians awoke to the fact that faith in Jesus and magic incantations and spells are totally incompatible. Dependence on charms, secret names, and occult practices is sinful. Many <u>confessed</u> their secret evil deeds openly. Many Christians who had secretly hung on to some of their old superstitions after believing in Jesus took dramatic and costly steps to sever the old evil connections. They brought magical scrolls, "Ephesian Letters," lists of angelic names, and occult paraphernalia and, as Ephesus watched, these once-prized items valued at fifty thousand days' wages—several million dollars—went up in holy smoke!

> The power of the Word of God was demonstrated most dramatically when the Ephesian believers confessed their evil practices and burned the other books and sources to which they looked for wisdom and hope. They burned their bridges behind them and gave themselves in exclusive allegiance to Christ. What are some things you hesitate to "burn" in order to be really honest and committed to the Lord? What would it cost to let them go?

> **Acts 19:21–22** After all this had happened, Paul decided to go to Jerusalem, passing through Macedonia and Achaia. "After I have been there," he said, "I must visit Rome also." He sent two of his helpers, Timothy and Erastus, to Macedonia, while he stayed in the province of Asia a little longer.

Missionary Eyes

Watching the bonfire of proof that the Gospel was taking root in Ephesus, Paul's squinty missionary eyes got that faraway look. *"I must visit Rome!"* He would stay on a little longer to direct "mopping up" operations in Ephesus. Timothy and Erastus headed for Macedonia and Corinth to urge <u>the collection</u> of financial aid for hard-pressed Christians in Israel. Paul would take the money to Jerusalem, then head for Rome.

KEY POINT

In the twenty-first century wholehearted, no-strings-attached surrender to Jesus still sets people free and gives them real joy.

☞ **GO TO:**

1 John 1:9 (confessed)

Something
to Ponder

☞ **GO TO:**

Romans 15:25–28;
 1 Corinthians 16:1–4;
 2 Corinthians 8 and 9
 (the collection)

> **Acts 19:23–24** About that time there arose a great disturbance about **the Way**. A silversmith named Demetrius, who made silver shrines of Artemis, brought in no little business for the craftsmen.

Love Is A Many-Splendored Space Rock

Ephesus was the capital, not only of occultism and witchcraft, but of idolatry. The city's greatest claim to fame was the temple of Artemis (alias: Diana or Aphrodite), goddess of love, fertility, and nourishment (see illustration, page 225). The magnificent structure was larger than a football field. Its roof was supported by 127 sixty-foot-high stone columns. Scores of priests and prostitute-priestesses served worshipers and tourists from all over the world. The temple was the center of everything in Ephesus, including religion, the arts, and banking.

If you were a true Artemis-worshiper, the goddess was the most beautiful relic in the world. Her temple contained an image of her *"which fell from heaven"* (see Acts 19:35)—a meteorite resembling, to believing eyes, the form of a many-breasted woman. To clearer eyes she was an old, cold, black rock, full of lumps and crannies where spiders spun their webs.

> **Acts 19:25** He called them together, along with the workmen in related trades, and said: "Men, you know we receive a good income from this business."

Love Month

The "lusty month of May" brought the annual monthlong Festival of Artemisia, honoring the goddess. Nearly the whole province converged on Ephesus to worship, compete, and have a high old time! It was the State Fair, Olympics, World Series, Miss America Pageant, and Mardi Gras rolled into one.

It was a time of high religious fervor, and it was a time to spend money. Souvenir manufacturers and merchants depended on Artemisia for their year's profits (a lot like Christmas!). Thousands bought trinkets and medals to remember the occasion. Especially popular were wooden, silver, or gold images of the goddess and the temple.

Artemis, the Fertility Goddess

This drawing depicts a statue of Artemis that was recovered at Ephesus, showing her multiple breasts or possibly eggs. Thousands of tourists visited her temple in Ephesus and often bought replicas of the goddess and the building. This brought lots of money to the city's artisans.

Acts 19:26–28 "And you see and hear how this fellow Paul has convinced and led astray large numbers of people here in Ephesus and in practically the whole province of Asia. He says that man-made gods are no gods at all. There is danger not only that our trade will lose its good income, but also that the temple of the great goddess Artemis will be discredited, and the goddess herself, who is worshiped throughout the province of Asia and the world, will be robbed of her divine majesty."

When they heard this, they were furious and began shouting, "Great is Artemis of the Ephesians!"

Bankrupting The Many-Breasted Lady

It is possible the riot of the silversmiths erupted at the Festival of Artemisia. In his speech, Demetrius, president of the local brotherhood of silversmiths, quoted Paul as saying that man-made gods are *"no-gods"* (Acts 19:26)! The *"divine majesty"* (Acts 19:27) of their dear old space-rock maiden was at stake. Demetrius touched a most sensitive nerve by pointing out that, with the shrinkage of the silver shrine and trinket business, Christianity was also becoming a royal pain in the pocketbook.

The smiths and salesmen ran into the streets shouting the cult cry voiced by worshipers in the temple: *"Great is Artemis of the Ephesians!"*

The screaming smithies of Ephesus represent all who oppose spirituality, morality, or justice when profit margins are threatened. In our modern world, there is ample evidence that idolatry of the bottom line is alive and well.

THE BIG PICTURE 🔍

> **Acts 19:29–41** When the craftsmen took their demonstration to the streets, many citizens joined them. Paul's friends, Gaius and Aristarchus were seized. Provincial **officials** friendly to Paul urged him not to confront the mob. When the Jews pushed Alexander forward to speak, they shouted him down. For two hours in the city stadium they shouted, "Great is Artemis of the Ephesians!" The riot ended when the town clerk took charge, warned the crowd of repercussions from Rome, and dismissed the assembly.

Twenty-Five Thousand "Rahs!" For The No-God

Shoppers in the marketplace joined the demonstration. The mob rushed into the twenty-five-thousand-seat, open-air theatre. Many had not the foggiest idea what all the fuss was about (Acts 19:32), but it was exciting and everybody was doing it—so they joined in. They didn't want to miss whatever was happening.

Unable to find Paul, the crowd nabbed a couple of his team members, Gaius and Aristarchus. Paul, never one to run from a chance to share the Gospel, wanted to face the mob. But cooler heads convinced him to stay away (Acts 19:30–31).

Jewish leaders, concerned the demonstration might turn anti-Semitic, pushed Alexander, a Jewish metalworker, into the the-

Something to Ponder

☞ **GO TO:**

Colossians 3:5
(idolatry of the bottom line)

officials: ten-member council called "Asiarchs"

☞ **GO TO:**

Romans 16:23;
1 Corinthians 1:14
(Gaius)

Acts 20:4; 27:2;
Colossians 4:10;
Philemon 24
(Aristarchus)

2 Timothy 4:14–15
(Alexander)

ater, to explain the difference between Jews and Christians. (Most Romans saw Christianity not as a separate religion but as a Jewish sect.) When the crowd saw he was Jewish, they screamed themselves hoarse in a two-hour holy howl for their beloved bosomed boulder.

Hooray For Roman Justice!

Finally, the city clerk, executive officer of the town council, quieted the crowd with a somber warning that brought visions of sword-swinging legionnaires marching through the streets of Ephesus. Rome took a dim view of riots. If anyone had a grievance against anyone, the legitimate way to handle it was to take him to court. The silversmiths' demonstration could get the town in a peck of trouble and its magistrates fired.

"This meeting is adjourned!" the clerk said.

Repeatedly in Acts and in church history since that time to the present, the Lord has used honest judges and government officials to protect his people who are under attack.

William Barclay: [The town clerk] saved Paul and his companions but he saved them because he was saving his own skin. . . . Paul wished to face the mob but they would not let him. Paul was a man without fear. For the silversmiths and the town clerk it was safety first; for Paul it was always safety last.[9]

What Others are Saying:

Study Questions

1. What was missing in the faith and experience of the twelve disciples Paul discovered in Ephesus (Acts 19:1–5)?
2. Why did Paul stop teaching in the synagogue and move his meeting to Tyrannus's hall? What happened while Paul taught there?
3. What unusual and costly thing did the new Christians at Ephesus do to break free from their old superstitious and sinful life patterns and to demonstrate their commitment to Christ? What was the result?
4. What were Demetrius and the silversmiths so mad about? What form of modern "idolatry" do they represent?

- At Ephesus, Paul met twelve men who appeared to be Christians. They were disciples of John the Baptist, who had never experienced Christ coming in to live in them. When Paul baptized them in Jesus' name, the Holy Spirit came into their lives. (Acts 19:1–7)

- Paul taught in the Ephesian synagogue until opposition against the Gospel hardened. Then he took his base of operations to the lecture hall of Tyrannus. From there, the message of Jesus was taken to people all over the city and province. (Acts 19:8–10)

- Strange things happened in Ephesus as the Gospel spread. Items of Paul's clothing brought healing. Unbelievers using Jesus' name were attacked by a demon they tried to exorcise. Occult books were burned in a huge bonfire. (Acts 19:11–20)

- Christianity had such a powerful impact in Ephesus it threatened to bankrupt craftsmen and sellers of pagan artifacts. The metalworkers demonstrated against Paul. This led to a riot that was finally quelled by the town officials. (Acts 19:21–41)

ACTS 20: THE VULNERABLE AMBASSADOR

Let's Get Started

Even before the wild demonstration at the Ephesian festival of Artemis, Paul's eyes were already fixed on Rome, capital of the world (see Acts 19:21–22). Beyond Rome he hoped to go to Spain and plant churches in the western Mediterranean area (see Romans 15:24–28). He took a roundabout route to reach his goal. And as Luke tells it, every stop Paul made, everything he said and did on the way to Rome, had a ring of finality.

> **Acts 20:1** When the uproar had ended, Paul sent for the disciples and, after encouraging them, said good-by and set out for Macedonia.

Man In Motion

The riot of the silversmiths had shown Paul his continued presence in Ephesus would create more problems for the young Ephesian church. After three years (see Acts 20:31) it was time to move. He called the believers together, encouraged them to keep the faith, and said his final *adios*.

> **Acts 20:2–3a** He traveled through that area, speaking many words of encouragement to the people, and finally arrived in Greece, where he stayed three months.

Bolstering The Brotherhoods

☞ **GO TO:**

Acts 14:21–25; 15:36, 40; 16:4–5; 18:23 (revisiting)

From the start of his apostolic ministry, Paul had followed the pattern of <u>revisiting</u> churches he'd helped establish. On these return visits he did six things.

1. He talked a lot (Acts 20:2). "Many words" in Greek indicates more than quantity. It means breadth and fervor. He fine-tuned their theology and built a fire under their faith.

2. He encouraged them (Acts 20:2). "Encouragement" in Greek is persuasion, cheer, and comfort. Paul lifted their spirits in the face of the persecutions and pressures and gave them solid reasons to keep on believing.

3. He strengthened them (see Acts 18:23). "Strengthened" means Paul validated and invigorated their faith, taught them to rest confidently in the Lord.

4. He appointed elders for them (Acts 14:23). He identified spiritually mature people and gave them authority to shepherd the Christian flock.

5. He prayed for them (see Acts 14:23; 20:36; Ephesians 1:15–23).

6. He committed them to the Lord (see Acts 14:23; 20:32). "Committed" means Paul handed control and care of each church to the Lord. He would travel on but Jesus would be their Leader and Savior.

JESUS CHRIST CEO

The Lord's leadership strategy includes giving the church gifted, spiritually mature people who help keep it on track. *"It was he [Christ] who gave some to be apostles, some to be prophets, some to be evangelists, and some to be pastors and teachers, to prepare God's people for works of service, so that the body of Christ may be built up . . . "* (Ephesians 4:11–12). These people do not do the church's work for it; they prepare and encourage the church to do its work.

What Others are Saying:

Audrey I. Girard: Every individual and church has the responsibility to seek God's guidance by praying, reading the Bible and listening for that inner conviction that the Holy Spirit promises (see John 16:13).[1]

> **Acts 20:3b–5** Because the Jews made a plot against him just as he was about to sail for Syria, he decided to go back through Macedonia. He was accompanied by Sopater son of Pyrrhus from Berea, Aristarchus and Secundus from Thessalonica, Gaius from Derbe, Timothy also, and Tychicus and Trophimus from the province of Asia. These men went on ahead and waited for us at Troas.

Never Go It Alone

The early church practiced the principle of spiritual teamwork Jesus had taught his disciples. Paul never traveled alone. At least eight men made the trip to Jerusalem with him.

- Sopater—Alias: Sosipater. Home church: Berea. Paul's relative (see Romans 16:21).

- Aristarchus—Home church: Thessalonica. Paul's coworker (see Acts 19:29). Was with him in prison and on the voyage to Rome (see Acts 27:2).

- Secundus—Home: Thessalonica.

- Gaius—Home church: Derbe. Probably became a Christian when Barnabas and Paul first visited there (see Acts 14:20–21).

- Timothy—Home church: Lystra (see Acts 16:1). Paul's spiritual "son" (see 1 Timothy 1:2). Permanent member of Paul's team.

- Tychicus—Home: Asia province. Carried messages from Paul to the churches (see Ephesians 6:21–22; Colossians 4:7–8).

- Trophimus—Home: Asia. Focus of controversy in Jerusalem that led to Paul's arrest (see Acts 21:29).

- Luke—His presence is revealed by references to "us" and "we" (Acts 20:5–6).

These men represented Gentile churches that raised relief money for struggling Jewish believers. They apparently linked up with Paul in Corinth (where he'd spent three months), intending to travel from there to Antioch (Syria) and then on to Jerusalem, in time for the Jewish Passover. There are good reasons why such an entourage should make this particular trip with Paul:

1. The cash they carried was enough to tempt many a robber. A corps of burly Christian men could better assure its safe arrival than a scrawny rabbi (Paul) traveling alone.
2. Christian giving is not merely a transfer of money. It's a response of loving hearts <u>sharing themselves</u>. Each church wanted its contribution to have a face.

☞ **GO TO:**

2 Corinthians 8:1–5
(sharing themselves)

Don't Take Unnecessary Risks

The assassination plot was discovered just as Paul and the others were about to sail from Greece to Syria. A ship carrying Jewish pilgrims to Jerusalem for the Passover would have provided the ideal opportunity to get rid of the man some considered "Public Enemy Number One" by simply throwing him overboard. "Paul was a man who always walked with his life in his hands."[2]

Discovering the plot, Paul gave up his plans to get to Jerusalem for Passover. He did not board the ship but, taking Luke with him, hoofed it overland to Philippi. The other men, serving as decoys, boarded the original ship and got off at Troas to wait for Paul and Luke (Acts 20:5). The assassins assumed Paul was with them. By the time they discovered otherwise, they were at sea.

☞ **GO TO:**

Philippians 1:20–26;
Psalm 6:4–5 (no help)

Remember This . . .

Paul risked his life for Jesus again and again. But martyrdom was not something he courted. He was willing to die for his faith but avoided death as long as he possibly could. The Lord had given him a job to do, and his first priority was to finish that job (see Acts 20:24). He'd be <u>no help</u> to anyone if he were dead!

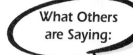

What Others are Saying:

William G. Bixler: The early church did not advocate voluntary martyrdoms . . . Jesus himself . . . advised fleeing when persecution was imminent.[3]

Persecution & Martyrdom—The early church encouraged flight to escape persecution and warned against rushing into voluntary martyrdom.[4] Paul escaped from Damascus (Acts 9:25); Peter, from Herod (Acts 12:17). Paul used Roman citizenship to avoid assassination (Acts 25:1–11).

In Uganda, 400,000 Ugandan Christians were martyred, disappeared, or fled the country between 1971–1976 under Idi Amin's rule. One of the escapees, Daniel Kyanda, now represents Christian Solidarity International in Nairobi, Kenya, working to prepare Africans for future persecutions.[5]

> **Acts 20:6** But we sailed from Philippi after the Feast of Unleavened Bread, and five days later joined the others at Troas, where we stayed seven days.

Plan B: Jerusalem By Pentecost

According to the revised plan, Paul and Luke sailed from Philippi after the Feast of Unleavened Bread. In A.D. 57, the twin feasts of Passover and Unleavened Bread were celebrated in Jerusalem on April 7–14. The next big festival would be Pentecost, six weeks later. Paul celebrated Passover in Philippi. From there he and Luke took a ship to Troas to rejoin the team.

> **Acts 20:7–8** On the first day of the week we came together to break bread. Paul spoke to the people and, because he intended to leave the next day, kept on talking until midnight. There were many lamps in the upstairs room where we were meeting.

Sunday Go-To-Meetin' In The Early Church

Luke's record of this visit gives a rare glimpse of a regular early church meeting. It looks more like a family gathering than a formal "worship service." That's as it should be. After all, Jesus promised his followers more than to be part of an audience. He said they'd have a family—brothers and sisters, parents and children (see Mark 10:29–30). In the face of life's pressures, only a family can meet the Christians' need for support.

- They met on Sunday. This is the first New Testament reference to the <u>first day</u> as the regular meeting time for Christians (see GWLC, pages 180–181).

- They ate together. Early Christians celebrated the Lord's Supper (Holy Communion) as part of a potluck meal (love feast).

- They met at night. This was probably to accommodate slaves who could only come when the day's work was done.

- They met three floors up (Acts 20:9). Early church meetings were held in the homes of members. Wealthy homes often had a third story loft. Many people also lived in three-story concrete tenements in which poorer families occupied the third floor.

 GO TO:

1 Corinthians 16:2 (first day)

- The length of the meeting was not regulated by the clock (Acts 20:7, 11). More important issues were in focus. This was the last chance to hear from the apostle Paul.

What Others are Saying:

John O. Gooch: In the first century, the Lord's Supper included not only the bread and the cup but an entire meal. As part of the meal, neighbors who had quarreled made peace again. . . . When worship was ended, Christians took home the consecrated bread so that those who couldn't attend worship could partake of the Lord's Supper. In North Africa, Christians took home the bread so they could celebrate the sacrament *every day* with their families.[6]

> **Acts 20:9–12** Seated in a window was a young man named Eutychus, who was sinking into a deep sleep as Paul talked on and on. When he was sound asleep, he fell to the ground from the third story and was picked up dead. Paul went down, threw himself on the young man and put his arms around him. "Don't be alarmed," he said. "He's alive!" Then he went upstairs again and broke bread and ate. After talking until daylight, he left. The people took the young man home alive and were greatly comforted.

Sleeping In Church Can Be Dangerous

Young Eutychus may have put in a hard day's work before coming to the meeting. The place was lit with smoky oil lamps (Acts 20:8). The atmosphere was stuffy. Sometime after midnight, Eutychus fell asleep and fell out the window! He landed on the stone pavement three stories down! Dr. Luke may be the one who pronounced him dead.

☞ **GO TO:**

1 Kings 17:21–23
(Elijah-like)

Elijah-like, Paul stretched himself over the lad's body. "He's alive!" he announced. They all went back upstairs and ate together. Paul started talking again and didn't stop till the sun came up! (And you thought your pastor's sermons were long!)

Something to Ponder

In a family gathering, neatness doesn't count much. Setting tables, eating, doing dishes, wiping up spilled food, changing diapers, handling tough questions, rescuing young men who fall out the window! It's very likely Paul's teaching was not an all-night lecture. (That'd be enough to put a whole congregation to sleep!) He taught in the Jewish style—the style of Jesus—interspersing teaching with questions and interaction. What counts when Christians gather is to meet God, remember Jesus, yield to the Spirit, build relationships, and leave better equipped to live the life and share the story.

One Sunday morning in San Antonio, Audrey and I visited a new church meeting in a movie theater. The meeting included a series of minor "speed bumps." For starters, the theater operator failed to unlock the place so preparations could be made for worship and Sunday school. The key finally showed up well past time for the service to start. The young congregation waited in the cold (some more than an hour), but no one left. They chatted and shivered together until the doors were open. Inside, there were problems with the sound system, the lights, the overhead projector. When time for the sermon came, only five minutes remained before they were scheduled to vacate the building for the first movie. But through it all the congregation of about a hundred sang, prayed, laughed, and enjoyed the adventure. Destruction of the structure actually affirmed their commitment to the new church and one another.

In this life difficulties are bound to occur, and there's nothing like a Eutychus falling out the window now and then to keep a congregation in touch with reality!

What Others are Saying:

Philip Yancey: Anyone can form a club; it takes grace, shared vision, and hard work to form a community. The Christian church was the first institution in history to bring together on equal footing Jews and Gentiles, men and women, slaves and free. . . . Church is one place . . . that brings together generations: infants still held at their mother's breasts, children who squirm and giggle at all the wrong times, responsible adults who know how to act appropriately at all times, and senior citizens who drift asleep if the preacher drones on too long.[7]

> **Acts 20:13–17** We went on ahead to the ship and sailed for Assos, where we were going to take Paul aboard. He had made this arrangement because he was going there on foot. When he met us at Assos, we took him aboard and went on to Mitylene. The next day we set sail from there and arrived off Kios. The day after that we crossed over to Samos, and on the following day arrived at Miletus. Paul had decided to sail past Ephesus

> to avoid spending time in the province of Asia, for he was in a hurry to reach Jerusalem, if possible, by the day of Pentecost. From Miletus, Paul sent to Ephesus for the elders of the church.

A Gathering Of Herdsmen

The Acts storyteller, Luke, obviously kept a log or diary of each day's travels. The morning after the all-night meeting, Paul stayed in Troas when the rest of the team set sail. The ship would stop at Assos, a twenty-mile hike from Troas (Acts 20:13–14). He'd catch up there. He probably wanted to check on Eutychus before he left or get rejuvenated by some aerobic walking.

Here we learn of Paul's desire to reach Jerusalem before Pentecost. Because of limited time and because his name was still "mud" in some Ephesian circles, Paul called for leaders of the Ephesian church to join him for a farewell muster at Miletus, thirty miles from Ephesus. The ship on which Paul had booked passage would be anchored at Miletus for a few days. Luke's minutes of the meeting provide the only example in Acts of Paul's preaching to *Christians*.

Paul uses three terms in his message to identify church leaders. In the first century, all three "titles" refer to the same *local* church office.

☞ **GO TO:**

Titus 1:5–9 (elders)

1 Timothy 3:1–7 (overseers)

Ephesians 4:11; 1 Peter 5:1–3 (shepherds)

- *Elders* (Acts 20:17). This was the traditional term for Jewish community and religious leaders. It emphasizes the need for church leaders to be spiritually mature.
- *Overseers* (Acts 20:28). This emphasizes the leaders' role as guides and protectors watching over God's people to guard them from spiritual danger. Synonym: guardian.
- *Shepherds* (Acts 20:28). The Greek word means one who feeds, pastures, tends a flock; shepherd or herdsman. It emphasizes a leader's role as caregiver. Synonym: pastor.

> **Acts 20:18** When they arrived, he said to them: "You know how I lived the whole time I was with you, from the first day I came into the province of Asia."

The Visible Church Leader

In his "farewell address" to the Ephesian elders, Paul did not explain a Bible passage or offer insights into the meaning of some pithy Greek word. He did not appeal to their intellects or list ten rules for effective church leadership. He took the risk of talking about *himself*, his record, his ministry, his fears and tears and hopes. He believed and demonstrated a very important principle that distinguishes Jesus-style leadership from all others: The Christian leader does not merely *tell* people the way they should live, but in the way he himself lives, he <u>shows</u> them the way.

If the shepherd-overseers of Ephesus wanted to know how to live and work, they needed to remember how Paul lived and worked. Paul was sure enough of himself to dare to say, "Follow me!"

KEY POINT

Good Christian leaders walk the walk they talk.

☞ **GO TO:**

Luke 6:39–40 (shows)

Audrey I. Girard:

Let the beauty of your Grace be reflected in our face
And let no one doubt to Whom we belong.[8]

> **Acts 20:19–21** "I served the Lord with great humility and with tears, although I was severely tested by the plots of the Jews. You know that I have not hesitated to preach anything that would be helpful to you but have taught you publicly and from house to house. I have declared to both Jews and Greeks that they must turn to God in repentance and have faith in our Lord Jesus."

What Others are Saying:

The Way I Was

As the visible, vulnerable Christian leader he was not cold, aloof, or distant. He got down and dirty, up close and personal, where they could see and know him . . . warts and all!

- In the face of personal danger he did the Lord's work with humility and intensity (Acts 20:19).
- No matter the cost in <u>lost reputation</u> and <u>public outrage</u>, he didn't hesitate to tell people what they *needed* to hear (Acts 20:20).
- He pursued his evangelistic and teaching ministry everywhere anyone would listen—both *"publicly and from house to house"* (Acts 20:20).
- He invited people, regardless of ethnic and cultural background, to leave their sins, turn to God, and put their faith in Jesus as Lord (Acts 20:21).

☞ **GO TO:**

Acts 19:9 (lost reputation)

Acts 19:23–31 (public outrage)

☞ **GO TO:**

2 Corinthians 5:14
(compelled)

Acts 20:22–27 "And now, <u>compelled</u> by the Spirit, I am going to Jerusalem, not knowing what will happen to me there. I only know that in every city the Holy Spirit warns me that prison and hardships are facing me. However, I consider my life worth nothing to me, if only I may finish the race and complete the task the Lord Jesus has given me—the task of testifying to the gospel of God's grace.

"Now I know that none of you among whom I have gone about preaching the kingdom will ever see me again. Therefore, I declare to you today that I am innocent of the blood of all men. For I have not hesitated to proclaim to you the whole will of God."

What's Coming Down The Pike

This was good-bye. Paul had spent seven or eight years establishing churches on both sides of the Aegean Sea. He had done his job. He would never return.

The statement, *"I am innocent of the blood of all men"* was Paul's very Jewish way of saying he had faithfully carried out his spiritual responsibility. He'd explained the saving plan of God completely. If people of Ephesus chose to reject the Gospel and be lost from God, the guilt was theirs, not his! As <u>God's watchman</u>, he had not failed to sound the alarm.

☞ **GO TO:**

Ezekiel 2:16–21; 33:1–9
(God's watchman)

What Others are Saying:

Howard Marshall: As the watchman who warns people faithfully of the coming of an enemy is not guilty if they choose to ignore the warning, so it is with Paul as a preacher of the gospel. Paul's assurance was derived from his confidence that he had faithfully preached the gospel in every particular; he had dealt with the whole of God's plan of salvation.[9]

JESUS CHRIST CEO

In Acts 20:22 Paul uses a phrase that shows how the Lord Jesus reveals the direction he wants his people to go and the things he wants them to do: *"compelled by the Spirit."* In the original Greek this means the Spirit of Christ (Holy Spirit) living in the Christian provides the moral motivation to do the right thing, the thing Jesus wants us to do. Christians are not forced by outward rules and regulations or expectations, but *"the compelling motivation for our choices comes from within."*[10]

> **Acts 20:28–31** "Keep watch over yourselves and all the flock of which the Holy Spirit has made you overseers. Be shepherds of the church of God, which he bought with his own blood. I know that after I leave, savage wolves will come in among you and will not spare the flock. Even from your own number men will arise and distort the truth in order to draw away disciples after them. So be on your guard! Remember that for three years I never stopped warning each of you night and day with tears."

What Every Church Needs Is A Good Sheepdog!

Sometimes elders, overseers, shepherds of the church would be better described as "sheepdogs." There are dangers out there. "_Savage wolves_" eager to decimate the flock. Leaders must guard themselves and the church against the ravages of faith destroyers. Here's Paul's argument:

1. You didn't choose your job—you're an overseer because the Holy Spirit "_made you_" one (Acts 20:28).
2. God <u>bought and paid</u> for the church with "_his own blood._" (Jesus' death was God **redeeming** his people.) The church flock belongs to God, not the shepherds (Acts 20:28).
3. Some people (some hearing Paul say these words!) want to possess the church for themselves. They will push themselves forward and "_distort the truth_" to get the flock to follow them _instead of God_ (Acts 20:29–30).
4. This persistent danger calls for impassioned watchfulness and warnings (Acts 20:31).

Healthy church growth not only involves adding disciples, leaders, and locations but also subtracting harmful influences, attitudes, and teachings.

> **Acts 20:32–35** "Now I commit you to God and to the word of his grace, which can build you up and give you an inheritance among all those who are sanctified. I have not coveted anyone's silver or gold or clothing. You yourselves know that these hands of mine have supplied my own needs and the needs of my companions. In everything I did, I showed you that by this kind of hard work we must help the weak, remembering the words the Lord Jesus himself said: 'It is more blessed to give than to receive.'"

☞ **GO TO:**

1 Timothy 1:3–7; 4:1–3; 2 Timothy 3:6–9; 4:3–4; 1 Peter 5:8–9 (wolves)

1 Corinthians 6:19–20; 7:23; Revelation 5:9 (bought and paid)

redeeming: _buying people's freedom from sin_

CHURCH GROWTH

You're In Good Hands With The Almighty

Paul again reminds the Ephesian pastors of the example of his life and ministry:

- He did not micro-manage the churches. He trusted the well-being, protection, and progress of the church <u>to God</u>, his Word, and his grace. He did not depend on his own efforts to produce change and mature Christians. He trusted God's grace at work in his people.
- He served without the thought of material gain.
- He wasn't afraid to get his hands dirty to support himself and others.
- He worked hard to <u>help the weak</u>.
- He got joy and fulfillment from a giving-rather-than-receiving lifestyle.

☞ **GO TO:**

Acts 14:23 (to God)

1 Corinthians 9:22 (help the weak)

Everyone who accepts Jesus' invitation to follow him is called to full-time Christian living, fully developed Christian character, and wholehearted commitment to the Lord. If Paul was called to lay his life on the line for the witness of God's grace through Jesus, so are we.

Something to Ponder

What Others are Saying:

Ruth Bell Graham: Pashi, from India, was a college student. When he was presented with the claims of Christ, Pashi told me, "I would like to believe in Christ. But we have never seen a Christian who was like Christ." . . .

I asked . . . Dr. Akbar Haqq, a brilliant Christian who had been president of a school of Islamic studies in India . . . "How would you answer Pashi? What would you say?"

"That is simple," he answered decisively. "I would tell Pashi, 'I am not offering you Christians. I am offering you Christ.'"[11]

> **Acts 20:36–38** When he had said this, he knelt down with them all and prayed. They all wept as they embraced him and kissed him. What grieved them most was his statement that they would never see his face again. Then they accompanied him to the ship.

Bon Voyage!

This is all too personal! These are not dutiful employees waving good-bye to a respected boss and mentor. There's too much emotion—too much personal pain at seeing Paul go. It's another indication that Paul's leadership style was not to run things from above or to demand obedience in order to fulfill the boss's personal goals. Paul had involved himself personally in their lives, given himself to them, in such a self-revealing, honest, caring way that it lifted their relationship with him to a much higher, closer, more personal level.

When Paul left with the announcement that they would never see him again, they broke down and cried! Paul was no scary "authority figure." He was their spiritual father and a friend with whom their lives had become interwoven in a rich tapestry of love.

Remember This . . .

Jesus said those who learn from him become like him (see Luke 6:40). New Testament leadership follows this pattern. It is not merely a matter of transmission of facts and principles and motivating people by a system of rewards and pressures. It is the passing of a quality of life from the leader to those he or she leads.

What Others are Saying:

John Oxenham:

> Wish me "Bon Voyage!"
> As you do a friend
> Whose joyous visit finds its happy end.
> And bid me both "a Dieu!"
> And "au revoir!"
> Since, though I come no more,
> I shall be waiting there to greet you,
> At His Door.[12]

Study Questions

1. Identify the five characteristics of the church meeting in Troas.
2. Who fell asleep and fell out the window?
3. Identify three "titles" for local church leaders used in Acts 20:17–38, and tell what aspect of Christian leadership each emphasizes.
4. Let's play "Who Wants to Be a Church Leader?" according to Acts 20:28–31.
   - The $1,000 question: Who really chooses a church leader for his or her job?

a. The congregation

b. The leader himself or herself

c. The leader's wife

d. The Holy Spirit

- The $10,000 question: Who owns the church and why?
  a. The pastor because of his position
  b. The congregation because it gives money
  c. God because he shed his blood
  d. The bank because it holds the mortgage

- The $100,000 question: Because of danger from people who distort the truth to get people to follow them instead of God, what's a church leader to do?
  a. Be on guard
  b. Don't rock the boat
  c. Resign and move to another church
  d. Warn people of the danger

CHAPTER WRAP-UP

- Paul left Ephesus for Macedonia where he encouraged the Christians. With several companions, he planned to travel to Jerusalem with a gift for needy Jewish believers. A plot against his life delayed his departure until after the Passover. (Acts 20:1–6)

- At a stopover in Troas, Paul went to the Sunday gathering of the local church and preached till midnight. A youth named Eutychus fell to his death from the third-story window. Paul revived him and preached on till the sun came up. (Acts 20:7–12)

- At a stopover in Miletus, Paul gathered the leaders of the Ephesian church together for a final farewell. (Acts 20:13–17)

- He told the Ephesian elders to follow his example. He talked about his willingness to die for the Gospel. He warned the Ephesian church of coming trouble for them and reminded them of their responsibility to protect God's flock. (Acts 20:18–31)

- Paul committed them to God's care, reminded them of his unselfish, giving lifestyle while among them, and quoted a saying from Jesus found nowhere else in the Bible. They saw him off with hugs, kisses, and tears. (Acts 20:32–38)

Part Four

CHAINED WITNESS

"Being a good Christian, Engineer Joe passed out tracks during his break."

ACTS 21:1–22:29: STARING DOWN DANGER

Let's Get Started

The Ephesian church leaders wept openly as they escorted Paul to the ship and kissed him good-bye (see Acts 20:37–38). Jerusalem was calling him like a Star Trek tractor beam. Paul loved the Holy City. No other place on earth held such attraction to Jews or inspired such yearning and intense loyalty.

For Paul this trip to <u>Mount Zion</u> held more danger and at the same time more opportunity than any before in his life. He knew (see Acts 20:23) he would probably leave Jerusalem in chains—possibly even in a coffin! But he felt compelled to go there—no matter the risks!

☞ **GO TO:**

Psalm 48:2
(Mount Zion)

> **Acts 21:1–6** After we had torn ourselves away from them, we put out to sea and sailed straight to Cos. The next day we went to Rhodes and from there to Patara. We found a ship crossing over to Phoenicia, went on board and set sail. After passing Cyprus and passing to the south of it, we sailed on to Syria. We landed at Tyre, where our ship was to unload its cargo. Finding the disciples there, we stayed with them seven days. Through the Spirit they urged Paul not to go on to Jerusalem. But when our time was up, we left and continued on our way. All the disciples and children accompanied us out of the city, and there on the beach we knelt to pray. After saying good-by to each other, we went aboard the ship, and they returned home.

Don't Go, Paul, Don't Go!

Luke's logbook records the voyage from Miletus, site of Paul's farewell meeting with the Ephesian elders, to Caesarea, the seaport nearest Jerusalem. Incidents at two of the stops along the way tested Paul's commitment to face what lay ahead and assured him his fellow Christians cared.

The first incident took place at the Phoenician seaport town of Tyre. The disciples, *"through the Holy Spirit,"* urged Paul not to go to Jerusalem.

"Through the Holy Spirit" does not mean the Spirit said, "Don't go!" In Acts 20:22 Paul specifically says the Spirit "compelled" him to go. The Holy Spirit in his fellow Christians made them sensitive to his danger and <u>produced</u> the love they had for him. Awareness and concern were expressed through special **gifts** of the Spirit. But going to Jerusalem in the face of danger was Paul's personal response to the clear directions from the Lord for which he alone must answer.

> **Acts 21:7–9** We continued our voyage from Tyre and landed at Ptolemais, where we greeted the brothers and stayed with them for a day. Leaving the next day, we reached Caesarea and stayed at the house of Philip the evangelist, one of the Seven. He had four unmarried daughters who prophesied.

A Family Of Preacher-Girls

The team's host in Caesarea was Philip, one of the seven appointed twenty years earlier to feed Jerusalem's poor (Acts 6:1–6). What a reunion this was! The last time Paul and Philip were mentioned in the same paragraph, Philip was running for his life with Paul (then called Saul), the Christian-hater, in hot pursuit! After preaching around the country, Philip settled in Caesarea and raised four <u>daughters</u> who were **"prophetesses."**

Ajith Fernando: Luke's mention of Philip's daughters highlights the fact that people not regarded as being of high status did have positions of prominence in the church. The breaking of human barriers is one of the main subthemes of Acts. Luke has given <u>prominence to women</u> in different ways. . . . The present passage records single women exercising what the New Testament regards as a key gift for the church (Acts 21:9). . . . Acts teaches us that

---

☞ **GO TO:**

Galatians 5:22–23 (produced)

Romans 12:6–8; 1 Corinthians 12:1–11, 27–31 (gifts)

gifts: abilities, sensitivities, graces enabling people to do God's work

☞ **GO TO:**

Acts 2:17–18 (daughters)

Acts 1:14; Acts 6:1–7; Acts 9:36–42; Acts 16:15; Acts 18:18–19 (prominence to women)

What Others are Saying:

prophetesses: women gifted to speak God's message

---

women, especially women marginalized by society, have a prominent role in fulfilling the agenda of the kingdom.[1]

EARLY CHURCH WOMEN—Philip's preacher-daughters later moved with their father to the Ephesus area where they lived to old age and were valued by the second-century church as sources of information about early Judean Christianity.

> **Acts 21:10–11** After we had been there a number of days, a prophet named Agabus came down from Judea. Coming over to us, he took Paul's belt, tied his own hands and feet with it and said, "The Holy Spirit says, 'In this way the Jews of Jerusalem will bind the owner of this belt and will hand him over to the Gentiles.'"

Detour! There's A Muddy Road Ahead

Luke reports the arrival in Caesarea of the Christian prophet <u>Agabus</u> with a message for Paul. Agabus, fresh from Jerusalem, knew the atmosphere in the Holy City. In the <u>style of Old</u> Testament prophets, he pantomimed his prophecy, tying his own hands and feet with Paul's **belt** and forecasting that in Jerusalem the owner of the belt would be tied up and turned over to godless people.

Lawrence O. Richards: In Acts 20:22 Paul confessed to being in the dark about what would happen to him in Jerusalem. . . . But then came a word of prophecy! Paul would face hostility. He would be bound. But he would survive to be handed over to the Gentiles, and so ultimately fulfill his mission to that world. A warning? No, a word of grace, and a reminder that even men of great faith, like Paul, need encouragement from the Lord. As do we all.[2]

> **Acts 21:12–14** When we heard this, we and the people there pleaded with Paul not to go up to Jerusalem. Then Paul answered, "Why are you weeping and breaking my heart? I am ready not only to be bound, but also to die in Jerusalem for the name of the Lord Jesus." When he would not be dissuaded, we gave up and said, "The Lord's will be done."

☞ **GO TO:**

Acts 11:27–30 (Agabus)

1 Kings 11:29–31; Isaiah 20:3–4; Jeremiah 13:4; 27:2–3; Ezekiel 4, 5:1–4 (style of Old)

What Others are Saying:

belt: *leather sash worn around outer robe to keep it close to the body while working*

KEY POINT

Ultimately, our decisions must be guided by the Holy Spirit, not the emotions and opinions of other people.

"I'd Rather Die On My Feet Than Live On My Knees!"

The scene that followed Agabus's prophecy was emotional. Paul's friends begged him to avoid Jerusalem. But <u>like Jesus</u> on the way to Jerusalem for the last time (see GWLC2, pages 8–9, 131), he refused to turn back. He'd burned his bridges behind him. His life was <u>expendable</u>. And he had <u>a job</u> to do: to bring the good news to Jews and Gentiles—a mission in fulfillment of which Paul considered chains and death a reasonable price to pay (Acts 20:24; 21:13).

The argument ended with a shrug of shoulders and a prayer of <u>commitment</u>, *"The Lord's will be done"* (Acts 21:14).

Ajith Fernando: People who love us may try to shield us from the cross. We take community life seriously, but at times our own people will take stands that must be rejected.[3]

Dietrich Bonhoeffer: As we embark upon discipleship we surrender ourselves to Christ in union with his death—we give over our lives to death. Thus it begins; the cross is not the terrible end to an otherwise God-fearing and happy life, but it meets us at the beginning of our communion with Christ. When Christ calls a man, he bids him come and die.[4]

> **Acts 21:15–20a** After this, we got ready and went up to Jerusalem. Some of the disciples from Caesarea accompanied us and brought us to the home of Mnason, where we were to stay. He was a man from Cyprus and one of the early disciples.
>
> When we arrived at Jerusalem, the brothers received us warmly. The next day Paul and the rest of us went to see James, and all the elders were present. Paul greeted them and reported in detail what God had done among the Gentiles through his ministry.
>
> When they heard this, they praised God.

The Good News: Paul Arrives In The Holy City

Arrangements had been made for Paul and his team to stay at the home of a transplanted Cypriot Jew named Mnason. Mnason had been part of the Jerusalem church from its beginning. *"One of the early disciples"* (Acts 21:16) indicates he may have been one of

☞ **GO TO:**

Matthew 16:21
(like Jesus)

Acts 20:24; 21:13
(expendable)

**What Others
are Saying:**

Matthew 28:19–20;
Acts 9:15–16 (a job)

Matthew 26:39; Luke
11:2 (commitment)

the original three thousand believers (see Acts 2:41). It was easier for a foreign-born Jew than for a Judean-born Jew to host Gentiles.

After unpacking at Mnason's pad, the travelers met **James** and the Jerusalem elders. They presented the gift from the Gentile churches (see Romans 15:25; Acts 24:17). Luke doesn't mention the gift. Evidently the gift seemed incidental compared with the exciting things Paul had to report about God's work among the pagans:

James: Jesus' half-brother, leader of the Jerusalem church elders

- Opening Europe (Macedonia, Greece) to the Gospel (see Acts 16)
- Introducing Athenian philosophers to their "unknown God" (see Acts 17)
- Transforming lives in Corinth (see Acts 18; 1 Corinthians 6:10–11)
- The bonfire of magic books and occult paraphernalia in Ephesus (see Acts 19)

The Gentile brothers with Paul shared their spiritual experiences and verified his report. The Jewish brothers responded with worship.

> **Acts 21:20b** Then they said to Paul: "You see, brother, how many thousands of Jews have believed, and all of them are zealous for the law."

Jews For Jesus

The Jerusalem elders shared the good news that *"many thousands"* of Jews had put their faith in Jesus. The original word is *myriads*—literally, "tens of thousands."

With the addition of the phrase, *"and all of them are zealous for the law,"* the elders delicately introduced their greatest concern about Paul's arrival.

The Bad News: Paul Arrives In The Holy City

Not everyone, even among the Christians, was happy to see Paul sauntering into town with that mixed crew of Jew and Gentile buddies of his. It was almost time for the Feast of Pentecost, and Jewish feasts always ignited nationalist fire and anti-Gentile sentiment. Anti-Gentile attitudes were magnified by hunger and deprivation. When crops failed across the empire, pervasive anti-Semitic prejudice assured that trade in essential foodstuff would go to other places before it came to "troublesome Israel."

Jews hated Romans and other Gentiles for leaving them to starve. These anti-Gentile sentiments made it tricky for the Jerusalem Christians to accept help from the Gentile Christians.

> **Acts 21:21** "They have been informed that you teach all the Jews who live among the Gentiles to turn away from Moses, telling them not to circumcise their children or live according to our customs."

The Scuttlebutt About Paul

The elders knew these rumors were untrue. Paul never told Jewish Christians to stop being Jewish. He taught that Gentile Christians should "not deny their cultural heritage and assume that by becoming 'Jewish' they would be more pleasing to God."[5] This teaching was consistent with the <u>church's decision</u> to free Gentiles from the Law (Acts 21:25). What Paul taught is clear from the things he did and wrote:

- A person's standing before God is not based on circumcision but faith and <u>new creation</u> (see Galatians 2:15–16; 5:6; 6:15).
- To circumcise or not to circumcise one's son is a matter of parental choice (see Acts 16:3; 1 Timothy 1:1, and WBFM, pages 113–114).
- A Christian Jew is free to observe Jewish traditions and feast days (see Acts 18:18; 20:6, 16; Romans 14:2–8).
- Winning people to Christ is more important than observance of religious traditions (see 1 Corinthians 9:20–21). To communicate the Gospel, Paul accommodated both Jewish and Gentile preferences, depending on which he was trying to reach.

In his autobiography, *Just as I Am,* Billy Graham tells of receiving the invitation to conduct a preaching mission in 1984 in the Soviet Union. He was not certain he should accept it, because a previous visit had been misused for propaganda purposes.

As he struggled with his decision, he thought of the apostle Paul and his desire to preach the Gospel in Rome, the seat of

☞ **GO TO:**

Acts 15:19
(church's decision)

John 3:3–8;
2 Corinthians 5:17
(new creation)

**Something
to Ponder**

infamous Nero's empire. Just before retiring one night he read Paul's statement in 1 Corinthians 9:20–21 from *The Living Bible*:

"When I am with the Jews I seem as one of them so that they will listen to the Gospel and I can win them to Christ. When I am with Gentiles who follow Jewish customs and ceremonies I don't argue, even though I don't agree, because I want to help them. When with the heathen I agree with them as much as I can, except of course that I must always do what is right as a Christian. And so, by agreeing, I can win their confidence and help them too."

Dr. Graham wrote: "During the night, I woke up with these words clearly in my mind. They seemed to be God's direct answer to my quandary. When morning came . . . I had a settled peace about going."[6]

The daring, go-anywhere spirit of the twentieth century's greatest evangelist is traceable, at least in part, to the same theology of "accommodation for the sake of communication" that helped make Paul the first century's greatest evangelist. To both, winning people to Christ was more important than observance of arbitrary and limiting traditions and protocols. Both were willing to reach people outside the envelope of their own culture, even if it meant being misunderstood and criticized.

> **Acts 21:22** "What shall we do? They will certainly hear that you have come, . . ."

Christian Fiddlers On The Roof

Christian Jews in Jerusalem were in a precarious position. They knew Jesus fulfilled the Jewish rituals. They knew salvation was based on faith in him, his death and resurrection. Yet, they remained loyal to the traditions—Jesus filled the old rites with new meaning!

But Israel was divided about Jesus (one-third believed; two-thirds did not). Most Jewish leaders rejected Christ. Pressures on believers to renounce the new faith or get out of Judaism were intensifying. A decade after Paul's visit, Christian Jews would find themselves **excommunicated** from the Temple!

excommunicated: censured, denied access, excluded from Jewish religious life

> **Acts 21:23–25** ". . . so do what we tell you. There are four men with us who have made a vow. Take these men, join in their purification rites and pay their expenses, so that they can have their heads shaved. Then everybody will know there is no truth in these reports about you, but that you yourself are living in obedience to the law. As for the Gentile believers, we have written to them our decision that they should abstain from food sacrificed to idols, from blood, from the meat of strangled animals and from sexual immorality."

Polishing Paul's Image

Jerusalem's Christian leaders hoped that if Paul could be seen in the Temple carrying out Jewish religious rituals, doubts about his **orthodoxy** could be diffused. Their plan called for him to participate in the purification rites of four Jewish Christians.

The <u>Nazarite vow</u>, which is apparently what the four were doing, was a ritual expressing gratitude for God's special blessing. It involved abstaining from eating meat and drinking wine for thirty days, during which the hair was allowed to grow. The last seven days were spent in the Temple. Offerings were made—a lamb for a sin offering, a ram for a peace offering, unleavened bread, cakes made of fine flour and oil, a meat offering, and a wine offering—not an inexpensive process. Finally, the hair of the vow-taker was cut and burned with the sacrifice as an offering to God. If you saw a guy leaving the Temple with his head shaved, chances are he wasn't just being "cool." He had just said "Thanks, God!" by taking the Nazarite vow.

Jewish law allowed a person who had not done the thirty days of self-denial to join in the Nazarite ceremonies of others by participating in their **purification rites**, paying their expenses, and going through the last seven days with them. Even though he didn't do the whole Nazarite thing, paying the Nazarites' expenses was considered an especially fine, godly thing to do.

That is what Paul was asked to do (Acts 21:24).

> **Acts 21:26** The next day Paul took the men and purified himself along with them. Then he went to the temple to give notice of the date when the days of purification would end and the offering would be made for each of them.

orthodoxy: *devotion to an accepted set of beliefs and practices*

☞ **GO TO:**

Numbers 6 (Nazarite vow)

purification rites: *required of pilgrims from pagan lands before participating in temple worship*

Caught In The Act Of Making Peace

Paul's show of solidarity with the four Nazarites was consistent with his "theology of accommodation." His reasons for following the elders' public relations scheme included these ideas:

- To express confidence in the wisdom of the Jerusalem elders

- To preserve peace in the church

- To ease tensions between Christian Jews and their culture

- To remove barriers to acceptance of the Gospel by Jews

- To open the way for the elders to accept aid from the Gentiles

- To express unity between Gentile and Jewish wings of the church

- To demonstrate loyalty to his Jewish roots

Willingness to accommodate the likes and dislikes of others, where accommodation does not hinder spiritual growth or violate some clear instruction of the Lord, is part of a sound church growth strategy.

William Barclay: It is the sign of a great man that he can subordinate his own wishes and views for the sake of the church. There is a time when compromise is not a sign of weakness but of strength.[7]

Acts 21:27–30 When the seven days were nearly over, some Jews from the province of Asia saw Paul in the temple. They stirred up the whole crowd and seized him, shouting, "Men of Israel, help us! This is the man who teaches all men everywhere against our people and our law and this place. And besides, he has brought Greeks into the temple area and defiled this holy place." (They had previously seen Trophimus the Ephesian in the city with Paul and assumed that Paul had brought him into the temple area.)

The whole city was aroused, and the people came running from all directions. Seizing Paul, they dragged him from the temple, and immediately the gates were shut.

☞ **GO TO:**

1 Corinthians 9:19–23; 10:23–33; Romans 14:1–15:7 (theology of accommodation)

CHURCH GROWTH

What Others are Saying:

Peace Process Boomerangs!

The Jerusalem Christian elders' scheme backfired. With the Nazarites in the Temple for seven days, Paul was highly visible. Old enemies—Jews from Asia Province who'd failed to silence him in Ephesus (see Acts 19:8–10)—recognized him. They grabbed him, shouting that he was guilty of teaching anti-Judaism and adding the inflammatory accusation that he'd brought pagans into the Temple! Both charges were 100 percent baloney.

Katie, Bar The Door!

Gentiles were not allowed in the Temple. They could only come to the outer Court of the Gentiles (see illustration, page 38). Between the outer and inner courts was a fence. On the fence was a sign in Greek and Latin: "No foreigner may enter within the barricade which surrounds the temple and enclosure. Anyone who is caught trespassing will bear personal responsibility for his ensuing death."[8]

The Roman occupation government did not allow Jews to execute anyone without the governor's permission with this exception; a Gentile (even a Roman) who crossed the fence line was a dead man!

Earlier, the Asian Jews had seen Paul and Trophimus, a Greek, together in the city and assumed Paul had brought him into the Temple.

Hearing the accusations, people rushed Paul and dragged him out into the Court of Gentiles. Immediately the gates slammed shut.

Bible scholars see the shutting of the temple gates as a symbol of the deliberate choice of leaders and people of Israel to shut their hearts, minds, and religious life to God, his message and his Messenger. The Temple was now ripe for destruction. In A.D. 70, less than a decade later, destruction came.

Something to Ponder

☞ **GO TO:**

Acts 28:25–27 (shut their hearts)

Luke 21:6 (destruction)

officers: centurions

> **Acts 21:31–36** While they were trying to kill him, the news reached the commander of the Roman troops that the whole city of Jerusalem was in an uproar. He at once took some **officers** and soldiers and ran down to the crowd. When the rioters saw the commander and his soldiers, they stopped beating Paul.
> The commander came up and arrested him and or-

dered him to be bound with two chains. Then he asked who he was and what he had done. Some in the crowd shouted one thing and some another, and since the commander could not get at the truth because of the uproar, he ordered that Paul be taken into the barracks. When Paul reached the steps, the violence of the mob was so great he had to be carried by the soldiers. The crowd kept shouting, "Away with him!"

Roman Justice To The Rescue!

Just northwest of the temple area overlooking the Court of Gentiles was the Fortress Antonia, built by Herod and named in honor of Roman General Mark Antony. The fortress served as barracks for a thousand Roman soldiers deployed under the command of a **tribune**, to keep the peace at feast times. The fortress was connected to the Court of Gentiles by two flights of stairs, strategically close so the garrison could intervene quickly at the first sign of civil disturbance.

Rome demanded civil order in its provinces. A riot was a serious breach of the **Pax Romana** carrying serious repercussions.

When word of the uproar reached the tribune, at least two hundred soldiers stormed down the steps to where the mob was beating Paul. When the rioters saw the troops, swords drawn, they quickly backed away.

Since Paul was the focus of the ruckus, the tribune ordered him chained. When the tribune asked the crowd what crime Paul had committed, he got a confused cacophony of shouted accusations that made no sense. He ordered the prisoner inside the fortress for questioning. As Paul was being led away, the crowd again lunged at him, trying to tear him from the soldiers, screaming for his death! The mob became so violent, the soldiers had to pick Paul up bodily and carry him up the stairs.

William Barclay: There was never a time when Paul was nearer death than this and it was the impartial justice of Rome which saved his life.[9]

Persecution & Martyrdom—Attacks by angry mobs are not foreign to the Christian experience. In the 1970s in Berkley, Hubert Lindsey preached to radical students on the campus of the University of California. The cover of his book, *Bless Your Dirty Heart*, reports: "'Holy

---

☞ **GO TO:**

Luke 23:18
(Away with him!)

tribune: *commander of one thousand troops with ten centurions*

Pax Romana: *Roman peace enforced by a powerful military*

What Others are Saying:

Hubert,' as they dubbed him, has been beaten senseless, kicked, mocked, and spat upon countless times for his belief, yet his spirit remains undaunted, and perhaps his greatest witness is the degree to which he truly loves his enemy."[10]

> **Acts 21:37–22:2** As the soldiers were about to take Paul into the barracks, he asked the commander, "May I say something to you?"
>
> "Do you speak Greek," he replied. "Aren't you the Egyptian who started a revolt and led four thousand terrorists out into the desert some time ago?"
>
> Paul answered, "I am a Jew, from Tarsus in Cilicia, a citizen of no ordinary city. Please let me speak to the people."
>
> Having received the commander's permission, Paul stood on the steps and motioned to the crowd. When they were all silent, he said to them in Aramaic: "Brothers and fathers, listen now to my defense."
>
> When they heard him speak to them in Aramaic, they became very quiet.

The Tenacious Truth Teller

This conversation reveals some interesting facts:

- Paul was multilingual. He spoke Greek, universal language of the Roman Empire, and Aramaic, everyday language of Palestinian Jews (Acts 21:37, 40; 22:2). As a trained rabbi, he was also fluent in Hebrew, the language of the Old Testament.

- When the trouble started, the tribune jumped to the conclusion that Paul was an Egyptian assassin who had led *"four thousand terrorists"* in a failed revolt in A.D. 54. The Egyptian was on both the Jewish and Roman "Ten Most Wanted" lists.

- Paul came to Jerusalem with one consuming passion: to share the good news of Jesus Christ with his countrymen (see Acts 9:15). A less Christ-obsessed man would be yelling, "Please! Get me to the ER!" Paul was asking, *"Please let me speak to the people."*

The tribune, hoping to get information to report to his superiors on the reason for the riot, granted Paul's request. A wall of

terrorists: "dagger men"; whose tactic was to mingle with festival crowds, stab pro-Roman Jews, then disappear into the crowd

☞ **GO TO:**

Galatians 2:20 (Christ-obsessed)

tough legionnaires kept the crowd from coming too close. The beat-up, upbeat little Jew from Tarsus stood at the top of the stairs. Surprisingly, the crowd fell silent at the wave of his hand and the sound of his voice speaking their language. *"Brothers and fathers,"* he began. These were the same words Paul had heard the martyr Stephen speak to begin his defense (see Acts 7:2).

KEY POINT

When speaking about Jesus, speak in language listeners can understand.

> **Acts 22:3–5** Then Paul said: "I am a Jew born in Tarsus of Cilicia, but brought up in this city. Under Gamaliel I was thoroughly trained in the law of our fathers and was just as zealous for God as any of you are today. I persecuted the followers of this Way to their death, arresting both men and women and throwing them into prison, as also the high priest and the Council can testify. I even obtained letters from them to their brothers in Damascus, and went there to bring these people as prisoners to Jerusalem to be punished."

The Saul/Paul Of Tarsus Story

Paul called it *"my defense"* (Acts 22:1). It was the story of his conversion. Acts contains two other accounts of this same story: Luke's third person report in Acts 9:1–19 and another first person account before Governor Festus and King Agrippa 2 in Acts 26:4–23. It's a model for Christians telling the stories of their personal spiritual journeys.

Who I Was

Paul was a Jew. He never forgot his <u>national identity</u>. He identified with his listeners.

* A Roman citizen—*"Born in Tarsus."*
* A citizen of Jerusalem—*"Brought up"* in the Holy City, probably arrived at age thirteen for rabbinical education.
* A lawyer and rabbi—*"Trained in the law"* under the famed Pharisee teacher, <u>Gamaliel</u>, renowned as "the **glory** of the law."
* Zealous for God—"Like you!" he added. The zeal was real, but misguided.
* Persecutor of Christians—He hunted down, arrested, jailed, and even killed *"the followers of **this Way**"*—Jesus' followers.

☞ **GO TO:**

2 Corinthians 11:22; Philippians 3:4–5 (national identity)

Acts 5:34 (Gamaliel)

John 14:6; Acts 9:2; 22:4 (this Way)

glory: *radiance, reflection, image*

this Way: *term for Christians emphasizing their unique way of living*

> **Acts 22:6–16** Paul tells the story of how God got his attention, corrected his understanding, blinded him, sent Ananias to heal him, and transformed him into a messenger for God.

How I Met Jesus

Paul, known as Saul at the time of his conversion, told what happened on his way to Damascus to hunt Christians (Acts 9). It was high noon. A blazing light dazzled him and knocked him down. A voice called his name. The speaker was Jesus who, until that moment, Saul believed was dead. Not only did Saul hear the voice, but he _saw_ the resurrected Lord Jesus—person to person (Acts 22:14–15).

Ananias, a Christian believer highly respected by both Jews and Christians in Damascus, came to see the blinded, shaken Saul. He restored Saul's sight, assured him God had **chosen** him and that he wasn't dreaming—he'd _really_ seen Messiah Jesus. He gave Saul God's assignment: Tell everyone you meet about Jesus.

Ananias instructed Saul how to begin his walk with Jesus: (1) Call on Jesus for salvation and cleansing from your sins; (2) be baptized as an outward sign of your <u>new life</u>; and (3) act _now_!

☞ **GO TO:**

Acts 26:16; 1 Corinthians 9:1; 15:8; Galatians 1:16 (saw)

Ephesians 1:4; Romans 8:28–29 (chosen)

2 Corinthians 5:17; Ephesians 2:1 (new life)

chosen: "handpicked"[11]

> **Acts 22:17–21** "When I returned to Jerusalem and was praying at the temple, I fell into a trance and saw the Lord speaking. 'Quick!' he said to me. 'Leave Jerusalem immediately, because they will not accept your testimony about me.'
>
> "'Lord,' I replied, 'these men know that I went from one synagogue to another to imprison and beat those who believe in you. And when the blood of your martyr Stephen was shed, I stood there giving my <u>approval and guarding</u> the clothes of those who were killing him.'
>
> "Then the Lord said to me, 'Go; I will send you far away to the Gentiles.'"

☞ **GO TO:**

Acts 7:58; 8:1 (approval and guarding)

How My Life Has Changed Since I Met Jesus

From what Paul said before his voice was drowned out by renewed demands for his death, we detect these changes:

- Paul did not stop being Jewish. The difference was that now when he prayed Jesus met him.

- Paul could now hear the Lord's voice directing his life.

- Paul saw his sins clearly and was honest in admitting them.
- When he talked about sins committed before he met Christ, he discovered the Lord was <u>no longer concerned</u> about his past, only his present and future.
- Paul had been trained to teach Jews God's law. But now the Lord sent him to teach pagans God's grace.

☞ **GO TO:**

Hebrews 10:17;
1 John 1:9
(no longer
concerned)

Johnny Cash: A few years ago I was hooked on drugs. I dreaded to wake up in the morning. There was no joy, peace, or happiness in my life. Then one day in my helplessness I turned my life completely over to God. Now I can't wait to get up in the morning and study my Bible. Sometimes the words out of the Scriptures leap into my heart. This does not mean that all my problems have been solved, or that I have reached any state of perfection. However, my life has been turned around. I've been born again![12]

What Others are Saying:

> **Acts 22:22–23** The crowd listened to Paul until he said this. Then they raised their voices and shouted, "Rid the earth of him! He's not fit to live!"
>   As they were shouting and throwing off their cloaks and flinging dust into the air, . . .

First-Century Religious Hot Button

At the mention of the Gentiles, Paul struck the raw nerve that triggered the riot in the first place. The crowd remembered why they wanted to kill him. The horror of his "crime" swept over them again: Taking a filthy heathen, a lawless, godless, ceremonially unclean, unblessed, despised, hell-bound Gentile into the house of God! In "righteous" rage they tore off their cloaks and shook the dust off them as a sign of condemnation. In horrified grief over the imagined desecration of the sacred place, they threw dust into the air till the Court of Gentiles was a choking cloud of suspended dirt.

William Barclay: If Paul had preached the yoke of Judaism to the Gentiles all would have been well; it was because he preached the grace of Christianity to them that the Jews were enraged.[13]

What Others are Saying:

> **Acts 22:24–29** . . . the commander ordered Paul to be taken into the barracks. He directed that he be flogged and questioned in order to find out why the people were shouting at him like this. As they stretched him out to flog him, Paul said to the centurion standing there, "Is it legal for you to flog a Roman citizen who hasn't even been found guilty?"
>
> When the centurion heard this, he went to the commander and reported it. "What are you going to do?" he asked. "This man is a Roman citizen."
>
> The commander went to Paul and asked, "Tell me, are you a Roman citizen?"
>
> "Yes, I am," he answered.
>
> Then the commander said, "I had to pay a big price for my citizenship."
>
> "But I was born a citizen," Paul replied.
>
> Those who were about to question him withdrew immediately. The commander himself was alarmed when he realized that he had put Paul, a Roman citizen, in chains.

Citizen Paul

Standard interrogation procedure under Roman justice was not questioning with one's lawyer present. To get at the truth in the shortest time possible, Roman police simply stretched the accused spread-eagle on the ground and literally whipped the livin' stuffin' out of him until he either died from it or was willing to say whatever it took to get the torture to stop! This is what Paul was facing when he played his trump card!

The attitude of the Romans changed quickly when they learned Paul was a freeborn Roman <u>citizen</u>. Everyone from the commander and centurion to the scourge-wielding dog-faced soldier suddenly backed off in shock at how close they'd come to mistreating a fellow Roman without due process. It was a serious crime to chain or flog a Roman citizen. The commander could lose his military commission or even his life.

Roman Citizenship

A Roman citizen was treated as if he were a resident of the city of Rome.

Advantages of Roman Citizenship

- A Roman citizen was subject only to Roman courts and laws.

☞ **GO TO:**

Luke 20:22–25;
 Romans 13:1–8;
 Ephesians 2:19;
 Philippians 3:20
 (citizen)

- A Roman citizen was protected from interrogation by torture or imprisonment before trial.
- A Roman citizen was free to travel anywhere in the empire he wished to travel.
- A Roman citizen was under the protection of the local Roman garrison in any city in the empire.

Four Ways One Became a Roman Citizen

1. By birth in a free Roman city, such as Tarsus or Philippi.
2. By birth to parents who were Roman citizens.
3. By having citizenship conferred in recognition of special service to the emperor or empire.
4. By bribing an official who could grant citizenship (this is how the tribune in Acts 22:28 obtained it).

Stanley Hauerwas and William H. Willimon: The church is a colony, an island of one culture in the middle of another. In baptism our citizenship is transferred from one dominion to another, and we become, in whatever culture we find ourselves, resident aliens.[14]

What Others are Saying:

Study Questions

1. How did Agabus pantomime his prophecy concerning Paul's arrest in Jerusalem? How did Agabus know what Paul would face? How did Paul's response to the prophecy differ from his Christian friends' response?
2. What did James and the Jerusalem church elders want Paul to do to prove he was not anti-Jewish? Why did Paul go along with their plan?
3. Identify the three main points in Paul's conversion story (Acts 22:1–21).
4. Identify three of the five changes that took place in Paul's life as a result of his encounter with Jesus (Acts 22:17–21).

CHAPTER WRAP-UP

- As Paul headed for Jerusalem, he knew he was headed for danger. Fellow Christians tried to convince him not to go. Agabus prophesied his arrest and that he would be turned over to the Romans. (Acts 21:1–14)
- In Jerusalem Paul met with church leaders. After exchanging

reports of God's work among Gentiles and Jews, they proposed a plan for Paul to participate in purification rites to put down rumors that he was guilty of anti-Jewish teaching. (Acts 21:15–19)

- The plan backfired. Paul was recognized in the Temple by his enemies, who falsely accused him of anti-Jewish teaching and taking a Gentile into the Temple. A riot ensued. Roman soldiers rescued Paul from the murderous mob. (Acts 21:20–36)

- Paul asked the Roman commander to let him speak to the people from the top of the fortress stairs. He told the story of his conversion. When he mentioned being sent to the Gentiles, the crowd again erupted in cries for his death. (Acts 21:37–22:23)

- Just as the Romans were about to interrogate him by flogging, Paul told them he was a Roman citizen. The torture stopped. Paul was taken into protective custody and treated with greater respect. (Acts 21:24–29)

ACTS 22:30–23:35: PAUL'S TICKET TO RIDE

Let's Get Started

According to Acts, the presence of Jesus Christ in a person can change his or her life from a road to nowhere to high adventure. In the final chapters, Luke traces the journey of Paul from one dramatic event to another. With each paragraph risks increase, intrigue deepens, action intensifies. We observe the little Jew from Tarsus ultimately rising—soaring like an eagle—above it all. One dangerous, painful, or horrific situation after another becomes an opportunity to tell the story the early Christians seemed ready to tell if it was the last thing they did!

As the drama unfolds, we see with increasing clarity one emerging reality: Jesus Christ is alive! He is present with his people in the midst of it all. And his presence turns calamity into a victory for believers and another chance for unbelievers to turn to God!

> **Acts 22:30–23:1** The next day, since the commander wanted to find out exactly why Paul was being accused by the Jews, he released him and ordered the chief priests and all the Sanhedrin to assemble. Then he brought Paul and had him stand before them.
>
> Paul looked straight at the Sanhedrin and said, "My brothers, I have fulfilled my duty to God in all good conscience to this day."

Who's On Trial Here, Anyway?

The day after Paul's arrest (see Acts 21:33), the tribune of the Roman garrison at Jerusalem summoned the Sanhedrin, Israel's supreme court, to a meeting to determine the exact nature of the charges against Paul. This seventy-member council was composed of high priests, city officials, and Pharisee, Sadducee, and Herodian party reps.

With Roman soldiers on alert nearby, the tribune escorted Paul, no longer in chains, into the council chamber.

The normal way to address the Sanhedrin was to say, "Rulers of the people and elders of Israel."[1] By saying *My brothers,* Paul declared himself an equal with the council. Before becoming a Christian he'd been deeply involved in Sanhedrin affairs, either as a Pharisee delegate or a rabbinical student. He had once been the Sanhedrin's "fair-haired boy."

☞ **GO TO:**

Acts 7:58; 8:1, 3;
9:1–2; 22:4–5
(fair-haired boy)

Assertions Of Innocence

The accusation of the Asian Jews who stirred up the previous day's riot was that Paul had brought Gentiles into the Temple and was teaching against Judaism (see Acts 21:28). In this meeting before the Sanhedrin those charges were never mentioned. Paul, taking control of his own trial, opened with a ringing plea of *Not guilty!*

> **Acts 23:2–5** At this the high priest Ananias ordered those standing near Paul to strike him on the mouth. Then Paul said to him, "God will strike you, you whitewashed wall! You sit there to judge me according to the law, yet you yourself violate the law by commanding that I be struck!"
>
> Those who were standing near Paul said, "You dare to insult God's high priest?"
>
> Paul replied, "Brothers, I did not realize that he was the high priest; for it is written: 'Do not speak evil about the ruler of your people.'"

Ananias—Spiritual Leader Or Flim-Flam Man?

Ananias had been the high priest for ten years. He was corrupt and violent. Jewish historian Josephus reports that Ananias sent servants to Judean farmers' threshing floors during harvest and illegally confiscated tithes that were supposed to go to the common priests.[2] Another source tells how he misappropriated sacrifices dedicated to God.

Infuriated by Paul's disregard of Sanhedrin protocols, Ananias ordered the sergeant-at-arms to hit him in the mouth! We can't be sure the blow ever landed, because Paul instinctively responded with verbal blows to stagger his opponent.

- Paul accused Ananias of breaking the law (Acts 23:3). Under Jewish law defendants were presumed innocent until proven guilty. To mistreat a person before trial was forbidden. Paul had not been properly charged, nor tried and convicted. The law also stated that to <u>strike</u> a fellow Israelite was to attack the glory of God![3]

- Paul called Ananias a fake. The metaphor "<u>whitewashed wall</u>" (Acts 23:3) pictured a cracked structure whose disintegration is thinly disguised by a coat of cheap paint. The high priest hid <u>hypocrisy</u> and wickedness behind a facade of religious piety.

- Paul didn't recognize Ananias as the legitimate high priest. He agreed that <u>insulting Israel's ruler</u> violated the Law. When he said, "I did not recognize him" (Acts 23:5), did he mean he wasn't physically familiar with the man or "I apologize for my unthinking outburst"? Or was he being sarcastic?—"I did not know a man as disreputable as this could hold the office of high priest!"

- Paul prophesied Ananias's judgment. He told the man who ordered him struck, "*God will strike you!*" (Acts 23:3). The prophesied judgment began a year later when he was removed from office. His ill-gotten wealth continued to give him influence. The final strike came in 66 A.D. at the point of assassins' daggers, as Jewish guerillas dragged him from his hiding place in an aqueduct and killed him.

☞ **GO TO:**

John 18:22–23 (strike)

Ezekiel 13:10–13; Matthew 23:7 (whitewashed wall)

Matthew 23:13 (hypocrisy)

Exodus 22:28 (insulting Israel's ruler)

F. F. Bruce: The warm impetuousness of a man [Paul] of like passions with ourselves is vividly portrayed in this trial scene, and there is no doubt who presents the more dignified bearing—Paul or the high priest.[4]

What Others are Saying:

Acts 23:6–9 Then Paul, knowing that some of them were Sadducees and the others Pharisees, called out in the Sanhedrin, "My brothers, I am a Pharisee, the son of a Pharisee. I stand on trial because of my hope in the resurrection of the dead." When he said this, a dispute broke out between the Pharisees and the Sadducees, and the assembly was divided. (The Sadducees say that there is no resurrection, and that there are neither angels nor spirits, but the Pharisees acknowledge them all.)

There was a great uproar, and some of the teachers of the law who were Pharisees stood up and argued vigorously. "We find nothing wrong with this man," they said. "What if a spirit or an angel has spoken to him?"

The Truth Will Drive You Crazy

Paul knew the makeup of the Sanhedrin like the back of his hand. Its seventy members were religious "experts." One thing you can count on is that religious scholars will argue at the drop of a Bible passage! Especially *this* bunch of experts.

The Sanhedrin

The Majority: Sadducee Party	The Minority: Pharisee Party
High priestly aristocracy	Experts in Jewish law
Roman sympathizers	Silent protesters against Rome
Accepted authority of only the **Pentateuch**	Accepted rabbinical **traditions** as authoritative
Believed in human free will	Believed in **predestination**
Denied existence of spirit world, angels, demons	Believed in spirit world, angels, demons
Denied life after death or resurrection	Believed in resurrection of the dead
A few became Christians (see Acts 6:7)	Many became Christians (see Acts 15:5)

Pentateuch: *first five books of the Bible*

traditions: *interpretations of rabbis, added religious rules*

predestination: *belief that events are determined by God ahead of time*

The Guts Of The Gospel

Paul's announcement that he was a second generation Pharisee on trial over the issue of the resurrection was like an apple thrown to a herd of pigs. It turned Israel's rulers into a scrapping aggregation of squealing creatures incapable of decision making!

Some think Paul's resurrection statement was designed to bring out the worst in the Sanhedrin. But there was more to it than trickery to create a diversion. Paul turned the spotlight on the real reason some Sanhedrin members wanted to terminate him. They could not prove him guilty of bringing Gentiles into the Temple or anti-Jewish teaching. What many (especially the Sadducean rulers) despised about him and all Christians was their teaching of the *resurrection*. If a person believed in the resurrection, it was possible to believe the Christians' claim that Jesus rose from the dead. And from there it was only a short distance to faith in Jesus as the Messiah, sent from God to redeem people from their sins and bring Judaism to its fulfillment.

The Resurrection—Good News or Grand Nuisance?

It's a pattern. As the early church's story is traced in Acts, the subject of resurrection repeatedly incites hostility and conflict.

Dig Deeper

- Acts 3:12–4:3—Peter and John teach the people about Jesus' resurrection. The Sadducees get all hot and bothered and throw them in jail.
- Acts 5:30–33—The Twelve mention the resurrection. Council members want to kill them.
- Acts 7:55–60—Stephen says he sees Jesus alive and standing at God's right hand. The council goes wild and stones him to death.
- Acts 17:32—Paul mentions the resurrection to the Athenian philosophers. They jeer him and walk out.

Why Was the Resurrection Such a Turn-Off?

The problem with the resurrection as the early Christians taught it—the Easter story—is that resurrection demonstrates Jesus is who he claimed to be. The fact that Jesus rose from the dead shows the following:

Dig Deeper

- Acts 2:24–36—He is <u>Lord</u> and Christ (Savior-King).
- Acts 3:15–16—His name can bring healing.
- Acts 4:10–12—<u>Salvation</u> (rescue from sin and separation from God) is found nowhere else. Jesus is the **capstone** of everything God is doing.
- Acts 5:29–32—He is Prince and Savior.
- Acts 13:37–39—Through him, sins are forgiven and people get right with God—something the law (human works) could never do.
- Acts 17:31—Jesus is God's appointed judge of the world.

☞ **GO TO:**

Romans 1:4 (Lord)

1 Corinthians 15:14–22 (salvation)

capstone: *keystone that holds the whole building together*

It is not the resurrection idea itself that drives people crazy. It is what the resurrection says about Jesus. A theoretical Jesus who exists on the level of ideas, religious traditions, institutional trappings, and history does not disturb most people. But a Jesus who died for the world's sins, rose from

Remember This . . .

KEY POINT

Believing Jesus is alive
means you have to do
business with him!

the dead, and presently lives in his followers, calling for real
change in the way all people live—*that* Jesus cannot be ignored. *That* Jesus makes people mad.

> **Acts 23:10–11** The dispute became so violent that the
> commander was afraid Paul would be torn to pieces by
> them. He ordered the troops to go down and take him
> away from them by force and bring him into the bar-
> racks.
>   The following night the Lord stood near Paul and
> said, "Take courage! As you have testified about me in
> Jerusalem, so you must also testify in Rome."

The Resurrection—Up Close And Personal

That night, back in the safety of the fortress, Paul reflected on the
events of the last two days. He'd boldly challenged the powerful
men of Israel. He'd thrown the council into pandemonium with
one volley of truth. He'd declared the resurrection of Jesus. But
after being mauled by an angry crowd, he may have been experiencing a healthy dose of discouragement. No one had been converted. His presence and words in the Holy City only seemed to
inspire rage and conflict. And what of his dreams of witnessing in
Rome?

At that moment the reality of the resurrection stood beside him
in the cell! The Lord Jesus came to him and turned his questions
into promises.

At decisive points in his walk of faith, Paul heard the Lord say
what he most <u>needed</u> to hear. In this jailhouse vision Jesus gave at
least four reassurances:

☞ **GO TO:**

Acts 16:9; 18:9–10;
27:23–24 (needed)

1. Jesus was with Paul.

2. Paul had accomplished what he'd come to Jerusalem to
   do—*"carry [Jesus'] name . . . before the people of Israel"*
   (Acts 9:15). His testimony at the top of the stairs (Acts
   21:40–22:21) and declaration of faith in the resurrection
   in the Sanhedrin (Acts 23:6) fulfilled the assignment. *"You
   have testified about me in Jerusalem,"* the Lord said.

3. Paul would get to Rome and fulfill his dream of telling
   the Jesus story there, as in Jerusalem (Acts 23:1). Prison
   would not keep him from being Christ's witness!

4. Paul would leave Jerusalem *alive*.

JESUS CHRIST CEO

With Jesus' comforting appearance to Paul in his jail cell, we (and Paul) are assured that everything that is happening—the anger and error of religious men, the military force of pagan Rome, the events that have brought Paul to this point, and all that will follow—is being used by the Lord (Romans 8:28) to position Paul to do what he longs to do—witness for Christ to the most powerful man in the world, the Roman emperor.

What Others are Saying:

John McRay: Paul may have spent as much as 25% of his time as a missionary in prison.[5]

Billy Graham: God does not always deliver us out of catastrophe, but he promises to be with us throughout.[6]

Henry Alford: So one crumb of divine grace and help [was] multiplied to feed five thousand wants and anxieties [for Paul].[7]

Something to Ponder

A ninety-five-year-old woman in our town died, and I was asked to preach the funeral sermon. Knowing she was a Christian, I decided to preach on the resurrection. I based my message on what Jesus told Martha after the death of her brother. *"I am the resurrection and the life. He who believes in me will live, even though he dies; and whoever believes in me will never die"* (John 11:25–26).

It soon was obvious what I was saying was not pleasing some mourners. A few minutes into my sermon a sister of the deceased approached the pulpit and told me to stop.

"I can't," I said, "I need to finish the message." Loud male voices in the audience said "Either stop, or you're outta here!"

Deciding I'd rather walk out than be carried, I closed with a prayer that summed up my unfinished sermon. Some family members apologized for the others. The woman who'd arranged for me to preach was in tears. I assured her I did not blame her and I forgave them all.

Following the hearse to the cemetery, I remembered times when Paul and others stirred up anger and confusion by mentioning the resurrection. It eased my pain a little to know I was in good company. But as I drove back to town after the interment I felt really bad. Then a wonderful thing happened.

I dropped off some clothing at a local charity and was getting back in my vehicle when I heard a woman's voice: "No, you can't hug the man. He's all dressed up and you're all dirty!"

I looked around and saw a young woman crossing the street with a chubby little boy about five years old who had obviously been playing in the mud. I got out of my car and said, "Lady, I'm really hurting, and I *need* a hug!" With his mother's permission, the little boy ran to me and we gave each other a warm (mucky) hug.

As I drove away, I cried. In that muddy embrace, the reality of the resurrection was confirmed. Jesus is alive. Through a muddy little angel he healed my pain.

> **Acts 23:12–15** The next morning the Jews formed a conspiracy and bound themselves with an oath not to eat or drink until they had killed Paul. More than forty men were involved in this plot. They went to the chief priests and elders and said, "We have taken a solemn oath not to eat anything until we have killed Paul. Now then, you and the Sanhedrin petition the commander to bring him before you on the pretext of wanting more accurate information about his case. We are ready to kill him before he gets here."

Get Paul!

Frustrated in their attempt to lynch Paul at the Temple and unable to press charges against him because of Sanhedrin infighting, his enemies concocted another assassination plot. More than forty men—probably **Zealots**—bound themselves together in a rash pact: They would not eat or drink until Paul was dead by their hand! Ruling members of the council—mostly Sadducees—joined the conspiracy.

The oath taken by these dagger men probably followed a familiar Jewish pattern: "So may God do to us, and more also, if we eat or drink anything until we have killed Paul."[8]

> **Acts 23:16–22** But when the son of Paul's sister heard of this plot, he went into the barracks and told Paul.
> Then Paul called one of the centurions and said, "Take this young man to the commander; he has some-

Zealots: militant party committed to protecting Judaism by violence

☞ **GO TO:**

Numbers 30:2 (pact)

thing to tell him." So he took him to the commander.

The centurion said, "Paul, the prisoner, sent for me and asked me to bring this young man to you because he has something to tell you."

The commander took the young man by the hand, drew him aside and asked, "What is it you want to tell me?"

He said: "The Jews have agreed to ask you to bring Paul before the Sanhedrin tomorrow on the pretext of wanting more accurate information about him. Don't give in to them, because more than forty of them are waiting in ambush for him. They have taken an oath not to eat or drink until they have killed him. They are ready now, waiting for your consent to their request."

The commander dismissed the young man and cautioned him, "Don't tell anyone that you have reported this to me."

Cat's Out Of The Bag

Not much is known about Paul's family. His father was a Pharisee (see Acts 23:6) and a Roman citizen from Tarsus. Paul mentions relatives in greetings to Christians in Rome (see Romans 16:7, 11, 21), but we can't be sure he's speaking of *spiritual* or *blood* relatives. Since so little is said of his immediate family it is usually assumed that when he became a Christian his family disowned him, and are included in his statement that for Christ's sake *"I have lost all things"* (Philippians 3:8).

We know from Acts 23:16 that Paul had a sister, whose son, a young man—a boy or a teenager—was in Jerusalem. We don't know if he or his mother was a believer, but he obviously cared what happened to his uncle. Somehow the lad got wind of the conspiracy and went to the Fortress Antonia to blow the wannabe assassins' cover.

After telling what he knew to Paul, he was taken to the tribune, who responded with uncharacteristic gentleness and listened carefully as the boy revealed what he knew about the conspiracy.

Christianity often spreads with the help of nonbelievers whose hearts are open to individual Christians they admire (see Matthew 10:40).

CHURCH GROWTH

Howard Marshall: The fact that the tribune *took* the boy *by the hand* has also been the subject of scholarly sarcasm: "Never was a tribune so amiable," said [one commentator]. But the impression we get is rather that the lad was quite young, and the tribune's action is appropriate. The ancient world would not have seen any incompatibility between his ordering Paul to be scourged and his kindly treatment of the boy.[9]

THE BIG PICTURE

> **Acts 23:23–33** Wasting no time the tribune assigned a force of 470 Roman legionnaires to escort Paul in the middle of the night to Antipatris, then on the next day to Caesarea. They carried a letter from Tribune Claudius Lysias to Felix, Roman governor of Judea, transferring Paul's case to the governor's jurisdiction.

Red-Eye To Caesarea

Quick action by the tribune changing the venue of Paul's trial from Jerusalem to Caesarea with a show of overwhelming force frustrated the assassins who must have felt silly for making their brash oath. Poor fools! They went without breakfast for nothing! Paul was long gone before they strapped on their cloaks and daggers the next morning. It's unlikely any starved because they were unable to keep their vow. The Jewish **Talmud** conveniently provided that such oaths could be annulled by getting a rabbi to cancel the obligation.

Paul's removal to Caesarea took the steam out of a problem that had created three days of high tension for the Jerusalem garrison. The commander's letter to the governor (Acts 23:27–30) followed the typical format of official first-century correspondence. Like any good politician, the noble tribune gave a spin to the facts making him look slightly more knowledgeable and in charge than he really was. Still, give Tribune Claudius Lysias a medal for effective crowd control and riot dousing.

Caesarea was about sixty miles (one hundred kilometers) northwest of Jerusalem. It was the governmental center of the province of Judea, and site of Herod's palace, which was occupied by Governor Marcus Antonius Felix.

The military escort with Paul left Jerusalem about 9:00 P.M. and traveled thirty-seven miles by forced march arriving at Antipatris before dawn. Next day the four hundred infantry and spearmen returned to Jerusalem. The cavalry took the prisoner the last twenty-seven miles.

Talmud: *ancient commentary on Old Testament laws*

> **Acts 23:34–35** The governor read the letter and asked what province he was from. Learning that he was from Cilicia, he said, "I will hear your case when your accusers get here." Then he ordered that Paul be kept under guard in Herod's palace.

First Stop On The Rugged Road To Rome

The cellblock of Herod's magnificent Caesarean palace was no royal guest suite. It was as ugly as the rest of the place was elegant. Paul slept on the floor wrapped in his own cloak, his hands manacled with a chain (see Acts 26:29). It was a miserable place, but safer than Jerusalem.

The governor would hear his case when his accusers arrived with formal charges. Paul's journey to Rome had begun as promised (Acts 23:11). God was using everything from theological arrogance to family loyalty to religious hatred to military power to Roman justice to spiritual vision, as he moved his witness to where he could use him best. In his letter to the Christians at Rome, Paul says he learned to see everything that happened as something useful in God's process of carrying out his grand design: *"And we know that in all things God works for the good of those who love him, who have been called according to his purpose"* (Romans 8:28).

KEY POINT

God can use all the happenings of our lives to accomplish good things.

Study Questions

1. In his response to the order that he be hit in the mouth, what four negative things did Paul say to or about Ananias, the high priest (Acts 23:3–5)?
2. Why did Paul's mention of the resurrection in the Sanhedrin create such turmoil? What is it about the resurrection that upsets people?
3. According to what is said about it in Acts, identify at least three things the resurrection reveals about Jesus.
4. Identify three of the four reassurances Jesus gave Paul when he visited him in the barracks.

CHAPTER WRAP-UP

- The Roman tribune called a meeting of the Sanhedrin to clarify charges against Paul. Paul claimed innocence. When the high priest ordered him struck, Paul struck back with charges and prophecies against the high priest. (Acts 22:30–23:5)

- Paul declared that the key issue that had gotten him into trouble was belief in the resurrection. The Sanhedrin became a shouting match between Pharisees who believed in resurrection and Sadducees who did not. (Acts 23:6–9)

- Roman troops again rescued Paul from being mauled by the warring council members. In his cell that night, Jesus reassured Paul he was doing what he'd been called to do and would soon witness in Rome. (Acts 23:10–11)

- Forty terrorists took an oath to kill Paul before they ate again. Some rulers joined the conspiracy. Paul's nephew discovered the plot and told Paul. (Acts 23:12–22)

- A large force of soldiers and cavalry escorted Paul to Caesarea, where he was turned over to Governor Felix for trial. (Acts 23:23–35)

ACTS 24–26: CHRIST'S AMBASSADOR ON TRIAL

CHAPTER HIGHLIGHTS

- Politics of Corruption
- Courtroom Strategy
- Too Close for Comfort
- Politics of Compromise
- Pomp and Circumstance
- Good News for the "Beautiful People"
- Wisecrack

Let's Get Started

Five days after his delivery to Herod's palace prison at Caesarea, the iron gates leading to Paul's cell clanged open. Two pairs of military boots stomped toward his cell. Two tough legionnaires hustled the little prisoner to Governor Felix's audience hall.

He stood in the great hall to face his accusers and his judge, on trial for his life. Always the Lord's promise echoed in the back of his mind: "You will testify for me in Rome" (see Acts 23:11).

In Acts, Roman justice is presented in a fairly favorable light. Even with its inconsistencies, the <u>system often worked</u> to the advantage of Paul and his team. As a Roman citizen he did not hesitate to demand the protections the system offered.

> **Acts 24:1** Five days later the high priest Ananias went down to Caesarea with some of the elders and a lawyer named Tertullus, and they brought their charges against Paul before the governor.

Politics Of Corruption

The governor was Marcus Antonius Felix. He was born a slave in the household of Antonia, mother of Claudius Caesar. Claudius freed him. In A.D. 38 he was appointed **procurator** of Judea. Felix married a succession of three wives, all princesses. The first was the granddaughter of Antony and Cleopatra, the name of the second is not known, and the third was Drusilla (Acts 24:24), youngest daughter of King Herod Agrippa 1.

☞ **GO TO:**

Acts 16:37–39; 18:16; 19:35–41; 22:25–29; 23:23–33 (system often worked)

procurator: ruler of a minor province

Roman historian Tacitus wrote that Felix "exercised kingly power with the mind of a slave."[1] His rule on Judea was marked by a series of insurrections, which he brutally crushed. The Jews hated him. His governance gave rise to the *sicarii* terrorists who assassinated Romans and Roman sympathizers. (The tribune at Jerusalem had assumed Paul was one of these terrorists when he had Paul arrested and jailed.)

> **Acts 24:2–9** When Paul was called in, Tertullus presented his case before Felix: "We have enjoyed a long period of peace under you, and your foresight has brought about reforms in this nation. Everywhere and in every way, most excellent Felix, we acknowledge this with profound gratitude. But in order not to weary you further, I would request that you be kind enough to hear us briefly.
>
> We have found this man to be a troublemaker, stirring up riots among the Jews all over the world. He is a ringleader of the Nazarene sect and even tried to desecrate the temple; so we seized him. By examining him yourself you will be able to learn the truth about all these charges we are bringing against him."
>
> The Jews joined in the accusation, asserting that these things were true.

Courtroom Strategy

Paul's accusers had hired a professional orator (that is, expert baloney slicer!) named Tertullus as prosecution counsel. Tertullus had a way with words! But very little regard for the truth.

Quick! Bring A Shovel!

Tertullus waxed eloquent about the *"long period of peace"* the province had enjoyed under Felix. Actually, few periods in Judean history were marred by more unrest and terrorism. Tertullus told how grateful the people were for the "reforms" instituted by Felix. The years A.D. 52–59 when Felix was procurator were years of unparalleled government corruption!

What a windbag! Did Tertullus actually believe that this unabashed attempt to manipulate the court through flattery would win the tough-minded Felix to his cause?

The delegation from Jerusalem charged Paul on three counts: First, he was a <u>worldwide troublemaker</u> (Greek: *loimos*—a pest, a

KEY POINT

Flattery is a manipulative substitute for truth, a warning of more lies to come.

☞ **GO TO:**

Acts 17:6
(worldwide troublemaker)

plague). Second, he was ringleader of the sect of the **Nazarenes**. Third, he violated the sanctity of the Temple by bringing in Gentiles. In the tradition of successful lawyers everywhere, Tertullus put his clients' unique spin on the facts. According to his made-for-the-courtroom yarn, the Jews narrowly averted disaster by taking Paul into custody (Acts 24:7). The lawyer-propagandist makes the lynch mob of Acts 21:30–31 sound like an orderly police action!

Nazarenes: *Hebrew and Arabic name for Jewish Christians*

THE BIG PICTURE

> **Acts 24:10–21** When Paul was allowed to speak, he boldly made his defense in a logical fashion. Paul told Tertullus what he did not do, what he did do, why he was in Jerusalem, and that there was no evidence to prove the charges against him.

Paul For The Defense

The defendant spoke respectfully and truthfully, foregoing the verbal **flatulence** with which Tertullus filled the courtroom. The charges against him were without substance (Acts 24:13). Here is his argument:

flatulence: *stomach gas*

1. What I'm not guilty of doing (Acts 24:12–13)
   - I did not argue with anyone.
   - I did not stir up trouble in the city.
2. What I admit (Acts 24:14–16)
   - I worship the God of Israel—a freedom granted by Roman law.
   - I follow *"the Way"*—lifestyle taught by Jesus of Nazareth.
   - My faith agrees with the Old Testament—*"the Law"* and *"the Prophets."*
   - I share hope of a future resurrection—as Old Testament patriarchs and prophets did.
   - I try to live with a clear conscience before God and man.
3. Why I came to Jerusalem (Acts 24:17)
   - I came with gifts to help the poor.
   - I came to worship—*"present offerings."*
4. What I was doing at the temple (Acts 24:18)
   - I was participating in a ceremony of cleansing in preparation for worship.

5. There is no evidence to prove the charges against me (Acts 24:19–20)

   - The Asian Jews who started this (Acts 21:28) should be here to be cross-examined if they have any charges to bring. But they are not here. Their allegations are invalid.
   - The Sanhedrin could not agree on the crime for which I should be charged (see Acts 23:7–9).

6. What I've done is no crime (Acts 24:21)

   - I am "guilty" of believing in the resurrection of the dead. This is why I am on trial! (Paul knew if Felix became convinced the issue had nothing to do with Roman law, but was about a point of Jewish theology, he'd throw the case out of court.)

> **Acts 24:22–23** Then Felix, who was well acquainted with the Way, adjourned the proceedings. "When Lysias the commander comes," he said, "I will decide your case." He ordered the centurion to keep Paul under guard but to give him some freedom and permit his friends to take care of his needs.

The Politics Of Expediency

As Felix responded to Paul's defense, the rough-and-tumble slave-turned-politician revealed thorough knowledge of the Jesus movement. Did he know some Christians? Caesarea had some live ones, including the Roman centurion Cornelius (see Acts 10) and evangelist Philip and his preacher-girls (see Acts 21:8–9). Some scholars think he got his information from his Jewish wife, Drusilla.

He could have dismissed the charges and let Paul go. Instead, to keep from offending the Sanhedrin, Felix postponed the verdict and left Paul in jail under the pretext of needing to hear more testimony.

Meanwhile, Paul was kept under guard, but given limited freedom. Roman jailhouse procedure was that a prisoner's food and personal needs were not provided. Paul's friends (Luke, Philip, and others) could visit and care for his needs.

> **Acts 24:24–26** Several days later Felix came with his wife Drusilla, who was a Jewess. He sent for Paul and listened to him as he spoke about faith in Christ Jesus. As Paul discoursed on righteousness, self-control, and the judgment to come, Felix was afraid and said, "That's enough for now! You may leave. When I find it convenient, I will send for you." At the same time he was hoping that Paul would offer him a bribe, so he sent for him frequently and talked with him.

Too Close For Comfort

It would be two years before Paul's trial resumed (Acts 24:27, 25:1). During that time, Paul received visitors and strengthened the Caesarean Christians from his place of confinement. Scholars believe Luke, who was with Paul, used these two years to gather information needed for his two books about the life of Christ and the early church.

During those two years, Paul and Felix had many conversations. The phrase *"at the same time"* hints that Felix had a divided heart. His talks with Paul betrayed a hungry heart with a genuine interest in Jesus. *"At the same time,"* corrupt politician that he was, he hoped Paul (whose family was wealthy) might grease his palms with a significant bribe to buy his freedom!

Drusilla, Beautiful, Rich, Powerful . . . And Starving!

Acts 24:24 reports that Felix's third wife, Drusilla, joined her husband in some of the conversations with Paul. Drusilla was Jewish. She was the daughter of King Herod Agrippa 1 (see Acts 12). Drusilla was sixteen when Felix seduced her and convinced her to leave her Jewish husband for him. Now at nineteen she was a beautiful woman who had already experienced what wealth, power, social advantage, and self-indulgence could provide.

> Even people who look like they have it "together" need Christ. Early Christians knew this and used every opportunity, including their own difficulties, to share the good news with others.

Don't Call Me—I'll Call You!

You can bet your last shekel Paul's chitchats with Felix and Drusilla were not little sermonettes, comedy routines, or heady discussions on how many angels can dance on the head of a pin! Paul

KEY POINT

Christian witnesses leave people free to make their own decisions about Christ—even if they make the wrong one!

CHURCH GROWTH

zeroed in on themes of *"faith in Jesus Christ . . . righteousness, self-control and the judgment to come"* (Acts 24:24–25). In other words, Paul talked about God's love demonstrated in Jesus, God's moral and spiritual demands, and the need for personal redemption—with a little hellfire and damnation thrown in for good measure.

The hair stood up on the back of Felix's dirty neck! He ended one conversation with the famous line: *"That's enough for now! You may leave. When I find it convenient, I will send for you."* We know they talked many times. We don't know if Felix or Drusilla ever found it "convenient" to trust in Jesus. We do know <u>God loves</u> dirty politicians and self-indulgent beauty queens!

☞ **GO TO:**

Romans 5:6–8
(God loves)

☞ **GO TO:**

Luke 18:24–25;
1 Timothy 6:9–10
(hard for the rich)

Remember
This . . .

Ajith Fernando: Felix's behavior gives us at least three reasons why it is so <u>hard for the rich</u> and powerful to enter the kingdom of God. (a) They are able to camouflage their insecurity by pretending to be in control of their lives (Acts 24:25). . . . (b) The rich and powerful are often controlled by an insatiable greed, and they usually find convenient ways to express this (Acts 24:26). . . . (c) Those who are at the top feel that they have to please many people if they want to stay in their position and thrive in society (Acts 24:27).[2]

Paul and the early Christians turned courtroom appearances into fulfillment of Jesus' call to carry his name everywhere. Their accusers, who demanded the Christians answer for their faith, often found *themselves* on trial in the court of their own consciences.

> **Acts 24:27** When two years had passed, Felix was succeeded by Porcius Festus, but because Felix wanted to grant a favor to the Jews, he left Paul in prison.

The Noble Roman Replaces The Brutal Ex-Slave

Felix's talent for bad government went too far. Racially driven mob violence broke out between Jews and Greeks in Caesarea. Felix gave his approval as thousands of Jews were killed and the houses of the wealthy were sacked. (He may have taken a cut of the loot for himself.) Rome recalled him. His corruption in office never led to official charges because his brother, a close friend of Caesar, used his influence to hide discrepancies in provincial accounts.

Felix was out. Festus replaced him as governor. But Paul was still stuck in the palace prison.

Porcius Festus (not to be confused with Matt Dillon's deputy) doesn't get many lines in the history books. He was appointed Procurator of Judea in A.D. 59 or 60. A kinder, gentler man to deal with a bitterly divided province, he was committed to Roman justice and an expert in the art of political compromise.

 Persecution & Martyrdom—Long, unjust imprisonments (like Paul's) are a regular feature of Christian history. January 1952 in Shanghai, Watchman Nee was arrested by the Chinese Communist Religious Affairs Bureau and charged with "imperialist intrigue," "counter-revolutionary activities hostile to government policy" as "an enemy of the people"[3]—in other words, he was a Christian leader. After twenty years in prisons and labor camps (five years longer than his sentence), he was released in April 1972 and died less than two months later.

> **Acts 25:1–8** Three days after arriving in the province, Festus went up from Caesarea to Jerusalem, where the chief priests and Jewish leaders appeared before him and presented the charges against Paul. They urgently requested Festus, as a favor to them, to have Paul transferred to Jerusalem, for they were preparing an ambush to kill him along the way. Festus answered, "Paul is being held at Caesarea, and I myself am going there soon. Let some of your leaders come with me and press charges against the man there, if he has done anything wrong."
>
> After spending eight or ten days with them, he went down to Caesarea, and the next day he convened the court and ordered that Paul be brought before him. When Paul appeared, the Jews who had come down from Jerusalem stood around him, bringing many serious charges against him, which they could not prove.
>
> Then Paul made his defense: "I have done nothing wrong against the law of the Jews or against the temple or against Caesar."

KEY POINT

We often spend more time and energy to gain favor with humans than with God.

Politics Of Compromise

"Poor old hate-filled men!"[4] Eugenia Price calls Jewish leaders still harboring their bitterness and pressing their allegations against Paul. When Festus arrived they tried to get him to return Paul to Jerusalem for trial. They had no intention of trying him. Although their brash fast had obviously been called off, the two-year-old plot by forty assassins to terminate Paul was still alive and breathing fire (Acts 25:3; 23:12–15).

After the two-year postponement, the trial resumed in Caesarea. Like turkey vultures flocking to road kill, Sanhedrin leaders clustered around the prisoner, flapping and pecking. From Paul's one-liner defense (Acts 25:8) we can surmise the nature of their complaints—breaking Jewish law; desecrating the Temple; violating Caesar's decrees. The one about Caesar's decrees had been added since the trial before Felix. It's the charge to which Festus would pay most attention. Again, none of the accusations were provable and no evidence was offered.

> **Acts 25:9–12** Festus, wishing to do the Jews a favor, said to Paul, "Are you willing to go up to Jerusalem and stand trial before me there on these charges?"
>
> Paul answered, "I am now standing before Caesar's court, where I ought to be tried. I have not done any wrong to the Jews, as you yourself know very well. If, however, I am guilty of doing anything deserving death, I do not refuse to die. But if the charges brought against me by these Jews are not true, no one has the right to hand me over to them. I appeal to Caesar!"
>
> After Festus had conferred with his council, he declared: "You have appealed to Caesar. To Caesar you will go!"

"To Caesar You Will Go!"

Festus's proposal to move the trial to Jerusalem was the politics of compromise, pure and simple. He knew no Roman law had been violated (Acts 25:18–19). As new governor he simply wanted to avoid upsetting Jewish leaders his first month in office.

Paul knew he'd never get a fair trial in Jerusalem. He hadn't forgotten the murder pact. Roman law provided that if a case being tried—especially a capital case—was beyond the competence of a provincial governor, a Roman citizen had the right of *provocatio ad Caesarem*—appeal to the emperor. Only murderers, pirates, or bandits caught in the act were denied this right. The Jewish leaders' charge that Paul had violated Caesar's decrees opened the way for his bold and strategic legal move: *"I appeal to Caesar!"*

Caesar: emperor

The current **Caesar** was Nero. Paul's trial took place in the fifth year of Nero's reign, during the early years when he ruled well and under the wise influence of the Stoic philosopher Seneca. Nero's insane crusade against Christians did not begin until five years later.

THE BIG PICTURE 🔍

> **Acts 25:13–22** King Herod Agrippa 2 from the neighboring province of Chalcis (part of modern Lebanon) and his sister Bernice paid a state visit to welcome Festus, the new governor. Agrippa was considered an expert in Jewish affairs. Festus was unfamiliar with Jewish customs and theology, and uncertain as how to proceed with Paul's appeal to Caesar, so he asked the king's advice. Agrippa revealed he would like to hear Paul for himself. So a hearing was arranged for the next day.

Pomp And Circumstance And All That Jazz

Legally, the hearing was unofficial, since Agrippa had no jurisdiction in the case. Unofficial or not, it became a grand spectacle (Acts 25:23). Agrippa and Bernice put on their purple robes and golden crowns. Festus dressed in the scarlet cape worn by Roman governors on high state occasions. Agrippa was attended by his royal entourage and surrounded by Caesarean Jewish leaders, all dressed to kill. With Festus came the captains of the five cohorts stationed at Caesarea, along with an escort of legionnaires at attention.[5]

Agrippa's full name was Marcus Julius Agrippa 2. He was the great grandson of Herod the Great who slaughtered the babies of Bethlehem (see Matthew 2:16) and son of Herod Agrippa 1 who beheaded James (Acts 12:2). With his appointment by the Romans as "King of Chalcis" came the right to appoint Jewish high priests. He knew the Jews well and was deeply interested in Jewish theology.

Bernice's full name was Julia Bernice (Latin: Veronica). She was not Agrippa's wife, but his younger sister. Rumors persisted of an incestuous relationship between them. For her activities on behalf of the Jews before the **fall of Jerusalem**, she was later revered as "Julia Bernice, the great queen."

fall of Jerusalem: *A.D. 70, Romans slaughter thousands of Jews; destroy city and Temple*

Simon Kistemaker: The contrast between the dazzling garb of the high and mighty and the humble clothes of the chained prisoner suddenly becomes meaningless, for Paul displays the quiet dignity of a man with a message.[6]

What Others are Saying:

EARLY CHURCH WOMEN—There is no record of Bernice or Drusilla putting their faith in Christ. We know they were hungry to know about him. Their interest and urging may have influenced the male leaders around them to call Paul to testify repeatedly.

> **Acts 25:23b–27** At the command of Festus, Paul was brought in. Festus said: "King Agrippa, and all who are present with us, you see this man! The whole Jewish community has petitioned me about him in Jerusalem and here in Caesarea, shouting that he ought not to live any longer. I found he had done nothing deserving of death, but because he made his appeal to the Emperor I decided to send him to Rome. But I have nothing definite to write to His Majesty about him. Therefore I have brought him before all of you, and especially before you, King Agrippa, so that as a result of this investigation I may have something to write. For I think it is unreasonable to send on a prisoner without specifying the charges against him."

Send In The Clown!

When the beautiful, rich, and powerful had paraded in and assumed the places in the room demanded by the protocols of the day, Procurator Festus called for Paul to be brought in. The little tentmaker from Tarsus, hands in chains, stood before the king and the high muckymucks of Caesarea. It was high drama and great entertainment.

Festus explained the purpose of this fancy-but-informal hearing: Paul had appealed to Caesar. Before sending him to Rome, it was necessary to prepare an official report documenting the case. This imposing **aggregation**—especially King Agrippa—had been invited to help the governor prepare the wording of the report.

aggregation: group

THE BIG PICTURE

> **Acts 26:1–18** As he began his defense before Agrippa, Paul acknowledged the king's familiarity with Jewish customs and theology, and then proceeded to tell his story. Initially he had opposed Jesus and mistreated Christians. But Jesus confronted him on his way to persecute Christians in Damascus, and his life was totally changed. Jesus called him to go to both Jews and Gentiles and tell them their lives could be changed and they could be forgiven too.

GOD'S WORD FOR THE BIBLICALLY-INEPT

Early Christians on Trial in Acts

Scripture Record	Defendant(s)	Judge(s)	Sentence or Result
Acts 4:1–22	Peter and John	Sanhedrin	Threatened and released
Acts 5:17–40	The Twelve	Sanhedrin	Flogged and released
Acts 6:8–7:60	Stephen	Sanhedrin	Death by stoning
Acts 12:1–2	James (the apostle)	Herod Agrippa 1	Beheaded
Acts 12:3–19	Peter	Herod Agrippa 1	Escaped, never tried
Acts 16:19–39	Paul and Silas	Philippian magistrates	Caned, jailed overnight
Acts 17:6–9	Jason and brothers	Thessalonian city officials	Posted bond
Acts 18:12–17	Paul	Gallio	Case thrown out
Acts 19:23–41	Paul, Gaius, Aristarchus	Ephesian mob (unofficial)	Dismissed
Acts 21:27–22:22	Paul	Temple mob (unofficial)	Rescued by Roman troops
Acts 23:1–10	Paul	Sanhedrin	Hung jury (no decision)
Acts 24:1–23	Paul	Felix	Postponed, Paul in jail two years
Acts 25:1–12	Paul	Festus	Appealed to Caesar
Acts 25:1–26:32	Paul	Festus and Agrippa 2	Sent to Rome

Good News For The "Beautiful People"

Paul felt "fortunate" to be able to tell his story (Acts 26:2). Sharing the good news of Jesus with an audience of movers and shakers was better than a trip to Disneyland!

Once again Paul insisted he was on trial because he believed in the resurrection. From childhood his personal hope of spiritual survival had always depended on Israel's survival as a nation. A member of Judaism's strictest sect, Pharisee, he was committed to the Law—"God's thunder from the mountain . . . carved in stone, written on parchment, etched on the heart of Israel"[7]—and Judaism's survival (Acts 26:4–6).

Resurrection <u>hope</u> is deeply embedded in the history of Israel. God has raised Israel repeatedly! (The modern world watched him do it again with the establishment of the present state of Israel in 1948.) In fact, it is *incredible* that any Jew should ever *"consider it incredible that God raises the dead"* (Acts 26:6–8).

Paul had believed Jesus was a threat to the survival of Judaism and should be opposed. So he threw himself lock, stock, and barrel into what he thought was <u>God's work</u>. He attacked Jesus' **"saints,"** jailed and voted to kill them, tried to force them to **blaspheme**, and tracked them down in foreign cities (Acts 26:9–11).

☞ **GO TO:**

Job 19:25–27; Ezekiel 37:1–14 (hope)

Philippians 3:4–6 (God's work)

saints: *ordinary believers in Jesus*

blaspheme: *renounce faith in Jesus*

Paul was on his way to Damascus armed with arrest warrants. Jesus confronted Paul, knocked him flat on his face, exposed his inner struggle against the Holy Spirit, personally introduced himself, and sent Paul to share with Jews and non-Jews alike what he'd seen and heard (Acts 26:12–18).

Paul's orders from God included a summary of what Jesus does for people (Acts 26:18):

- Opens their eyes making them <u>able to see</u> things they never saw before
- Turns them from spiritual darkness (deceit, evil) <u>to light</u> (transparency, holiness)
- <u>Transfers</u> them from the **power** of Satan to the power of God, making them able to live obediently, victoriously
- Gives them forgiveness of sins and a share with the **sanctified**, recreating and purifying their lives as they trust in Jesus

Early Christians refused to let another person's immoral lifestyle hinder them from sharing Jesus' love with that person.

> **Acts 26:19–23** "So then, King Agrippa, I was not disobedient to the vision from heaven. First to those <u>in Damascus</u>, then to those in Jerusalem and in all Judea, and to the Gentiles also, I preached that they should repent and turn to God and prove their repentance by their deeds. That is why the Jews seized me in the temple courts and tried to kill me. But I have had God's help to this very day, and so I stand here and testify to small and great alike. I am saying nothing beyond what the prophets and Moses said would happen—that the Christ would suffer and, as the first to rise from the dead, would proclaim light to his own people and to the Gentiles."

One Vision, One Master

"I was not disobedient to the vision!" Paul had seen the crucified Jesus alive. In fact, Jesus' Spirit had invaded the feisty Pharisee's heart and life (see Acts 9:17). As soon as he knew what the Lord wanted him to do, Paul began doing it with the same intensity with which he'd persecuted Christians (see Acts 9:19–22).

☞ **GO TO:**

John 3:3 (able to see)

John 3:19–21; 1 John 1:5–7 (to light)

Colossians 1:12–14 (transfers)

power: *rule, kingdom*

sanctified: *set apart as special, holy*

CHURCH GROWTH

☞ **GO TO:**

Acts 9:19–25 (in Damascus)

Paul's gung ho obedience and effectiveness in communicating God's law-free grace to Gentiles and Jews was, in fact, the reason behind the attack against him in the Temple. *"That is why the Jews seized me in the temple courts and tried to kill me,"* Paul said (Acts 26:21). Their hostility could be traced to envy over the life-changing results of his ministry in Ephesus (see Acts 19:8–20).

As proof he had violated neither Judaism's laws nor Caesar's decrees, Paul repeated the main points of the message he preached everywhere. He was not merely defending himself—he was offering Agrippa and the others the hope that goes with resurrection.

- All people must repent and prove their heart change by their life change (Acts 26:20).
- Jesus fulfilled the predictions of the Old Testament prophets (Acts 26:22).
- He <u>suffered</u> on the cross to pay the penalty for human sin (Acts 26:23).
- He <u>rose</u> from the dead, the first to do so (Acts 26:23).
- Christ alive is active in the lives of Jews and Gentiles, showing them <u>light</u>—revealing God (Acts 26:23).

☞ **GO TO:**

Isaiah 53:5–6 (suffered)

Psalm 16:9–10 (rose)

Isaiah 60:1–3 (light)

What Others are Saying:

F. F. Bruce: From the moment when he heard the words, *"I am Jesus,"* Paul knew but one Master. Henceforth for him to receive a command from that one Master was to set about obeying it.[8]

Billy Graham: There is one great fact which gives the Christian assurance in the face of death: the *resurrection of Jesus Christ.* It is the physical, bodily resurrection of Christ that gives us confidence and hope. Because Christ rose from the dead, we know beyond doubt that death is not the end, but is merely the transition into eternal life.[9]

> **Acts 26:24–25** At this point Festus interrupted Paul's defense. "You are out of your mind, Paul!" he shouted. "Your great learning is driving you insane."
> "I am not insane, most excellent Festus," Paul replied. "What I am saying is true and reasonable."

In Touch With Reality

Agrippa knew the Jews and had studied their theology. The Romans considered him an expert adviser on Judaism. He understood what Paul was saying. Festus, on the other hand was in over his head! When Paul pressed the issue of Jesus rising from the dead, it was too much for the pragmatic Roman mind to process. "You're crazy, Paul!" he shouted. "You think too much!" (Acts 26:24, paraphrased).

Paul was highly educated and intellectually brilliant. In Festus's opinion (or was it a derisive joke?) superior learning had driven the prisoner over the edge. No sensible man would turn his whole nation against him (see Acts 25:24) for such fantastical philosophical foolishness. *Resurrection! Bah humbug!*

Paul used two Greek words to defend what he'd been saying (Acts 26:25): *aletheias*—"true," in harmony with reality[10]; and *sophrosunes*—"reasonable," <u>mentally sound</u>.

☞ **GO TO:**

2 Timothy 1:7
(mentally sound)

Something to Ponder

> When a person knows Jesus, nothing makes more sense than that Jesus is alive! His being alive is what makes life in this crazy world finally make sense. To genuinely link up with God is to be in touch with reality.

What Others are Saying:

Charles H. Spurgeon: To be laughed at is no great hardship to me. I can delight in scoffs and jeers. Slanders are my glory. But that you should turn from mercy, this is my sorrow. Spit on me, but, oh, repent! Laugh at me, but, oh, believe in my Master! Make my body as dirt of the streets, but damn not your own souls![11]

THE BIG PICTURE 🔍

> **Acts 26:26–32** Paul asked, "King Agrippa, do you believe the prophets?" Agrippa responded, "Do you think that in such a short time you can persuade me to be a Christian?" Paul said he prayed to God the people listening to him would all become Christians. The dignitaries left, convinced Paul did not deserve to be in prison.

The Wisecrack Heard 'Round The World

It's a story repeated in the court appearances of early Christians—the judges find themselves on trial. Paul is right. Agrippa knew the Old Testament prophets. Not only that, the events that fulfilled the ancient prophecies were well known in Israel. The stories of Jesus' miracles, death, and resurrection were common knowledge, not a secret carefully kept from the public (Acts 2:22).

The community of Christian believers was not a secret society, but highly visible and active.

Paul knew the truth: Agrippa *believed*! That is, he was intellectually convinced Jesus fulfilled the prophets' predictions. He was in a catch-22. What was the king to say? If he said he believed the prophets, Paul would say, "Surely, then, you accept Jesus as the Messiah!" If he said he did not believe the prophets, it would be politically disastrous for his relationship with the Jews he's trying to govern. To complicate matters, the Roman governor had just equated Christianity with insanity.

Agrippa comes up with a wisecrack that brings down the house! "Keep this up much longer and you'll make a Christian out of me!"[12] (Acts 26:28). Ha! Ha! Ha?

Paul was not laughing. *"Short time or long—I pray God that not only you but all who are listening to me today may become what I am [a follower of Jesus], except for these chains"* (Acts 26:29). With that Paul smiled and raised his right hand, and with it the left arm of the silent soldier standing beside him, to whom he was manacled wrist to wrist with what Eugene Peterson calls "prison jewelry"![13]

The beautiful people paraded from the room as they'd entered—each with secret questions he or she would answer before God. They agreed: Paul's imprisonment was unjust. Nonetheless these "powerful" people were too politically and morally weak to free him. He was a step closer to preaching the Gospel in Rome (Acts 26:30–32).

What Others are Saying:

Lawrence O. Richards: Strip away the palaces and the jewels, the pomp and fine clothes, and we realize that history's beautiful people are as frail and empty as the rest. They search among the world's treasures, but cannot find anything that will give their lives meaning, or give themselves a value divorced from material possessions. . . . How desperately *every* human being needs to look beyond what the world has to offer, to find true fulfillment in a personal relationship with God.[14]

Crosspoint: Believing requires more than our minds. Believing requires our hearts and our wills. Believing requires that our passions line up with the words we have said and the testimonies we have made. Believing requires hard work as we submit all that we are to the one who can transform us into people of faith.[15]

Study Questions

1. On what three counts did Tertullus and the Jerusalem leaders charge Paul before Felix? What charge was added in the trial before Festus?
2. In answering the charges before Felix, what two reasons did Paul give for coming to Jerusalem? What was he doing at the Temple when the crowd tried to kill him?
3. Identify four things Jesus does for people according to Acts 26:18.
4. What issue did Paul press that made Festus say Paul was insane? What did Paul insist King Agrippa already believed?
5. What wisecrack did Agrippa use to avoid answering Paul's question about believing the prophets?

CHAPTER WRAP-UP

- Paul appeared before Governor Felix, in Caesarea. Paul pleaded not guilty, repeating his contention that he was on trial because he believed in the resurrection. (Acts 24:1–21)

- Felix postponed his verdict and kept Paul in prison for two years. Felix had several conversations with Paul. He trembled with fear as Paul spoke. (Acts 24:1–26)

- Felix was recalled. Festus took his place. He asked Paul if he'd be willing to be tried in Jerusalem. Knowing of the assassination plot, Paul used his Roman citizen's right of appeal to Caesar. (Acts 25:1–12)

- King Agrippa visited Festus. A meeting was scheduled to hear Paul. Paul told an audience of government and military leaders about his conversion. (Acts 25:13–26:23)

- When Paul spoke of Jesus' resurrection, Festus called him "crazy." Paul asked Agrippa if he believed the prophets, and the king responded with the joke-line: "Almost you persuade me to be a Christian!" (Acts 26:24–32)

ACTS 27: DANGEROUS PASSAGE

Let's Get Started

King Agrippa agreed with Governor Festus that Paul had done nothing worthy of capital punishment or imprisonment. He could have been released but for one thing: He had appealed his case to the Roman emperor (see Acts 26:30–31). The appeal took the decision out of the governor's hands. Roman law required that an appeal to Caesar had to be carried to completion. Paul would stand trial in Rome. Unmentioned at this point by the author of Acts were the facts (already in evidence to the reader of Acts) that (1) a radical assassination squad still waited outside to "welcome" Paul with daggers (Acts 23:12; 25:2–3); and (2) the Lord had told him in a vision (Acts 23:11) that he was on his way to Rome to witness for Christ. He'd be traveling courtesy of Roman justice, under whose protection he sat in jail.

The trip to Rome would be made by sailing ship, by far the fastest form of long-distance travel from the eastern to western Mediterranean. If you like a good sea story, you'll be captivated by Luke's masterpiece of descriptive writing in Acts 27. It's a salty yarn in the tradition of sections of Melville's *Moby Dick*. The language of this tale shows the author knew the sea well. Because of this and other clues in Acts some scholars theorize Luke had spent at least part of his medical career as a ship's surgeon. We know he took several sea voyages with Paul, including this in Acts 27. (Luke tells us he was there by his use of "we" and "us.")

F. F. Bruce: Luke's narrative of the voyage and shipwreck of Paul on his way to Italy is a small classic in its own right.[1]

> **What Others are Saying:**

James Smith: No sailor would have written in a style so little like that of a sailor; no man not a sailor could have written a narrative of a sea voyage so consistent in all its parts, unless from actual observation.[2]

> **Acts 27:1–2** When it was decided that we would sail for Italy, Paul and some other prisoners were handed over to a centurion named Julius, who belonged to the Imperial Regiment. We boarded a ship from Adramyttium about to sail for ports along the coast of the province of Asia, and we put out to sea. Aristarchus, a Macedonian from Thessalonica, was with us.

Anchors Aweigh!

Agrippa advised Festus on wording for official documents sent to Rome with Paul (see Acts 25:26–27). Legal documents prepared, the prisoners at Caesarea were turned over to a centurion named Julius of the honored Imperial Regiment. Troops of the Imperial Regiment were all Romans recruited in Italy and were trusted with special assignments for the emperor.

The Roman fleet had no passenger ships. Passengers sailed aboard cargo ships as space was available. This voyage (see illustration, page 293) would take place on three ships: a **coaster** from Caesarea to Myra (Acts 27:2–5) and two Egyptian grain ships on regular runs from Alexandria to Rome (Acts 27:6–28:1; Acts 28:11–13).

coaster: ship that sailed close to land and called at ports along the coast

Edwin M. Yamauchi: The ships left when the winds and omens were favorable. The expense for passage was not high; it cost a family but two drachma (about two days' wages) to sail from Alexandria to Athens. The fare included the provision of water and cabins but not food.[3]

Paul's Loyal "Slaves"

Luke, as noted, was with Paul on this voyage. Another apostolic coworker, Aristarchus the Macedonian, was also there. It is possible Luke signed on as ship's doctor. Another intriguing possibility mentioned by some scholars is that both Luke and Aristarchus went as Paul's slaves. Roman law permitted prominent Roman citizens under arrest to take with them one or two slaves to care for their personal needs.

Paul's Voyage to Rome

This map shows the route of Paul's last journey beginning in Caesarea and Sidon. He boarded a ship at Caesarea, sailed close to land and then toward Crete, was shipwrecked at Malta, and traveled to Rome. The inset shows the way the ship was blown off course at Crete.

The possibility that two men might actually volunteer to become slaves in order to stay with Paul on one of his most dangerous trips reveals the surprising depth of their love for the apostle and the Lord they all served!

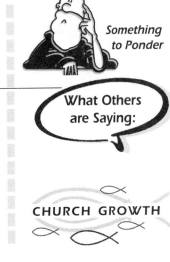

Something to Ponder

W. M. Ramsay: [Luke and Aristarchus would have gone] not merely performing the duties of slaves . . . but actually passing as slaves. In this way not merely had Paul faithful friends always beside him; his importance in the eyes of the centurion was much enhanced, and that was of great importance.[4]

What Others are Saying:

Continuous church growth depends on the willingness of Christians to make personal sacrifices and to go to the ends of the earth to tell the Jesus story.

CHURCH GROWTH

Nothing convinces people that Christianity is real like the lengths to which Christians will go to express their love.

> **Acts 27:3** The next day we landed at Sidon; and Julius, in kindness to Paul, allowed him to go to his friends so they might provide for his needs.

Society Of Friends

In just one day at sea, Paul won the friendship of Centurion Julius. Luke calls him *"kindly Julius"* (Acts 27:3). When the ship called at the port of Sidon, Julius allowed Paul to leave the ship and visit *"his friends,"* the Sidonian Christians. The original Greek reads *"the* friends," another way early Christians referred to one another—like *"the Way"* (see Acts 24:22), *"the brothers"* (see Acts 28:15), or *"the disciples"* (see Acts 21:16).

lee: *side of an island sheltered from the wind*

> **Acts 27:4–9a** From there we put out to sea again and passed to the **lee** of Cyprus because the winds were against us. When we had sailed across the open sea off the coast of Cilicia and Pamphylia, we landed at Myra in Lycia. There the centurion found an Alexandrian ship sailing for Italy and put us on board. We made slow headway for many days and had difficulty arriving off Cnidus. When the wind did not allow us to hold our course, we sailed to the lee of Crete, opposite Salmone. We moved along the coast with difficulty and came to a place called Fair Havens, near the town of Lasea.
> Much time had been lost, and sailing had already become dangerous because by now it was after the Fast.

Rough Sailing

The safe Mediterranean sailing season was summer—May to September. Sailing from east to west after mid-September was considered "iffy," impossible by November, and suicidal from November to February. For weeks between November and March cloudy skies hid the sun and stars on which first-century sailors depended for their bearings. Without sextant or compass, staying on course was impossible. Most of Paul's voyage took place *"after the Fast"* (Acts 27:9), Yom Kippur, the Jewish Day of Atonement, which in that year, A.D. 59, was late—October 5, well into the scary season!

When they put to sea after the Sidonian stopover, late summer winds from west and northwest made going north and west difficult. To take advantage of the steady westward current along the south coast of Asia Minor (modern Turkey) and night breezes from the shore, the ship hugged the coast of Cilicia and Pamphylia. When westerly winds made progress impossible, the ship lay at anchor in the shelter of the coastline. Finally, they arrived at Myra, a chief port of the imperial grain service.

There the centurion found an Alexandrian ship headed for Rome with a load of Egyptian corn or wheat and put his soldiers and prisoners aboard.

Egypt was Rome's "granary." Hundreds of thousands of tons of grain were shipped to the Imperial City on what, for that day, were huge ships (see illustration below). **Fore** and **aft** these vessels were basically the same shape. Rudderless, they were steered with two huge paddles on each side of the stern. Power depended on a single gigantic square sail made of heavy Egyptian linen or animal hides stitched together. They were *not* designed for sailing against the wind—which is exactly what sailors faced on this ill-fated voyage in early October A.D. 59.

fore: *ship's bow or front*

aft: *ship's stern or rear*

Egyptian Grain Ship

Paul was a prisoner put aboard an Egyptian grain ship such as this one. The biggest ships were 140–180 feet long, 36–45 feet wide, and 33–45 feet deep with a cargo capacity of up to 1,200 tons of grain. Some ships had more than one figurehead, usually a carving of a god. Castor and Pollux, twins of the constellation Gemini, were the favorite gods and good luck sign of mariners.

With difficulty the ship made the port of Cnidus, a peninsula on the southwest coast of Asia Minor. From there they intended to sail directly to Crete and along the north side of the island, then to Italy. But a persistent **nor'wester** off Cnidus forced them to give up the direct course. They sailed south to the leeward side of Crete and struggled along the south coast, arriving at Fair Havens well into the danger season.

nor'wester: *northwest wind*

> **Acts 27:9b–12** So Paul warned them, "Men, I can see that our voyage is going to be disastrous and bring great loss to ship and cargo, and to our own lives also." But the centurion, instead of listening to what Paul said, followed the advice of the **pilot** and of the owner of the ship. Since the harbor was unsuitable to winter in, the majority decided that we should sail on, hoping to reach Phoenix and winter there. This was a harbor in Crete, facing both southwest and northwest.

pilot: *helmsman, navigator*

By The Time I Get To Phoenix

Paul was a tentmaker not a seaman, but he was an experienced sea traveler who had already been through underline three shipwrecks! He urged officers of the ship to winter at Fair Havens. Adequate accommodations could be found in the nearby city of Lasea (Acts 27:8). From personal experience he warned of loss of ship and lives. Later, an angel revealed to him that the ship would wreck, but with no loss of life (see Acts 27:24).

☞ **GO TO:**

2 Corinthians 11:25 (three shipwrecks)

The centurion, senior military officer on board, would make the final decision. He chose to rely on the wisdom and experience of the ship's owner (who was probably also ship's captain) and the pilot who knew these waters like the back of his hand. The fact that Phoenix (modern Phenika) would be safer and more comfortable for spending the winter tipped the scales. The decision was made to sail the fifty miles along the coast to Phoenix and winter there.

(The best laid plans of mice and men . . . and all that!)

> **Acts 27:13–15** When a gentle south wind began to blow, they thought they had obtained what they wanted; so they weighed anchor and sailed along the shore of Crete. Before very long, a wind of hurricane force, called

> the "northeaster," swept down from the island. The ship was caught by the storm and could not head into the wind; so we gave way to it and were driven along.

Euroquilo!

Phoenix was west from Fair Havens, around the southwestern tip of Crete, then a short distance north across the Gulf of Messara. A gentle southern breeze was the answer to the sailors' prayers. Hugging the shore for a few hours would put them safely into their winter haven. But not even the saltiest salt pulling ropes and hoisting sail on that ship could have predicted what happened next, even though it was "a common occurrence in those seas," according to nautical expert James Smith.[5]

At the center of the island of Crete rose Mount Ida. Without warning the south wind changed as a violent northwest wind roared down the slopes of the mountain—"*a wind of hurricane force.*" The NIV calls it "*northeaster.*" The Greek-speaking sailors called it "*Euroquilo,*" a hybrid Greek word combining *Euros* (east wind) with *Aquilo* (north wind). It described well the wild, unpredictable, twisting motion of sea and clouds caused by contrary currents of air moving opposite directions at high speed.[6]

The unexpected arrival of *Euroquilo* meant that when the ship tried to turn north around Cape Matala to reach Phoenix, she would be turning directly into the fierce gale—something the big grain ships simply were unequipped to do in heavy seas. All they could do was to run with the wind. They suddenly found themselves being driven hard *away* from land. She would never see Phoenix!

> **Acts 27:16–17** As we passed the lee of a small island called Cauda, we were hardly able to make the lifeboat secure. When the men had hoisted it aboard, they passed ropes under the ship itself to hold it together. Fearing that they would run aground on the sandbars of Syrtis, they lowered the sea anchor and let the ship be driven along.

Lay To On The Starboard Tack!

Twenty-five miles (forty kilometers) south of Crete lay the tiny isle of Cauda. The leeward side of the island gave slight and temporary relief from the fiercest blast of the *Euroquilo*. This gave the crew an opportunity to perform some precautions. Above the roar of the storm commands something like these were given:

- "Hoist the lifeboat!" The *"lifeboat"* was a single wooden dinghy towed astern of the main vessel. By now it was full of water, making securing it more difficult.

- "Winch the hawsers!" This was known as "frapping" the ship. It involved passing ropes or cables (called "hawsers") under the ship, and drawing them tight with winches to keep the ship from breaking its back ("hogging") and to prevent the wood-plank hull from coming apart.[7]

- "Drop the sea anchor!" A "drift anchor" dragged astern slowed the ship's descent as she plunged down from the crest of wave after wave. The reason for deploying this anchor was the fear that the winds, if they continued for several days, might drive the ship across the Mediterranean into an area of sandbars called "the Greater Syrtis" off the African Coast west of Cyrene, a legendary ships' graveyard!

- "Lay to on the **starboard tack**!" To slow her further the ship was turned so her right side was to the wind.[8] This done, the best they could do was *"let the ship be driven along."*

starboard: *right side of a ship looking forward (port: left side)*

tack: *ship's direction*

> **Acts 27:18–20** We took such a violent battering from the storm that the next day they began to throw the cargo overboard. On the third day, they threw the ship's tackle overboard with their own hands. When neither sun nor stars appeared for many days and the storm continued raging, we finally gave up all hope of being saved.

Davy Jones's Locker: *bottom of the ocean*

jettisoned: *threw overboard to lighten ship*

mainsail: *principal sail on the main mast*

yard: *long wooden member (spar) that maintains spread of the top of a square sail*

Congratulations! You've Won 276 Tickets To Davy Jones's Locker!

During the next three days two last-gasp actions were taken in hope of saving the lives of the 276 passengers and crew (that's how many Acts 27:37 says were on board) before they visited **Davy Jones's Locker**. First, some of the cargo was thrown overboard. Two days later the relentless storm raged on, and the ship showed more signs of breaking up. So together, crew and passengers (note the use of "we") **jettisoned** some of the ship's tackle—probably the heavy **mainsail** and **yard**. Frantic last rites for a dying ship!

Night and day storm clouds hid the sun and stars so the pilot could not tell where they were. The ship was taking on water and riding low in the water.

Luke's terse statement expresses the terrified resignation that gripped everyone on board: *"We finally gave up all hope of being saved"* (Acts 27:20).

> **Acts 27:21–26** After the men had gone a long time without food, Paul stood up before them and said: "Men, you should have taken my advice not to sail from Crete; then you would have spared yourselves this damage and loss. But now I urge you to keep up your courage, because not one of you will be lost; only the ship will be destroyed. Last night an angel of the God whose I am and whom I serve stood beside me and said, 'Do not be afraid, Paul. You must stand trial before Caesar; and God has graciously given you the lives of all who sail with you.' So keep up your courage, men, for I have faith in God that it will happen just as he said to me. Nevertheless, we must run aground on some island."

Admiral Paul

Seasick and demoralized the crew and passengers hung on to whatever they could to keep from being washed overboard, and waited for the ship to be swamped. In the midst of this milieu of hopelessness Paul talked with God. It was two-way communication:

1. The phrase, *"God has graciously given you the lives of all who sail with you,"* indicates Paul had prayed not just for himself but for the other 275 who shared his situation. (Believers <u>instinctively</u> pray in the predicaments of life.) It may have been a <u>terrified shout</u> as he struggled with the others to save the ship, a <u>silent wish</u>, a specific <u>request</u>, or a sigh of <u>resignation</u> to God's will.

2. God's response was communicated by an angel:
   - "Remember God's <u>promise</u>: You *will* stand before Caesar in Rome. (It's only reasonable: How can you do that if you go down with this ship?)
   - "The ship will be destroyed."
   - "No one will die in the shipwreck."

☞ **GO TO:**

1 Thessalonians 5:17 (instinctively)

Matthew 14:30 (terrified shout)

Psalm 37:4; John 15:7 (silent wish)

Philippians 4:6 (request)

Matthew 8:2; Luke 22:42; Acts 21:14 (resignation)

Acts 22:11 (promise)

Armed with this revelation and promise, Paul became the doomed ship's unofficial "admiral." As the storm raged, he stood up, hanging on to some rigging to keep from being thrown off his feet by the pitching ship. After an irresistible "I told you so!" the "admiral" issued an incredible order: "Cheer up, fellas! We're gonna make it!" He passed on the angel's message and ended with a shout of confidence, *I have faith in God!*

Billy Graham: When the "evil day" comes, we do not have to be dependent upon the circumstances around us, but rather on the resources of God![9]

KEY POINT

With God there's no such thing as a "hopeless situation"!

JESUS CHRIST CEO

The situation appeared so hopeless it was understandable for even Christian men to think they were beyond help. But in the midst of the blackest, stormiest night, the Lord sent a messenger to reveal he was in control—even a shipwreck could not sink his program for reaching the world with his message of love.

> **Acts 27:27–29** On the fourteenth day we were still being driven across the Adriatic Sea, when about midnight the sailors sensed they were approaching land. They took soundings and found that the water was a hundred and twenty feet deep. A short time later they took soundings again and found it was ninety feet deep. Fearing that we would be dashed against the rocks, they dropped four anchors from the stern and prayed for daylight.

The Sound Of Land

The tempest had driven the drifting ship for two weeks! The Adriatic Sea mentioned is the first-century name for the central Mediterranean, distinguished from the "Gulf of Adria" to the north, known today as the Adriatic Sea.[10] In the middle of the pitch-dark fourteenth night, the sailors, whose ears were tuned to the sounds of sea, *"sensed they were approaching land."* One ancient manuscript of this story says, "the land was resounding" (Acts 27:27). In other words, they heard breakers!

Approaching the bay the breakers were especially violent and noisy. Standard practice as the ship approached land was to check the depth of the water at half-hour intervals.[11] Depth soundings confirmed the ship was being driven toward an unknown shore.

Four anchors were dropped from the stern to keep the ship from crashing against shoreline rocks. The anchors pointed her toward the shore in preparation for beaching at dawn.

> **Acts 27:30–32** In an attempt to escape from the ship, the sailors let the lifeboat down into the sea, pretending they were going to lower some anchors from the bow. Then Paul said to the centurion and the soldiers, "Unless these men stay with the ship, you cannot be saved." So the soldiers cut the ropes that held the lifeboat and let it fall away.

Rats Try To Leave The Sinking Ship

Pretending to deploy more anchors, the crew decided they'd have a better chance of survival if they took the only lifeboat and skedaddled. There were no other lifeboats. This one was only large enough for the crew. In the sailors' ratty scheme the soldiers and passengers would be left behind to go down with the ship!

Paul realized what was happening and warned the centurion that the safety of everyone on board depended on the sailors staying with the ship and doing what they alone were trained to do—sail! A couple of whacks by legionnaires' swords and the mariners' malevolent escape scheme washed away with the deserted dinghy.

What Others are Saying:

F. F. Bruce: By this time the centurion had learned that it was unwise to disregard Paul's advice, although his advice was probably misinterpreted when the soldiers cut the hawsers and let the dinghy go adrift. The dinghy could have been very useful in getting the ship's company ashore had it proved impossible to beach the ship. . . . However, the centurion may have decided that the soldiers' action was the most effective way of keeping the sailors on board.[12]

> **Acts 27:33–38** Just before dawn Paul urged them all to eat. "For the last fourteen days," he said, "you have been in constant suspense and have gone without food—you haven't eaten anything. Now I urge you to take some food. You need it to survive. Not one of you

will lose a single hair from his head." After he said this, he took some bread and gave thanks to God in front of them all. Then he broke it and began to eat. They were all encouraged and ate some food themselves. Altogether there were 276 of us on board. When they had eaten as much as they wanted, they lightened the ship by throwing the grain into the sea.

Breakfast With The Admiral

What was just ahead would require all the strength they could muster. So Paul urged the passengers and crew to do something they hadn't done for two weeks—eat. Again he assured them all would survive. Like a Jewish father beginning a family meal, he took bread, thanked God, broke the bread, and began to eat. As they ate they caught some of Paul's confident spirit. After their predawn breakfast, they threw the last of the cargo into the sea to raise the ship in the water so she'd run closer to shore before being beached.

What Others are Saying:

William Barclay: Into the tempest there seems to come a strange calm. The man of God has somehow made others sure that God is in charge of things. The most useful people in the world are those who, being themselves calm, bring to others the secret of confidence.[13]

Audrey I. Girard: Confidence in God is better caught than taught.[14]

☞ **GO TO:**

Genesis 18:26–32 (presence)

bay: now called "St. Paul's Bay"

F. F. Bruce: Human society has no idea how much it owes, in the mercy of God, to the presence in it of righteous men and women.[15]

Acts 27:39–41 When daylight came, they did not recognize the land, but they saw a **bay** with a sandy beach, where they decided to run the ship aground if they could. Cutting loose the anchors, they left them in the sea and at the same time untied the ropes that held the rudders. Then they hoisted the foresail to the wind and made for the beach. But the ship struck a sandbar and ran aground. The bow stuck fast and would not move, and the stern was broken to pieces by the pounding of the surf.

Shipwreck!

By dawn's early light the pilot saw a sandy beach. *"They"*—the pilot and owner-captain—decided to try to run the ship aground on the beach. The cables on the aft anchors were cut, the **foresail** (which hadn't been jettisoned in Acts 27:19) was hoisted to the wind. The battered ship picked up speed as she headed for land. It never made the beach. Her bow stuck fast in an offshore sandbar. The storm-churned surf immediately tore the stern to splinters.

foresail: *small sail used to aid steering*

> **Acts 27:42–44** The soldiers planned to kill the prisoners to prevent any of them from swimming away and escaping. But the centurion wanted to spare Paul's life and kept them from carrying out their plan. He ordered those who could swim to jump overboard first and get to land. The rest were to get there on planks or on pieces of the ship. In this way everyone reached land in safety.

Grab A Plank, Mates, And Swim Fer Yer Life!

Roman military discipline made soldiers responsible for their prisoners. If they escaped, the guards were given the penalty intended for the fugitive. An escaped prisoner could mean death for the guard on whose watch he got free. Killing prisoners was one way to assure that none escaped! To save Paul's life, the centurion called a halt to this mass execution before it could happen. And he ordered everyone to abandon ship.

As the ship disintegrated, 276 passengers and crew swam or floated on parts of the wreckage. All crawled out of the surf, soaking wet, bone weary, and greatly relieved to be alive!

W. M. Ramsay: Thus the foreship was held together, until every passenger got safe to dry land. Only the rarest conjunction of favorable circumstances could have brought about such a fortunate ending to their apparently hopeless situation.[16]

What Others are Saying:

Ajith Fernando: Christ . . . does not immunize Christians from problems that others in the world also face. Sometimes he miraculously delivers Christians from such situations, while at other times he gives Christians courage to endure natural and other disasters. We thank him for performing miracles but also for his sufficient grace that provides endurance <u>in the midst</u> of storms.[17]

☞ **GO TO:**

2 Corinthians 12:7–10 (in the midst)

John Greenleaf Whittier:
> Here in the maddening maze of things,
> When tossed by storm and flood,
> To one fixed ground my spirit clings,
> I know that God is good![18]

Study Questions

1. Name two Christians who accompanied Paul on his voyage to Rome. What were they likely willing to do in order to go with him?
2. What made sailing so difficult? When did Paul's ship reach Fair Havens, Crete? Why did the ship's owner and pilot decide to sail on to Phoenix?
3. Identify three parts of the message the *"angel of God"* brought Paul in the midst of the storm.
4. What happened when sailors tried to escape in the lifeboat? What did the centurion do when soldiers wanted to kill prisoners to keep them from escaping? Why?

CHAPTER WRAP-UP

- Paul and other prisoners sailed the first leg of their journey to Rome aboard a "coasting vessel." Luke and Aristarchus were with Paul. At Sidon, the centurion allowed Paul to visit Christian friends. (Acts 27:1–3)

- At Myra they boarded an Egyptian grain ship. Contrary winds made staying on course impossible. At Fair Havens, Crete, Paul urged them to stop for the winter. The ship's owner and pilot overruled him. (Acts 27:4–12)

- When a southern breeze began to blow, they set sail for Phoenix but never got there. A sudden hurricane-force wind (*Euroquilo*) swept down from the northeast, and the ship was caught in a terrible storm. (Acts 27:13–20)

- All on board gave up hope of survival. But an angel gave Paul God's promise that, though the ship would be lost, everyone on board would survive. (Acts 27:21–26)

- On the fourteenth stormy night sailors sensed land was near. They tried to escape in the only lifeboat, leaving passengers to go down with the ship. Paul told the centurion, who cut the lifeboat adrift to keep the crew aboard. (Acts 27:21–34)

- Before beaching the boat Paul urged them all to eat. At dawn the ship was headed to the beach. It struck a sandbar, stuck fast, and broke up in the waves. The centurion ordered everyone to abandon ship and to swim or grab a plank and float to shore. All 276 aboard survived! (Acts 27:35–44)

ACTS 28: THE UNCHAINED TRUTH

Let's Get Started

Sailors, soldiers, prisoners, and other passengers from the Alexandrian corn ship lay drenched and exhausted amid the splintered wreckage of their ship, on a strange beach even their pilot did not recognize (see Acts 27:39). The realization that they had actually survived two weeks of endless struggle to survive, at the mercy of tempestuous seas, must have, in itself, seemed incredible. Were they dreaming, or was this solid ground beneath them? And when the count was taken and it was discovered that all on board had made it to shore alive, incredulity must have given way to sheer astonishment and joy.

> **Acts 28:1–2** Once safely on shore, we found out that the island was called Malta. The islanders showed us unusual kindness. They built a fire and welcomed us all because it was raining and cold.

Hope Island

The survivors discovered they had washed up on the small island of Malta. Luke's original word to describe *"the islanders"* is *barbaroi,* literally translated "barbarians." In the first century that did not mean they were uncivilized. Greek-speaking people used the word to refer to non-Greek-speaking people. These islanders turned out to be quite civil. Survivors found a blazing fire, built by the islanders, waiting to warm them.

> **Acts 28:3–6** Paul gathered a pile of brushwood and, as he put it on the fire, a viper, driven out by the heat, fastened itself on his hand. When the islanders saw the snake hanging from his hand, they said to each other, "This man must be a murderer; for though he escaped from the sea, Justice has not allowed him to live." But Paul shook the snake off into the fire and suffered no ill effects. The people expected him to swell up or suddenly fall dead, but after waiting a long time and seeing nothing unusual happen to him, they changed their minds and said he was a god.

Shakin' Snake

As Paul gathered a bunch of brushwood to add to the fire he inadvertently picked up a poisonous snake, a viper, stiffened by the cold. (It's interesting that today there are no poisonous snakes on the island.) As he laid wood on the fire, the snake revived by the warmth, grabbed Paul's hand with its fangs. Paul shook it off into the fire.

Superstitious islanders watched for the worst to follow. They'd no doubt heard the story of the murderer who escaped a shipwreck on the Libyan coast but **Justice** caught up with him when he died of a viper's bite.[1] As they watched Paul shake the snake into the fire, they concluded he too was a murderer getting what he deserved. To their surprise, Paul did <u>not drop dead</u> from the venom. The Maltese then decided he must be <u>a god</u>!

Justice: goddess of retribution

☞ **GO TO:**

Mark 16:18 (not drop dead)

Acts 14:8–13 (a god)

> **Acts 28:7–10** There was an estate nearby that belonged to Publius, the chief official of the island. He welcomed us to his home and for three days entertained us hospitably. His father was sick in bed, suffering from fever and dysentery. Paul went in to see him and, after prayer, placed his hands on him and healed him. When this had happened, the rest of the sick on the island came and were cured. They honored us in many ways and when we were ready to sail, they furnished us with the supplies we needed.

Winter Of Hope And Healing

The islanders took the survivors into their homes. Paul and Luke were entertained for three days at the home of Publius, Malta's top government official. While there, Paul prayed for Publius's father who was sick with dysentery. He got well. Word of this spread, and Paul and Luke (notice "us," Acts 28:10) spent the winter healing the island's sick. Knowing Paul's compulsion for sharing Christ, we can be sure medical treatment and healing were dispensed with rich doses of the good news.

JESUS CHRIST CEO

Shipwrecked, still a prisoner, and stuck for three months on a strange island, Paul and Luke found themselves with opportunities for ministry arranged, not by their careful planning, but by the secret sovereign arranging of the Lord.

> **Acts 28:11–13** After three months we put out to sea in a ship that had wintered in the island. It was an Alexandrian ship with the figurehead of the twin gods Castor and Pollux. We put in at Syracuse and stayed there three days. From there we set sail and arrived at Rhegium. The next day the south wind came up, and on the following day we reached Puteoli.

On The "Road" Again

Another Egyptian grain ship had wintered on Malta. The ship was decorated with figures (see illustration, page 295) for good luck. When the ship sailed in early February, Centurion Julius put his prisoners and soldiers aboard. Early February was usually considered too early to resume Mediterranean sailing. But according to the Roman writer, Pliny,[2] ships sailing near shore could put to sea after February 8 when westerly and southerly winds began to blow.

It was forty miles—a one-day trip—to Syracuse, main port of the island of Sicily. From Syracuse the ship sailed to the toe of the Italian peninsula, putting in at Rhegium. Another day's sailing brought it to Puteoli, which, in the first century, was the busiest port in southern Italy, located in the most sheltered part of the Bay of Naples. There passengers disembarked and traveled the rest of the way to Rome on the famous Appian Way.

> **Acts 28:14–15** There we found some brothers who invited us to spend a week with them. And so we came to Rome. The brothers there had heard that we were coming, and they traveled as far as the Forum of Appius and the Three Taverns to meet us. At the sight of these men Paul thanked God and was encouraged.

The Roman Welcoming Committee

serendipity: unexpected, delightful happening

Evidently Centurion Julius had a week's worth of official red tape to attend to before continuing to Rome. In a welcome **serendipity** it was discovered there were some Christian brothers in Puteoli. Paul and his companions were permitted, under guard, to spend the week with them.

meet: Greek: official delegation welcoming a dignitary

Evidently the Puteoli Christians sent word to Rome that Paul had arrived. Two delegations of Christians hiked down the Appian Way to **meet** and escort him to Rome. The Forum (marketplace) of Appius was forty-three miles from the capital. *Tres Tabernae* (*"the Three Taverns"*) was a familiar Appian Way stopping place thirty-three miles from Rome.

Who Started The Church At Rome?

The best guess is that the church at Rome got its start when Roman Jews heard Peter preach in Jerusalem on the Day of Pentecost, A.D. 30 (see Acts 2:10). No doubt some were among the three thousand who believed in Jesus as Messiah and were baptized that day (see Acts 2:41). They had returned home to share the good news and began meeting as believers.

Paul's friends, Aquila and Priscilla, were from Rome and would have told him about the Christians there (see Acts 18:2).

Three years before his arrival, Paul wrote his letter to the Roman Christians in which he expressed his longing to come to Rome and share with them for mutual encouragement (see Romans 1:8–13 and GWRM, pages 12–14). At last he was looking into the faces of Roman Christians. The dream was becoming a living reality.

What Others are Saying:

William Barclay: The Christian is never alone. (1) He has the consciousness of the unseen cloud of witnesses around him and about him. (2) He has the consciousness of belonging to a worldwide fellowship. (3) He has the consciousness that wherever he goes there is God. (4) He has the certainty that his Risen Lord is with him.[3]

JESUS CHRIST CEO

Through his **omnipresent** Spirit, the Lord leads and empowers people in many places at once to be witnesses and to function as the church. Because he is not limited to time and space, God may direct Christians to a traveler in all sorts of strange and faraway places.

omnipresent: present everywhere

THE BIG PICTURE 🔍

> **Acts 28:16–22** Upon arrival in Rome Paul was placed under house arrest. Three days after arrival in Rome, Paul introduced himself to the leaders of the Jewish community. He told them about his arrest and appeal to Caesar. He declared he was a prisoner *"because of the hope of Israel."* They responded that they'd heard nothing bad about him and they'd like to hear what he had to say.

☞ **GO TO:**

Acts 23:8; 24:15;
  26:6–8
  (hope of Israel)

"Friends, Romans, Countrymen, Lend Me Your Ears!"

hope of Israel: national survival, renewal, eternal life through the risen Jesus

While awaiting trial in Rome, Paul was allowed to rent his own house (perhaps working with leather or making tents to provide funds). He was still a prisoner, chained twenty-four hours a day, wrist-to-wrist, to a soldier of the Praetorian Guard (Acts 28:20).

"A prominent individual, or one expected to be released, might be kept under house arrest if he or she could afford the rent. In Rome, where housing prisoners was excessively expensive, Paul was given the privilege of house arrest, and he paid the rent himself. . . . He probably lived in a third-floor apartment; first floors were used for shops, and the second floor was expensive."[4]

Many people came to see him. As each guard stood his watch, he overheard Paul's conversations and watched him. In one of his letters Paul reports that the whole Praetorian Guard had come to know he was *"in chains for Christ"* (Philippians 1:12–14). Some of these soldiers may have become Christians (see Philippians 4:22).

Through many years, in city after city, Paul offered the Gospel to Jews before anyone else. He never gave up hope that his countrymen would believe in Jesus as Messiah. The story almost always had the same ending—some Jews believed and joined the Jesus movement, others refused to believe and dug in their heels in bitter opposition to Christ. It happened again in Rome.

Roman Jews had heard nothing bad about Paul (Acts 28:21)—amazing, considering the bitterness against him in Jerusalem. Here are possible reasons for this happy lack of negative communication: (1) A letter or representative may have been delayed by the complexities of winter travel; (2) Jerusalem leaders realized they didn't have a chance of success after failing to convict Paul in Judea; or (3) Roman law could make life difficult for unsuccessful prosecutors, and they didn't want to take the risk.[5]

They'd heard nothing bad about Paul, but the Roman Jews did have some unfavorable hearsay information about the Christian movement (Acts 28:22).

THE BIG PICTURE

> **Acts 28:23–27** The Jewish leaders arranged a meeting and large groups of people came to where Paul was staying. From dawn to dusk Paul told them about Jesus Christ, trying to convince them that Jesus was Messiah by quoting from the Law of Moses and from the Prophets.

Same Song, Same Sour Notes

The leaders arranged an extended meeting with Paul at his rented place. From morning till evening he told the story of Jesus, explaining how Jesus' life, death, and resurrection fulfilled Old Testament promises concerning the Messiah. It wasn't a monologue. That wasn't the Jewish way nor Paul's style. There were tough questions. Hot debates. Demands for proof. Appeals to believe and welcome Jesus as Savior and Lord.

Some became convinced and believed in Jesus (Acts 28:24).

Others refused. In Acts 28:26–27 Paul quoted and applied to them the dire words God gave the prophet Isaiah for his unbelieving generation in Isaiah 6:9–10.

healing: *wholeness, cure from sin's sickness, restoration of relationship with God*

Something to Ponder

> Many people, Jews and Gentiles, do not believe because they *choose* not to believe, they *deliberately* close their eyes, ears, and hearts, and harden themselves against the truth about themselves and God's plan for their spiritual **healing**.

What Others are Saying:

William Barclay: There is something wonderful in the fact that to the end of the day, wherever he went, Paul began with the Jews. For rather more than thirty years now they had been doing everything they could to hinder him, to undo his work, and even to kill him: and even yet it is to them first he offers his message. Is there any example of undefeatable hope and unconquerable love like this act of Paul when, in Rome too, he preached first to the Jews?[6]

For the probable contents of Paul's daylong session with the Jews at Rome, check these passages:

Acts 13:17–41; 17:2–3; 26:4–23.

Dig Deeper

For the Old Testament messianic prophecies that early Christians quoted when talking with Jews, check these passages:

Christian Quote	Old Testament Source
Acts 2:16–21	Joel 2:28–32
Acts 2:25–28	Psalm 16:8–11
Acts 2:34–35	Psalm 110:1
Acts 3:22–23	Deuteronomy 18:15, 18–19
Acts 3:25	Genesis 22:18
Acts 4:11	Psalm 118:22
Acts 4:25–26	Psalm 2:1–2
Acts 8:32–33	Isaiah 53:7–8
Acts 13:33–35	Psalm 2:7; Isaiah 55:3; Psalm 16:10

> **Acts 28:28, 30–31** "Therefore I want you to know that God's salvation has been sent to the Gentiles, and they will listen!"
> For two whole years Paul stayed there in his own rented house and welcomed all who came to see him. Boldly and without hindrance he preached the kingdom of God and taught about the Lord Jesus Christ.

☞ **GO TO:**

Acts 13:48 (will listen)

No Chain Can Hold The Truth!

Rejecting Jews left the meeting in disarray. (Some manuscripts add a twenty-ninth verse that reads: "After he said this, the Jews left, arguing vigorously among themselves.") The door they chose to slam shut became a swinging door, wide open to the Gentiles. For two years Paul waited in Rome for his appeal to be heard before Emperor Nero. He welcomed all comers, all the while coupled to Roman soldiers day and night by a chain. He told everyone who visited about the good news of Jesus and the difference in people's lives the kingship and practical reign of God could make.

None of this was any secret to the Roman authorities, yet no official attempt was ever made to stop it. In the Greek manuscript of Acts, the last word is *axolutos*—"without hindrance." A wonderful note, considering Paul's physical situation. The Ambassador of Christ was chained, but the good news was unchained!

What Others are Saying:

William Barclay: This rejection of Jesus by the Jews is the very thing which has opened the door to the Gentiles. There is a purpose in everything; on the helm of things is the hand of the unseen steersman—God.[7]

The End?

This is where the book stops. With Paul under house arrest in Rome.
"Print it!"
But . . . we wish Luke had told us more.
What happened at the trial? Did Paul witness for Jesus to Nero? What happened to the early Christians? We are left to get our information from other sources. But for Luke it was like Income Tax Day: "Gotta get it postmarked before midnight!" The deadline for publication had arrived.
Luke ends with a note of triumph: *"Preaching the kingdom of God, and teaching those things which concern the Lord Jesus Christ, with all confidence, no man forbidding him"* (Acts 28:31 KJV).
But the rest of the story is left untold in the Bible narrative. In reality, Luke cannot write the end because the story is still being told in the twenty-first century, in the lives of the Christians today.

Paul In Rome: The Rest Of The Story

Acts gives only a glimpse of what happened in Rome. Beginning in the chained ambassador's unchained heart, from his rented house, the Gospel <u>quietly invaded</u> the city and the empire. From prison Paul accomplished four things vitally important to the spread of the Gospel:

☞ **GO TO:**

Matthew 13:33; Luke 17:20–21 (quietly invaded)

1. He wrote. While under house arrest in Rome, Paul wrote letters to (1) Philippians, (2) Ephesians, (3) Colossians, and (4) Philemon.

2. He directed a team of ambassadors for Christ.

   • Luke and Aristarchus were with him (see Acts 27:1–2). Luke stayed to the end (see 2 Timothy 4:11).

   • Timothy came and went with apostolic instructions for churches (Philippians 1:1; Colossians 1:1; Philemon 1).

   • Tychicus served Paul's needs; he delivered Paul's letter to the Ephesians (Ephesians 6:21).

- Epaphroditus spent time with Paul and brought money to supply his needs (Philippians 4:18).
- John Mark became Paul's valued aide and ministered with him in Rome (Colossians 4:10; 2 Timothy 4:11).

3. He personally introduced people to Jesus. (1) The soldiers of the Praetorian Guard all knew Paul was in chains because of Christ (Philippians 1:13); some became believers. (2) Paul's fearless preaching while in chains inspired his fellow Christians to witness more boldly (Philippians 1:14). (3) Members of Caesar's personal staff (relatives and others) became believers (Philippians 4:22).

4. He witnessed to Caesar. There is no New Testament record of an appearance before the emperor, unless it was the trial Paul refers to in 2 Timothy 4:16–17. In God's message to Paul during the storm, he promised Paul would stand trial before Caesar (Acts 27:23–24). We may assume the Lord kept that promise as he did the promise that no lives would be lost in the shipwreck (Acts 27:44).

JESUS CHRIST CEO

You'd think being under arrest would stifle a man's witness and keep him from effective ministry. But Jesus knows what he's allowing. Powerfully, God worked through Paul in prison. Had he not been confined, the busyness of ministry may have delayed the writing of the New Testament letters so vital to our Christian faith. Members of his team may have remained overly dependent on Paul and failed to find their own ministries. Paul's experience reveals: No confinement can stop the Lord's work!

Lawrence O. Richards: Apparently the Jews in Jerusalem did not forward any charges against him. After the statutory wait established by Roman law, Paul was simply released in A.D. 63. For the next few years Paul continued to evangelize, perhaps going to Spain as he had wanted (see Romans 15). Paul wrote letters to Timothy and Titus during this period.

Paul was later arrested. He writes his second letter to Timothy during this imprisonment, and it is clear he expects death. Tradition tells us that Paul was executed in Rome, probably around A.D. 68. But when Paul went to meet his Lord, he left a church which had spread throughout the Roman Empire, with hundreds of thousands who had come to know Christ through the missionary effort begun by this small but great man.[8]

What Others are Saying:

To The Ends Of The Earth

When you stop to think about it, Acts 28 was a pretty good place to stop. With Christ on the offensive in Rome, the table of contents for Luke's early church history, outlined by Jesus in Acts 1:8, reached its climax:

1. *"You will receive power when the Holy Spirit comes on you"*—story in Acts 1:12–2:4.

2. *"You will be my witnesses in Jerusalem"*—story in Acts 2:5–7:60; Acts 22:1–23:10.

3. *"You will be my witnesses . . . in all Judea and Samaria"*—story in Acts 8:1–11:18.

4. *"You will be my witnesses . . . to the ends of the earth"*—story in Acts 11:19–21:14; 23:11–28:31.

CHURCH GROWTH

Acts is the story of people responding to God's invitation to be rescued from alienation from him by believing and acknowledging Jesus as Lord of their lives (see Acts 9:3–5; 26:19).

The truth by which they find their way to God is found in the Bible, which they consider to be the Word of God (see Acts 2:16–36). Their lives are shaped by its teachings (see Acts 15:13–21; 19:18–20). Their sole aim in life is to glorify God and tell the story of Jesus to everyone, depending on the Spirit to lead and enable them (see Acts 4:29; 20:24; Ephesians 1:12).

As they catch that vision—the vision Jesus himself gives them—they do not live as "rugged individuals," but live and work in the context of the family of faith (see Acts 2:41–47; 20:1–11). The fellowship of the living church becomes the "matrix for mission"—the place where spiritual maturity is encouraged and Christ's vision is born in his followers, and from which Christ's witnesses emerge to tell the world!

What Others are Saying:

Richard C. Halverson: At Pentecost . . . by the supernatural power of the Holy Spirit, those 120 individual disciples were galvanized into one, inseparable, indivisible, indestructible living organism—the body of which Christ is the head. They literally became members of one another, needing one another, responsible to one another as the members of a physical body are responsible and necessary to each other. . . .

What that first century world saw was a phenomenon of people of all walks of life loving one another, praying for one another. Slaves and free men were in that community. Rich and poor were in that fellowship. Roman citizens and non-Roman citizens were in that community. Members of the establishment and those violently opposed to the establishment were part of that community. The intelligentsia and the illiterate were members of that community. To the utter amazement of the world outside, they were bound together in an unexplainable love and unity.[9]

 Persecution & Maryrdom—Emperors would come and go. Anti-Christian forces would be fierce. Fiery persecutions, including ten ordered by Roman emperors, would try to silence the truth. Courage would always be demanded of witnesses. It is today.

The Gospel impacted not only Rome but the world. The Christian movement expanded quietly—one person at a time confessing faith in Jesus as Savior and Lord.

Two and a half centuries after Acts 28, in A.D. 313, Emperor Constantine officially called an end to persecution of Christians. Eleven years later, in A.D. 324, the emperor himself confessed his faith in Christ and declared his intention to make Christianity the religion of the Roman Empire.

Today the cost of following Christ is still high. It is estimated that more Christians have been martyred for Christ in the last half of the twentieth century than in the first three centuries of the church.

Today the last unreached peoples on earth to hear the Gospel are within reach through modern technology. The *"ends of the earth"* will soon know the impact of Jesus' message. And <u>then</u>?

Within a few years of Luke's writing Acts 28, Paul was martyred for his faith. Acts 28:31 could serve as his epitaph. What do you need to be building into your life right now, so that your faith in Christ will be what people remember about you when you die?

Luke's story of the early church is designed to give Christian witnesses in the twenty-first century insights into their resources in the Holy Spirit, hope in the storms into which following Jesus inevitably led, and peace in the relentless working of God to fulfill his divine plan to bring people of all nations to their knees at the <u>feet of Christ</u>.

☞ **GO TO:**

Matthew 24:14, 27, 30–31 (then)

Ephesians 1:9–10, 22; Philippians 2:9–11; Colossians 1:17–20; Revelation 4:1–14 (feet of Christ)

Something to Ponder

Remember This . . .

Billy Graham: As we have seen in this book, Pentecost was the day of power of the Holy Spirit. It was the day the Christian church was born. We do not expect that Pentecost will be repeated any more than that Jesus will die on the cross again. But we do expect pentecostal blessings when the conditions for God's moving are met, and especially as we approach "the latter days." We as Christians are to prepare the way. We are to be ready for the Spirit to fill and use us.[10]

Study Questions

1. When a poisonous snake bit Paul's hand what did the Maltese islanders think? What did they expect to happen to him? When it didn't, what did they conclude?

2. What did Paul mean when he quoted the verses from Isaiah 6:9–10 to the people who rejected Christ (Acts 28:25–27)?

3. With what note of triumph does Luke end his story of the early church's witness to the world in Acts 28:31?

4. Identify three or four things his New Testament letters reveal Paul accomplished in Rome in addition to what is reported in Acts 28.

CHAPTER WRAP-UP

- Survivors of Paul's wrecked ship washed up on the island of Malta. Islanders were kind. Paul and Luke ministered to the sick. (Acts 28:1–10)

- Centurion Julius took prisoners and soldiers aboard an Egyptian ship from Malta to Puteoli. Two groups of Romans came to escort Paul to Rome. (Acts 28:11–15)

- In Rome Paul lived under house arrest. Leaders and members of the Jewish community came and listened to his message. Sharp division developed among them about Jesus. (Acts 28:16–27)

- Having given Jews first chance Paul then took the Gospel to Gentiles. He remained under arrest and preached Christ without government hindrance. (Acts 28:28–31)

- Paul's ministry in Rome was effective. He wrote letters, directed apostolic teams, and won many to Christ. Luke ends his telling of the story of the early Christians as the *"ends of the earth"* phase of Christian witness was just getting underway. (Acts 1:8)

APPENDIX A—TIMELINE OF PAUL'S LIFE

Birth and early adult life

Born in Tarsus	A.D. 6
Studies in Jerusalem, becomes a Pharisee	A.D. 20–30
Persecutes Jesus' followers in Jerusalem	A.D. 30–33

Conversion and early Christian experience

Meets Jesus on Damascus Road	A.D. 33
Flees persecution in Damascus	A.D. 36
Persecuted in Jerusalem, flees to Tarsus	A.D. 36–44
With Barnabus in Antioch, teaches	A.D. 44–46
Goes to Jerusalem for famine relief	A.D. 46

Missions Trips

First missions trip to Cyprus and Galatia with Barnabas	A.D. 47–48
Argues for Gentile freedom from the Law at Jerusalem Council	A.D. 49
Second missions trip to Asia Minor and Greece with Silas	A.D. 49–52
Begins third missions trip	A.D. 52
Founds church at Ephesus	A.D. 52–55
Travels through Greece, returns to Jerusalem	A.D. 55–59

Arrest, imprisonment, and martyrdom

Arrest in Jerusalem, jailed in Caesarea	A.D. 59
Trials before Felix and Festus, appeals to Caesar	A.D. 59–60
Voyage to Rome, shipwreck	A.D. 60
Under house arrest in Rome	A.D. 60–62
Released, travels (perhaps to Spain)	A.D. 62–64
Rearrested, martyred in Rome in Nero's persecution	A.D. 64

APPENDIX B—THE ANSWERS

ACTS 1: LIGHTING THE FUSE

1. Jesus got his power to teach and work from the Holy Spirit. (Acts 1:2)
2. Baptism with the Spirit changes a person into Christ's likeness (2 Corinthians 3:18); cleanses from sin (Acts 15:8); and fills with the Spirit's presence and character (Acts 2:4) by placing the person into the stream of Christ's resurrection life (Romans 8:2) and making him or her a member of Christ's body (1 Corinthians 12:13).
3. Major offensives in Jesus' strategy for world conquest call for Christians to be witnesses (1) in Jerusalem, (2) in Judea and Samaria, and (3) to the ends of the earth. (Acts 1:8)
4. The people in the upper room were constantly in prayer. (Acts 1:14)
5. Judas's replacement must be someone who (1) met the risen Jesus, (2) knew Jesus well by being with him during his earthly ministry, and (3) knew and could work with the other apostles (Acts 1:21–22). Joseph and Matthias met the qualifications (Acts 1:23).
6. After listening to the job description and qualifications, they prayed for the Lord to reveal his choice (Acts 1:24) and cast lots to see whom he had chosen (Acts 1:26).

ACTS 2: FIREWORKS AT THE FIESTA

1. When the Spirit came, the disciples heard wind (Acts 2:2) and saw fire (Acts 2:3). They were filled with the Spirit and enabled to speak new languages (Acts 2:4).
2. The gift of tongues is the ability, given by the Holy Spirit, to speak a language one was unable to speak before (Acts 2:6, 11). It allowed communication with people who otherwise could not have understood their message (Acts 2:5–11). In new languages they communicated God's wonders (Acts 2:11). Reactions included bewilderment (Acts 2:6), amazement (Acts 2:7, 12), questions (Acts 2:7–8, 12), perplexity (Acts

2:12), discussion (Acts 2:12), ridicule (Acts 2:13), and slander (Acts 2:13). More information on speaking in tongues is found in 1 Corinthians 12–14.
3. The resurrection proves Jesus is Lord and Christ. (Acts 2:36)
4. The gift of the Holy Spirit is given to all who respond to the invitation to repent, declare faith in Jesus (baptism is a sign of faith), and receive forgiveness of sins.
5. Early believers devoted themselves to (1) apostles' teaching, (2) fellowship, (3) bread breaking (sharing meals and the Lord's Supper), and (4) prayer. (Acts 2:42)
6. Early believers expressed oneness and love by making available everything they had to meet each other's needs (Acts 2:44). If they had nothing to give, they sold something and gave the proceeds (Acts 2:45).
7. Luke reports, *"The Lord added to their number daily"* (Acts 2:47).

ACTS 3–4: SETTIN' THE WOODS ON FIRE

1. The man at the Beautiful Gate asked for money (Acts 3:3). Peter and John gave him healing (verses 6–8). The power to heal came through faith in Jesus' name (verse 16).
2. To act "in Jesus' name" means to act under authority from Jesus; consistent with his person, character, goals, values, and instructions; with motives and desires in harmony with his motives, desires, and will. (John 14:12–14, 26; 16:23–24; 1 John 5:14–15)
3. Two reasons given in Acts 4:2 for the arrest of Peter and John are (1) they taught the people, and (2) they proclaimed Jesus' resurrection. Sadducees wanted to stop the resurrection teaching because they didn't believe in the resurrection (Luke 20:27).
4. When Peter and John were ordered not to teach in Jesus' name, they insisted (1) they had to do what was right in God's sight, and (2) they could not help telling what they had seen. (Acts 4:19–20)
5. Jerusalem Christians demonstrated love and solidarity by (1) considering their material possessions as

belonging to the community of believers, (2) sharing what they had, (3) selling property and houses to get money for distribution to the needy (Acts 4:32, 34–37). In this way (4) all known needs were met (verse 34).

ACTS 5: THE PERFECT CHURCH—NOT!

1. Satan was behind Ananias and Sapphira's hypocrisy (Acts 5:3). They lied to the Holy Spirit, God (Acts 5:3–4). Giving was not demanded; Peter told Ananias the land belonged to him and the proceeds were his to do with as he pleased (Acts 5:4).
2. An "obvious" miracle is one in which natural laws seem to be suspended. Example: Opening the eyes of the blind (John 9:32), healing a lame man (Acts 3:6–8). A "hidden" miracle is one in which God shapes and uses natural events and processes to accomplish his purposes (Romans 8:28; Acts 2:5, 44–47; 4:32, 34).
3. Facts about Christian healing ministry observed in Acts 5:12–16 include these: (1) Like Jesus, they gave healing high priority. (2) Ministry to the sick was evidence of God's power at work (Acts 5:12). (3) Healings were done through the apostles (Acts 5:12) and others (Acts 5:16). (4) Healing ministry makes the church attractive (Acts 5:16).
4. The priests were jealous because of crowds coming to the apostles (Acts 5:16–17). An angel of the Lord let them out of jail (Acts 5:19). They went directly to the Temple and started preaching Jesus again, as the angel had instructed them to do (Acts 5:21).
5. A Pharisee named Gamaliel spoke in favor of letting the apostles go (Acts 5:34–39). His fellow teachers called him "The Beauty of the Law."
6. The apostles rejoiced because they'd been *"counted worthy of suffering disgrace"* for Jesus (Acts 5:41).

ACTS 6–7: A TEMPLE TO DIE FOR

1. Qualifications for people caring for the poor were being well known, being full of the Holy Spirit, and being wise. (Acts 6:3)
2. Christian beliefs were twisted to form charges against Stephen: (1) The Temple isn't the only place people can meet God (John 4:23–24; Matthew 18:20). (2) The Law and Temple are fulfilled (fully understood) in Christ (Matthew 5:17). (3) The Holy Spirit writes God's laws on people's minds and hearts (Hebrews 8:10; 10:16). (4) God's grace is not exclusively for Jews, but also for Gentiles (Matthew 28:19; Acts 2:39).

3. Stephen said his accusers were guilty of persistent resistance against the Holy Spirit (Acts 7:51); persecution and martyrdom of the prophets (Acts 7:52); betrayal and murder of the Messiah (Acts 7:52); and disobedience of the Law they claimed to defend (Acts 7:53).
4. As he died Stephen prayed, *"Lord, Jesus receive my spirit"* (Acts 7:59) and *"Lord, do not hold this sin against them"* (Acts 7:60). As he died Jesus prayed, *"Father, into your hands I commit my spirit"* (Luke 23:46) and *"Father, forgive them"* (Luke 23:34).

ACTS 8: SCATTERGUN!

1. God used Saul's persecution to get Christians to take Christ to Judea and Samaria. (Acts 8:1, 4)
2. Crowds heard Philip preach and saw his miracles. Many believed in Jesus and were baptized. His most notable "convert" was Simon the magician. (Acts 8:5–13)
3. Three things that were different were (1) the apostles prayed for them (Acts 8:15); (2) the delay between believing in Jesus and receiving the Spirit (Acts 8:16); and (3) the need for the apostles to lay hands on them when the Spirit was given (Acts 8:17). It was important for the apostles to be there (1) to assure the Samaritans they were accepted; (2) to demonstrate the apostles' authority; (3) to assure Jewish Christians that Samaritans were true followers of Christ.
4. Simon was confused about (1) God's grace—he thought he could buy it (Acts 8:18–20); (2) power—the difference between magic and the Holy Spirit's power; (3) ministry—he saw it as showmanship (Acts 8:21); and (4) the purpose of the Spirit's work—he saw it as a means of personal gain.

ACTS 9: U-TURN ON STRAIGHT STREET

1. Jesus confronted Saul with the question: "Why do you persecute me?" (Acts 9:4). The spiritual principle revealed by the question is that Jesus and his followers are one—to persecute Jesus' follower is to persecute Jesus.
2. The five spiritual processes involved in Saul's spiritual reconstruction/conversion were these: (1) personal encounter with Jesus; (2) forgiveness by Jesus and others for the harm he'd done to Christians (Acts 9:17); (3) filling with the Spirit (Acts 9:17); (4) baptism (Acts 9:18); and (5) commissioning as Christ's ambassador (Acts 9:15).
3. At first Saul was rejected because the Jerusalem be-

lievers thought Saul's conversion was a new attempt to infiltrate their group. Barnabas listened to Saul's story, believed him, and introduced him to the others. (Acts 9:26–27)

4. As a result of Peter's healing of Aeneas and raising of Tabitha, many people in and around Lydda and Joppa heard the Gospel and believed in Jesus. (Acts 9:35, 42)

ACTS 10–11: PETER GOES WALL CRASHING

1. In his vision Peter saw a sheet containing animals he believed were unclean. The voice told him to *"kill and eat"* the so-called unclean animals. When he protested the voice said: *"Do not call anything impure that God has made clean."* (Acts 10:11–15)

2. To show his change of mind, Peter (1) welcomed the Gentiles (Acts 10:23); (2) returned to Caesarea with them, no questions asked (Acts 10:23, 29); (3) entered the house of the Gentile Cornelius (Acts 10:25, 27); (4) confessed his change of mind (Acts 10:28–29); and (5) declared the Gospel's inclusiveness (Acts 10:34–35).

3. Witnesses who went to Antioch shared the good news about Jesus with Gentiles. (Acts 11:20)

4. Barnabas's ministry accomplished four things: (1) affirmed God's work (Acts 11:23); (2) introduced people to Jesus (Acts 11:24); (3) linked him up with Saul (Acts 11:25–26); and (4) discipled (trained and taught) new converts (Acts 11:26).

5. Visible proofs of grace that may have caused Antiochenes to call disciples "Christians" include (1) willingness to cross racial, cultural, and social barriers to share Christ (Acts 11:20); (2) unity based on accommodation to each others' differences; (3) eagerness to grow (Acts 11:26); and (4) generosity (Acts 11:18–30).

ACTS 12: KING OF HOT AIR AND MAGGOTS

1. James was *"put to death with the sword"* (beheaded) (Acts 12:2). This persecution was different because it was the first attack on the church by a secular government.

2. To get Peter out of jail, the church got together and prayed (Acts 12:5). Groups met at members' homes; one prayer group met at Mary's house (Acts 12:12).

3. In response to their prayers, an angel was sent to Peter to wake him up and lead him to freedom (Acts 12:6–10). The real power is in the hands of God, the Lord of the church, who can overrule the plans and orders of kings and governments.

4. When Rhoda said Peter was at the door she got two responses: (1) You're crazy! (2) It's his angel (Acts 12:15). What their responses reveal about their prayers is that they prayed and God answered even though their prayers and faith were not perfect or doubt-free.

5. Herod Agrippa's fraudulence was revealed when he let the Phoenicians call him a god. (Acts 12:22–23)

ACTS 13–14: WORLD AMBASSADORS

1. Two types of ministry used by the shepherds (pastors) of Antioch were prophecy and teaching: prophecy is communicating God's message; teaching is explaining the meaning and application of God's message. (Acts 13:1)

2. When they got together, the prophets and teachers worshiped the Lord and fasted. While they were together the Holy Spirit told them to set Barnabas and Saul apart for a wider mission. (Acts 13:2)

3. Paul told the sorcerer (1) he was a child of the devil; (2) he was an enemy of all that is right; (3) he was full of deceit; (4) he always made right seem wrong and wrong seem right; and (5) the Lord was against him. (Acts 13:10–11)

4. After the lame man's healing, the people of Lystra thought Barnabas and Paul were the pagan gods Zeus and Hermes (Acts 14:11–12). To show they were human the apostles tore their clothes and went into the crowd so they could be seen up close (Acts 14:14–15).

5. A testimony to God's reality and kindness that all humans can see is the natural world—rain, sunshine, seasons, crops, supply of food, and things that give joy. (Acts 14:17)

ACTS 15: OUTSIDERS CRASH THE CHRISTIAN PARTY

1. When the legalistic teachers came to Antioch, Paul and Barnabas debated them (Acts 15:2). The controversy was about whether people are saved by faith or by keeping religious laws (Galatians 2:15–16).

2. The six points Peter stressed were these: (1) God initiated the outreach to the Gentiles (Acts 15:7). (2) God verified his acceptance by giving them the Holy Spirit (Acts 15:8). (3) God makes no distinction between Jews and Gentiles, purifying the hearts of both by faith (Acts 15:9). (4) Laying law on people God has accepted amounts to questioning God (Acts 15:10). (5) If the Law is an impossible burden to Jews, it makes no sense to expect Gentiles to live by

it (Acts 15:10). (6) The law never saved anyone—both Jews and Gentiles are saved through grace (Acts 15:11).

3. James was convinced the Gentiles should be accepted because of (1) God's actions (Acts 15:14), and (2) God's Word (Acts 15:15–18).

4. Two accommodations Gentiles were asked to make in order to make fellowship with their Jewish brothers easier were these: (1) Don't serve food that has been offered to idols before being sold in the market. (2) Don't serve meat that has not been properly bled. (Acts 15:20)

5. The issue that led to the breakup of Paul and Barnabas was whether or not John Mark should accompany them on their next missionary journey.

ACTS 16: JAILHOUSE ROCK

1. Four "higher principles" that guided Paul are (1) personal obedience to Christ (2 Corinthians 10:5); (2) living by the spirit, not the letter of the Law (2 Corinthians 3:6); (3) accommodation on nonessentials (1 Corinthians 9:19–23); and (4) love (1 Corinthians 13:4–8).

2. Two reasons Tim submitted to "the surgery" were (1) to assure Jews that following Christ didn't mean to stop being Jewish, and (2) to assure credibility with Jews.

3. Paul and the team were convinced by a vision that going to Macedonia was God's will (Acts 16:9–10). Luke joined the team. We know because he, as author, uses first person pronouns "we" and "us" when describing team movements (Acts 16:10–12).

4. Three whose stories are in Acts 16 are (1) Lydia, a wealthy businesswoman trading in purple cloth (Acts 16:14–15); (2) the demon-possessed girl who was a fortune-teller and slave (Acts 16:16); and (3) the jailer who was a middle-class Roman soldier (Acts 16:23–34).

5. Paul and Silas answered, *"Believe in the Lord Jesus, and you will be saved—you and your household"* (Acts 16:31). As proof of his conversion (Acts 16:33–34), the jailer (1) made amends, washing their wounds; (2) was baptized with his family; (3) shared table fellowship with Paul and Silas; and (4) experienced joy.

ACTS 17: JUNKYARD OF THE GODS

1. Thessalonian enemies accused Christians of (1) causing trouble, (2) defying Caesar's decrees, and (3) promoting a king to replace Caesar. (Acts 17:6–7)

2. In contrast to others, the Bereans eagerly received the message and studied the Scriptures to see if the message was true. (Acts 17:11)

3. Paul's starting place in his Mars Hill speech was the altar *"To an Unknown God"* (Acts 17:23).

4. The statements from Paul's Mars Hill speech are as follows:
   a. People are dependent on God for *"life and breath and everything else"* (Acts 17:25).
   b. God is *"not far from each one of us"* (Acts 17:27).
   c. *"In him we live and move and have our being"* (Acts 17:28).
   d. *"We are his offspring"* (Acts 17:28).

5. Areopagus members sneered when Paul mentioned the resurrection. (Acts 17:32)

ACTS 18: SIN CITY SAINTS

1. In Corinth Paul linked up with Aquila and Priscilla (Acts 18:2). They were tentmakers, Jews, and Christians (Acts 18:2–3).

2. Paul went to the home of Titius Justus, next door to the synagogue, to continue preaching. Crispus, synagogue president, believed and followed Christ, along with his entire family. Many Corinthians believed and were baptized. (Acts 18:7–8)

3. The three reasons the Lord gave Paul for staying in Corinth and continuing to preach were (1) the Lord was with him, (2) the Lord would protect him, and (3) the Lord had people in Corinth who would respond to the message. (Acts 18:9–10)

4. Apollos was influenced and helped by Aquila and Priscilla. He was a good orator, comfortable in public debates. (Acts 18:25, 28)

ACTS 19: FREEDOM AND FURY IN THE CITY OF THE NO-GODS

1. Missing elements in the faith and spiritual experience of the "Ephesian twelve": They had not heard of the Holy Spirit, so they had not received him. (Acts 19:2)

2. Paul stopped teaching at the synagogue when people became obstinate, refused to believe his message, and slammed the Christian way of life (Acts 19:9). During the two years he taught at Tyranus's hall, *"all the Jews and Greeks who lived in the province of Asia heard the word of the Lord"* (Acts 19:10).

3. The new Christians at Ephesus broke free from their superstitious ways and demonstrated commitment to Christ by burning their occult and magic books (Acts 19:17–19). Result: The *"word of the Lord spread widely and grew in power"* (Acts 19:20).

4. Demetrius and the silversmiths were angry because the number of people turning to Christ was depleting the profits of their Artemis trinket business (Acts 19:23–27). They represent people today who oppose spirituality, morality, and justice when profit margins are threatened—the "idolatry of the bottom line."

ACTS 20: THE VULNERABLE AMBASSADOR

1. Five characteristics of the church meeting at Troas were (1) they met on Sunday, (2) they ate together, (3) they met at night, (4) they met in a third-floor room, and (5) the length of the meeting was not regulated by the clock. (Acts 20:7–11)
2. A young man named Eutychus fell asleep and fell out of the window. (Acts 20:9)
3. The three "titles" for local church leaders mentioned in Acts 20 are (1) elders (Acts 20:17)—emphasizes the need for leaders to be spiritually mature; (2) overseers (Acts 20:28)—emphasizes their role as guides and protectors; and (3) shepherds (Acts 20:28)—emphasizes leaders' role as caregivers.
4. The "final answer" to the $1,000 question: d. The Holy Spirit (Acts 20:28). The "final answer" to the $10,000 question: c. God, because he shed his blood (Acts 20:28). The "final answer" to the $100,000 question: a. Be on guard, *and* d. Warn people of the danger (Acts 20:31).

ACTS 21:1–22:29: STARING DOWN DANGER

1. Agabus bound his own hands and feet with Paul's belt and said, "In this way the Jews of Jerusalem will bind the owner of this belt" (Acts 21:11). The Holy Spirit revealed this to him. Paul's friends begged him not to go to Jerusalem, but the prophecy only strengthened Paul's determination to go (Acts 21:12–14).
2. The elders asked Paul to join the purification rites of four men (Acts 21:21–25). The main reason he agreed was his "theology of accommodation"—his personal commitment to adapt to the preferences and desires of both Jews and Gentiles to remove barriers to the Gospel so he could win them to Christ (1 Corinthians 9:19–23).
3. Paul's three main points were these: (1) Who I was; (2) how I met Jesus; and (3) how my life has changed since I met Jesus.
4. Changes in Paul's life after his encounter with Christ were these: (1) Jesus met him when he prayed (Acts 22:17–18). (2) The Lord was leading him (Acts 22:18, 21). (3) He could be honest about his sins (Acts 22:19–20). (4) He discovered the Lord was not concerned about his past but about his present and future (Acts 22:21). (5) He was able to tell people about God's grace (Acts 22:21).

ACTS 22:30–23:35: PAUL'S TICKET TO RIDE

1. In his response to Ananias's order to hit him in the mouth, Paul (1) accused Ananias of breaking the law (Acts 23:3); (2) called him a fake—a *"whitewashed wall"* (Acts 23:3); (3) refused to recognize him as legitimate high priest (Acts 23:5); and (4) prophesied that God would strike him (Acts 23:3).
2. Paul's mention of the resurrection threw the Sanhedrin into turmoil because Pharisees believed in it and Sadducees did not. What upsets people about the resurrection is that it reveals things about Jesus that make him difficult to ignore. (Romans 1:4)
3. According to Acts, the resurrection reveals (1) Jesus is Lord and Christ (Acts 2:24–36); (2) his name heals (Acts 3:15–16); (3) salvation is in him (Acts 4:10–12); (4) he is Prince and Savior (Acts 5:29–32); (5) he forgives sins and puts people right with God (Acts 13:37–39); and (6) he is God's appointed judge (Acts 17:31).
4. Jesus' visit (Acts 23:11) reassured Paul that (1) the Lord was with him; (2) Paul had accomplished what he came to Jerusalem to do—testify about Jesus to the people of Israel; (3) Paul would witness in Rome; and (4) Paul would leave Jerusalem alive.

ACTS 24–26: CHRIST'S AMBASSADOR ON TRIAL

1. In the trial before Felix (Acts 24:5–7), Tertullus accused Paul of (1) being a troublemaker; (2) being ringleader of the Nazarene sect; and (3) violating the Temple (Acts 21:28). Before Festus they also said Paul violated Caesar's decrees (Acts 25:8).
2. On trial before Felix, two reasons Paul gave for coming to Jerusalem were (1) to bring gifts to the poor, and (2) to "present offerings" (Acts 24:17). When the crowd attacked him, he was participating in a cleansing ceremony (Acts 24:18).
3. Four things Jesus does for people (Acts 26:18) are (1) opens their eyes, (2) turns them from darkness to light, (3) transfers them from the power of Satan to God, and (4) gives them forgiveness of sins and a share with the sanctified (holy, special to God).
4. Festus said Paul was insane when he insisted that Jesus rose from the dead (Acts 26:23). Paul said King Agrippa believed the prophets (Acts 26:27).
5. The wisecrack Agrippa used to avoid answering Paul's question about believing in the prophets was, *"Do*

you think that in such a short time you can persuade me to be a Christian?" (Acts 26:28).

ACTS 27: DANGEROUS PASSAGE

1. Two Christians who accompanied Paul to Rome were Luke (note "we" in Acts 27:1–2), and Aristarchus (Acts 27:2). Luke and Aristarchus may have gone as Paul's slaves.
2. Sailing was difficult because *"the winds were against"* them (Acts 27:4). They reached Fair Havens *"after the Fast"* (Acts 27:9)—after Yom Kippur, the Day of Atonement, October 5, A.D. 59. The owner and pilot decided to sail on to Phoenix because accommodations were better there for spending the winter (Acts 27:11–12).
3. The angel (1) reminded Paul of God's promise that he would testify for Jesus in Rome, (2) revealed that the ship would be lost, but (3) no one traveling with Paul would die in the shipwreck. (Acts 27:21–26)
4. When sailors tried to escape, Paul told the centurion they had to stay on board if everyone was going to be saved (Acts 27:30–32). When soldiers decided to kill the prisoners, the centurion stopped them. He wanted to spare Paul (Acts 27:42–43).

ACTS 28: THE UNCHAINED TRUTH

1. When the snake bit Paul, the Maltese thought he was a murderer getting justice (Acts 28:4). They expected him to die (Acts 28:5–6). When he didn't, they concluded he was a god (Acts 28:6).
2. By quoting from Isaiah (Acts 28:25–27) Paul said that people do not believe in Jesus Christ because they *choose* not to believe, *deliberately* close their eyes, ears, and hearts, and harden themselves against the truth about themselves and God's plan for their spiritual healing.
3. Luke's final note of triumph is to tell of Paul's bold, unhindered preaching of the kingdom of God and teaching about the Lord Jesus Christ. (Acts 28:31)
4. Paul's letters reveal that, in Rome, in addition to what is reported in Acts 28, Paul (1) wrote New Testament letters (Philippians, Ephesians, Colossians, and Philemon); (2) directed a team of Christian workers (Acts 27:1–2; Philippians 1:1; 4:18; Colossians 1:1; 4:10; 2 Timothy 4:11; Philemon 1; Ephesians 6:21); (3) personally introduced people to Jesus (Philippians 1:13–14; 4:22); and (4) witnessed to Caesar (Acts 27:23–24; 2 Timothy 4:16–17).

APPENDIX C—THE EXPERTS

Henry Alford—Dean of Canterbury, England; author of *The New Testament for English Readers* Bible commentary.

Vickie Baker—Poet, Denver, Colorado.

William Barclay—New Testament scholar and writer; Professor of Divinity and Biblical Criticism at the University of Glasgow; author of many books, including the multivolume *Daily Study Bible* commentary on all the New Testament books.

Venerable Bede—Seventh- and eighth-century Bible scholar and hymn writer.

Bernard of Clairvaux—Tenth-century monk, theologian, mystic, and spokesman for medieval Christianity; author of *Twelve Steps to Humility.*

Paul Billheimer—Radio preacher and Bible college president.

William G. Bixler—Clinical psychologist in Manassas, Virginia.

Dietrich Bonhoeffer—German theologian, cofounder of the Confessing Church in Germany, martyred by the Nazis for resistance against Nazi persecution of Jews.

F. F. Bruce—Scottsman, preeminent evangelical scholar of the post-World War 2 era, president of Society for Old Testament Studies and Society for New Testament Studies.

Johnny Cash—Country western singer, song writer, and film producer.

Michael Card—Contemporary Christian author, composer, performer, and recording artist, lives in Nashville, Tennessee.

Oswald Chambers—Principal of Bible Training School, London; founder of two YMCA desert camps in Egypt during World War 1 where he ministered to British soldiers.

Robert E. Coleman—Professor of Evangelism at Trinity Evangelical Divinity School, Deerfield, Chicago; author.

Charles Colson—Founder of Prison Fellowship Ministries, presidential aide under Richard Nixon, columnist, author.

Cyril of Jerusalem—Fourth-century Christian writer.

J. R. Dumelow—Minister, Bible scholar, teacher at Queens College, Cambridge, England.

Gene Edwards—Founding pastor, the Church at Goleta, Goleta-Isla Vista, California; author.

Epimenides—Cretan philosopher and poet, 600 B.C.

Ajith Fernando—President of Youth for Christ, Sri Lanka; author of the NIV Application Commentary on Acts.

J. A. Findlay—British theologian, author.

Mark Galli—Editor of *Christian History* magazine.

Audrey I. Girard—Elementary teacher and intervention specialist; Christian song writer; assistant to author of *The Life of Christ—God's Word for the Biblically-Inept,* volumes 1 and 2, and *Acts—God's Word for the Biblically-Inept.*

John O. Gooch—Editor of youth resources for the United Methodist Publishing House, Nashville; author.

Billy Graham—International crusade, radio, and TV evangelist, he has presented the Gospel face-to-face to more people than any man in history; author of many inspirational classics read by millions; founder of *Christianity Today* and *Decision* magazines.

Ruth Bell Graham—Author, poet, contributor to *Decision* magazine; wife of evangelist Billy Graham.

Michael Green—Principal, St. John's College, Nottingham, England.

Henry Halley—Author of the well-known and widely used *Halley's Bible Handbook,* which has sold two million copies.

Richard C. Halverson—Chaplain of the United States Senate; pastor of Fourth Presbyterian Church, Washington, D.C.; author.

Stanley Hauerwas—Professor of theological ethics at the Divinity School, Duke University, Durham, North Carolina.

Flavius Josephus—First-century Jewish historian.

Craig S. Keener—Bible scholar and historian, expert on cultural and historical background of the Bible.

John Kennedy—Educated at the Universities of London and Glasgow, ministered in India and Japan and other Asian countries; no relation to the former U.S. president.

Sue Monk Kidd—Author, retreat leader, wife, and mother.

Simon Kistemaker—Professor of New Testament at Reformed Theological Seminary; author.

Festo Kivengere—Anglican Bishop of the diocese of Kigezi in Uganda; recipient of the International Freedom Prize and the St. Augustine Cross.

C. J. Klausner—Jewish scholar.

"Holy Hubert" Lindsey—Campus evangelist at the University of California at Berkley during the stormy 1960s and 1970s.

George MacDonald—Nineteenth-century writer, contemporary with Dickens, Emerson, Longfellow, Tennyson, and Whittier; fantasy writer who helped start C. S. Lewis on his journey to God.

J. Gresham Machen—Professor of New Testament, Westminster Theological Seminary, Philadelphia.

Howard Marshall—Senior Lecturer in New Testament Exegesis, University of Aberdeen, Scotland.

Kilian McDonnell—Founder/president of Institute for Ecumenical and Cultural Research; consultant, Pontifical Council for Promoting Christian Unity.

John McRay—Professor of New Testament and archaeology at Wheaton College, Illinois.

Keith Miller—Author of books on personal spiritual renewal, including *A Taste of New Wine*.

Watchman Nee—Twentieth-century Chinese Christian preacher; author, Nee To-sheng.

John Oxenham—poet.

John Pollock—Cambridge educated clergyman, Billy Graham's authorized biographer; lives in Devonshire, England.

Eugenia Price—West Virginia-born contemporary author of best-selling novels and devotional Bible studies.

W. M. Ramsay—Englishman, Bible historian, expert in historical background of the Bible, author of many books.

Lawrence O. (Larry) Richards—Theologian, Bible scholar, ecclesiologist, author of 175 books, including Bible commentaries and reference works for pastors, church leaders, teachers, laymen and youth; General Editor of *God's Word for the Biblically-Inept* series.

Samuel Rutherford—Scottish pastor and theologian.

Basilea Schlink—Founder of the Evangelical Sisters of Mary, Darmstadt, Germany.

Ronald J. Sider, Ph.D.—Yale University; president of Evangelicals for Social Action; professor of theology at Eastern Baptist Seminary.

James Smith—Nineteenth-century yachtsman, student of classical scholarship, expert on early Mediterranean sailing, author of a major book on Luke's account of Paul's sea voyages and shipwreck.

Howard Snyder—Formerly Dean of Free Methodist Seminary in São Paulo, Brazil; Director of Light and Life Men International; author of books on church renewal.

Charles H. Spurgeon—Famed nineteenth-century preacher and pastor of Park Street Church, London.

Krister Stendahl—Professor of Divinity Emeritus, Harvard University and Bishop Emeritus of Stockholm, Sweden.

John R. W. Stott—British Evangelist, scholar and Christian statesman; for many years rector of All Souls Church, London.

Tertullian—Second- and third-century Christian apologist, theologian.

Paul Tournier—Practicing psychiatrist in Geneva, Switzerland.

Jim Wallis—Editor of *Sojourners* magazine; author of books on Christian social action.

Walter Wangerin—Award-winning author; holder of the Jochum Chair at Valparaiso University in Indiana where he is a writer-in-residence.

Charles Wesley—Brother of John Wesley the founder of Methodism, eighteenth-century hymn writer who wrote thousands of theologically rich hymns, many of which are still sung by Christians today.

Maude De Joseph West—Sunday school teacher at Westminster Presbyterian Church, Fresno, California, short story writer.

John Greenleaf Whittier—Nineteenth-century American editor, poet, and abolitionist born in Massachusetts; sometimes called "the Quaker poet."

Dallas Willard—Professor at the University of Southern California's School of Philosophy; visiting professor at the University of Colorado.

William H. Willimon—Professor of the Practice of Christian Ministry, Duke University, Durham, North Carolina.

Sherwood Wirt—Founding editor, *Decision Magazine*; author, Presbyterian minister.

Edwin M. Yamauchi—Professor of history at Miami (Ohio) University.

Philip Yancey—Editor-at-large of *Christianity Today* magazine; best-selling author.

> Note: To the best of our knowledge, all of the above information is accurate and up to date. In some cases we were unable to obtain biographical information.
>
> —THE STARBURST EDITORS

ENDNOTES

Acts 1: Lighting the Fuse

1. Flavius Josephus, *The Wars of the Jews,* 7 vols. of *The Works of Flavius Josephus,* translated by William Whiston (Grand Rapids, MI: Associated Publishers & Authors, n.d.).
2. Maude De Joseph West, *Saints in Sandals* (Grand Rapids, MI: Baker, 1975), 9.
3. William Barclay, *The Gospel of Luke* (Philadelphia: Westminster, 1956), 2.
4. Ben Wirthington III, "Primary Sources," *Christian History* 17, no. 3 (issue 59): 18.
5. Howard A. Snyder, *Community of the King* (Downers Grove, IL: InterVarsity, 1977), 12.
6. Billy Graham, *The Holy Spirit: Activating God's Power in Your Life* (New York: Warner, 1976), 32.
7. F. F. Bruce, *The New International Commentary on the New Testament: The Book of Acts* (Grand Rapids, MI: Eerdmans, 1988), 36.
8. Graham, *The Holy Spirit,* 14.
9. William Barclay, *The Acts of the Apostles* (Philadelphia: Westminster, 1975), 11.
10. Snyder, *Community of the King,* 16–17.
11. I. Howard Marshall, *The Acts of the Apostles* (Grand Rapids, MI: Eerdmans, 1980), 62.
12. Sue Monk Kidd, "Learning to Wait on God: Prayer," *Daily Guideposts, 1989* (Carmel, NY: Guideposts, 1988), 131.
13. Eugene Peterson, *The Message* (Colorado Springs, CO: NavPress, 1993), 210.
14. Lawrence O. Richards, *Victor Bible Background Commentary: New Testament* (Wheaton, IL: Victor, 1994), 280.

Acts 2: Fireworks at the Fiesta

1. Michael Card, *Immanuel: Reflections on the Life of Christ* (Nashville, TN: Thomas Nelson, 1990), 24.
2. Graham, *The Holy Spirit,* 45.
3. Richards, *Victor Background Commentary,* 280.
4. Dallas Willard, *The Divine Conspiracy* (San Francisco: Harper, 1998), 279.
5. Paul Tournier, *The Person Reborn* (New York: Harper & Row, 1966), 4.
6. Cyril of Jerusalem, quoted in *Crosspoint* 12, no. 3 (fall 1999): 16.
7. *The Amplified Bible* (Grand Rapids, MI: Zondervan, 1958), 424.
8. Kilian McDonnell, "The Spirit and the Believer," *Crosspoint* 12, no. 13 (fall 1999): 17.
9. Graham, *The Holy Spirit,* 140–141.

10. Krister Stendahl, "Come Holy Spirit—Renew the Whole Creation," *Crosspoint* 12, no. 3 (fall 1999), 13–14.
11. Ajith Fernando, *NIV Application Commentary: Acts* (Grand Rapids, MI: Zondervan, 1998), 96.
12. Watchman Nee, *A Table in the Wilderness* (Wheaton, IL: Tyndale, 1965), reading for January 16.
13. Barclay, *Acts,* 26–27.
14. George MacDonald, quoted in *NRSV Classics Bible* (Grand Rapids, MI: Zondervan, 1996), 1273.
15. Audrey I. Girard, from the song "My Sweet Messiah," copyright 1997 by the composer.
16. J. Gresham Machen, *The Christian Faith in the Modern World* (Grand Rapids, MI: Eerdmans, 1947), 63.
17. Bruce, *Acts,* 69.
18. Liddell & Scott, *Greek-English Lexicon* (London: Oxford/Clarendon, 1944), 607.
19. Tertullian, *Apologeticus,* quoted in Philip Schaff, *The History of the Christian Church,* vol. 2: *Anti-Nicene Christianity* (Grand Rapids, MI: AP & A, n.d.), 167.
20. Lawrence O. Richards, *A Theology of Christian Education* (Grand Rapids, MI: Zondervan, 1975), 30.
21. Sherwood Wirt, *Afterglow* (Grand Rapids, MI: Zondervan, 1975), 82.
22. Tertullian, *Apology,* chapter 39, quoted in *Crosspoint* 13, no. 2 (fall 2000): 27.
23. Jim Wallis, *Agenda for Biblical People* (San Francisco: Harper & Row, 1984), 65.
24. Snyder, *Community of the King,* 124–125.

Acts 3–4: Settin' the Woods on Fire

1. *The Revell Bible Dictionary* (Old Tappan, NJ: Revell, 1990), 142.
2. Richard C. Halverson, *Relevance: The Role of Christianity in the Twentieth Century* (Waco, TX: Word, 1968), 87–88.
3. Bruce, *Acts,* 82.
4. Walter Wangerin, *The Book of God* (Grand Rapids, MI: Zondervan, 1996), 847.
5. Peterson, *The Message,* 214.
6. Nee, *Table,* October 14.
7. John R. W. Stott, *The Cross of Christ* (Downer's Grove, IL: InterVarsity, 1986), 59–60.
8. C. J. Klausner, *From Jesus to Paul* (London: Allen & Unwin, 1944), 282–283.
9. Peterson, *The Message,* 215.
10. Barclay, *Acts,* 42.

11. West, *Saints in Sandals,* 34.
12. Fernando, *Acts,* 170.
13. Ronald J. Sider, *Rich Christians in an Age of Hunger* (Downer's Grove, IL: InterVarsity, 1977), 103.
14. Wallis, *Agenda for Biblical People,* 71.
15. Graham, *The Holy Spirit,* 282.
16. Wallis, *Agenda for Biblical People,* 71.

Acts 5: The Perfect Church—Not!
1. Charles Colson, *The Body: Being Light in Darkness* (Dallas: Word, 1992), 130.
2. Barclay, *Acts,* 44–45.
3. Fernando, *Acts,* 199.
4. Graham, *The Holy Spirit,* 298.
5. Peterson, *The Message,* 216.
6. Colson, *The Body,* 382–384.
7. Richards, *Bible Background Commentary,* 288.
8. Ibid., 289.
9. Peterson, *The Message,* 217.
10. J. A. Findlay, quoted in Bruce, *Acts,* 115.
11. William L. Saunders, "Genocide in Sudan," *Crosspoint* 13, no. 2 (fall 2000): 43.
12. John McLaughlin, on PBS's *The McLaughlin Group,* December 29, 2000.
13. Bruce, *Acts,* 117–118.
14. West, *Saints in Sandals,* 44.

Acts 6–7: A Temple to Die For
1. Gene Edwards, *The Early Church* (Goleta, CA: Christian Books, 1974), 69.
2. Richards, *Background Commentary,* 291.
3. Keith Miller, *A Second Touch* (Waco, TX: Word, 1967), 154.
4. Sherwood Eliot Wirt, *Jesus, Man of Joy* (Nashville, TN: Nelson, 1991), 71.
5. Peterson, *The Message,* 218.
6. Ibid.
7. Fernando, *Acts,* 236.
8. Billy Graham, *Peace with God* (New York: Pocket Books/Permabooks, 1955), 204.
9. Barclay, *Acts,* 52.
10. Colson, *The Body,* 114, 116.
11. Bruce, *Acts,* 135.
12. Fernando, *Acts,* 256.
13. Festo Kivengere, "Love Triumphs in Suffering," *Crosspoint* 13, no. 2 (fall 2000): 17.

Acts 8: Scattergun!
1. Bruce, *Acts,* 161.
2. Barclay, *Acts,* 63.
3. Everett Ferguson, "Did You Know," *Christian History* 9, no. 3 (issue 27): inside front cover.
4. Halley, *Bible Handbook,* 465.
5. Robert E. Coleman, *The Master Plan of Evangelism* (Old Tappan, NJ: Revell, 1964), 102–103.
6. Graham, *The Holy Spirit,* 318.
7. Barclay, *Acts,* 141.
8. Audrey I. Girard, from her unpublished journals.
9. Bruce, *Acts,* 170.
10. Acts 8:20, J. B. Phillips, *The New Testament in Modern English* (New York: Macmillan, 1972), 250.
11. Bruce, *Acts,* 166, citing Justin Martyr and Terullian.
12. Nee, *Table,* June 26.
13. New American Standard Bible marginal note.
14. Barclay, *Acts,* 69.

Acts 9: U-Turn on Straight Street
1. Kivengere, "Love Triumphs in Suffering," 17.
2. Quoted in James Reapsome, "Persecuted Christians Today," *Christian History* 9, no. 3 (issue 27): 37.
3. *Acts of Paul,* quoted in Stephen M. Miller, "Bald, Blind, and Single?" *Christian History* 14, no. 3 (issue 47): 33.
4. Price, *Learning to Live,* 65.
5. Barclay, *Acts,* 71.
6. John R. W. Stott, *Basic Christianity* (Grand Rapids, MI: Eerdmans, 1998), 125–126.
7. Barclay, *Acts,* 71.
8. Ibid., 72.
9. Billy Graham, *How to Be Born Again* (Waco, TX: Word, 1977), 162–163, 165–166.
10. Basilea Schlink, *Ruled by the Spirit* (London: Oliphants, 1969), 50–51.
11. Fernando, *Acts,* 311.

Acts 10–11: Peter Goes Wall Crashing
1. Barclay, *Acts,* 79.
2. West, *Saints in Sandals,* 80.
3. John Kennedy, *The Torch of the Testimony* (Bombay: Gospel Literature Service, 1965), 3–4.
4. *The Analytical Greek Lexicon* (Grand Rapids, MI: Zondervan, 1970), 147.
5. Richards, *Background Commentary,* 290.
6. *Revell Bible Dictionary,* 228.
7. Schlink, *Ruled by the Spirit,* 115.
8. Fernando, *Acts,* 328–329.
9. Bruce, *Acts,* 217.
10. Fernando, *Acts,* 338.
11. *Good News Bible: The Bible in Today's English Version* (New York: American Bible Society, 1976), Acts 11:2.
12. Fernando, *Acts,* 339.
13. Edwards, *The Early Church,* 162.
14. Ibid., 167–168.
15. *Revell Bible Dictionary,* 450.
16. West, *Saints in Sandals,* 92.

Acts 12: King of Hot Air and Maggots
1. Samuel Rutherford, quoted in Billy Graham, *Till Armageddon: A Perspective on Suffering* (Waco, TX: Word, 1981), 115.
2. Ibid., 108, 110.
3. Mrs. Howard Taylor, *The Triumph of John and Betty Stam* (Chicago: Moody, 1935), 136.
4. James Reapsome, Evangelical Mission Information Service, "Persecuted Christians Today," 37.
5. Vegetius, *On Military Affairs,* quoted in Bruce, *Acts,* 234.
6. Barclay, *Acts,* 94.
7. Reapsome, "Persecuted Christians Today," 37.
8. Paul Billheimer, *Destined for the Throne* (Ft. Washington, PA: Christian Literature Crusade, 1975), 52.
9. Charles Wesley, from the hymn, "And Can It Be?"
10. Peterson, *The Message,* 231.
11. Nee, *Table,* February 25.
12. Bruce, *Acts,* 237.
13. Flavius Josephus, *Antiquities of the Jews,* Book 19, 8:2.
14. West, *Saints in Sandals,* 102–103.

Acts 13–14: World Ambassadors
1. Oswald Chambers, *My Utmost for His Highest* (Grand Rapids, MI: Discovery House, 1963), 290.
2. Edwin M. Yamauchi, "How Far Did Paul Travel?" *Christian History* 14, no. 3 (issue 47): 18.

3. Peterson, *The Message,* Acts 13:8.
4. Bede, *Commentary on Acts,* quoted in Bruce, *Acts,* 249.
5. Graham, *The Holy Spirit,* 294.
6. Wangerin, *Book of God,* 848.
7. Barclay, *Acts,* 100–101.
8. J. R. Dumelow, *Commentary on the Holy Bible* (New York: Macmillan, 1923), 836.
9. Oswald Chambers, *So Send I You* (Ft. Washington, PA: Christian Literature Crusade, 1930), 163.
10. Barclay, *Acts,* 110.
11. Fernando, *Acts,* 404.
12. Billheimer, *Destined,* 133.

Acts 15: Outsiders Crash the Christian Party
1. Marshall, *Acts,* 249.
2. Peterson, *The Message,* 237.
3. Barclay, *Acts,* 114–115.
4. Ibid., 115.
5. Bruce, *Acts,* 296 (footnote).
6. West, *Saints in Sandals,* 133.
7. Richards, *Background Commentary,* 302.
8. Marshall, *Acts,* 249.
9. Larry Richards, *Bible Difficulties Solved* (Grand Rapids, MI: Revell, 1993), 323.
10. Fernando, *Acts,* 433–434.

Acts 16: Jailhouse Rock
1. R. W. Emerson, "Essay on Self-Reliance," *Essays, Lectures and Orations* (London: n. p., 1848), quoted in Bruce, *Acts,* 304.
2. Barclay, *Acts,* 114–115.
3. Fernando, *Acts,* 433 n. 11.
4. Bruce, *Acts,* 308.
5. Fernando, *Acts,* 433.
6. Pollock, *Apostle,* 124.
7. Barclay, *Acts,* 124.
8. *Christian History* 7, no. 3 (issue 19): 37.
9. Barclay, *Acts,* 127.
10. Richards, *Background Commentary,* 307.
11. Howard Marshall, "Acts," in *Eerdmans Handbook to the Bible,* ed. David and Pat Alexander (Grand Rapids, MI: Eerdmans, 1973), 561.

Acts 17: Junkyard of the Gods
1. J. B. Phillips, *The New Testament in Modern English* (New York: Macmillan, 1972).
2. Marshall, "Acts," 562.
3. Barclay, *Acts,* 127.
4. Bruce, *Acts,* 323.
5. Billy Graham, *The Jesus Generation* (Grand Rapids, MI: Zondervan, 1971), 117–118.
6. Reapsome, "Persecuted Christians Today," 37.
7. Fernando, *Acts,* 469.
8. Calvin Miller, *The Singer* (Downer's Grove, IL: InterVarsity, 1975), 106.
9. *Revell Bible Dictionary,* 510.
10. Marshall, "Acts," 562.
11. Digenes Laertius, *The Lives of Eminent Philosophers* vol. 1, 110; Plato, *Laws;* Aristotle, *The Art of Rhetoric* (Book 3, 17:10); quoted in Richardson, *Eternity in their Hearts,* 14–21.
12. Don Richardson, *Eternity in Their Hearts* (Ventura, CA: Regal, 1981), 24.
13. Bruce, *Acts,* 337.
14. Peterson, *Message,* 243.
15. Epimenides, quoted in Richards, *Background Commentary,* 308.

16. Michael Green, "Early Christian Preaching," *Eerdmans Handbook,* 555.
17. Bruce, *Acts,* 343.
18. West, *Saints in Sandals,* 163.
19. John Pollock, *Apostle,* 155.

Acts 18: Sin City Saints
1. Pollock, *Apostle,* 161–162.
2. Bruce, *Acts,* 346.
3. Ibid.
4. Bernard of Clairvaux, quoted in Richard Foster, *Celebration of Discipline* (San Francisco: Harper, 1978), 110.
5. Maria, in Rogers and Hammerstein's *The Sound of Music.*
6. Seneca, quoted in Barclay, *Acts,* 137.
7. Bruce, *Acts,* 354.
8. Barclay, *Acts,* 139.
9. Vickie Baker, Denver, Colorado, quoted in "The Quiet Heart," *Decision,* October 2000, 41.

Acts 19: Freedom and Fury in the City of the No-Gods
1. John Kennedy, *The Torch of the Testimony* (Bombay: Gospel Literature Service, 1965), 238.
2. Peterson, *The Message,* 245.
3. Graham, *The Holy Spirit,* 178–179.
4. Ibid., 143.
5. Bruce, *Acts,* 366.
6. Peterson, *The Message,* 245.
7. Richards, *Background Commentary,* 309.
8. Mark Galli, "Did You Know?" *Christian History* (issue 57): inside front cover.
9. Barclay, *Acts,* 147.

Acts 20: The Vulnerable Ambassador
1. Girard, from her unpublished journals.
2. Barclay, *Acts,* 148.
3. William G. Bixler, "How the Early Church Viewed Martyrs," *Christian History* 9, no. 3 (issue 27): 30.
4. Everett Ferguson, "Did You Know?" *Christian History* 9, no. 3 (issue 27): inside front cover.
5. Reapsome, "Persecuted Christians Today," 37.
6. John O. Gooch, *Christian History* 12, no. 1 (issue 37): 2.
7. Philip Yancey, *Christianity Today,* May 20, 1996, 80.
8. Audrey Girard, from the song "Reflection of Grace," *Adult Teaching Guide* (Wheaton, IL: Scripture Press, March-May 1997). Property of the composer: Audrey Girard, P.O. Box 5148, Lake Montezuma AZ 86342. All rights reserved.
9. Marshall, *Acts,* 333.
10. Lawrence O. Richards, *Expository Dictionary of Bible Words* (Grand Rapids, MI: Zondervan, 1985), 181.
11. Ruth Bell Graham, *Decision,* October 2000, 39.
12. John Oxenham, "A Dieu! And Au Revoir," *Lines to Live By* (Nashville, TN: Nelson, 1972), 81.

Acts 21:1–22:29: Staring Down Danger
1. Fernando, *Acts,* 554–555.
2. Richards, *Background Commentary,* 312–313.
3. Fernando, *Acts,* 555.
4. Dietrich Bonhoeffer, *The Cost of Discipleship,* quoted in *Christian History* (issue 32): 29.
5. Richards, *Background Commentary,* 213.
6. Graham, *Just as I Am,* 613–614.
7. Barclay, *Acts,* 156.
8. Bruce, *Acts,* 409.
9. Barclay, *Acts,* 157.

10. "Holy" Hubert Lindsey, *Bless Your Dirty Heart,* ed. Howard G. Earl (Plainfield, NJ: Logos, 1973), back cover.
11. Peterson, *The Message,* 252.
12. Johnny Cash, quoted in Billy Graham, *How to Be Born Again,* 153.
13. Barclay, *Acts,* 162.
14. Stanley Hauerwas and William H. Willimon, *Resident Aliens: Life in the Christian Colony* (Nashville, TN: Abingdon, 1989), 12.

Acts 22:30–23:35: Paul's Ticket to Ride
1. Barclay, *Acts,* 164.
2. Josephus, *Antiquities of the Jews* 20:206, quoted in Bruce, *Acts,* 425.
3. Barclay, *Acts,* 164.
4. Bruce, *Acts,* 426.
5. John McRay, "Stench, Pain, and Misery—Life in a Roman Prison," *Christian History* 14, no. 3 (issue 47): 14.
6. Billy Graham, "What Will You Do When Disaster Comes?" *Decision,* November 2000, p. 3.
7. Alford, *The New Testament for English Readers,* 806.
8. Bruce, *Acts,* 431.
9. Marshall, *Acts,* 368.

Acts 24–26: Christ's Ambassador on Trial
1. Tacitus, quoted in Bruce, *Acts,* 437.
2. Fernando, *Acts,* 587–588.
3. Angus L. Kinnear, *Against the Tide* (Eastbourne, Sussex, England: Victory Press, 1973), 208.
4. Eugenia Price, *Learning to Live from the Acts,* 131.
5. Barclay, *Acts,* 175.
6. Simon Kistemaker, *New Testament Commentary: Exposition of the Acts of the Apostles* (Grand Rapids, MI: Baker, 1990), 884.
7. West, *Saints in Sandals,* 228.
8. Bruce, *Acts,* 467–468.
9. Billy Graham, *Till Armageddon: A Perspective on Suffering* (Waco, TX: Word, 1981), 200.
10. Richards, *Background Commentary,* 315.
11. Charles H. Spurgeon, *"New Park Street Pulpit,"* vol. 4 (Pasadena, TX: Pilgrim Publications, 1970), quoted in "Life Lived on the Edge," *Decision,* October 2000, 40.
12. Peterson, *The Message,* 260.
13. Ibid.

14. Richards, *Background Commentary,* 317.
15. "Concerning the Word of Life," *Crosspoint* 13, no. 2 (summer 2000): 75.

Acts 27: Dangerous Passage
1. Bruce, *Acts,* 474.
2. James Smith, *The Voyage and Shipwreck of St. Paul* (London: Longmans, Green, 1848, 1880), quoted in E. F. Harrison, *The Acts of the Apostles: A Commentary* (Philadelphia: Westminster, 1971), 412.
3. Ewin M. Yamauchi, "On the Road with Paul," *Christian History* 14, no. 3 (issue 47): 18.
4. W. M. Ramsay, *St. Paul the Traveler,* quoted in Bruce, *Acts,* 477–478.
5. Smith, *Voyage and Shipwreck,* 102.
6. Bruce, *Acts,* 485.
7. Marshall, *Acts,* 408–409.
8. Bruce, *Acts,* 486.
9. Billy Graham, *Hope for the Troubled Heart* (Minneapolis: Grason, 1991), 177.
10. Bruce, *Acts,* 489–490.
11. Smith, *Voyage and Shipwreck,* 121.
12. Bruce, *Acts,* 491.
13. Barclay, *Acts,* 186.
14. Girard, from her unpublished journals.
15. Bruce, *Acts,* 488.
16. W. M. Ramsay, *St. Paul the Traveller and the Roman Citizen* (London: Hodder & Stoughton, 1895, 1920), 341.
17. Fernando, *Acts,* 617.
18. John Greenleaf Whittier, quoted in ibid.

Acts 28: The Unchained Truth
1. Bruce, *Acts,* 498.
2. Pliny, *Natural History,* quoted in ibid., 500.
3. Barclay, *Acts,* 190.
4. McRay, "Stench, Pain, and Misery," 14.
5. Fernando, *Acts,* 625.
6. Barclay, *Acts,* 191–192.
7. Ibid., 192.
8. Richards, *Handbook,* 599.
9. Richard C. Halverson, *How I Changed My Thinking about the Church* (Grand Rapids, MI: Zondervan, 1972), 41–42.
10. Graham, *The Holy Spirit,* 328.

INDEX

Boldface numbers refer to defined (What?) terms in the sidebar.

on Spirit-filled Christians, 90
on suffering for Christ, 194
Graham, Ruth Bell, on offering
	Christ, 240
Grecian, 67–**68**, 71, 108–109
Greek(s), **4**, **68**, **126**
	(*See also* Gentiles)
Green, Michael, on Christianity
	and paganism, 200
Grinding of teeth, **81**
Growth, spiritual (*see* spiritual:
	growth)
Gulf :
	of Adria, 300
	of Messara, 297

H

Halley, Henry, on the persecution
	of Saul, 88
Hall of Hewn Stone, **43**, 61–64
Halverson, Richard C.:
	on giving what you have, 39
	on Pentecost, 314
Hands, laying on (*see* laying on of
	hands)
Harmony:
	of believers, 58–59, 129
	with nature, 196
Harvest (*see* Pentecost)
Hatred, 59, 157
Hauerwas, Stanley, and Willimon,
	William H, on the Church
	as a colony, 261
Head, **12**
	(*See also* Jesus Christ: headship
	of)
Healing, **310**
	of Aeneas, 109–110
	of the beggar (*see* beggar)
	of cripples, 91, 157
	of evil spirits (*see* evil spirits:
		casting out)
	of the paralytic, 37–41, 44
	of Saul (*see* Saul: conversion of)
	of the sick, 60, 67, 221, 306–
		307
	spiritual, 310
	of Tabitha, 110–111
	(*See also* miracles)

Heaven, 4, 79, 101
Hebraic Jews, 67–68, 71
Hebrew(s), **20**, **76**
	book of, 139
	language, 101
	nation (*see* Israel)
Hedonism, **203**
Hell, **95**
Hermes, **157**
Hermon, Mount (*see* Mount:
	Hermon)
Herod:
	Agrippa 1, 45, 49, 132–136,
		139–141, 232, 275, 279,
		285
	Agrippa 2, 257, 283–289, 291–
		292
	the Great, **114**, 283
	palace of, 272–273, 275
Heterogeneous, **128**
High council (*see* Sanhedrin)
Hillel, Rabbi, 207
His name, **121**
Hitler, 141
Holy City, 95, 100
Holy Land, **125**
	(*See also* Jerusalem)
Holy place, 76–80
	(*See also* Temple)
Holy Spirit:
	baptism of the (*see* Baptism: of
		the Holy Spirit)
	called by the, 32
	as comforter, 8, 29
	coming of the, 93
	as counselor, 8
	encouraged by the, 109
	energy of the, 7, 10, 35
	filled with the, 19–29
	fruit of the, 55
	gift of the, **8**
	guidance of the, 4, 8, 18, 118,
		230
	and Jesus, 8–10
	power of the, 9–10, 29–30, 46,
		94, 214, 314
	resisting the, 80
	voice of the (*see* voice of the
		Spirit)

waiting on the, 10, 15
witness of the, 62
work of the, 7–8, 22, 30–31,
	94
Homosexuality (*see* sexual
	immorality: homosexuality)
Honesty, 53–57
Hope of Israel, **309**
House:
	church, 67, **137**–139
	of God (*see* tabernacle;
		Temple)
Household, **183**
Humility, 237
Hymns, 185
Hypocrisy, 31, 55–60, 65, 174,
	265

I

Iconium, 155–156, 178
Ida, Mount (*see* Mount: Ida)
Identification, **72**
Idi Amin, 141
Idolatry, **77**
	in Athens, 195–201
	in Ephesus, 224–226
	Gentiles and, 169–170
	of the Israelites, 77
	in Lystra, 157–159
Idols, **195**
Illusions, 92
Immersion, 97
	(*See also* baptism)
Imperial Regiment, 292
Imprisonment (*see* persecution)
Impure Jews, **113**
Incantations, **215**
Incest, 157
Incarnation (*see* Jesus Christ:
	birth of)
Independence, 107
India, 10, 240
Individualism, 107
Indwelling (*see* Holy Spirit: filled
	with the)
Infused, **81**
Insects, 117
Insurrection, 3
Intercedes, **12**

in Troas, 233–235
visions of (*see* visions: of Paul)
Paupers, 16
Pax Romana, **255**
Penalty, death (*see* death: penalty)
Pentecost, **20**–25, 249, 308, 314–316
Perea, 17
Perga, 151
Persecution:
  of the apostles, 64
  by arrest, 42, 47
  of the early church, 57, 87–90, 124, 132–141
  effects of, 67
  & Martyrdom, 61, 65, 82, 88, 100, 133, 134, 141
  of Paul (*see* Paul: arrested)
  of Peter (*see* Peter: in prison)
  of prophets, 80
  protection from, 64, 209–210
  ridicule as, 26
  of Silas (*see* Silas: in prison)
  torture, 47, 65, 260
Peru, 194
Peter, 13
  in Caesarea, 119–123
  and Cornelius, 115–122
  healing of, 37–40, 109–111
  at the Jerusalem Council, 165, 167
  in prison, 41–46, 134–138, 232, 267
  preaching of, 26, 41
  and the sorcerer, 92
  visions of (*see* visions: of Peter)
Peterson, Eugene, 48, 166, 289
Pharisee(s), **63**, 165–**166**, 264–266, 285
Pharoah, **20**, **76**
Phenika, 296
Philemon, 312
Philip:
  the apostle, 13–14
  the evangelist, 59, 71, 91–98, 246, 278
  of Macedon, 182
  of the Seven (*see* Philip: the evangelist)

Philippi, 181–189, 192, 232–233
Philippians, 208, 312
Philosophers, philosophy:
  in Athens, 196–201
  in Corinth, 204, 210
  in Ephesus, 220
  (*See also* Seneca)
Phoenicia, 124–125, 140, 164, 245
Phoenix, 296–297
Phrygia, 24, 216
Piety, 38
Pilate, Pontius, 40, 45, 48–49, 153
Pilgrimage, 79, 95
Pilot, **296**
Plague, 197–198
Pleasure, 196, 204, 215
Pliny, 307
Politarchs, **193**
Pollock, John:
  on Corinth, 204
  on Paul in Athens, 201
  on Paul's second missionary journey, 181
Pollux, 295, 307
Pontus, 24
Poor, 67–70, 73
  (*See also* beggar)
Portico (*see* Solomon's Colonnade)
Poseidon, 204
Post bond, **193**
Potluck, **33**
Poured out, **20**
Power, **286**
Power of attorney, **39**
Praetorian Guard, 309
Praising God, 35
Prayer:
  devoted to, 32, 34
  importance of, 15, 17, 35, 73
  Jewish times of, 37
  and the Holy Spirit, 48–49
  Lord's, 5
  and miracles, 59, 135–138
  power of, 141, 147
Preaching, 33
  (*See also* apostles: teaching)
Prejudice:
  against Gentiles, 113–130

against Grecian Jews, 68
healed from, 71
against Jews, 250
against Samaritans, 91
Price, Eugenia:
  on the Sanhedrin, 281
  on Saul's obsession, 101
Pride, 54, 107
Priest:
  conversion of, 72
  high, 43, 49, 60–62
Priests, **42**
  (*See also* Sanhedrin)
Prince, 63–**64**
Priscilla and Aquila:
  in Corinth, 205–206
  in Ephesus, 211–213, 216
  in Rome, 213, 308
Proconsul, **149**–151, **210**
Procurator, **275**, 281, 284
Procorus, 71
Promise, **19**
  (*See also* God: promise of)
Promised land, **76**
Property, **184**
Prophecy, **146**
  of David (*see* David: prophecies of)
  about famine, 129–130
  Messianic, 12, 30, 41, 80, 95–96, 153, 169, 218, 310–311
  as miracles, 58
  about Paul, 247–248
  student of, 14
Prophesy, **27**
Prophetesses, **246**
Prophets, **130**
  in Antioch, 145
  Isaiah (*see* Isaiah)
  Old Testament, 287–288
  writings of the, 310
Propitious, **140**
Proselytes, 115
Proselytes of the Gate, **192**
Prostitutes:
  in Corinth, 204–205, 210
  male, 209
  priestesses, 224
  (*See also* sexual immorality)

Province of Asia (*see* Asia, province of)
Psalms, 16, 48
Ptolemais, 246
Publius, 306–307
Pulpit, **219**
Purification rites, **252**
Purple cloth (*see* dye)
Puteoli, 307–308
Pyrrhus, 231
Pythian, **197**
Python, **183**

Q

Quicana Indians, 194

R

Rabban, **63**
Rabbi, 46, 205, 272
Rain, 158
Ram, 252
Ramsay, W. M.:
    on Paul's slaves. 293
    on the shipwreck, 302
Rape, 65
Reconciliation, 39
Redeeming, **239**
Rejection, 76
Religion, 29
Religious, **191**
Religious establishment, **134**
Renounce, 100
Reputation, 237
Responsibility, 55
Resurrection of the dead:
    controversy about, 266–270
    disbelief about, 201, 288
    and Jesus (*see* Jesus Christ:
        resurrection of)
    Jesus' miracles involving, 111
    hope because of, 287
    Paul's belief in, 277–278
Revelation, 220
Revell Bible Dictionary, the, on
    beggars in the Bible, 38
Reverence, 56
Revolution, 3, 15
Rhegium, 307
Rhoda, 137–139

Rhodes, 245
Richards, Larry:
    on Christian education, 33
    on miracles, 58
    on Paul's hypocrisy, 174
Richards, Lawrence O.:
    on Agabus's prophecy, 247
    on casting lots, 18
    on fulfillment, 289
    on the Jerusalem Council,
        171
    on Paul in Rome, 313
    on ritual cleanliness, 117
Ridicule, 194
Right, **95**
Righteousness, 8, 279–280
Righteous One, **80**
    (*See also* Jesus Christ)
Right hand, 12, **28**, **63**, 81
Riot:
    in Berea, 195
    in Ephesus, 226–227, 229
    in Jerusalem, 254–259, 264
    about Stephen, 81–82
    in Thessalonica, 192–193
Ritual, 31
River, Nile (*see* Nile River)
Roadblocks, 180
Rock of Execution, 82
    (*See also* death: penalty)
Rock, the (*see* Peter)
Roman colony, **182**
Roman:
    citizenship, 260–261
    Empire, 3, 11, 100, 109, 125
Rome:
    church in, 185, 205–206, 308
    Paul in (*see* Paul: in Rome)
    Paul's desire to go to, 181
    trip to, 291–308
    visitors from, 24
Russian Orthodox, 134
Rutherford, Samuel, on persecu-
    tion, 133

S

Sabbath:
    Paul preaching on the, 152,
        154, 192

praying on the, 182
    prophecies read on the, 30, 169
Sabbath day's walk, **13**
Sacrificed to idols, **170**
Sacrifices:
    animal, 20
    child, 157
    evening, 37
    morning, 37
Sadducees, 41–**42**, 60, 264–266,
    270
Saints, **109**, **285**
Salamis, 147–149
Salmone, 294
Salome, 14
Salvation, **27**, **44**, 128
    from sin (*see* sin: saved from)
    through faith, 165, 251
    through grace, 167
Samaria, 89, 91, 164
    witnesses in, 9–10, 89, 113, 314
Samaritans, 59, 91
    prejudice against (*see* preju-
        dice: against Samaritans)
Samos, 235
Samothrace, 181
Sanctified, **209**, **286**
Sanhedrin, **43**
    the apostles before the, 61–64
    authority of, 100
    in Caesarea, 282
    disagreement within the, 270,
        278
    Paul before the, 263–267
    Peter and John before the, 43–
        46
    Stephen before the, 74–81
    trials of the, 285
Sapphira, 53, **54–57**
Satan, 55, 121, 150, 184, 286
Saul:
    in Antioch, 126–130, 145–146,
        163–164, 171–172
    blindness of (*see* blindness: of
        Saul)
    conversion of, 101–106, 205,
        257–258, 284–285
    persecution of, 81–82, 87–89,
        99–101, 257, 284–285

Books by Starburst Publishers®
(Partial listing—full list available on request)

The ***God's Word for the Biblically-Inept*™** series is already a best-seller with over 100,000 books sold! Designed to make reading the Bible easy, educational, and fun! This series of verse-by-verse Bible studies, topical studies, and overviews mixes scholarly information from experts with helpful icons, illustrations, sidebars, and time lines. It's the Bible made easy!

Acts—God's Word for the Biblically-Inept™
Robert C. Girard

An important book of history, Acts recounts the ascension of Jesus into heaven, the spread of Christianity throughout the Roman Empire, and the rapid growth of the church—despite the persecution of Paul and other apostles. A must-read for anyone interested in learning more about the early days of the church without getting bogged down in complicated language and confusing details.
(trade paper)   ISBN 189201646X   **$17.99**

The Bible—God's Word for the Biblically-Inept™
Larry Richards

An excellent book to start learning the entire Bible. Get the basics or the in-depth information you are seeking with this user-friendly overview. From Creation to Christ to the Millennium, learning the Bible has never been easier.
(trade paper)   ISBN 0914984551   **$16.95**

Daniel—God's Word for the Biblically-Inept™
Daymond R. Duck

Daniel is a book of prophecy and the key to understanding the mysteries of the Tribulation and end-time events. This verse-by-verse commentary combines humor and scholarship to get at the essentials of Scripture. Perfect for those who want to know the truth about the Antichrist.
(trade paper)   ISBN 0914984489   **$16.95**

Genesis—God's Word for the Biblically-Inept™
Joyce L. Gibson

Genesis is written to make understanding and learning the Word of God simple and fun! Like the other books in this series, the author breaks the Bible down into bite-sized pieces making it easy to understand and incorporate into your life. Readers will learn about Creation, Adam and Eve, the Flood, Abraham and Isaac, and more.
(trade paper)   ISBN 1892016125   **$16.95**

Health & Nutrition—God's Word for the Biblically-Inept™
Kathleen O'Bannon Baldinger

The Bible is full of God's rules for good health! Baldinger reveals scientific evidence that proves the diet and health principles outlined in the Bible are the best for total health. Learn about the Bible diet, the food pyramid, and fruits and vegetables from the Bible! Experts include Pamela Smith, Julian Whitaker, Kenneth Cooper, and T. D. Jakes.
(trade paper)   ISBN 0914984055   **$16.95**

John—God's Word for the Biblically-Inept™
Lin Johnson

From village fisherman to beloved apostle, John was an eyewitness to the teachings and miracles of Christ. Now, readers can join in an easy-to-understand, verse-by-verse journey through the fourth and most unique of all the Gospels. Witness the wonder of Jesus, a man who turned water into wine, healed the blind, walked on water, and raised Lazarus from the dead.
(trade paper)   ISBN 1892016435   **$16.95**

Life of Christ, Volume 1—God's Word for the Biblically-Inept™
Robert C. Girard

Girard takes the reader on an easy-to-understand journey through the Gospels of Matthew, Mark, Luke, and John, tracing the story of Jesus from his virgin birth to his revolutionary ministry. Learn about Jesus' baptism, the Sermon on the Mount, and his miracles and parables.
(trade paper)   ISBN 1892016230   **$16.95**

Life of Christ, Volume 2—God's Word for the Biblically-Inept™
Robert C. Girard

Life of Christ, Volume 2, begins with events recorded in Matthew 16. Read about Jesus' transfiguration, his miracles and parables, triumphal ride through Jerusalem, capture in the Garden of Gethsemane, and his trial, crucifixion, resurrection, and ascension. Find out how to be great in the kingdom of God, what Jesus meant when he called himself the light of the world, and what makes up real worship.
(trade paper)   ISBN 1892016397   **$16.95**

Mark—God's Word for the Biblically-Inept™
Scott Pinzon

The shortest of all the Gospels, Mark focuses on Jesus' actions. Telling the story of the adult Jesus from the time of his baptism by John the Baptist to his crucifixion and resurrection, readers will learn about the Book of Mark in simple, vivid terms that will bring it to life like never before!
(trade paper)   ISBN 1892016362   **$17.99**

Men of the Bible—God's Word for the Biblically-Inept™
D. Larry Miller

Benefit from the life experiences of the powerful men of the Bible! Learn how the inspirational struggles of men such as Moses, Daniel, Paul, and David parallel the struggles of men today. It will inspire and build Christian character for any reader.

(trade paper)   ISBN 1892016079   **$16.95**

Prophecies of the Bible—God's Word for the Biblically-Inept™

Daymond R. Duck

God has a plan for this crazy planet, and now understanding it is easier than ever! Best-selling author and end-time prophecy expert Daymond R. Duck explains the complicated prophecies of the Bible in plain English. Duck shows you all there is to know about the end of the age, the New World Order, the Second Coming, and the coming world government. Find out what prophecies have already been fulfilled and what's in store for the future!

(trade paper)   ISBN 1892016222   **$16.95**

Revelation—God's Word for the Biblically-Inept™

Daymond R. Duck

End-time Bible prophecy expert Daymond R. Duck leads us verse by verse through one of the Bible's most confusing books. Follow the experts as they forge their way through the captivating prophecies of Revelation!

(trade paper)   ISBN 0914984985   **$16.95**

Romans—God's Word for the Biblically-Inept™

Gib Martin

The best-selling *God's Word for the Biblically-Inept™* series continues to grow! Learn about the apostle Paul, living a righteous life, and more with help from graphics, icons, and chapter summaries.

(trade paper)   ISBN 1892016273   **$16.95**

Women of the Bible—God's Word for the Biblically-Inept™

Kathy Collard Miller

Finally, a Bible perspective just for women! Gain valuable insight from the successes and struggles of such women as Eve, Esther, Mary, Sarah, and Rebekah. Interesting icons like "Get Close to God," "Build Your Spirit," and "Grow Your Marriage" will make it easy to incorporate God's Word into your daily life.

(trade paper)   ISBN 0914984063   **$16.95**

   •   Learn more at www.biblicallyinept.com   •

An Expressive Heart: Stories, Lessons, and Exercises Inspired by the Psalms

Edited by Kathy Collard Miller

An intimate book of inspirational lessons from the best-selling editor of the *God's Abundance* collection. Each selection includes a passage from the poetic Book of Psalms, an inspirational story, lesson, quotation, and idea for personal journaling with room to write. The Psalms provide an unmatched guide for anyone who wants to know God better, and *An Expressive Heart* will help you say what's on your heart.

(trade paper)   ISBN 1892016508   **$12.99**

A Growing Heart: Stories, Lessons, and Exercises Inspired by Proverbs

Edited by Kathy Collard Miller

The profound truths of Proverbs provide wisdom for making good choices in life. Each selection includes a verse from Proverbs, an inspirational story, teaching, quotation, and an idea for journaling with room to write. Lessons will guide the reader on topics such as discipline, friendship, love, parenting, wealth, and work.

(trade paper)   ISBN 1892016524   **$12.99**

Cheap Talk with the Frugal Friends

Angie Zalewski and Deana Ricks

A collection of savvy tips and tricks for stretching the family dollar from celebrity thrifters, Angie Zalewski and Deana Ricks, known as the Frugal Friends by their radio and television audiences. This book features twenty-nine chapters on various topics, including automotive, beauty care, cleaning products, dating, decorating, entertainment, medicine, pet care, and sporting goods. Includes advice on eliminating credit card debt, making extra money, and organizing the home. Finally, a practical way to save money with without compromising convenience or lowering lifestyle standards!

(trade paper)   ISBN 1892016583   **$9.99**

Stories for the Spirit-Filled Believer

Edited by Cristine Bolley

It's one thing to know that God is real. It is quite another to have profound and on-going experiences that confirm that belief. In this awesome collection of stories, Cristine Bolley compiles the real-life testimonies of believers who have heard God's voice and responded. This volume includes stories from today's most dynamic charismatic personalities: Oral Roberts, Beth Moore, T. D. Jakes, Joyce Meyer, and more. Each selection contains a Scripture verse, true story, and a prayer. Sure to inspire readers to listen for God's voice in their own lives.

(trade paper)   ISBN 1892016540   **$13.99**

God Things Come in Small Packages: Celebrating the Little Things in Life

Susan Duke, LeAnn Weiss, Caron Loveless, and Judith Carden

Enjoy touching reminders of God's simple yet generous gifts to brighten our days and gladden our hearts! Treasures like a sunset over a vast sparkling ocean, a child's trust, or the crystalline dew on a spider's web come to life in this elegant compilation. Such occasions should be celebrated as if gift wrapped from God; they're his hallmarks! Personalized Scripture is artfully combined with compelling stories and reflections.

(cloth)   ISBN 1892016281   **$12.95**

God Things Come in Small Packages for Moms: Rejoicing in the Simple Pleasures of Motherhood

Susan Duke, LeAnn Weiss, Caron Loveless, and Judith Carden

The "small" treasures God plants in a mom's day shine in this delightful book. Savor priceless stories, which encourage us to value treasures like a shapeless, ceramic bowl presented with a toothy grin; a child's hand clinging to yours on a crowded bus; or a handful of wildflowers presented on a hectic day. Each story combines personalized Scripture with heartwarming vignettes and inspiring reflections.

(cloth)   ISBN 189201629X $12.95

God Things Come in Small Packages for Friends: Exploring the Freedom of Friendship

LeAnn Weiss, Susan Duke, and Judy Carden

A heartwarming combination of true stories, paraphrased Scripture, and reflections that celebrate the simple yet cherished blessings shared between true friends. This series combines the beauty of gift books with the depth of devotionals. Includes reflective meditation, narrative vignettes detailing powerful moments of revelation, and encouraging scripture passages presented as letters to a friend.

(cloth)   ISBN 1892016346 $12.95

God Things Come in Small Packages for Women: Celebrating the Unique Gifts of Women

LeAnn Weiss, Susan Duke, and Judy Carden

Women will experience God's love like never before through wonderfully paraphrased Scripture, true stories, and reflections, which celebrate the unique character of women. Includes reflective meditation, narrative vignettes detailing powerful moments of revelation, and encouraging scripture passages presented as letters from God.

(cloth)   ISBN 1892016354 $12.95

The Weekly Feeder: A Revolutionary Shopping, Cooking, and Meal-Planning System

Cori Kirkpatrick

A revolutionary meal-planning system, here is a way to make preparing home-cooked dinners more convenient than ever. At the beginning of each week, simply choose one of the eight preplanned menus, tear out the corresponding grocery list, do your shopping, and whip up each fantastic meal in less than 45 minutes! The author's household management tips, equipment checklists, and nutrition information make this system a must for any busy family. Included with every recipe is a personal anecdote from the author emphasizing the importance of good food, a healthy family, and a well-balanced life.

(trade paper)   ISBN 1892016095 $16.95

God Stories: They're So Amazing, Only God Could Make Them Happen

Donna I. Douglas

Famous individuals share their personal, true-life experiences with God in this beautiful new book! Find out how

God has touched the lives of top recording artists, professional athletes, and other newsmakers like Jessi Colter, Deana Carter, Ben Vereen, Stephanie Zimbalist, Cindy Morgan, Sheila E., Joe Jacoby, Cheryl Landon, Brett Butler, Clifton Taulbert, Babbie Mason, Michael Medved, Sandi Patty, Charlie Daniels, and more! Their stories are intimate, poignant, and sure to inspire and motivate you as you listen for God's message in your own life!

(cloth)   ISBN 1892016117 $18.95

Treasures of a Woman's Heart: A Daybook of Stories and Inspiration

Edited by Lynn D. Morrissey

Join the best-selling editor of *Seasons of a Woman's Heart* in this touching sequel where she unlocks the treasures of women and glorifies God with Scripture, reflections, and a compilation of stories. Explore heartfelt living with vignettes by Kay Arthur, Elisabeth Elliot, Emilie Barnes, Claire Cloninger, and more.

(cloth)   ISBN 1892016257 $18.95

Seasons of a Woman's Heart: A Daybook of Stories and Inspiration

Edited by Lynn D. Morrissey

A woman's heart is complex. This daybook of stories, quotes, Scriptures, and daily reflections will inspire and refresh. Christian women share their heartfelt thoughts on seasons of faith, growth, guidance, nurturing, and victory. Includes Christian writers Kay Arthur, Emilie Barnes, Luci Swindoll, Jill Briscoe, and Florence Littauer.

(cloth)   ISBN 1892016036 $18.95

Stories of God's Abundance for a More Joyful Life

Compiled by Kathy Collard Miller

Like its successful predecessor, *God's Abundance*, this book is filled with beautiful, inspirational, real-life stories. Those telling their stories of God share Scriptures and insights that readers can apply to their daily lives. Renew your faith in life's small miracles and challenge yourself to allow God to lead the way as you find the source of abundant living for all your relationships.

(trade paper)   ISBN 1892016060 $12.95

More of Him, Less of Me

Jan Christiansen

Subtitled: *A Daybook of My Personal Insights, Inspirations & Meditations on the Weigh Down™ Diet.* The insight shared in this year-long daybook of inspiration will encourage you on your weight-loss journey, bring you to a deeper relationship with God, and help you improve any facet of your life. Each page includes an essay, Scripture, and a tip-of-the-day that will encourage and uplift you as you trust God to help you achieve your proper weight. Perfect companion guide for anyone on the Weigh Down™ diet!

(cloth)   ISBN 1892016001 $17.95

What's in the Bible for . . .™

From the creators of the **God's Word for the Biblically-Inept™** series comes the innovative **What's in the Bible for . . .™** series. Scripture has certain things to say to certain people, but without a guide, hunting down *all* of what the Bible has to say to you can be overwhelming. Borrowing the user-friendly format of the **God's Word for the Biblically-Inept™** series, this new series spotlights those passages and themes of Scripture that are relevant to particular groups of people. Whether you're young or old, married or single, male or female, this series will simplify the very important process of applying the Bible to your life.

What's in the Bible for . . .™ Couples *Kathy Collard Miller and D. Larry Miller*   **WBFC**
(trade paper)   ISBN 1892016028   **$16.95**

What's in the Bible for . . .™ Women *Georgia Curtis Ling*   **WBFW**
(trade paper)   ISBN 1892016109   **$16.95**

What's in the Bible for . . .™ Mothers *Judy Bodmer*   **WBFM**
(trade paper)   ISBN 1892016265   **$17.99**

What's in the Bible for . . .™ Teens *Mark Littleton and Jeanette Gardner Littleton*   **WBFT**
(trade paper)   ISBN 1892016052   **$16.95**

• **Learn more at www.biblicallyinept.com** •

Purchasing Information

www.starburstpublishers.com

Books are available from your favorite bookstore, either from current stock or special order. To assist bookstores in locating your selection, be sure to give title, author, and ISBN. If unable to purchase from a bookstore, you may order direct from STARBURST PUBLISHERS®. When ordering please enclose full payment plus shipping and handling as follows:

Post Office (4th class)
$4.00 with a purchase of up to $20.00
$5.00 ($20.01–$50.00)
9% of purchase price for purchases of $50.01 and up

United Parcel Service (UPS)
$5.00 (up to $20.00)
$7.00 ($20.01–$50.00)
12% ($50.01 and up)

Canada
$5.00 (up to $35.00)
15% ($35.01 and up)

Overseas
$5.00 (up to $25.00)
20% ($25.01 and up)

Payment in U.S. funds only. Please allow two to four weeks minimum for delivery by USPS (longer for overseas and Canada). Allow two to seven working days for delivery by UPS. Make checks payable to and mail to: **Starburst Publishers®**, P.O. Box 4123, Lancaster, PA 17604. Credit card orders may be placed by calling 1-800-441-1456, Mon–Fri, 8:30 A.M. to 5:30 P.M. Eastern Standard Time. Prices are subject to change without notice. For a catalog send a 9 x 12 self-addressed envelope with four first-class stamps.